Literature, Culture and Society

Second edition

Andrew Milner

LONDON AND NEW YORK

First published 1996 by UCL Press

Second edition published 2005 by Routledge
2 Park Square, Milton Park, Abingdon, Oxon OX14 4RN

Simultaneously published in the USA and Canada
by Routledge
270 Madison Ave., New York, NY 10016

Routledge is an imprint of the Taylor & Francis Group

Typeset in Gill Sans and Sabon by Taylor & Francis Books Ltd

Printed and bound in Great Britain by TJ International Ltd, Padstow, Cornwall

British Library Cataloguing in Publication Data
A catalogue record for this book is available from the British Library

Library of Congress Cataloging in Publication Data
A catalog record for this book has been requested

ISBN 0–415–30784–8 (hbk)
ISBN 0–415–30785–6 (pbk)

Literature, Culture and Society

As cultural studies has grown from its origins on the margins of literary studies, it has tended to discard both literature and sociology in favour of a focus on the semiotics of popular culture. *Literature, Culture and Society* makes a determined attempt to re-establish the connections between literary studies, cultural studies and sociology.

Andrew Milner provides a lucid critical overview of the various theoretical approaches to textual analysis, from hermeneutics to post-modernism, and presents a substantive account of the processes by which literary, film and television texts are produced and consumed.

This new second edition has been fully revised and updated. There are entirely new sections on major theorists and critical approaches including Bourdieu, Žižek and psychoanalysis, Moretti and world systems theory. Existing case studies of *Genesis*, *Paradise Lost*, *Frankenstein* and *Blade Runner* have been updated and there are new case studies of Karel Čapek's *Rossum's Universal Robots*, Fritz Lang's *Metropolis*, Chris Carter's *The X-Files* and Joss Whedon's *Buffy the Vampire Slayer*.

Andrew Milner is Professor in the Centre for Comparative Literature and Cultural Studies at Monash University in Melbourne, Australia. His recent publications include *Cultural Materialism* (1993), *Class: Core Cultural Concepts* (1999), *Re-Imagining Cultural Studies* (2002) and *Contemporary Cultural Theory* (third edition, 2002).

This book is dedicated to the memory of:

my father, John Milner (1923–2003), a Flight Sergeant in wartime RAF Bomber Command and one of thousands of captured Allied aircrew force-marched across Lithuania, Poland and Germany in the closing months of the Second World War, who taught me about socialism, internationalism and anti-militarism;

my mother, Dorothy Ibbotson (1921–88), who taught me about life, love and happiness, about the joys and terrors of Protestant faith, about class and how the coal-owners cruelly oppressed the mineworkers and their families;

my friend and colleague, Marie Maclean (1928–94), who taught me about comparative literature, speculative fiction, feminism and Mary Shelley;

my friend and publisher, John Iremonger (1944–2002), who taught me about books, the book trade and writing.

All four died of cancer. Why is that you can never find an earth-shattering scientific invention when you really need one?

Contents

Tables

Acknowledgements

The first edition of *Literature, Culture and Society* was published in 1996 by University College London Press. I remain indebted to Nicholas Esson and Stephen Gerrard for all their hard work on that book. This second edition has been fully revised and rewritten, its argument and empirical materials systematically updated, and the length increased from about 81,000 to 100,000 words. Of the six main chapters, the first and the fifth remain substantially unchanged; the last is almost entirely new, apart from the discussion of *Blade Runner*; and each of the others has been very extensively revised. I am grateful to Rebecca Barden and Lesley Riddle at Routledge for their work on this edition.

As always, I am crucially indebted to my partner, Verity Burgmann, and to our sons, David, James and Robert, for their emotional and personal support. I am also indebted to friends, colleagues and students in and around the Centre for Comparative Literature and Cultural Studies at Monash University and to the staff at the Monash University Library, including the Rare Book Library. Special thanks are due to Roland Boer, Jeff Browitt, Ross Farnell, Wallace Kirsop, Andrew Padgett, Kate Rigby, David Roberts, Millicent Vladiv-Glover, Chris Worth and Gail Ward.

Chapter 1

Literature, culture and the canon

We all know what literature is: it is writing. Which is why women's groups, political parties, trade unions and churches tend to set up 'literature stalls' to display their published writings. But this is not what is meant by literature as a 'subject' to be studied in schools and colleges, 'Literature' as distinct not only from political or religious pamphlets, but also from 'fiction'. In the English language, the earliest senses of the word 'literature' clearly anticipated both contemporary usages. From the fourteenth to the eighteenth century, it denoted 'both an ability to read and a condition of being well-read' (Williams 1976a: 151). Thus all available writing was indeed literature, just as it still is on literature stalls, and yet, in a society in which most adults were unable to read and where literacy remained a mark of social privilege, what was read, 'polite learning', carried with it connotations that prefigured the later sense of 'English literature' as an academic discipline. It is only from the eighteenth century, however, that we can trace an 'attempted and often successful specialization of *literature* to certain kinds of writing...understood as well-written books but...even more clearly understood as well-written books of an *imaginative* or *creative* kind' (ibid.: 152).

Raymond Williams here caught much of the sense of what English teachers in secondary, further and higher education in Britain, the

United States and throughout the English-speaking world have often meant by literature. Yet this new specialist meaning remained radically incoherent. As Williams noted, Carlyle and Ruskin, who wrote neither novels nor poems nor plays, belonged to English literature; and, we might add, Joss Whedon's scripts for *Buffy the Vampire Slayer* – an imaginative creation, surely – do not. Indeed, this radical incoherency is one of the more striking features of the many and varied attempts to define literature in terms of some property or another assumed to inhere in its objects of study. The most common such attempt was that to which Williams referred, in which literature was understood as essentially a matter of imaginative creation, fundamentally fictive rather than factual in character. The implicit premise that philosophy, science and history are somehow neither imaginative nor creative is very obviously indefensible. But the central claim that literature is fictive rather than factual remains similarly problematic, not only because Carlyle counts and Whedon doesn't, but also because much that is at the very core of English literature is quite possibly 'fact'.

Consider, for the moment, Milton's sonnet on his blindness:

> Cyriack, this three years' day these eyes, though clear
>   To outward view of blemish or of spot,
>   Bereft of light their seeing have forgot;
>   Nor to their idle orbs doth sight appear
> Of sun or moon or star throughout the year,
>   Of man or woman. Yet I argue not
>   Against Heav'n's hand or will, nor bate a jot
>   Of heart or hope, but still bear up and steer
> Right onward. What supports me, dost thou ask?
>   The conscience, friend, to have lost them overplied
>   In liberty's defense, my noble task,
> Of which all Europe talks from side to side.
>   This thought might lead me through the world's vain masque,
>   Content though blind, had I no better guide.

The poem is addressed to 'Cyriack', that is, to Milton's friend and former pupil Cyriack Skinner, a real person born in 1627 who died in

1700. It was written, presumably early in 1655, some three years into Milton's blindness, just as the poet claims. Obviously Milton cannot have known for sure that his eyes were not disfigured, but it isn't difficult to imagine that he had been so reassured by friends or relatives. It is certainly true that he was blind and we have no reason at all to doubt the claim that his response to blindness had been essentially one of fortitude. As to the explanation that he had been sustained in this fortitude by the knowledge that his sight had been lost in the defence of liberty, we may perhaps doubt that this was so, but we cannot reasonably doubt that Milton believed it so. He had been appointed 'Latin secretary' to the English revolutionary government in 1649, and both *Eikonoklastes*, published in English in October of that year, and the Latin *Pro Populo Anglicano Defensio*, published in February 1651, had enjoyed the status of semi-official defences of the new English republic. His sight had finally failed in 1652, sacrificed, as Milton thought, to his labours on behalf of the Commonwealth. If Milton's account of his own reputation might perhaps be accused of exaggeration, a twentieth-century historian would nonetheless insist that 'Milton's *Defence of the People of England* enjoyed a fantastic success. Salmasius [Milton's opponent] was held to be Europe's greatest scholar; Milton was unknown outside his own country. Yet by general consent David beat Goliath' (Hill 1977: 182). Where, then, is the fiction in Milton's poem?

Literary studies: classics, comparative literature, English literature

If literature is not necessarily fictive, then what is it? There are many theories as to the nature of 'literariness' and we shall have cause to refer to these in chapter two. For the moment, however, let us settle for the simplest of definitions, that literature is what 'literary studies' actually studies. By literature I will mean, then, in the first instance at least, not so much a particular type of text as a particular type of intellectual practice. Literary studies and English literature are not necessarily coextensive. But the way most people in most Anglophone countries mostly learn about literature is still through English literature. We should note, however, the presence of two other relatively well-established academic discourses on literature, 'comparative literature' and 'classics'. Until well into the nineteenth century, academic literary studies in European universities had invariably meant classics, that is, the study of Ancient Greek and Latin languages and literatures. Unsurprisingly, this was true of both Oxford and Cambridge; but even in as 'new' a country as Australia, neither of the two oldest universities, Melbourne and Sydney, taught English at their foundation, whilst both taught classics.

Moreover, when the idea of studying 'modern literature' was first canvassed it was very often as comparative literature, that is, as the study of literature in ways that go beyond particular national and linguistic boundaries (Remak 1961: 3). Comparative literature developed as a discipline, in the first place at least, primarily in France and in Germany. But Matthew Arnold, whose *Culture and Anarchy* is often cited as one of the founding inspirations for English literature, had clearly understood modern literature as essentially comparative rather than national in scope. Indeed, he appears to have been the first to use the term in English (Wellek and Warren 1976: 46). In the United States, courses in comparative literature were taught at Cornell from 1871 and Michigan from 1887, and the first chair established at Harvard in 1890. In New Zealand, one of the first occupants of the Chair of Classics and English Literature at Auckland was the leading comparatist H. M. Posnett (Bassnett 1993: 22; cf. Posnett 1973). In Australia, Melbourne appointed a professor of 'English, French and German Language and Literature' (that is, in fact, comparative literature) in 1882; Sydney followed suit in 1887 with, again, a chair of 'Modern Literature' (including literature in other European languages). In the long run, however, British and Commonwealth universities would overwhelmingly specialise in English literature. Comparative literature would be reborn and renewed in the post-Second World War years, but as a minority discipline within literary studies, mainly located in France, Germany and, above all, the United States: at the beginning of the twenty-first century the American Comparative Literature Association listed 145 departments or programmes in American universities (Spivak 2003: 6).

Of the three 'literary' disciplines, English literature at first sight seems the most intellectually improbable. Comparative literature, like classics, normally requires an extensive training in foreign languages (in this case usually modern European languages). By comparison, there seems little obvious point in an academic study of the novels, plays and poetry of your own time, your own place and your own language. Where is the scholarship in studying what many would do for pleasure anyway? In 1887 E. A. Freeman, the Regius Professor of History at Oxford, opposed the establishment of a university English school precisely on the grounds that 'we do not want...subjects which are merely light, elegant, interesting. As subjects for examination, we must have subjects in which it is possible to examine' (Palmer 1965: 99). English literature, Freeman assumed, could not possibly be examinable because all such 'chatter about Shelley' was essentially a matter of personal taste. How, then, did English literature win out over comparative literature and classics? The short answer is through a concerted campaign in the early twentieth century, organised by the 'English Association', to encourage the teaching of English in Britain and the wider Empire. It proved extraordinarily successful: Oxford appointed its first 'literary' professor of English in 1904; Melbourne re-established Modern Literature as a chair of English in 1911; Cambridge appointed its first professor of English Literature in the same year and established an independent 'English School' in 1917; Sydney established a separate chair of English Literature in 1921. The latter two dates – 1917 and 1921 – are especially significant, for it was above all the First World War that enabled English studies to establish its credentials as *the* central kind of literary discourse. Unlike classics – and, even more especially, unlike comparative literature – English was a discipline whose patriotism could be more or less assured. Its development was thus inextricably connected to that of modern English nationalism (Baldick 1983: 86–106) and its wider extension, greater British imperial nationalism.

Literature as value: the canon, criticism, minority culture

Both comparative literature and English literature sought to define their respective subject matters in terms of a 'canon' of authoritatively 'literary' texts: *Weltliteratur*, or 'world literature', on the one hand, the

'English tradition' on the other. The term 'canon' (spelt with two rather than three 'n's) denotes a set of officially recognised 'sacred' books. In Christian theology, it had referred to the books of the Bible recognised by the Church as genuine and divinely inspired, and therefore 'true', as distinct from the *apocrypha*, those other texts (extra gospels and so on) claimed by some to be divinely inspired but nonetheless finally rejected by the Church. Literary critics never claimed a literally sacred status for their canon: Shakespeare might have been great, but he wasn't actually God. By analogy, however, the literary canon was normally seen as 'authentic' and 'inspired' in ways that other (merely 'fictional') texts were not. Such distinctions between more or less authentic and more or less inspired texts are, of course, judgements of value rather than statements of fact. But insofar as literary studies understood itself as the study of great literature, such value judgements entered into the very definition of its subject matter, and thereby took on the quasi-objectivity of what might be termed a pseudo-fact.

Unlike most other disciplines in the academic curriculum, English literature – and comparative literature, where it existed – was essentially and centrally a matter of valuation. This is not to suggest that other disciplines are merely matters of value-free 'fact'. Quite the contrary, knowledge in the human sciences is almost always connected to value judgements, especially those articulated to wider systems of social belief and wider structures of social interest. But although value judgements and interests certainly provide much of the inspiration for research in history, geography or anthropology, the subject matter of these disciplines remains in principle analytically separable from those judgements and interests. Historians study periods of which they disapprove, geographers countries they dislike, anthropologists tribal religions they disbelieve. Literature teachers, by contrast, have not normally wasted very much time on books, or even types of book, they deem not to be literature, that is, not 'great' (or 'fine'). As Franco Moretti rather nicely put it: 'if everyone behaved like literary critics who only study what they 'like', doctors might restrict themselves to studying only healthy bodies and economists the standard of living of the well-off' (Moretti 1988: 14). Literature as an academic discipline was not so much 'informed' by value judgements as positively *satu-*

rated in values, to the extent that any attempt to eliminate them, such as is occasionally recommended by 'positivistic' thinkers in other fields, would have been to eliminate the discipline itself. For literary studies was the study, not of writing *per se*, but of valued writing.

Moreover, literature's disciplinary focus had typically fallen, not on how to write valued writing, but on how to *value* it. As one historian of the discipline commented, 'the real content of the school and college subject which goes under the name "English Literature" is not literature in the primary sense, but *criticism*' (Baldick 1983: 4). We all know what criticism means: it is hostile commentary. Which is why politicians and business leaders, union officials and even university professors tend to see it as 'carping' or 'ill informed'. Again, however, this is not what has normally been meant by literary 'criticism' as practised in schools and colleges. Here criticism became the study of how to 'appreciate' writing. And since the books chosen for study were normally already deemed valuable, hostility itself disappeared almost altogether from criticism, to be replaced by a much more positive induction into a particular set of already available literary values. The logic of this procedure is caught very nicely in Baldick's conclusion that:

> The critical approach, which refuses to accept what is offered simply at face value, which will not rest satisfied with things as they are, was squeezed into a narrowly literary criticism; social criticism in particular was blunted to conform with the implicit norm of literary 'sensibility', and put in the service of social consensus. The title of 'criticism' was usurped by a literary discourse whose entire attitude was at heart uncritical. Criticism in its most important and most vital sense had been gutted and turned into its very opposite.
>
> (Baldick 1983: 234).

It was as such uncritical criticism, then, that literary studies attempted to make sense of itself and to make sense for others.

The case for teaching examined courses in English literature is far from self-evident. Academic disciplines are normally justified in terms of their value as either knowledge-producing or skill-producing enterprises. In the latter case, examination procedures are conventionally justified as devices by which to exclude incompetent or inadequately trained practitioners from the profession or trade in question. In the former, the rationale is less obvious: the harm that might be done by unleashing an inadequately trained historian into the world is by no means readily apparent. But it appears to derive from the assumption that some test of acquired familiarity becomes necessary as a check on the adequacy of the pedagogical process itself. Undoubtedly there is much that is open to question in all of this. But assuming the validity of the argument, one can still ask what new skill or new knowledge is involved in English literature. At primary and perhaps even at secondary school level certain basic language skills can indeed be learnt by students. And even at university or college certain new knowledges, about the history of the English language for example, may very well be made available. However, the core of the discipline, the reading and appreciation of English literature, entailed no obviously new skills or knowledges. English students were typically asked to do what many people did anyway, that is, to read and appreciate novels, plays and poems. It was rather as if one were asked to pass examinations in television-watching or rock-concert attendance.

What eventually came to distinguish studying English at university from reading books on the train was therefore the ability to 'discriminate', 'evaluate' and 'criticise'. And these skills were in fact examinable, but only on the condition that criteria of literary value could be found to which both teachers and students could, or at least should, subscribe, and which had some greater validity than criteria already available to the untrained reader. In general English teachers certainly tended to behave as if such criteria were available. But the key words here are 'as if': it was not that English teachers argued explicitly for any given theory of aesthetics, rather that their teaching practices only remained intelligible if one assumed the existence of some such implicit aesthetic. The peculiar double bind by which English studies insisted on the absolute importance of an aesthetic that was somehow absent rather than present is directly traceable to the work of F. R. Leavis, perhaps the single most important figure in the twentieth-century history of the discipline. When challenged by the philosopher René Wellek to defend his own position 'abstractly', Leavis replied that: 'My whole effort was to work in terms of concrete judgements and particular analyses: "This – doesn't it? – bears such a relation to that; this kind of thing – don't you find it so? – wears better than that" ' (F. R. Leavis 1962a: 215). The authentic reader responding authentically to the authentically literary text was apparently in no need of any abstract theory of aesthetics because the truly literary work spontaneously elicited from the mature literary reader a properly aesthetic response.

But what if it didn't? What if one were to reply to Leavis: 'No, I don't really think this does bear such a relation to that; no, I'm sorry but I don't find it so, I rather think that the other kind of thing wears better'? What if one were to insist with Freeman that chatter about Shelley was essentially a matter of personal taste? Then, of course, the entire procedure collapsed into mutual unintelligibility and perhaps even mutual recrimination. Such incidents were never entirely unfamiliar to teachers of English. For this was more or less exactly what happened whenever first-year students, invited to respond spontaneously to the literary work and strongly discouraged from reading the available secondary criticism, volunteered their own spontaneous responses, only to discover that these were not the types of spontaneous response the English Department had been seeking. The cultivated theoretical inarticulacy of this Leavisite aesthetic was thus not merely one of its most distinctive features, but also a distinctive source of anxiety for the student novitiate in English studies. It is difficult enough to learn the habits of a new and unfamiliar discipline even when these are formulated explicitly; when carefully left unstated they became doubly worrisome.

More than any other single figure, Leavis provided apparently good reason for studying English literature, as distinct from comparative literature or classics. He argued that it was in language itself, in its most literary moments of articulation, that the truths of a particular national culture were most clearly formed. For Leavis, the English language in its 'Shakespearean use' was possessed of the distinctive and peculiar property that its 'words seem to do what they say' (F. R. Leavis 1972a: 58). It followed, then, that the proper subject matter of literary studies lay in the Englishness of the language itself. Moreover, the Englishness of the language was, in turn, an expression of the Englishness of the people and of their erstwhile 'common culture'.

The true values of a national culture were sustained by literary language, he insisted, by 'the changing idiom, upon which fine living depends, and without which distinction of spirit is thwarted and incoherent'. 'By "culture"', he added, 'I mean the use of such a language' (F. R. Leavis 1948: 145). It should be no surprise that in the 1960s, when confronted by a proposal to include foreign writers in a new course on the novel, Leavis would argue that to study Proust and Kafka 'would be a misdirection. There is nothing relevant there' (Williams 1984: 117).

For Leavis, literary and non-literary culture were inextricably connected: in a healthy culture there is, 'behind the literature, a social culture and an art of living' (F. R. Leavis 1962a: 190). Cultural health thus entailed a kind of 'organic' unity between sophisticated and popular cultures, between literature and life. In 'seeing off' classics and comparative literature, Leavis had actually appealed from the literary to the social, and incidentally from the sophisticated to the popular; but only retrospectively so, since he also subscribed to a theory of cultural decline which insisted that the Industrial Revolution had led to cultural levelling and standardisation. English literature justified itself as the best self of the national (and imperial) culture: that was how it had managed to sideline classics and comparative literature. But in so doing it had to invoke 'culture' in the social as well as the aesthetic sense of the term, culture as 'way of life', as well as culture as art. It came increasingly to define itself against contemporary ways of life, of course, and in favour of a (largely mythical) way of life located in the pre-industrial, historical past. Thus 'literature' as art became counterposed to 'fiction' as popular commodity. But the issue had been broached nonetheless: English literature was about culture as well as about literature. Sooner or later, academics trained in English were bound to become curious about what lay beyond the canon. Sooner or later they were likely to take a more serious interest in popular culture itself. This was precisely the route toward 'cultural studies' eventually taken by both Raymond Williams and Richard Hoggart.

For comparative literature, by contrast, the literary canon was international rather than national in range and scope. The discipline thus gave pride of place to what Goethe had termed *Weltliteratur*. Writing in 1828, he enthusiastically anticipated that:

> our present active epoch with its increasing communication between nations might soon hope for a world literature.
>
> (Goethe 1973: 7)

The radical edge to such intellectual cosmopolitanism was as apparent in the nineteenth century as today. Indeed, the century's two most famous radicals, Karl Marx and Friedrich Engels, would use exactly the same word, in more or less exactly the same sense, in the opening section of their *Communist Manifesto*:

> The bourgeoisie has through its exploitation of the world market given a cosmopolitan character to production and consumption in every country. To the great chagrin of Reactionists, it has drawn from under the feet of industry the national ground on which it stood.... And as in material, so also in intellectual production. The intellectual creations of individual nations become common property. National one-sidedness and narrow-mindedness become more and more impossible, and from the numerous national and local literatures, there arises a world literature.
>
> (Marx and Engels 1967: 83–4)

As the German text makes clear, the exactness of the resemblance is not an effect of mistranslation:

> Daß bei der gegenwärtigen höchst bewegten Epoche und durchaus erleichterter Kommunikation eine Weltliteratur baldigst zu hoffen sei.
>
> (Goethe 1950: 895)

> Die Bourgeoisie hat durch die Exploitation des Weltmarkts die Produktion und Konsumption aller Länder kosmopolitisch gestaltet. Sie hat zum großen Bedauern der Reaktionäre den nationalen Boden der Industrie unter den Füßen weggezogen.... Und wie in der materiellen, so auch in der geistigen Produktion. Die geistigen Erzeugnisse der einzelnen Nationen werden Gemeingut. Die nationale Einseitigkeit und Be-schränktheit wird

> mehr und mehr unmöglich, und aus den vielen nationalen und lokalen Literaturen bildet sich eine Weltliteratur.
>
> (Marx and Engels 1959: 466)

Indeed, I am tempted to the observation that the regret of reactionists – chagrin is nicer, but not literally accurate – might well be the point of comparative literature. Certainly, this seems to be Moretti's view when he observes, in a commentary deriving in part from Goethe, in part from Marx and Engels, that 'there is no other justification for the study of world literature...but this: to be a thorn in the side, a permanent intellectual challenge to national literatures' (Moretti 2000: 68).

Moretti is too smart, however, not to see the obvious problem that, if national literary canons are radically selective, insofar as they are constructed around what literary critics happen to 'like', then this will necessarily be even more so for a world canon. 'What does it mean, studying world literature?', he writes:

> I work on West European narrative between 1790 and 1830.... Not really, I work on its canonical fraction, which is not even one per cent of published literature...there are thirty thousand nineteenth-century British novels out there, forty, fifty, sixty thousand – no-one really knows, no-one has read them, no-one ever will. And then there are French novels, Chinese, Argentinian, American.... Reading 'more' is always a good thing, but not the solution.
>
> (Moretti 2000: 55)

His own solution, clearly prefigured in earlier essays on the sociology of literary form, even more so in his recent attempts at a cultural geography of the modern novel (Moretti 1998), is to move from criticism to social science, here represented by Immanuel Wallerstein's world-system theory. This isn't exactly what Hoggart and Williams had intended by cultural studies, nor what their successors have come to define as such, but it does represent a roughly analogous theoretical shift: from text to context; and from prescriptive criticism to what Williams called 'the complex seeing of analysis' (Williams 1989a: 239).

The inspirational effects of literary cosmopolitanism have sometimes been substantial: witness Edward Said's insistence that: 'Survival...is about the connections between things.... It is more rewarding – and more difficult – to think concretely and sympathetically, contrapuntally, about others than only about "us" ' (Said 1993: 408). But English literary nationalism could be equally inspirational: Martin Green, for example, saw Leavis as 'intensely and integrally British...his voice has echoes of the best things in my parents' England' (Green 1959: 506–7). Even a left-wing opponent would concede that Leavis's work had established 'new standards of discrimination' and 'permanently altered complacent traditional receptions of English poetry and the English novel' (P. Anderson 1992: 97). Literary humanism has become increasingly discredited, nonetheless, primarily as a result of what we might term the radical 'postmodernisation' of contemporary intellectual culture. The term 'postmodernism' has acquired a very large number of meanings: in the language of semiology, it is a radically 'polysemic' sign. But, however we define it, there can be little doubt that postmodern culture has entailed the collapse precisely of those antitheses between high and low, elite and popular, which were inscribed into the founding statutes of the disciplines of English and comparative literature. Zygmunt Bauman has argued that the social role of the contemporary intellectual shifted from that of 'legislator' to 'interpreter' (Bauman 1992: 1–24). 'The postmodernity/modernity opposition', he wrote, 'focuses on the waning of certainty and objectivity grounded in the unquestioned hierarchy of values...which makes the questions of objective standards impracticable and hence theoretically futile' (ibid.: 24). For Bauman, this change, in which academic thought effectively abandoned its traditional function of policing the boundaries of cultural authority, has been absolutely central to the postmodern inflection in contemporary culture. In itself this is hardly cause for regret: the older literary humanisms had clearly hardened into an irredeemable elitism, contemptuous, by turn, of 'mass culture', of 'foreign' or at least 'non-Western' literature, even sometimes of their own students. But when contemporary cultural theory celebrates the pluralism of the postmodern condition, and with it the collapse of older institutionalised claims to authoritative cultural judgement, it necessarily also celebrates the end of literature as literature teachers had hitherto understood it.

This is not to suggest that literature, in the sense of writing, becomes thereby an unsuitable object for academic study. To the contrary, writing, reading and the various associated social practices which facilitate them are immensely important human activities. In their aggregate they represent the particular fashion by which, within any given literate society, what Fredric Jameson has termed 'the all informing process of *narrative*...the central function or *instance* of the human mind' (Jameson 1981: 13) comes to be socially institutionalised. Literature in this sense will, of course, continue to command the attention of any body of scholarship worth the name. Humanist literary criticism has thus been progressively superseded by much less prescriptive versions of literary studies which have sought to analyse and explain how writing is written, read, distributed and exchanged. Thus reformulated, literary studies threatens to become part of a much wider intellectual enterprise, variously designated as 'cultural sociology' or, as we have seen, 'cultural studies'. For if literature is no longer the 'canonical' other of non-literature, as in the old antitheses between literature and fiction, minority culture and mass civilization, then it becomes merely some texts amongst many, each in principle analysable according to analogous intellectual procedures and operations.

From literary to cultural studies: the sociological turn

The term 'culture' has a long and varied history, 'cultural studies' rather less so, but both have been intimately connected with the history of literature. By 'cultural studies' I mean, again, a particular academic discipline, the discourse about 'culture', as distinct from 'literature', which began to develop during the 1950s and 1960s, initially on the margins of literary studies. The name came from Hoggart and was thus a specifically British coinage, but the intellectual orientation was much more generally European. I have argued elsewhere that cultural studies is best understood as a 'social-scientific' approach to the study of all textualised meanings, whether elite or popular, literary or non-literary (Milner 2002: 5). Defined thus, it can plausibly be read as deriving from, or at least significantly anticipated by, three relatively distinct intellectual formations: in Germany, Frankfurt School Critical Theory (especially the work of Theodor Adorno); in England, the 'left Leavisism' of Williams and Hoggart; and, in France, Roland Barthes's rewriting of existentialism as a semiology of demystification. The key foundational texts were Adorno and Horkheimer's *Dialektik der Aufklärung*, published in 1944, Barthes's *Mythologies*, published in French in 1957, Hoggart's *The Uses of Literacy* and Williams's *Culture and Society 1780–1950*, published in 1957 and 1958, respectively. These three intellectual formations, each with its own distinctive national history, will have cause to detain us on more than one occasion in the argument that follows. For now, however, note only that, where literary studies had focused attention on one particular kind of culture, 'high' literature, this new kind of 'cultural studies' would be concerned in principle with all kinds.

According to Williams, culture was 'one of the two or three most complicated words in the English language' (Williams 1976a: 76). In *Culture and Society* he identified four kinds of meaning that attach to the word, referring respectively to: an individual habit of mind; the intellectual development of a whole society; the arts; and the whole way of life of a group of people (Williams 1963: 16). The distinction which most fascinated him, however, was that between the latter two meanings. The concept of culture, he would later note, had 'played a crucial role in definitions of "the arts" and "the humanities", from the first sense...an equally crucial role in definitions of the "human sciences" and the "social sciences", in the second sense' (Williams 1977: 17). When Williams and Hoggart first began to broach the subject matter of what would become cultural studies, they each began to shift focus from the first to the second sense of the term, thus inaugurating what we might well describe in retrospect as a 'sociological turn' in British literary studies. Where traditional literary studies had defined literature as a timeless, 'aesthetic' category, cultural studies would tend to see cultural value as socially constructed. From its inception, then, cultural studies would be interested in the interplay between cultural texts, cultural identity and such conventionally 'sociological' indicators of social inequality as class, gender, race and ethnicity.

Sociology itself had hitherto been a very un-English affair, clearly overshadowed in both British and imperial universities by the immediately cognate discipline of anthropology. In principle, sociology and 'social anthropology' seem to be engaged in much the same exercise, since both claim to be the 'science of the study of society'. In practice, however, the differences had often been considerable. Sociology had tended to study 'modern', 'complex', 'industrial' societies, that is, in effect, 'white' people; anthropology 'primitive', 'simple', 'tribal' societies, that is, in effect, 'black' people. Sociology had tended to opt for quantitative, statistical methods of analysis, seen as somehow more appropriate to 'mass' societies; anthropology for qualitative, 'ethnographic' methods, normally based on 'participant observation' and 'fieldwork', seen as somehow more appropriate to relatively isolated, 'small-scale' societies. Anthropology had reached its heyday – unsurprisingly – in Britain and France during the period of European high imperialism, roughly from the 1880s to the Second World War. The world's two largest empires provided the world's most successful anthropologists with the field for their 'fieldwork'. Sociology, by contrast, had a rather more complex and chequered career. The term '*sociologie*' had been coined in the early nineteenth century by the French social philosopher August Comte. It had become institutionalised as a recognised academic discipline at much the same time as English literature, neither in England nor the Empire, but in Germany, France, Italy and the United States: Emile Durkheim was appointed to a chair at Bordeaux in 1896, and at the Sorbonne in 1902; Max Weber at Freiburg from 1893, and at Heidelburg from 1896; Vilfredo Pareto at Lausanne from 1894; Gaetano Mosca at Turin from 1895, later at Rome. The first Sociology Department in the United States, headed by Robert Park, was established at the University of Chicago in 1892.

If both anthropology and sociology imagined themselves as the study of society, then the obvious question becomes: what exactly is society? For anthropology, the answer was fairly straightforward: it was everything to do with human social life, work, kinship, art, religion, government and so on. This rather grand claim could be sustained partly because the societies studied were indeed relatively small-scale. Once the anthropologists had lived with their selected tribe for a year or two they could indeed 'know' quite a lot about all of these or, at the very least, plausibly imagine themselves to do so. It was sustained also by the absence of any serious academic competition to threaten the boundaries of anthropological knowledge. By and large, the Nuer of the southern Sudan remained the private preserve of anthropology in general and Professor E. E. Evans-Pritchard in particular (Evans-Pritchard 1940, 1951, 1956), since there were neither Nuer economists nor political scientists, art historians nor musicologists attempting to muscle in on the research. For anthropology, the object of study was indeed, in Williams's phrase, 'a whole way of life'. What made a way of life whole, however, for most anthropologists were the *values* that bound the tribe together as a collectivity, especially the tribal religion. More often than not, then, social anthropology turned out to be cultural anthropology. This type of ethnographic research could in principle also be applied to relatively well-defined 'bits' of larger-scale societies and, in fact, has been so applied by contemporary cultural studies, especially to the study of what are often termed 'spectacular youth subcultures' (Hall and Jefferson 1976; Hebdige 1979; Willis *et al.* 1990). But in general anthropologists themselves have tended to stick to their tribespeople. This may well explain why their discipline has become increasingly unwelcome in formerly colonised societies, where the new elites almost invariably prefer not to think of themselves as tribalised.

For sociology, the societies studied were much larger (the United States is the paradigmatic instance) and the academic competition much more ferocious. If sociology simply couldn't study everything, then what would it study? The short answer turned out to be 'values': in practice, mainstream sociological thinking tended toward the view that the 'essence' of the social, what held society together, was in fact the 'common value system'. The most influential mid-twentieth-century sociological thinker was almost certainly Talcott Parsons, Professor of Sociology at Harvard. Looking back on the legacy of European sociology, in its variously French, German and Italian versions, at the beginning of his own career, he concluded that the discipline had developed around a growing recognition of 'the conception of a common system of ultimate values as a vital element in concrete social life' (Parsons 1949: 469). A common system of ultimate values is rather less than a whole way of life, of course, but it is another sense of the term 'culture', nonetheless, that of a particular social sub-system, functioning alongside the economic and political sub-systems. Where literary studies had self-consciously defined itself as a humanity, an 'arts' subject, sociology imagined itself as a social science (anthropologists were often much less certain). Indeed, Comte is widely credited as the author, not only of sociology, but also of 'positivism', that is, the doctrine that society and the human condition can be studied by means roughly analogous to the methods of the natural sciences. The true 'founding father' of French sociology, who presided over its institutionalisation in the universities, wasn't so much Comte, however, as Durkheim. And Durkheim too had aspired to 'scientificity', enjoining would-be sociologists, in his famous *Rules of Sociological Method*, to 'Consider social facts as things' (Durkheim 1964: 14). This approach led sociology into the search for 'objective' ways of 'measuring' values 'quantitatively'.

Typically, then, sociological research came to involve the design of a standard questionnaire with which to survey a more or less random sample of respondents so as to discover their 'values', as indicated by the responses to the questions. These questions were framed in ways that allowed for quasi-quantitative measurement, for example boxes ranging from 'Strongly agree' to 'Strongly disagree' by way of 'Don't know'. The responses were measured in percentage terms and correlated against such variables as age, gender, class and so on. Unlike literary studies, neither anthropology nor sociology had much problem incorporating popular culture into its subject matter: for anthropology, almost all culture was in some sense 'popular' (or at least 'common'); for sociology, popular cultural preference was merely yet more grist to its statistical mill. But the sociological approach remained oddly external to the culture it studied, happy to discover the age, gender and class of the average *Star Trek* fan, measured to two decimal places, but unable to suggest very much as to what *Star Trek* was actually 'about'. If literary studies had long since discovered that it couldn't stand popular culture, then sociology would discover that it couldn't *under*stand it. The stage was set, then, for English literature to turn toward sociology and begin to think about what a contemporary cultural studies might become.

English studies had inherited a tradition of peculiar ambivalence in the face of sociology. It was often obliged to recognise, with Leavis, that 'a real literary interest is an interest in man, society and civilization' (F. R. Leavis 1962a: 200) and is thus in a sense sociological. Yet it also often insisted, again with Leavis, that 'no "sociology of literature"...will yield much profit unless informed and controlled by a real and intelligent interest – a first-hand critical interest – in literature' (ibid.: 198). The key term in this last sentence is 'critical'. What Leavis and many other literary critics feared in sociology was the dead hand of a positivist empiricism which would suppress the literary, the critical, the aesthetic, which would subordinate literature itself to the imperatives of what Leavis later came to term 'technologico-Benthamite' civilisation (F. R. Leavis 1972b: 33). This was not simply, as it has sometimes been presented, a matter of Leavis's insistence on the importance of the 'internal' analysis of the text itself, as opposed to 'external' analyses of the text's various contexts. More importantly, what was at stake was the centrality of evaluation, as applied to both texts and contexts. Such questions are indeed important and are typically suppressed in much positivist sociology. But nonetheless, and despite Leavis, there is nothing distinctively 'literary' about the nature of a mind which might pose them.

Indeed, there is no reason at all why sociology should not be properly 'critical'. Criticism, we have observed, is a matter of evaluation, and evaluations are politically and socially committed, because politically and socially located. Adorno's colleague Max Horkheimer defined his own 'critical sociology', in opposition to 'traditional' positivist sociology, as 'an essential element in the historical effort to create a world which satisfies the needs and powers of men...the theory never aims simply at an increase of knowledge as such. Its goal is man's emancipation from slavery' (Horkheimer 1972: 245–6). Despite the sexism of the terms – in the English translation at least – this notion of criticism has the clear advantage over Leavis in that it incorporates the everyday sense of criticism as hostile. A critical cultural studies, like a critical sociology, would be characterised, above all, by a sustained hostility to whatever 'slaveries' may impede the continuing cause of human emancipation. If this appears to take the sociological turn too far from literature, then we should recall the much-quoted thesis of another of Adorno's colleagues, Walter Benjamin: 'There is no document of civilization which is not at the same time a document of barbarism'

(Benjamin 1973a: 258). Where the subject matter of literary studies had been 'civilization', as Benjamin uses the term here, and that of sociology (very often the 'barbarism' of structured social inequalities), then cultural studies would attempt to deal systematically with both.

Hoggart's *The Uses of Literacy* marked the point at which post-Leavisite English studies shifted emphasis from 'literature' to 'culture'. For Hoggart, it was to be the general culture of the working class, rather than the specifically literary culture of the Leavisian 'minority', that would be analysed, valorised and sometimes also elegised. His achievement was thus to divest Leavisism of something of its cultural elitism, if not of its nostalgia. This shift was to register even more fully, however, in Williams's *Culture and Society* and in *The Long Revolution*, first published in 1961. In the 'Conclusion' to *Culture and Society*, Williams had rejected the Leavisite notion of a distinctively valuable minority culture. A culture, he wrote, 'is not only a body of intellectual and imaginative work; it is also and essentially a whole way of life' (Williams 1963: 311). Here, he expanded the range of the concept 'culture' to include the 'collective democratic institution', that is, the trade union, the co-operative and the working-class political party (ibid.: 313). In *The Long Revolution* he would seek to map out the historical emergence of modernity through the interrelated processes of the democratic revolution, the Industrial Revolution, and the 'cultural revolution' of the extension and democratisation of communications (Williams 1965: 10–12).

Cultural studies is today emerging as a discipline in its own right, with all this means in terms of professional associations, journals, departments and 'centres'. The Birmingham Centre for Contemporary Cultural Studies, founded in 1964 by Hoggart, then still Professor of English Literature at Birmingham, and later headed by Stuart Hall, clearly paved the way for much of this. But cultural studies has already escaped the peculiarities of its British origins. If not quite the 'genuinely global movement' Simon During describes (1999: 11), it has nonetheless grown into a putatively international discipline, with a serious intellectual presence, stretching beyond Europe, the Americas and Australia, into India, Taiwan and Korea. In England itself, cultural studies emerged out of literary studies essentially by way of a very simple move: by shifting attention from an exclusive focus on the canon of high literary texts to an in-principle inclusive focus on all cultural texts, Williams and Hoggart attempted no more than to expand the subject matter of English literature to include 'popular culture'. English literary criticism had constructed the popular, not as part of 'English', however, but as the discipline's excluded antithetical other. Almost by default, then, 'the popular' became the subject matter of something else, the new proto-discipline of cultural studies. Given that both English and comparative literature continued to study and police their respective literary canons, cultural studies increasingly became preoccupied – in practice, as distinct from in principle – with popular culture, television soap operas, James Bond films, Superman comics, cyberpunk, Mills and Boon and so on. If the distinction between literature (and the other high arts) on the one hand and popular culture on the other had been simply and uncontroversially a matter of different kinds of text – for example the novel as distinct from the television programme – then there could have been a more or less straightforward division of labour between literary and cultural studies, defined in terms of these different objects of study. But, as we have seen, the 'literature' in English and comparative literature had never meant all writing, nor even all novels, but only valuable writing – which clearly posed the question: who does the valuing?

The distinction between literature and fiction, between 'elite' and 'popular' cultural forms, clearly overlaps with that between elite and non-elite social groups. Insofar as literary studies had insisted that literature was inherently valuable, and popular culture inherently less so, it tended toward a form of cultural elitism, deliberately privileging minority forms and values. Whilst this is analytically separable from social elitism, they were in practice normally deeply intertwined. As T. S. Eliot (an elitist on both counts) insisted, a cultural elite 'must...be attached to *some* class...it is likely to be the dominant class that attracts this élite to itself' (Eliot 1962: 42). Empirical sociological research has repeatedly confirmed that canonical literature tends to be valued by the more educated, more affluent and more powerful groups, fiction by the less well educated, less affluent and less powerful (cf. Bourdieu 1984). Such evidence can be read as meaning either that the dominant groups tend to have better taste in 'art' or that they have the power to define as 'art' whatever it is they tend to prefer. Pierre

Bourdieu concluded that the pedagogical procedures in French secondary and higher education in the humanities test not so much specific knowledges as access to an elite culture 'which is *given* to the children of the cultivated classes – style, taste, wit – in short, those attitudes and aptitudes which seem natural in members of the cultivated classes, and naturally expected of them precisely because...they are the *culture* of that class' (ibid.: 39). Bourdieu himself wrote as a declared opponent of such cultural elitisms. But the point is almost as readily conceded by their advocates: for Leavis, literary culture was necessarily a 'minority culture'. 'In any period', he wrote, 'it is upon a very small minority that the discerning appreciation of art and literature depends' (F. R. Leavis 1948: 143).

Where cultural studies has defined itself as the study of 'all' texts, minority or popular, it has sometimes been able to sidestep this issue. But insofar as it has become the study of popular culture in particular it has increasingly tended to argue for the inherent value of the popular, that is, to espouse a form of cultural populism. This is to broach the vexed question of the cultural politics of cultural studies. Where literary studies had inclined towards an often politically conservative cultural elitism, cultural studies has often displayed an equivalent commitment to various kinds of political radicalism. Williams's early work very clearly emerged from out of a sustained encounter between English literary criticism and socialist politics: he had come from a working-class (trade unionist and Labour Party) family background and had been repelled by the cultural elitism of English literature and by the contempt it directed at working-class culture. It is no accident that Hoggart – and, in France, Bourdieu – came from roughly similar backgrounds. This elision of politics and culture has been a recurring theme in cultural studies, which has often tended to align itself with political dissent, in the first place working-class socialism, but later also other kinds of 'new social movement' radicalism, for example feminism, ethnic multiculturalism and homosexual liberation.

Elitism, populism and immodest cultural studies

Note that there are two versions of cultural studies in play here: on the one hand an 'immodest' version, where the new discipline is defined in terms of a new methodology connecting the study of the popular to the study of the literary; on the other a 'modest' version, defined in terms of its subject matter, that is, as the study of popular culture. Despite Williams's and Hoggart's own clearly immodest intentions, the more general immediate impulse within cultural studies was to turn away from literature and toward culture, still understood in essentially Leavisite terms as non-literature. Certainly, the work of the Birmingham Centre acquired an increasingly 'sociological' character, especially after Hall's appointment as Director in 1968. In retrospect, however, this 'separate development' of an institutionally distinct, non-literary cultural studies alongside a still theoretically inviolate English literature appears not so much as radical innovation but as unhappy compromise. For the real promise of cultural studies had always been contained, not in the discovery of a new empirical subject matter, but in a 'deconstruction' of the very theoretical boundaries that hitherto demarcated literature from fiction, art from culture, the elite from the popular. The eventual outcome of this deconstruction, postponed but not prevented by the resistances from within English, would be a 'double movement', in Anthony Easthope's phrase, by which 'literary study becomes increasingly indistinguishable from cultural studies' and 'cultural studies makes incursions into the traditionally literary terrain of textuality' (Easthope 1991: 65). Thirty years on from the first publication of *The Long Revolution*, the way seemed finally open to Easthope 'for a combined analysis of literary and non-literary texts as instances of signifying practice' (ibid.: 74). A cultural studies thus constituted would clearly understand literature not as the antithetical other of culture, but as one regional sub-system amongst others within the more general culture.

Both modest and immodest versions of cultural studies threatened the disciplinary integrity of traditional literary studies, but in rather different ways. The immodest version threatened to subsume literary studies as a regional specialism within cultural studies. The modest version tacitly agreed to leave English and comparative literature to get on with the traditional business of literary studies, but thereby simultaneously turned itself into a potential rival in the more general academic competition for students and funding. Much as modern literature had done *vis-à-vis* classics, modest cultural studies might simply supersede rather than subsume literary studies. Cultural studies has tended increasingly towards theoretical modesty, although both versions still remain in play. Which eventually succeeds will depend in large measure on how literature comes to be understood, both by literary studies and by cultural studies itself. Such matters are deeply controversial, of course, with opinions ranging from a radically elitist insistence on the absolute inviolability of the literary canon to a radically populist determination to ignore literature altogether. I want now to explore something of the logic of each of these options, represented paradigmatically by two contemporary writers, each with a claim to a certain authority in matters of theory: Harold Bloom, Professor of Humanities at Yale University in the United States; and Tony Bennett, the successor to Stuart Hall as Professor of Sociology at the Open University in England. Bloom is the author of an extensive corpus of literary criticism, including *The Anxiety of Influence* (1973) and *Poetry and Repression* (1976). His approach to literary criticism has been strongly influenced by Freudian psychoanalysis, but also – and ironically – by an encounter with the kind of 'post-structuralism' known as 'deconstruction'. Jacques Derrida, the deconstructionist *par excellence*, taught for many years in the Department of Comparative Literature at Yale, where he and Bloom met and in fact became co-contributors to one of the books generally held responsible for 'introducing' deconstruction to the North American literary public (Bloom 1979). Bennett is the author of an extensive body of work in cultural studies, including *Formalism and Marxism* (1979) and *Bond and Beyond: The Political Career of a Popular Hero* (Bennett and Woollacott 1987). His own approach had initially been influenced by a kind of 'structuralist' Marxism, but has increasingly come to embrace the kind of 'post-structuralism' associated with the work of the late Michel Foucault. Bloom and Bennett appear to agree about very little, except perhaps that literary studies and popular culture need have nothing to do with each other.

Bloom's *The Western Canon: The Books and Schools of the Ages* is an impressive defence of the idea of the canon, prompted by a perceived threat to literary studies from Derridean deconstruction and cultural studies. His *Shakespeare: The Invention of the Human* powerfully pits this most canonical of writers against contemporary 'cultural anthropology' and 'Theory' (Bloom 1999: 2). Bloom has no doubt that criticism, as he understands it, and literature are inextricably linked concepts. His purpose, he explains, is, at least in part, 'to combat the cultural politics, both Left and Right, that are destroying criticism and consequently may destroy literature itself' (Bloom 1994: 62). Without some kind of canon and without a body of criticism to account for that canon, there may well still be writing, but there will no longer be literature. He also has little doubt as to the direction from which the greater threat now emanates: 'Resentment', as he dubs it, the 'critics who value theory over the literature itself' (Bloom 1999: 9). These 'Feminists, Marxists, Lacanians, New Historicists, Deconstructionists, Semioticians' (Bloom 1994: 527) share a common hostility to the notion of a hierarchy of aesthetic value, in which some achieve greatness and some regrettably do not. Bloom's own argument rests on a very strong assumption as to the demonstrable 'reality' of inherent literary value. The 'phenomenon of surpassing literary excellence', he writes, is 'of such power of thought, characterisation and metaphor that it triumphantly survives translation and transposition and compels attention in virtually every culture' (ibid.: 52). And, for Bloom, Shakespeare is literary excellence at its most excellent. Indeed, this 'Shakespearean difference', as he terms it, is what finally defines the aim of literary study as 'the search for a kind of value that transcends the particular prejudices and needs of societies at fixed points in time' (ibid.: 62).

Shakespeare's greatness is thus fundamentally universal in character:

> he has become the universal canon, perhaps the only one that can survive the current debasement of our teaching institutions.... Every other great writer may fall away, to be replaced by the anti-elitist swamp of Cultural Studies. Shakespeare will abide.
>
> (Bloom 1999: 17)

Nor is this universality merely 'western': Shakespeare is at 'the center of the embryo of a world canon, not Western or Eastern and less and less Eurocentric' (Bloom 1994: 62–3). Thus *King Lear* is 'at the center of centers of canonical excellence', where 'the flames of invention burn away all context and grant us the possibility of what could be called primal aesthetic value, free of history and ideology' (ibid.: 65). Does this mean anything more than that Bloom really, really, likes *Lear*? Clearly it does for Bloom: primal aesthetic value, he assures us, is 'available to whoever can be educated to read and view it' (ibid.: 65). There is an obvious reply to this: that Bloom's 'whoever' is neither 'everyone' nor 'anyone', but rather, and quite specifically, a social elite. He acknowledges the problem, but counters with what I am tempted to describe as a kind of 'ultra-elitism' of his own. 'Partisans of Resentment might stress that only an elite can be so educated', he writes: 'As our more truthful moments inform us, it has become harder and harder to read deeply as this century grows older...even the elite tend to lose concentration as readers' (ibid.: 65). Which rather seems to suggest that not even the elite can be so educated.

Like Leavis before him, Bloom is eventually thrown back on not much more than the profession of literary studies, and by no means all of it. Admittedly, he is a much more boisterous character than Leavis, much less melancholic. But, like the Leavisites, he sees literature as in imminent danger of being 'levelled' out of existence. We live in a 'bad time', he writes with heavy irony, 'when teachers of literature teach everything except literature, and discuss Shakespeare in terms scarcely different from those employed for television serials or for the peerless Madonna' (Bloom 1999: 726). Elsewhere, he worries that literary studies 'as such' might not have much of a future:

> The study of Western literature will...continue, but on the modest scale of our current Classics departments. What are now called 'Departments of English' will be renamed departments of 'Cultural Studies', where *Batman* comics, Mormon theme parks, television, movies, and rock will replace Chaucer, Shakespeare, Milton, Wordsworth and Wallace Stevens.
>
> (Bloom 1994: 519)

We have to choose, then, between Batman and Chaucer, between television and Milton. Bloom knows, of course, that cultural studies is more than simply the study of popular culture, that the 'School of Resentment' has its eyes on literature too. But he is just as scathing about cultural studies approaches to canonical texts. 'French

Shakespeare', as he dubs Stephen Greenblatt's 'new historicist' approach, 'is just not Shakespeare' (Bloom 1999: 9). Insofar as it focuses on gender, ideology and so on, 'Resentment' is a typically contextual approach, Bloom observes, though this is in some ways a very odd thing to say of deconstruction, if not of feminism. He proceeds thence to speculate very rudely about his younger academic colleagues: 'I sometimes wonder if a critical preference for context over text does not reflect a generation made impatient with deep reading' (Bloom 1994: 65). As should be apparent, Bloom actually prefers modest to immodest cultural studies; that is, he prefers the version that will *not* deal with canonical literature. For he would rather that English wither on the vine than that it should ever be taught as a part of cultural studies.

I confess to some sympathy with many of the particular judgements in *The Western Canon*. Bloom's twenty-six central authors might not be mine, but nor thankfully are they either Eliot's or Leavis's: it is difficult not to applaud Milton's inclusion, for example. The notion of a 'world canon' nicely evades the more brutish forms of Anglocentric cultural chauvinism commonly associated with such bardolatry. Indeed, both Bloom's short list of twenty-six and his long list of 3,000 books by 850 authors derive from comparative literature rather than from English literature. In any case, the long list is so very long, and so very catholic, as to be readable as a curriculum rather than a canon. But the argument seems fundamentally misconceived, nonetheless, in what I take to be its two most fundamental premises: first, that there is a necessary opposition – and a necessary choice to be made – between literature and cultural studies; and second, that literary value is a transhistorical, essential property of all great art. As to the first, I do not even begin to understand why 'we' (meaning the academic institution of criticism rather than any particular group or individual therein) must necessarily choose between the study of minority and mass cultures. Quite the contrary, they are in practice interrelated in often very interesting ways and the study of each can cast light on the other. I will attempt to demonstrate something of this in Chapters 5 and 6, through the exploration of a network of contextual and intertextual connections between a group of elite and popular texts. As to the second question, I do not see how literary value – or any other kind of value – can ever exist independently of those doing the valuing. The 'literariness' of literature is not a property of a certain type of writing, but rather a function of the ways in which different kinds of writing are socially processed, both by writers themselves and by readers, publishers, booksellers, literary critics and so on. As Terry Eagleton has argued:

> There is no such thing as a literary work or tradition which is valuable *in itself*, regardless of what anyone might have said or come to say about it. 'Value' is a transitive term: it means whatever is valued by certain people in specific situations, according to particular criteria and in the light of given purposes.
>
> (Eagleton 1996a: 11)

Such valuations are not random, for, as Eagleton also insists, 'they have their roots in deeper structures of belief' (ibid.: 16). Whatever else literature may be, it is fundamentally a *social* construct, and moreover in historical terms a comparatively recent such construct at that.

The logic of Bloom's position also seems irresponsibly defeatist, insofar as it leads him to anticipate the decline of his own discipline with something quite close to relish. 'It was a mistake to believe that literary criticism could become a basis for democratic education', he argues: 'When our English and other literature departments shrink to the dimensions of our current Classics departments, ceding their grosser functions to the legions of Cultural Studies, we will perhaps be able to return to the study of the inescapable, to Shakespeare and his few peers' (Bloom 1994: 17). No doubt the 'we' in this sentence includes both Bloom himself and many of his colleagues at Yale, but it seems very unlikely to be extended to embrace the average liberal arts student at the average under-funded new university. Rather than expand literary studies to include Batman, Bloom will cheerfully watch it contract to the scale of classics. Yet classics barely exists in most secondary schools and is taught only as an increasingly marginal discipline within only a minority of Anglophone universities. No doubt both classics itself and English literature, redefined as a kind of classics without the training in languages, would continue to be taught at elite institutions such as Yale and Harvard or Oxford and Cambridge. But elsewhere the example of classics is surely deeply ominous, threatening at best to marginalise, at worst to eliminate literature almost altogether from the humanities curriculum. This isn't quite Lear's madness (with cultural studies cast as Cordelia); more Othello's (with literature as Desdemona):

> ...I had rather be a toad,
> And live upon the vapour of a dungeon,
> Than keep a corner in the thing I love
> For others' uses.
> (Shakespeare, *Othello*, III, iii, 270–3)

Bennett's *Outside Literature* is almost the theoretical obverse of *The Western Canon*, a negative 'cultural studies' critique of literary aesthetics, clearly predicated on similar assumptions about the social constructedness of literature to those in Eagleton. In a series of short essays written during the 1990s and in *Culture: A Reformer's Science* he also set out its ambitiously positive corollary, the case for a new kind of cultural sociology, recast as 'cultural policy studies'. Where Bloom had lumped Marxist critical theory together with feminism, deconstruction and semiology, Bennett was more discriminating. He sought to refute not only literary humanism, such as Bloom represents, but also Marxist 'ideology critique' of the kind practised by Eagleton. Marxism often claims to be 'historical' and 'materialist', Bennett noted, but Foucauldians, feminists and deconstructionists can 'say the same thing, and...with better credentials...for practising what they preach' (Bennett 1990: 36). Ironically, the central weakness of Eagleton's Marxism thus turned out to be its enduring loyalty to the legacy of humanist aesthetics. Marxism, Bennett concludes, 'is now virtually the only avenue through which the idealist concerns of bourgeois aesthetics retain a contemporary currency' (ibid.: 33) – which somehow seems to do justice neither to Eagleton nor to Bloom. Bennett widens this attack on Marxist critical theory into a more general critique of humanist aesthetics. Philosophical aesthetics misunderstands literary and artistic judgement as universal modes of cognition, he argues, whereas in reality these are only ever the socially specific application of the particular rules of value that happen to be shared by a particular valuing community. For Bennett, aesthetic discourse is thus merely one discourse of value amongst many others, such as sport or cuisine. Philosophical aesthetics 'fetishise the object of value' (ibid.: 160) because it mistakenly assumes that value inheres in the object valued, rather than in the valuing process.

Relative intolerance is characteristic of all discourses of value, Bennett notes, but, precisely because art is valued as inherently and qualitatively superior to cuisine or sport, its intolerance is absolute. 'In the case of aesthetic discourse', he writes:

> obliged to operate at the level of universality in order to establish the aesthetic as a distinctive mode of the subject's mental relation to reality...intolerance becomes absolute. Within such discourse, the subject who fails to appreciate correctly is regarded as being incompletely human rather than merely being excluded from full title to the membership of a specific valued and valuing community.
>
> (Bennett 1990: 165)

Not to appreciate rugby league football is merely not to be Northern English or New South Welsh. But not to appreciate the moral complexity of Leavis's 'Great Tradition' is somehow to fail in one's sense of the human situation and of the nature of life itself. Aesthetics thus necessarily deploys what Bennett termed a 'discourse of disqualification' (ibid.: 160) in relation to all those who will not conform to its edicts. To refuse to acknowledge the value of the aesthetic object demonstrates to the literary critic, not that the object is not valuable, but only that the valuer is not 'fit' to value. Aesthetics is thus little more than an ideology of intolerance, 'really useless knowledge', in Bennett's phrase (ibid.: 143). Bennett made much of the theoretical continuity between humanist literary criticism and Marxist critical theory, arguing that they share a common conception of criticism as 'a set of interpretive procedures oriented towards the transformation of the consciousness of individual subjects' (ibid.: 195). For Bennett, by contrast, the Foucauldian notion of the 'specific intellectual' requires that we 'pose questions of literary politics in ways that are sufficiently precise and focused to make a sustained difference to the functioning of literary institutions' (ibid.: 242, 286). It follows, then, that it is the institutional context, rather than the text as a discrete object in its own right, which most clearly warrants our attention, the 'truth/power symbiosis', as he terms it, again after Foucault. The outcome of all this would not only be cultural studies rather than literary studies, but cultural studies imagined in a very specific way, that is, as a kind of applied social science. Thus conceived, it will conduct its investigations 'with a view not only to undoing that symbiosis but also...[to] installing a new one in its place' (ibid.: 270). In practice, this turned out to mean the development of the supposedly 'really useful knowledge' of cultural policy studies. The 'cultural critic' must become the 'cultural engineer', Bennett suggested, 'less committed to cultural critique' as an instrument for changing consciousness than to 'modifying the functioning of culture by means of technical adjustments to its governmental deployment' (Bennett 1992: 406).

In *Culture: A Reformer's Science*, Bennett proceeded to argue that culture had become 'so deeply governmentalised' that it no longer made sense to think of it 'as a ground situated outside the domain of government...through which that domain might be resisted' (Bennett 1998: 30). Rather, 'intellectuals working in cultural studies needed to begin to "talk to the ISAs" – that is Althusser's famous Ideological State Apparatuses' (ibid.: 33). This, then, is what Bennett means by 'disciplining' cultural studies: 'allowing everyday life and cultural experience to be fashioned into instruments of government via their inscription in new forms of teaching and training' (ibid.: 51). I confess to some sympathy with his declaredly Foucauldian view that the object of study in cultural studies is 'the relations of culture and power' (ibid.: 53). But I doubt that either culture in general or higher education in particular is anything like so 'governmentalised' as Bennett suggests. For the notion of 'governmentality' here clearly refers to a much more explicitly 'statist' process than anything in Foucault (ibid.: 144; cf. Foucault 1991). And if governmentality is the work of the state in particular, rather than of power in general, then the most striking feature of postmodern 'late capitalism' is surely its opposite: the commodification and consequent 'degovernmentalisation' of cultural texts, practices and institutions. It is clear, in retrospect, that Bennett had initially imagined cultural policy studies in the service of left-of-centre governments committed to some kind of public intervention into the arts. The reality has been quite otherwise, however, much closer to that anticipated by cultural critics like Eagleton and Jameson. Even where substantial government sectors still persist, these are increasingly subject to what Jim McGuigan describes as 'the emergence and dissemination of a pervasive managerialist and market reasoning in the public sector itself' (McGuigan 1996: 2). As McGuigan concludes, policy debate in the cultural field is now framed by 'economic reductionisms and technological determinisms' to the extent that these inform even supposedly 'critical political economy of the media' (ibid.: 28). This is the process to which 'governmentalised' policy studies now seems irreparably committed, both in Britain and elsewhere. The only way out surely resides in some modest rehabilitation of the critical impulse, albeit not a return to Bloomian bardolatry. Bennett himself claims to find the prospect that cultural studies might become 'the heir of literary studies' positively 'depressing' (Bennett 1998: 52). Maybe, but its absorption and incorporation into the state apparatuses as policy studies is surely even more so.

For Bennett, the key issue is that between criticism, understood in essentially Leavisite terms as authoritatively prescriptive, and policy, understood as an exercise applied to populations by experts. A third alternative, however, would be to think of both as part of a more democratic process of debate and discussion containing significant inputs from 'below'. Hence McGuigan's interest in a 'broadly Habermasian perspective', located somewhere 'between theoretical critique and practical policy', which would base cultural policy studies on 'critical and communicative rationality' (McGuigan 1996: 1). But even he fails to appreciate the significance for this position of (literary or philosophical) textual criticism, as distinct from social critique. This is not simply a matter of ideology critique, in the more conventionally Marxian sense of the term, but also of its positively Leavisian or Bloomian moments. As Paul Jones has pointed out, literature figured in Williams's version of cultural studies as the site for an ' "emancipatory" ideology critique'. By this he meant the immanent analysis of the 'emancipatory promise' inherent in the utopian claims of ideologies, a promise which could turn them into a 'court of critical appeal', rather than merely a conservative ideological legitimation of the status quo (Jones 1999: 43–4). This procedure was of quite fundamental importance, not only to Williams, I would argue, but also to most radical cultural criticism, from Adorno and Marcuse to Eagleton, Said and Jameson. If we are 'to speak the truth to power', as Said enjoined us (1994: 71), then we can do so in the name of utopia as well as in opposition to ideology.

For Bennett, the recognition of the social constructedness of literature leads to a peculiar combination of cultural populism and managerialist elitism. The populism deliberately turns *against literature* – apparently the original title of Bennett's book (Bennett 1985: 49n.) – and towards what I have been calling modest cultural studies. The elitism transforms Foucault's quasi-anarchist critique of the Enlightenment into something close to its political antithesis. Indeed, what Bennett calls 'the Foucault effect' (Bennett 1998: 82–4) might much better be described as a delayed (technologico) 'Bentham effect'. A more interesting response, it seems to me, is that of Eagleton (and Williams): to insist that literature matters precisely *because* its value is made in and through history. To say that value is produced by the valuing community, rather than by the inherent properties of the valued text, is not necessarily to detract from the 'value' either of literature or of culture more generally. Why should art need to be transcendental in order to be either interesting or 'valued'? One can and should distinguish between texts and institutions – and between writers and readers, camera-operators and movie-goers – and all of these warrant study both in their interrelationships and independently. One can and should distinguish between different kinds of texts – 'print' as distinct from 'film', 'narrative' as distinct from 'lyric', and so on. And undoubtedly some texts are better than others when judged by the value criteria applied either by their own immediate audience or by subsequent audiences for subsequent readings. Perhaps, Shakespeare (and Mozart?) really are the greatest. But this is a meaningful proposition only insofar as we really can speak of a near-universal valuing community (humanity) able to sustain such judgements over a prolonged period of time. Whether or not judgements of this kind are ever in fact established remains an essentially empirical question. Is there such a universal consent to Bloom's valuation of Shakespeare? I doubt it, but remain open to persuasion.

The intelligentsia as a social class

This isn't exactly a theory of cultural value, although perhaps it should be. Writing from within a broadly cultural studies perspective, John Frow has proposed such a theory, located somewhere in the space between Bloomian literary absolutism and Bennett's neo-Foucauldian cultural relativism. The problem, as Frow defines it, was that of 'critical movement across the spaces between *incommensurate* evaluative regimes' (Frow 1995: 134). His solution to this 'problem of commensuration' borrows from Arjun Appadurai the concept of a 'regime of value', meaning 'a semiotic institution generating evaluative regularities under certain conditions of use, and in which particular empirical audiences or communities may be more or less fully imbricated' (ibid.: 144; cf. Appadurai 1986). The point about these institutions is that, although they can be correlated with such extratextual determinations as social position, they nonetheless have 'no directly expressive relation to social groups' (Frow 1995: 145). Logically, different regimes of value may be incommensurate, Frow acknowledges, but in the practicalities of social life they are in fact 'commensurated' by the institutions of mass education and mass culture. And these institutions are controlled by the 'knowledge class', that is, the class of intellectuals (ibid.: 155). By their very nature as intellectuals, this class is both enabled to speak (uneasily) 'for' others and possessed of a common class interest in what Frow terms 'the implementation of modernity'. His conclusion, though hedged with qualifications and finally left to a quotation from Alvin Gouldner, is that the intelligentsia has a necessarily 'progressive political potential', which informs its capacities for commensuration (ibid.: 164–5). It should be clear that this conclusion hinges on a prior assumption that the intelligentsia – writers, critics, academics and so on – constitutes a distinct social class, in the sociological sense of the term, an argument Frow develops in part by way of a critique of Bourdieu. For Frow, the intelligentsia is not, as Bourdieu had argued, a dominated part of the bourgeoisie, but rather a 'new middle class', a 'knowledge class' dealing in education-generated information (ibid.: 39–46, 121). It is 'a more or less coherent class in some respects, but not in others'; it is a 'weakly formed' class because formed around claims to knowledge rather than property; but it has a common class interest, nonetheless, in the 'institutions of cultural capital' (ibid.: 121, 125, 130).

Was Frow right to consider intellectuals as a social class in this specifically sociological sense? In contemporary common usage, an 'intelligentsia' is a collectivity of 'intellectuals', where the latter term clearly functions as a noun. From the fourteenth century until as late as the early nineteenth, however, 'intellectual' was much more commonly used in the English language as an adjective, more or less synonymous with 'intelligent'. Only at this late date did the word acquire a distinctly new and increasingly influential meaning as a noun referring to a particular kind of person, that is, to someone who 'thinks' (Williams 1976a: 140–2). The new usage was clearly elitist in its implied assertion that intelligence is the prerogative of a privileged few rather than a defining characteristic of the human condition. It succeeded, nonetheless, in capturing a part at least of an important and novel emergent social reality, that of the development in the late eighteenth and the nineteenth centuries of forms of cultural production increasingly dependent on the employment of increasingly specialised and increasingly professionalised cultural workers. It is this transformation and the subsequent substantial growth in the numbers employed in the culture industries which finally registers in the modern sense of the term 'intellectual' as referring, not to a certain type of person, but rather to a particular type of occupational role. This latter sense refers to *all* writers and journalists, actors and painters, priests and teachers, no matter what their own individual levels of 'intelligence', no matter what their own particular individual abilities and disabilities. If we accept that the term 'intellectual' refers to a particular kind of profession, rather than to a particular kind of person, then it may be that these professions, taken together in aggregate, constitute a distinctive social class such as the term 'intelligentsia' implies.

There has been much resistance to the notion. Writers working in the Marxist tradition, both socialists and sociologists, have almost invariably rejected the suggestion. For Marxism the central social category has been that of class, defined as any group which shares a common relation to the means of production; and intellectuals, most Marxists have agreed, share no such relation. Whichever of Marx's various models of class are used – whether the two-class model of the *Communist Manifesto* (bourgeoisie and proletarians), the three-class model of the last chapter of *Capital* (wage-labourers, capitalists and landowners) or the multi-class models of works such as the *Eighteenth Brumaire* (which incorporate the petty bourgeoisie, the peasantry and so on) – intellectuals only ever figure as members of and very often spokespeople for these other classes, rather than as members of any separate intellectual class (Marx and Engels 1967: 80; Marx 1974: 885; 1973: 238–45). This predilection to absorb the intelligentsia into the overall patterns of the general class structure is shared even by theorists as interested in the 'sociology of the intellectuals' as Gramsci. And it remained essentially unaffected by attempts to theorise the social position of the so-called 'new petty bourgeoisie' (Wright 1978: 61–83; Ehrenreich and Ehrenreich 1979). Feminist theorists have typically proven similarly resistant to the notion that intellectuals might possess a common group identity. For feminists it is not class but gender which represents the crucial line of fissure within society, and intellectuals therefore belong to and speak for at the very least their socially defined 'gender', and very possibly their biological 'sex'. If both Marxism and feminism reject the notion of a specifically intellectual social group in favour of other preferred social classifications, then more conservative cultural critics have often positively insisted on the cultural specificity of the intelligentsia. But this insistence is bought only at the price of a radical indifference to the social underpinnings of that specificity. Thus Eliot's 'élite' and the Leavises' 'minority' are not really sociological categories at all: they denote not a particular social group possessed of certain determinate empirical qualities, but rather a system of approbation, referring to certain particular valorised moral capacities. More recently, structuralisms and post-structuralisms have typically privileged the insight of the avant-garde intellectual. But they have done so in an oddly unreflexive fashion, which owed much more than is generally admitted to the more naive positivisms of the nineteenth century. The intellectual thus emerged not as a member of a particular social group, simultaneously enabled and constrained by the very fact of group membership, but rather as a locus of truth (even if, as in post-structuralism, this truth is only that there is no truth) situated outside society and outside discourse.

Yet for all this, not only Eliot and Leavis, Barthes and Foucault, but also Marx and Gramsci, de Beauvoir and Kristeva, remain clearly recognisable as 'intellectuals', and indeed most would almost certainly have happily assented to such a self-description. They are each intellectuals of a very distinctive kind, what Gramsci termed 'traditional' rather than 'organic' intellectuals. By this he referred to those ecclesiastics, administrators, scholars, scientists, theorists and philosophers who 'experience through an "*esprit de corps*" their uninterrupted historical continuity and their special qualification' and 'thus put themselves forward as autonomous and independent of the dominant social group' (Gramsci 1971: 7). In Gramsci's view this autonomy remains essentially illusory, and is in any case less characteristic of the historically more recent kinds of secular intellectual than of the older ecclesiastical intelligentsia (ibid.: 8). In both respects he seems to me mistaken. The rapid expansion of the modern university system and the coincidental decline in the power and prestige of organised religion have combined so as to secure for the new, secular, traditional intelligentsia an autonomy at least as assured as that of the ecclesiastics. Moreover, the entire traditional intelligentsia (in contradistinction to the 'organic' intellectuals either of the bourgeoisie or of the working class) now exercises a degree of institutional and discursive autonomy sufficient to constitute itself as a distinctive social group, if not exactly a social class in the strict Marxist sense of the term. For, of course, Marxists were right to insist that intellectuals occupy no common position in relation to the means of production: some are self-employed artisans (that is, petty bourgeois), some are wage- or salary-earning employees (that is, proletarians) and some perhaps are 'new petty bourgeois'. It can in fact be argued that knowledge itself has become a means of production in advanced capitalism and that intellectuals constitute a class by virtue of their common relation to it. Frow himself comes very close to this position (Frow 1995: 91–6). But the traditional intelligentsia, as we have described it, is much better characterised by its expertise in legitimation than by its possession of economically 'productive' knowledge: the surplus-generating qualities of academic 'deconstruction' are by no means at all clear, not even to the initiate.

The alternative tradition to the Marxist within modern social theory, which also makes use of the category of social class, is Weberian sociology. I refer here not to Weber's much cited redefinition of class in terms of market situation (1948: 181), which of itself seems to me positively unhelpful; but rather to his identification of a ' "social class" structure...composed of the plurality of class statuses between which an interchange of individuals on a personal basis or in the course of generations is *readily possible* and typically observable' (Weber 1964: 424). In short, what Weber means by a 'social class' is an aggregate of market positions that together take on the attributes of what he termed a 'status group' (Weber 1948: 187). As such, they also take on many of the characteristics Marx had accorded to classes understood as groups standing in common relation to the means of production, but which Weber denied to classes understood as groups occupying a common market situation. Unsurprisingly, Weber's account of the social class structure of contemporary capitalism runs closely parallel to Marx's: there are four such classes, Weber observes, the working class, the petty bourgeoisie, the privileged class, and the intelligentsia (Weber 1964: 427). Only the latter directly contradicts more conventionally Marxian accounts of the class structure of advanced capitalism. If we superimpose over each other Marx's and Weber's respective versions of the social class structure, the nett effect appears thus: on the one hand, there are classes such as the bourgeoisie and the proletariat which share both a common relation to the means of production and a regular interchange of individuals between market positions, and which thereby constitute, as it were, classes both in themselves and for themselves (Marx 1973: 239); on the other, there are classes such as the 'traditional' intelligentsia which share no common relation to the means of production but which nonetheless experience a regular interchange of individuals between market situations, and which thereby constitute classes for themselves, but not, paradoxically, classes in themselves. If this formulation appears clumsy, it succeeds nonetheless in identifying in the intelligentsia a group possessed of a very real sense of collective identity, an identity founded moreover on common material interests, but on material interests that are not those of a shared relation to the means of production.

What, then, are these material interests? How is this regular interchange of individuals between adjacent market situations in practice effected? The issue has been variously theorised: by English neo-Weberian sociology as the outcome of a shared monopoly over the means of certification (Parkin 1979: 47–8); by French neo-Durkheimian sociology as a function of the rate of exchange between economic and cultural capital within the dominant class (Bourdieu 1977: 183–97). But, however theorised, the system of higher education seems central to the social functioning of a relatively autonomous traditional intelligentsia. The emergence of a distinct intellectual class, we may hypothesise, remains crucially dependent on the prior expansion of higher education. In Marx's own time, then, the intelligentsia almost certainly did not constitute a separate social class, not even as defined by Weber. And it is only in the twentieth century that the central process of class formation finally occurred, and then only in the advanced capitalist societies. We must be careful not to overstate the case. There is, no doubt, some truth in Orwell's observation that the western intelligentsia became enamoured of Stalinism because it imagined the Soviet Union to represent 'a system which eliminates the upper class, keeps the working class in its place, and hands unlimited power to people very similar to themselves' (Orwell 1970a: 212). But, as Orwell himself recognised, such imaginings were essentially delusory. The intelligentsia was not some 'new class' on 'the road to class power', either in the East or in the West (Konrád and Szelényi 1979). It is rather one amongst many of those 'middle and intermediate strata' (Marx 1974: 885) whose histories interrupt but nonetheless do not determine the more 'epochal' transformations in the class structure. And it is so, I suspect, for the very simple reason that its lack of any common relation to any means of production ultimately disqualifies it from anything other than a minor role in a history that is, in the full Marxian sense of the term, a 'history of class struggle' (Marx and Engels 1967: 79). But if this is so at the epochal level which so preoccupied much Marxian and Weberian historical sociology, the intelligentsia remains nonetheless a significant social actor *within* that history of advanced capitalism which we still continue to inhabit. This isn't quite Frow's conclusion, though the two are by no means entirely incompatible. But he is much more sanguine than I as to the intelligentsia's capacity for quasi-altruistic commensuration between regimes of value. My own hermeneutic is much more suspicious, however, especially as it concerns the intersection between postmodern cultural theory and the politics of the so-called 'new social movements', a matter to which we will return on more than one occasion in the chapters that follow.

All of this leaves us, I think, with the inevitability of radically incommensurate regimes of value, and with the impossibility and undesirability both of canons and of counter-canons. It also leaves us, I hope, with the continuing possibility for intellectual work that will be organic to social groups other than the intelligentsia itself. The best kind of cultural studies, it seems to me, has never had any desire to substitute movies for Milton. Quite the contrary, it would study both. But it has insisted, first, that we should take all aspects of our contemporary culture very seriously, including film and television, for they surely take us seriously, if only in the sophistication of their attempts to manipulate our affections. And, second, it insists that there are more interesting ways to approach canonical literary texts than through acts of quasi-religious worship. In both respects, Williams's work still seems absolutely exemplary. For it was Williams more than any other individual who drafted the initial intellectual prospectus for a cultural studies that would include literary studies, that is, for what I have been calling the immodest version of cultural studies. Let me conclude by quoting from Williams's *The Long Revolution*. 'It was certainly an error', he wrote, 'to suppose that values or art-works could be adequately studied without reference to the particular society within which they were expressed' (Williams 1965: 61). His target here was Leavisite literary criticism, but the argument could just as easily be redirected at Bloom. Williams continued: 'it is equally an error to suppose that the social explanation is determining, or that the values and works are mere by-products' (ibid.: 61). His target here was Marxism, but the argument could just as easily be redirected against many forms of postmodern relativism, including Bennett's. Williams moves thence to what I take to be his central argument:

> The art is there, as an activity, with the production, the trading, the politics, the raising of families.... It is...not a question of relating

> the art to the society, but of studying all the activities and their interrelations, without any concession of priority to any one of them we may choose to abstract…I would define the theory of culture as the study of relationships between elements in a whole way of life. The analysis of culture is the attempt to discover the nature of the organization which is the complex of these relationships. Analysis of particular works or institutions is, in this context, analysis of their essential kind of organization, the relationships which works or institutions embody as parts of the organization of a whole.
>
> (Williams 1965: 61–3)

This still seems to me almost exactly right. Which is why the 'western canon' will almost certainly be far safer in the hands of an immodest cultural studies than in those of an English or comparative literature hell bent on turning itself into classics.

Chapter 2

Analytical strategies

In Chapter 1 we began to trace something of the recent history of the development away from literary studies and toward cultural studies, by way of what I described as a 'sociological turn'. We also noted how, in 'immodest' cultural studies at least, 'literary' texts and other cultural texts are seen as in principle analysable according to more or less analogous procedures. In this chapter, I want to examine some of the analytical strategies currently available to literary and cultural studies. The chapter begins with a consideration of three approaches deriving more or less directly from literary studies or from sociology: hermeneutics; cultural materialism and new historicism; and what I have loosely termed the sociology of culture. There is an obvious occasion for such inquiry, for, as we noted in the previous chapter, literary criticism and sociology were in effect the 'parent' disciplines of cultural studies. But there is a more than antiquarian interest at stake here since both disciplines continue to maintain an active 'presence' within the field. As Collini observed, only half jokingly, there are three main ways into cultural studies: from English, from social science, and from what he unkindly described as 'grievance' (Collini 1994: 3). These disciplinary boundaries have become much less consequential, however, even in their interdisciplinary afterthoughts, over the past thirty years. In the second part of the chapter, then, we move to a consideration of four approaches deriving from outside the older established disciplinary structures: Marxian and post-Marxian theories of 'ideology'; semiology and semiotics; psychoanalysis; and the cultural politics of 'difference' proposed by the new social movements. These politics and these movements have very often been cited as instances of a peculiarly contemporary 'postmodern condition'. The chapter concludes, then, with a glance at the more influential theories of postmodernism. All of this has an obvious general relevance to cultural studies, especially the more immodest varieties thereof, but will also have a more particular relevance to the analysis that follows in the succeeding chapters.

Hermeneutics

As we have seen, 'modern literature', in the sense of the systematic study of more or less historically recent, literary, 'high' art, had provided the subject matter for two major academic disciplines, English and comparative literature. Both had justified themselves on broadly 'humanist' grounds, as the study of the best that humans can create, conducted so as to learn the most we can about our common human condition. English literature was, of course, an overwhelmingly Anglophone affair, comparative literature much more cosmopolitan, albeit often distinctly Eurocentric. English literature has been a much less explicitly theorised discourse, perhaps because of its own institutional pre-eminence within the Anglophone academy, perhaps because of a more general empiricism within English academic life. Whatever the reason, the clearest theorisations of literary humanism derive not so much from English as from comparative literature, by way of the largely German tradition of 'philosophical hermeneutics'. The term 'hermeneutics' is generally used to refer to theories of 'interpretation', which take as their central problem how to 'understand' the more or less intended 'meanings' of others. Historically, its origins can be traced to the Reformation and to the Protestant insistence on the believer's right to interpret the Bible free from the authoritative dictates of the Catholic Church. In the first instance, then, what was to be interpreted was the religious canon itself, and for no less a purpose than to understand God's own intended meaning. This is obviously no small matter: if God speaks only the truth, as by definition he does, then the intended authorial meaning of his own texts must take an absolute priority over any subsequent readings.

Secularised by the Enlightenment, subjectivised by Romanticism and even rendered 'social scientific' by the late nineteenth-century neo-Kantian revival, hermeneutics has retained this emphasis on the interpretation of meaning. For literary hermeneutics, the relevant meaning was that intended, either consciously or unconsciously, by the author of the literary text. In Schleiermacher's phrase, the task was: 'To understand the text at first as well as and then even better than its author' (1985: 83). For historical and sociological hermeneutics, the relevant meaning would be that intended, again either consciously or unconsciously, by the social actor. So Weber's distinction between the natural and social sciences would devolve precisely upon the latter's concern with 'the empathic understanding' of 'psychological and intellectual (*geistig*) phenomena' (Weber 1949: 74). The hermeneutic tradition was refined and developed through Husserl's phenomenology and Heidegger's existentialism, reaching its most sophisticated recent articulation in the work of Gadamer. For Gadamer, as for Heidegger, both the interpreter and that which is to be interpreted are necessarily historically situated. This led Gadamer to a theoretical rehabilitation of the notion of 'tradition'. Historical consciousness is only possible, he concluded, insofar as historical tradition connects our 'horizon' with that of those we seek to understand: 'Our own past and that other past toward which our historical consciousness is directed help to shape this moving horizon out of which human life always lives and which determines it as heritage and tradition' (Gadamer 1990: 304). Although German hermeneutics has been powerfully present in comparative literature, it has been surprisingly uninfluential in English literature and Anglophone cultural studies. For English literature this has been, in part, no doubt an effect of the notorious insularity of Leavisism. But it remains surprising, nonetheless, if only because the hermeneutic tradition reproduces so many of English literature's characteristic tropes in more theoretically articulate form. This is so precisely because they are each literary humanisms.

For Eagleton, stern critic of Leavisite English and hermeneutics alike, this is sufficient reason to reject both: noting the parallels between Husserl and Leavis, he describes hermeneutic criticism as 'a kind of pure distillation of the blind spots, prejudices and limitations of modern literary theory as a whole' (Eagleton 1996a: 60); noting that between Gadamer and Eliot, he detects 'a grossly complacent theory of history' in which 'the alien is always secretly familiar' (ibid.: 73). Thus the very affinity between English literature and German hermeneutics seemed almost to have forewarned and forearmed cultural studies against the latter. Insofar as this effectively delivered it into the hands of structuralist and post-structuralist semiologies, it might well provide occasion for some regret.

The German tradition was neither so unregenerately fixated on the author nor so unregenerately elitist as cultural studies supposed. Jauss's 'aesthetic of reception', for example, developed a post-Gadamerian hermeneutic able to theorise the 'role of the reader' in ways that anticipated many of the insights of post-structuralism without thereby eliding the role of the writer. For Jauss, literary reception was a 'process of the continuous establishing and altering of horizons', where the 'new text evokes for the reader...the horizon of expectations and rules familiar from earlier texts' (Jauss 1982: 23). Like the post-structuralists, he recognised that literary meaning is constituted only in the act of reading. Here, however, reception is understood as occurring within a context of generic and other expectations shared in part by the text's author. Authorial intentions still matter, then, but they are decipherable, especially in the case of texts from the distant past, only in relation to the horizon of expectations of an anticipated readership, only 'against those works that the author...presupposed his contemporary audience to know' (ibid.: 28). Jauss himself defined the 'aesthetic distance' of a text as 'the disparity between the given horizon of expectations and the...new work' and proceeded to posit a strong distinction between properly 'literary' and merely 'culinary' texts, where the latter demand no horizonal change, merely 'fulfilling the expectations prescribed by a ruling standard of taste' (ibid.: 25). His own interests were with the 'high' literary text, of course, but the methods are just as applicable to the supposedly culinary. Indeed, there is no necessary connection between hermeneutics and an exclusive preoccupation with high culture. Ever since Schutz, sociological hermeneutics has embraced the 'phenomenology of everyday life' (cf. Schutz 1972; Berger and Luckman 1971). And if the texts of popular culture have their meanings, as clearly they do, then these too can be made available to hermeneutical analysis. Interestingly, Brooks Landon noted how, in the specific case of science fiction, 'an intention or author-centered theory of interpretation of written texts has...come to dominate the view of filmic adaptation prevalent in the community of...writers and readers' (Landon 1991: 95). He is understandably suspicious of what he sees as the outcome, a widespread assumption that 'the written text should control the manner and meaning of the filmed adaptation'. But there is surely something strangely elitist about the counter-insistence that hermeneutics should never be available to cultural studies, not even as one tool amongst many, not even in areas where popular audiences themselves systematically elicit 'the beliefs and intentions of writers...outside their works' (ibid.: 95).

There is nothing of any comparable theoretical sophistication in English literature: as we have seen, Leavis firmly resisted such attempts at systematic theorisation. But it is clear, nonetheless, that Leavisite English was in fact a kind of undertheorised literary hermeneutics: it too valued literary texts for the meanings they expressed; it too sought to understand those meanings through distinctly 'humanist' techniques of analysis, which it deliberately counterposed to the positivism of the natural and social sciences; it too believed this to be possible on account of our supposed 'common humanity'; it too relied on tradition as the medium through which that commonality is established and maintained. This approach was reserved for the literary canon alone, however: there is no equivalent in English literature to German hermeneutical sociology. To the contrary, as we noted in Chapter 1, Leavisite criticism had defined English precisely in terms of its opposition to contemporary popular culture. The classic instance is Q. D. Leavis's *Fiction and the Reading Public*, first published in 1932, where the techniques of analysis are those of sociology and social history rather than literary criticism. What mass-circulation newspapers had achieved, she eventually concluded, was 'to mobilize the people to outvote the minority...by working upon herd instinct' (Q. D. Leavis

1979: 151). As Baldick caustically commented, this was in effect a 'sociology of the herd' (Baldick 1983: 175).

Cultural materialism and new historicism

For the Leavises themselves, for their Leavisite followers and for much of English literature as a discipline, this antipathy toward popular culture became a cardinal principle of faith. It rested on the assumption that there was only *one* 'real' culture, the minority culture of the literary elite, and that all other culture was so essentially inferior as to warrant only hostility, contempt or 'sociological' explanation. If there is any one theme that guided the development of cultural studies from the 1960s on, it was the progressive dissolution of this notion of a single culture and its supersession by a notion of *cultures* in the plural. Such theoretical multiculturalism eventually extended to embrace the subcultures of gender and sexuality, race and ethnicity, generation and nationality. The first breach in the monolith was not, however, about any of these, but rather about *social class*. The realities of class difference can be readily apparent in British culture, and no more so than to those who have been socially mobile from one class to another. Both Williams and Hoggart had undergone precisely this experience and both brought it to bear in their responses to contemporary popular culture. In Hoggart's *The Uses of Literacy*, the problem of the mass media ceased to be a matter simply of 'levelling' and became also one of manipulation: 'these popular journals', he wrote, 'say the right things for the wrong reasons' (Hoggart 1958: 244). In Williams's *Culture and Society*, 'mass civilization' became not so much a fact of contemporary life as a way of misrepresenting it: 'There are in fact no masses; there are only ways of seeing people as masses' (Williams 1963: 289). Written slightly later, *The Long Revolution* was intended in part as a rejoinder to the pessimistic reading of cultural modernity developed by the Leavises. Though still accepting essentially Leavisite notions of literary value and still sharing in their alarm at the potentially damaging consequences of commercial culture, the book clearly rejected all definitions of culture as coextensive with minority literary taste.

It would be Williams, moreover, whose work would begin to define the subject matter of the new discipline of cultural studies. He had become increasingly aware of the interrelationships between texts and institutions, forms and technologies, in the workings of both 'high' and 'popular' culture. He had also begun to develop a critique of existing mass-media texts and institutions, which sought to identify the kinds of institution that might sustain a properly democratic communications system, a real rather than illusory 'common culture'. Where the Leavises remained irretrievably hostile to the media, Williams insisted that the new televisual technologies could become 'the contemporary tools of the long revolution towards an educated and participatory democracy' (Williams 1974: 151). In his work on drama, as in that on television, an awareness of the social conventionality of form was linked to a developing sense of the interrelationship between form and the technologies of performance. Dramatic convention, he concluded, is 'just this question of a relation between form and performance' (Williams 1973a: 398). Moreover, the distinction between high and low cultures came to seem increasingly problematic: 'There are very few absolute contrasts left between a "minority culture" and "mass communications" ', he would write; 'many minority institutions and forms have adapted, even with enthusiasm, to modern corporate capitalist culture' (Williams 1983: 134, 140).

A sense of the 'ordinariness' of culture led Williams to propose the notion of 'structure of feeling' as a mediating term between 'art' and 'culture'. A 'structure of feeling', he wrote, 'is the culture of a period: it is the particular living result of all the elements in the general organization' (Williams 1965: 64). Later still, it led him formulate the theoretical approach he would term 'cultural materialism': 'a theory of culture as a (social and material) productive process and of specific practices, of "arts", as social uses of material means of production' (Williams 1980: 243). From this perspective, cultural tradition became the 'selective tradition', a product of contemporary interests, rather than the legacy of history, as the Leavises had supposed. For Williams, culture had to be seen as 'the lived dominance and subordination of particular classes' and tradition as 'the most powerful practical means of incorporation' (Williams 1977: 110, 115). It is dependent upon identifiable 'institutions', moreover, and what he termed 'formations' or intellectual or artistic movements (ibid.: 117–20). If all culture is thus similarly 'material', then very little remains of the old Leavisite notion of 'literature'. It was essentially one of a series of 'evasions', Williams concluded, by which art and thinking about art separated themselves from the social processes which actually contained them (ibid.: 154). To such evasions, and to their often transparently elitist ideological functions, he counterposed a stress on 'the variability, the relativity, and the multiplicity of actual cultural practice' (ibid.: 153).

Like the Leavises, Williams saw language as at the centre of literary and cultural studies. But for Williams it was best understood 'as activity, as practical consciousness' (ibid.: 36). Whether spoken or written, language is not a 'medium', he argued, in the sense of an intermediate communicative substance, mediating between thought and expression, but rather a constitutive element of material social practice (ibid.: 158–9, 165). More particularly, 'Language is in fact a special kind of material practice: that of human sociality' (ibid.: 165). Linguistic signification is, then, a 'real and demonstrable activity', with its own distinctively material, and in a sense 'formal', properties. But these formal meanings function within 'lived and living relationships', which in turn '*make all formal meanings significant and substantial*' (ibid.: 167–8). Writing, he observed, is a special form of language, at once materially objectified and reproducible, its reproducibility necessarily dependent on the wider socio-cultural system (ibid.: 146, 170). This sense of the materiality of language was linked to a more general insistence on the materiality of form. For Williams, form was not so much a matter of classification as of social relationship: 'it is...a social process which...becomes a social product. Forms are...the common property...of writers and audiences or readers, before any communicative composition can occur' (ibid.: 187–8). Elsewhere this abstractly theoretical account is supplemented by a nuanced socio-formal analysis of the history of the drama and an attempt to distinguish three different 'levels of form', denoted, respectively, as 'modes', 'genres' and 'types' (Williams 1981: 148–80, 194–7). At each of these levels, form is by definition reproducible and culture thereby necessarily reproductive (ibid.: 184). But for Williams it was also necessarily productive: 'social orders and cultural orders must be seen as being actively made...unless there is...production and innovation, most orders are at risk' (ibid.: 201).

What for the Leavisites had been a 'literature', a canon of exemplary creative works expressive of a national tradition, became in Williams's cultural materialism a distinctive subset of socially specific, materially determinate forms and practices. Bereft of canon and national tradition alike, the obvious question arises as to what becomes of authorship, the ultimate guarantee for literary humanism, in principle at least, of the authoritative meaning of the literary work. Williams readily conceded the problematic status of the figure of the author (Williams 1977: 192), whilst insisting that authorship cannot be reduced to an effect either of textuality or of the institutionalised processing of texts. Rather, the central question remains that of the dynamic interrelationship between social formation, individual development and cultural creation (ibid.: 197). For Williams, then, the author as writer, though not as authoritative source or origin, remained, if not central, then at least not yet radically decentred. Like Jauss, but unlike much post-structuralism, Williams refused to reduce the moment of literary production to that of consumption: he continued to hold firmly to the irreducibility of authorship and readership, either to each other or to an amorphous 'textuality', and to the necessarily material sociality of each, both in themselves and in relation to each other. 'In this at once social and historical perspective', he wrote, 'the abstract figure of "the author" is...returned to these varying *and in principle variable* situations, relationships, and responses' (ibid.: 198).

Williams's work has been widely influential in literary and cultural studies on both sides of the Anglophone Atlantic (cf. Bennett 1989; Garnham 1983, 1988; Hall 1993; Lovell 1987; Williams and Said 1989; Wolff 1990, 1993). His most significant legacy to literary studies, however, has been through Eagleton, through Dollimore and Sinfield's self-declared 'cultural materialism', and through Greenblatt and Gallagher's so-called 'new historicism'. A former student of Williams, Eagleton's later writings redeployed and reapplied to very different contexts a whole set of essentially Williamsite categories. *The Ideology of the Aesthetic* (1990), for example, aimed to recover the negative and positive moments in the German 'aesthetic' tradition, just as Williams's *Culture and Society* had done for the English 'culturalist' tradition. As Eagleton noted, the latter was 'in fact derivative of

German philosophy' (1990: 11). *Heathcliff and the Great Hunger* (1995) is also a reworking of *Culture and Society*, but taking Irish literature rather than German philosophy as its primary object. The book builds on Williams in at least two respects: in its understanding of how Englishness and Irishness had been defined and constructed, in relation to and against each other, through the processes and projects of hegemony; and in its insistence that cultural representations can and should be measured against the historical referents to which they really do sometimes bear some relation. The opening chapter, for example, moves between the text of *Wuthering Heights*, the historical reality of the Irish Famine and its representation and non-representation in subsequent historiographical and literary texts (Eagleton 1995: 1–26). More recently, Eagleton's *Sweet Violence* (2003) has powerfully restated and generalised some of the key themes first explored in Williams's *Modern Tragedy* (1979a). This substantial body of work suggests the uses to which cultural materialism can be put in hands as creative as Eagleton's. The latter's own judgement warrants repetition here: 'the notion of cultural materialism is...of considerable value', he wrote, '...it extends and completes Marx's own struggle against idealism, carrying it forcefully into that realm ("culture") always most ideologically resistant to materialist redefinition' (Eagleton 1989: 169). If Williams's position sometimes seems archaic, Eagleton has recently observed, 'the problem in fact is that we have yet to catch up with it' (Eagleton 2000: 122).

Dollimore and Sinfield's *Political Shakespeare* (1994), subtitled *Essays in Cultural Materialism*, has proven so influential in Shakespeare studies as to prompt the very large claim that 'cultural materialism in Britain and New Historicism in America...now constitute the new academic order...in Renaissance studies' (Wilson 1995: viii). Both Dollimore and Sinfield have focused on substantive issues very different from those that concerned Williams, most especially (gay) sexuality. For Dollimore, cultural materialism was an important initial influence, but only as one 'perspective' amongst many (Dollimore 1991: 21). By contrast, Sinfield's guiding theoretical approach remained determinedly, if also 'dissidently', cultural materialist (Sinfield 1992: 8–10; 1998: 147–50). Indeed, in the opening chapter especially written for the second edition of what is probably still his most important book, he offers as succinct a summary as any of what exactly cultural materialism 'does':

> Cultural materialists investigate the historical conditions in which textual representations are produced, circulated and received. They engage with questions about the relations between dominant and subordinate cultures,...the scope for subaltern resistance, and the modes through which the system tends to accommodate or repel diverse kinds of dissidence. In this approach, the terms 'art' and 'literature'...are neither spontaneous nor innocent. They are...strategies for conferring authority upon certain representations, and hence upon certain viewpoints.
>
> (Sinfield 1997: xxiii)

The American new historicism is clearly also indebted to Williams, but much more importantly so to the work of Foucault (Greenblatt 1990: 2–3; 146–7). New historicist analysis typically brings literary and non-literary discourse into juxtaposition, so as to show how social power and historical conflict permeate the textuality of a society's literature. For example, Greenblatt sets the 'eucharistic anxiety' in *Hamlet* against the rhetoric of Protestant opposition to the Catholic Mass (Gallagher and Greenblatt 2000: 151–62). Clearly, this shares much common ground with cultural materialism.

Differences arise, however, over two main issues: the theoretical question as to the subversive potential of apparently subversive texts; and the epistemological question as to the status of the 'referent'. As to the first, the issue hinges on how to understand in/subordination, whether as always-already necessarily contained or as at least potentially resistive. In much of Greenblatt's work the apparently subversive moment in apparently subversive texts is read as ultimately affirmative of and complicit with the dominant discourse. The most famous instance is in his contribution to *Political Shakespeare*, which reads the subversive perceptions in the history plays as ultimately supportive of the kingly authority they appeared to question (Greenblatt 1994). For Sinfield, this new historicist insistence on the affirmative properties of apparently subversive texts amounts to an 'entrapment model' of ideology and power. The lines of disagreement can be overdrawn:

musing on whether sites of resistance are ultimately co-optable, Greenblatt commented simply that 'Some are, some aren't' (Greenblatt 1990: 165); confronting much the same issue, Sinfield concluded that 'there is no simple way through, but every reason to go on trying' (Sinfield 1994: 27). They are agreed, in short, that entrapment and dissidence are each theoretically possible. The difference is thus one of relative probabilities, but also therefore of intent and purpose and, hence, necessarily of politics.

The disagreements over the epistemological status of the referent are perhaps even more fundamental. For Greenblatt, 'methodological self-consciousness is one of the distinguishing marks of the new historicism', as opposed to the older historicisms 'based upon faith in the transparency of signs and interpretive procedures' (Greenblatt 1990: 158). Neither Dollimore nor Sinfield – nor Williams, nor Eagleton – believed in the transparency of either signs or interpretative procedures. But all four would have agreed that signs sometimes have referents and that texts can be used both to represent and misrepresent other extratextual 'realities'. The kind of analysis conducted by Williams in *The Country and the City* (1973b) or by Eagleton in *Heathcliff and the Great Hunger* (1995), where literary text and historical context are compared, in part so as to test the extent to which the texts misrepresent their contexts, tends to be precluded by the 'textualism' of new historicist criticism. For, as Ryan observes, insofar as 'new historicism turns history into a text', the price of this return to history 'is the evaporation of the world that produced all these words' (Ryan 1996: xiv).

The sociology of culture

In general, the institutionalised academic division of labour has ensured that the discipline of sociology would tend to steer clear of any too direct encounter with literature proper. As we noted in Chapter 1, sociology had been until comparatively recently a very un-British affair, concentrated above all in the United States, France and Germany. In France in particular it had understood itself as the 'science' of the study of the external 'facts' of social life. The pre-eminent French 'sociologist of literature' in the 1960s was Escarpit, whose work had determinedly confined itself to the externally defined 'social facts' of literature, especially as registered in the book trade. For Escarpit, it was 'only through the study of objective data, systematically exploited without preconceived ideas, that we may approach the literary fact' (1971: 18). Literary values were thus safely left to the literary critic, social facts to the sociologist. Where literary humanism had devoted itself to the particular work of the particular author, Escarpit's focus fell on the 'community of writers', understood in their aggregate as 'generations' and 'teams' (ibid.: 22, 25–8). Where literary humanism had been concerned with truly 'great' works, Escarpit deliberately extended the definition of literature to include all 'non-functional' writing (ibid.: 14). Where literary humanism had tended to valorise one version or another of what Jauss would mean by 'aesthetic distance', Escarpit was convinced that 'there can be no literature without a convergence of intentions between author and reader.... It is in this coincidence that literary success lies' (ibid.: 83).

In France, the major alternative to Escarpit's sociological positivism had been Goldmann's so-called 'genetic structuralism'. Like Escarpit, Goldmann had been influenced by the Durkheimian tradition: hence his definition of the discipline's subject matter as '*the study of the facts of consciousness*' (Goldmann 1970a: 36). But Goldmann owed a further debt to the legacy of German hermeneutics, which redirected his attention toward the subject matter of literary criticism, the literary text itself. Where Escarpit had evaded questions of aesthetic value, Goldmann set out to develop a sociological hermeneutics that could be applied precisely to the 'great' works of literary art. For Goldmann, the central task of the literary sociologist was thus to 'replace' the literary 'work' in 'historical evolution', studied 'as a whole', so as to 'bring out the work's objective meaning' (Goldmann 1964: 8). As in literary humanism more generally, he sought to understand the literary 'work' as the effect of an extratextual human agency. But where liberal humanism had discovered authoritative meaning in the intentionality of the individual author, he defined the subject of which the literary work is the object as necessarily collective or 'transindividual' in character. For Goldmann, as much as for later post-structuralisms, the individual author was already effectively decentred. But where structuralism and post-structuralism would relocate the locus of textual meaning around the reader, Goldmann opted to reconstitute the category of authorship at the 'higher' level of a quasi-Durkheimian 'collective consciousness'.

Moreover, Goldmann assumed that such group consciousnesses would normally entail a certain consciousness of social class. 'Every time it was a question of finding the infrastructure of a philosophy, a literary or artistic current', he wrote, 'we have been forced to consider...a social class and its relation to society' (Goldmann 1970a: 102). The crucial mediating agency between the life of a social class and the work of an individual writer was thus the 'world vision', that is, 'the whole complex of ideas, aspirations and feelings which links together the members of a social group...and which opposes them to members of other social groups' (Goldmann 1964: 17). The structures of intratextuality and intertextuality elucidated in structuralist accounts of literature were, in Goldmann's view, better understood as the central informing categories of such social-class world visions. Hence the general prospectus for a 'genetic structuralist' sociology of literature, which would establish a series of structural 'homologies' between the work of the individual writer, the world vision of the social group and the social situation in which the group finds itself. The term 'homology' here denotes a systematically patterned set of parallels between different objects of analysis, a parallelism so systematic in fact that, in the case of truly 'strict' homology, 'one might speak of one and the same structure manifesting itself on...different planes' (Goldmann 1975: 8). This definition of strict homology is taken from Goldmann's *Towards a Sociology of the Novel*. But his analyses are developed more persuasively for the looser homologies discovered in his studies of Kant, Pascal and Racine. Here he related the structure of the 'tragic vision' as a world vision, first, to the textual structures of the philosophical writings of Pascal and Kant and the theatre of Racine, second, to the social structures of seventeenth-century France and eighteenth-century Germany (Goldmann 1964: 89–163; 1971: 31–57). The power of his readings both of Jansenism and of Kantianism suggests something of the continuing theoretical purchase of this genetic structuralism. As an argument in and against high structuralism there is much to be said for Goldmann's theoretical humanism, for insofar as culture is indeed structured this is more plausibly the effect of human sociality than of some scientistically naturalising 'law of structure'. As Goldmann himself had insisted, in direct encounter with the leading figures of French high structuralism, 'structures are born from events and...except for the most formal characteristics, there is no permanence in these structures' (Goldmann 1970b: 99).

For Goldmann, social-class world visions could exist on two different planes, 'that of the *real* consciousness of the group...or that of their *coherent* exceptional expression in great works of philosophy or art' (Goldmann 1970a: 130). This coupling of coherence with exceptionality is fundamental to his argument: the coherent 'expression' in art of what is in everyday life only ever incoherent thereby represents the '*maximum of potential consciousness*' (ibid.: 103) of the group or class to which the artist belongs. He maintained, not only that all works of art do in fact coherently express such a world vision, but also that 'it is precisely because their work has such a coherence that it possesses...literary...worth' (Goldmann 1964: 98). This is suspect both as sociology and aesthetic, since there seems no good reason to suppose that either world visions or 'great' works of art are necessarily 'coherent'. Indeed, the long history of modernist and postmodernist valorisations of the 'transgressive', from the Russian Formalist espousal of defamiliarisation (Shklovsky 1965) through to Cixous's (1981) celebration of *écriture féminine*, suggests how powerfully persuasive the 'incoherent' may be. Which is not to say that in certain specific socio-discursive contexts, typically perhaps very different from those of our own postmodern 'late capitalism', an aesthetic of coherence such as Goldmann improperly seeks to universalise might well be locally acceptable. In the *Critique of Dialectical Reason* Sartre distinguishes between the alienated series, a collective wherein the forms of interior bonding between actors are determined by the passivity of scarce matter, and the fused group, in which forms of interior bonding are structured around the shared project of freedom, that is, of overcoming passivity and scarcity (Sartre 1976: 262–3, 340–1). Let me hypothesise that a Sartrean fused group would be the type of social group most likely to subscribe to a coherent totalisation such as interested Goldmann. Sartre's own example is the storming of the Bastille, but Goldmann's Jansenists would be analysable in very similar terms.

Insofar as the latter's 'genetic structuralist' readings actually work, then this is so, not because of the universal applicability of the method, but because of the quite specifically 'fused' nature of Jansenism.

Goldmann's sociology of literature remains significant in itself and as a source of inspiration, both positive and negative, to the kind of 'sociocriticism' developed by Cros (1988), Zima (2000) and their various co-workers in France and Canada (cf. Browitt 1996). But his fascination with the 'coherent' artwork remains pre-sociological, nonetheless: it is evidence of a much larger commitment to the notion of the 'aesthetic'. Like the Leavises, but unlike the later Williams, Goldmann continued to insist on a radical discontinuity between high 'art' on the one hand and popular commodity culture on the other. For an effective deconstruction of this 'distinction' French sociology would have to await the work of Bourdieu. Like Williams, Bourdieu came from an unusually plebeian and provincial background and, in some respects, their work is close in tone, purpose and subject matter. Certainly, when translated into English, Bourdieu's sociology had excited Williams's positive admiration. Bourdieu's reputation as a sociological thinker revolves around the 'theory of practice', in which he attempted to theorise human sociality as the outcome of the strategic action of individuals operating within a constraining, but nonetheless not determining, context of values. Famously, the term Bourdieu coined to describe this is 'the habitus', by which he meant 'an acquired system of generative schemes objectively adjusted to the particular conditions in which it is constituted' (Bourdieu 1977: 95). For Bourdieu, the habitus is simultaneously structured and structuring, materially produced, and, interestingly, very often generation-specific (ibid.: 72, 78). Like Williams, Bourdieu argued that modern capitalist societies were still class societies and that we can distinguish between the dominated classes (the working class, the peasantry) and the dominant. These distinctions are not simply matters of economics, however, but also of habitus. Moreover, according to Bourdieu, the dominant class, the bourgeoisie, is divided into two main fractions, a dominant fraction, which controls economic capital, and a dominated, which controls 'cultural capital'.

For Bourdieu, 'all practices, including those purporting to be disinterested or gratuitous', can be treated as 'economic practices directed towards the maximizing of material or symbolic profit' (ibid.: 183). The intelligentsia, the dominated fraction of the dominant class, are thus self-interested traders in cultural capital. The two fractions of the dominant class will have a common interest in maintaining their privileges *vis-à-vis* the dominated classes and, insofar as the symbolic system is necessary to secure social order, the economic bourgeoisie proper cannot simply dispense with cultural capital. But the two fractions will nonetheless be drawn into conflict over the rates of exchange between economic and cultural capital. Probably Bourdieu's most widely cited study and certainly the best example of his work in cultural sociology is *Distinction* (1984), an immensely ambitious exercise in theoretically informed empirical social research. The book was based on an extremely detailed sociological survey, conducted in 1963 and 1967–8 by interview and ethnographic observation, of the cultural preferences of over 1,200 people in Paris, Lille and a small French provincial town (Bourdieu 1984: 503). Analysing the sample data, he identified three main zones of taste: 'legitimate' taste, most widespread in the educated sections of the dominant class, where the predominant musical preferences, for example, included *Well-Tempered Clavier*, *Art of Fugue* and *Concerto for the Left Hand*; 'middle-brow' taste, more widespread amongst the middle classes, where musical preferences include *Rhapsody in Blue* and *Hungarian Rhapsody*; and 'popular' taste, widespread in the working classes, with preferences for *Blue Danube*, *La Traviata* and Petula Clark. The statistical correlation between zone of taste and class affiliation is clear from Bourdieu's own diagrams (ibid.: 17).

Much less obvious, however, is his argument to the effect that educational qualifications function as a condition of entry into the universe of legitimate culture, not simply as a training in the specific skills taught in educational courses. Bourdieu characterised legitimate taste in terms of its 'aesthetic disposition', that is, its disposition to assert the 'absolute primacy of form over function' (ibid.: 28, 30). Artistic and social 'distinction' are inextricably interrelated, he argued:

> It should not be thought that the relationship of distinction (which may or may not imply the conscious intention of distinguishing oneself from common people) is only an incidental component in

> the aesthetic disposition. The pure gaze implies a break with the ordinary attitude towards the world which, as such, is a social break.
>
> (Bourdieu 1984: 31)

The 'popular aesthetic', by contrast, is 'based on the affirmation of continuity between art and life' and 'a deep-rooted demand for participation' (ibid.: 32). Hence its hostility to representations of objects that in real life are either ugly or immoral. Bourdieu explained the difference between legitimate and other taste thus:

> The aesthetic disposition...presupposes the distance from the world...which is the basis of the bourgeois experience.... Economic power is first and foremost a power to keep economic necessity at arm's length.... The detachment of the pure gaze cannot be separated from a general disposition towards the 'gratuitous' and the 'disinterested'.... This affirmation of power over a dominated necessity always implies a claim to a legitimate superiority over those who...remain dominated by ordinary interests and urgencies.
>
> (Bourdieu 1984: 54–6)

If there is indeed a 'coherence' to art, for Bourdieu it was only ever that of a coherent attempt to sustain the boundaries of social exclusivity.

There is an apparent cynicism in Bourdieu, which applies as much to the specific cultural sector in which he worked, that is, the academy and the education system more generally, as to the art world. He analysed the academic profession as a competitive struggle for legitimacy and cultural distinction, which functioned so as to reproduce the central structures of social-class inequality. Whether applied to the world, to students or to academics, academic taxonomies were for Bourdieu 'a machine for transforming social classifications into academic classifications' (Bourdieu 1988: 207). He also stressed the central significance of the '*grandes écoles*' to the French social elite, their credentialism operating as a kind of 'state magic' for a supposedly rationalised society (Bourdieu 1996a: 374). Some of this apparent cynicism is belied in his later work by a quite explicit turn towards political engagement and activism (Bourdieu 1998, Bourdieu *et al.* 1999). Theoretically, he also struggled to find ways of thinking the role of the intellectual which would allow for his own developing aspiration to activism. Hence the interest in what he termed the 'corporatism of the universal', that is, the idea that intellectuals have a kind of collective self-interest in the defence of the culture sphere, which somehow translates into something close to a traditional humanist politics (Bourdieu 1989; 1996b: 339–48). The problem should be obvious, however: the approach ran contrary to his earlier scepticism about the intelligentsia's pretensions to distinction, whilst simultaneously understating the general moral significance of his own political interventions. Williams had moved away from English literature and towards cultural studies essentially by way of a critique of cultural elitism, whilst continuing to believe in the intrinsic interest and value of cultural texts, both popular and elite. By comparison, Bourdieu brought a conventionally sociological relativism to the study of culture, but supplemented the usual quantitative measurements with a healthy dose of (thinly disguised) cynical insight into the pretensions of privilege. Both have been of great value to contemporary cultural studies, both as provocation and inspiration. If forced to choose, however, I would put my money on Williams as the better guide: his much stronger sense of culture as about lived particularities seems finally more telling than all of Bourdieu's methodological sophistication.

Theories of ideology

The concept of ideology derives in the first instance from Marxism, from Marx himself in fact, who had used it to explore the connection between systems of belief and systems of material – especially class – interest. More generally, the term can also be applied to any set of shared assumptions and beliefs seen as in some sense 'governing' how people think and act. For Marx, a socially dominant set of such assumptions or beliefs, that is, a 'ruling ideology', was one imposed by the dominant institutions of a society in the interests of the dominant or ruling class and against other competing ideologies (Marx and Engels 1970: 64). I want to consider, not so much Marx's own theory of ideology, however, as those developed by the two major schools of twentieth-century 'Western Marxism', the so-called 'critical theory' of the German 'Frankfurt School' and Althusserian 'structural Marxism' in France. The Frankfurt School was a real academic institution, the Institut für Sozialforschung at the University of Frankfurt, founded in 1923, and its key figures have included Adorno, Horkheimer, Marcuse, Benjamin and, more recently, Habermas and Honneth. There was no equivalently Althusserian institution, but Althusser's theory of ideology nonetheless exercised a considerable influence over literary and cultural studies, both in France and internationally, during the 1960s and 1970s.

The term 'critical theory' was coined by the Frankfurt School to define their own position against what they had seen as the 'traditional theory' of mainstream sociology. Their work is often characterised as 'Marxist' and is indeed indebted to Marx in many significant aspects, not least the sense of mass culture as ideology. But it also owed much to Weberian sociology and Freudian psychoanalysis: from the former it inherited a suspicion of rationalism and a diagnosis of contemporary science and culture as (over-)rationalised; from the latter, the theory of the unconscious and the notion that social order functions in part by way of psychic repression. Nonetheless, the central theoretical concept remained that of ideology. For Adorno and Horkheimer, the two key figures in the School, modern capitalism had become a fully rationalised system of domination, its 'culture industries' institutions for the manufacture of manipulation. They argued that authentic art involved a necessary confrontation with already established traditional styles, 'inferior' work, merely the practice of imitation. 'In the culture industry', they concluded, 'imitation finally becomes absolute. Having ceased to be anything but style, it reveals the latter's secret: obedience to social hierarchy' (Adorno and Horkheimer 1979: 131). In short, the central function of the mass media is ideological manipulation in the interests of profit.

In *Dialectic of Enlightenment*, Adorno and Horkheimer discuss the technologies of the culture industries, noting how these typically involve the combination of a few production centres with many dispersed consumption points. The technological rationale for such organisation, they argued, is the rationale of domination (ibid.: 121), in which the cultural 'consumer' is made passive and manipulated. 'There is nothing left...to classify', they wrote: 'Producers have done it for him' (ibid.: 125). The culture industries' products are thus increasingly standardised and characterised by a predominance of 'effect' over 'idea', where the technical perfection of effects permits the ideological illusion that reality is as represented in the media. Hence, their startling observation that:

> Real life is becoming indistinguishable from the movies.... The...film...leaves no room for imagination or reflection on the part of the audience...hence the film forces its victims to equate it directly with reality.... They are so designed that quickness, powers of observation, and experience are undeniably needed to apprehend them...yet sustained thought is out of the question if the spectator is not to miss the relentless rush of facts.
>
> (Adorno and Horkheimer 1979: 126–7)

For almost all the writers associated with the Frankfurt School, avant-garde modernist art and music came to represent key sites of resistance to such cultural manipulation. Benjamin alone attempted to forge connections between the cultural avant-garde, on the one hand, and the new popular media, on the other, pitting the emancipatory potential of both against the traditional myth of the 'autonomous' work of art (Benjamin 1973b). Much more typical of the School, however, were Adorno and Horkheimer, for whom avant-garde art had represented a way towards freedom from a system of domination, which included and incorporated the culture industries and their mass culture.

In Adorno and Horkheimer, as in the Leavises, high art was privileged as a site of authenticity, mass culture anathematised and sociologically 'explained' as the site of manipulation. In Habermas, as in Williams, this antithesis is progressively undermined by a growing awareness of the institutional bases of all culture. Habermas's early work had sought to secure the emancipatory potential in Enlightenment reason from Adorno and Horkheimer's darkly pessimistic dialectic of Enlightenment. If Habermas was indeed a critical theorist in Horkheimer's sense of the term, seeking to discover the emancipatory potential in social forms, he nonetheless evaluated both the 'practical reason' of ethics and the social institutions of modernity much more positively than had Adorno and Horkheimer. For Habermas, reason is immanent within sociality, and especially within language: through the structure of language, he wrote, 'autonomy and responsibility are posited for us. Our first sentence expresses unequivocally the intention of universal and unconstrained consensus' (Habermas 1971: 314). This notion of unimpeded communication, which provided him with criteria by which to critique existing cultural reality, is very obviously of Enlightenment provenance. But for Habermas, as for Williams, Enlightenment reason was sustainable only by the novel institutional forms of cultural modernity. His interest in the peculiarity of these distinctive institutional arrangements had inspired his first major work, *The Structural Transformation of the Public Sphere*, published in 1962. Here, Habermas attempted to explain the socio-historical emergence, during the seventeenth and eighteenth centuries, of a distinctly middle-class, or 'bourgeois', public opinion, relatively independent of the absolutist-monarchical states. He traced the historical evolution of the institutions of public opinion through to their apparent decline in the modern social-welfare state, where state and society penetrate each other, producing an apparent 'refeudalization' (Habermas 1989: 231). The collapse of the liberal public sphere makes room for staged and manipulative publicity of the kind registered by Adorno and Horkheimer, he argued, but also clings nonetheless to the mandate of a critical public sphere (ibid.: 232). The problem for Habermas becomes, not that of the wholesale refusal enacted by the first generation of critical theorists, but rather of how to create new forms of critical public opinion within the institutional context already established by an increasingly 'organised' capitalism.

Art thus became for Habermas merely one institutional order amongst others. Following Weber, he viewed cultural modernity as characterised by 'the separation of the substantive reason expressed in religion and metaphysics into three autonomous spheres...science, morality and art' (Habermas 1985: 9). Capitalist societies have never been able to provide adequate motivation for their individual actors, Habermas argued, without resort to more traditional forms of typically religious belief, which have nonetheless become decreasingly effective over time (Habermas 1975: 77–8). Where religion had been by and large system-supportive, art and aesthetics seem much less obviously suited to this function: increasingly autonomous from both economics and politics, 'bourgeois' art collects together those human needs that cannot be met by either, which therefore become 'explosive ingredients built into the bourgeois ideology' (ibid.: 78). Avant-garde art thus 'strengthens the divergence between the values offered by the socio-cultural system and those demanded by the political and economic systems' (ibid.: 86). With the benefit of hindsight, it is difficult to avoid the supposition that Habermas had been over-impressed by the immediate impact of the 'counter-culture' of the 1960s. Returning to the problem in 1980, and rehearsing some of the themes outlined in Bürger's *Theory of the Avant-Garde* (1984), Habermas would come to the rather different conclusion that the historical avant-garde's attempt to force a reconciliation between art and life, by destroying the autonomy of art, had been doomed to failure. 'A reified everyday praxis can be cured', he wrote, 'only by creating unconstrained interaction of the cognitive with the moral-practical and the aesthetic-expressive elements. Reification cannot be overcome by forcing just one of those highly stylized cultural spheres to open up and become more accessible' (Habermas 1985: 11–12). As with Bürger, Habermas's final judgement on the avant-garde was much less sanguine than that in Adorno. These more specifically 'cultural' questions have been less central in Habermas's most recent work, which has become increasingly political in tenor, dealing by turn with immediately German problems, such as those posed by reunification, and more generally European problems, such as the relationship between the European Union and globalising capitalism (Habermas 1994, 1998a). But he remains Adorno's heir: confronted by the individualism of the so-called 'Berlin generation', he would insist on the need for 'a language capable of skewering the phenomena of the hour as mercilessly as Adorno did in the early days of the Federal Republic' (Habermas 1998b: 11). This is, at least in part, a call for ideology critique.

There are many other versions of the theory of ideology, all to some extent inspired by Marx, but the most important was almost certainly

Althusser's structuralist reworking of Gramsci's theory of 'hegemony'. Gramsci had used this last term to refer to the type of predominance of one social class over another which rests on a kind of constructed value consensus between the two classes. Stressing the interconnectedness of politico-economic coercion on the one hand and cultural hegemony on the other, he propounded the famous formula: 'State = political society + civil society, in other words hegemony protected by the armour of coercion' (Gramsci 1971: 263). Althusser would later rework this Gramscian distinction as that between the so-called 'repressive state apparatuses' and 'ideological state apparatuses', using the term 'apparatus' so as to draw attention to the institutions in which ideology is necessarily embedded. As in Williams and Habermas, so in Althusser culture was understood as existing only in and through concrete social institutions. Moreover, Althusser formulated his own distinctive explanation for the social function of ideology: to reproduce structured social inequality, or more specifically the 'relations of production', by ' *"constituting" concrete individuals as subjects*' (Althusser 1971: 171). Ideology thereby represents 'the imaginary relationship of individuals to their real conditions of existence' (ibid.: 162). For Althusser, art itself was not an ideology. '*I do not rank real art among the ideologies*', he wrote: 'Art (I mean authentic art, not works of an average or mediocre level) does not quite give us a *knowledge* in the *strict sense*...art makes us *see*...the *ideology* from which it is born...and to which it *alludes*' (ibid.: 221–2). Other Althusserian-inspired theorists were much less reticent, however, as to the possibilities of reading even high culture 'ideologically'. Althusser had developed a theory of symptomatic reading which sought to reconstruct the 'problematic' of the text (Althusser and Balibar 1970: 30–4), that is, the structure of determinate absences and presences which occasion it. For Macherey (1978), such readings could be directed at both literary and popular texts. Althusserianism thus 'alluded' to a prospective demystification of the artistic or literary text, which could expose ideology itself as the real object of art.

Arguing along roughly similar lines, Eagleton's *Criticism and Ideology* suggested that literature be understood as 'producing' ideology, in the sense that it performs it (Eagleton 1976: 64–9). 'The text is a tissue of meanings, perceptions and responses', he argued, 'which inhere in the first place in that imaginary production of the real which is ideology' (ibid.: 75). If this is so, then it will be true for both elite and popular texts, both literature and fiction. But, like Althusser before him, Eagleton retreated from the aesthetic relativism implicit in the position: rejecting the allegedly 'abstract egalitarianism' of cultural studies (ibid.: 162–3), he proceeded to endorse the notion of 'aesthetic value' itself and even much of the substantive content of the literary canon. 'All texts signify', he concluded, 'but not all texts are significant' (ibid.: 185). It is a nice line, but begs the most obvious of questions, significant *for whom*? The theory of ideology could very easily have led to a radical unravelling of the distinction between minority and mass cultures, since in principle both can be analysed 'ideologically', and this was certainly the direction suggested by Gramsci and Benjamin. But in Adorno and Horkheimer, on the one hand, and Althusserianism, on the other, authentic 'art' was somehow always exempt from the more radical effects of ideology critique: only popular culture truly betrays the logic of domination. Eagleton himself volunteered an immediate example of an 'inferior' text, the 'withered ideological matrix' of which 'simply precludes' the 'transformative textual production' which alone might 'redeem' it. With depressing predictability, it turns out to be 'the average love-story in a teenage magazine' (ibid.: 185). As Felperin once unkindly observed of Eagleton: 'you can take the boy out of Cambridge, but you cannot take Cambridge out of the boy' (Felperin 1985: 57). Althusserianism exercised a considerable fascination for radical critics, both socialist and feminist (cf. Barrett 1988), during the 1970s, but fell into disrepute after 1980, when Althusser killed his wife, Hélène, in what appears to have been a fit of madness. Eagleton himself has long since retracted his own erstwhile Althusserian sympathies (Eagleton 1989: 6). Claims for the continuing and allegedly 'postmodern' relevance of Althusser do surface from time to time (cf. Callari and Ruccio 1996), but seem increasingly eccentric. For, if Althusserianism was above all an attempt to read Marx as a structuralist, then its demise seemed probable, quite irrespective of the personal tragedy of the Althussers, once structuralism itself had begun to mutate into post-structuralism. It is to structuralism, then, especially in its crucial disciplinary manifestation as semiology, that we now turn.

Semiology and semiotics

Semiology (or semiotics, as it is sometimes known) takes as its fundamental premise the claim that the methods of structural linguistics can be generalised to apply to other aspects of culture. This entails understanding culture as a system of signs, analogous to the system of linguistic signs. Semiology is thus the science of the study of signs and of the communication of meaning through signs. Its origins can be traced back to the work in theoretical linguistics of Ferdinand de Saussure, who had argued that language should be understood as a structured system of 'signs', where each sign is intelligible only in relation to the other signs in the system. Rejecting the view that the linguistic sign is formed from the combination of a name with the thing to which it refers, the so-called 'referent', Saussure argued that a sign emerges from the union of the 'signifier', which is the sign's 'sound-image', that is, the marks on the paper or the sounds in the air, with the 'signified', which is not the referent, but rather the mental 'concept' that the signifier signifies (Saussure 1974: 66). Language is thus entirely a matter of social convention, in which the signifier and the signified, and the relations between them, are all arbitrary, each element in the language definable only in terms of its relation to other elements in the system of signs. If Saussure's own focus had fallen mainly on language, he had also foreshadowed the eventual creation of a more general science of signs, for which he coined the name 'semiology' (ibid.: 16). The new science would study the basis in social convention of much of human life, and the systems of rules, relations and structures that order it.

As with the theory of ideology, so too semiology threatened to dissolve the distinction between minority and mass cultures: both, after all, are 'only' systems of signs. In practice, however, much structuralist effort centred on the attempt to produce a supposedly 'scientific' understanding of the distinctively 'literary' aspects of the so-called 'literary system': Shklovsky argued that 'literariness' occurs when texts 'defamiliarise', or make strange, both previous literature itself and also the real world beyond the text (Shklovsky 1965: 12); Jakobson that language fulfils a 'poetic', or literary, function to the extent that it becomes self-conscious of itself as language (Jakobson

1960: 356–7). Barthes, perhaps the most famous of all semiologists, analysed popular culture as 'myth', that is, as a 'second order' semiological system, which functions as a social legitimation by 'giving an historical intention a natural justification...making contingency appear eternal' (Barthes 1973: 142). By contrast, his theory of literariness, like Jakobson's, valorised the attempt by modernist literature 'to substitute the instance of discourse for the instance of reality (or of the referent)' (Barthes 1970: 144). Later, Barthes would reformulate this as the distinction between 'readerly' and 'writerly' texts; later still, as that between 'the text of *plaisir*' and 'the text of *jouissance*'. Readerly texts are those that position the reader as passive consumer, for example realist fiction and, by extension, popular culture more generally; writerly texts those which demand that the reader actively participate as co-author of the text, typically avant-garde art (Barthes 1974: 4; 1975).

Elaborating on Barthes, Eco distinguished between 'closed' and 'open' texts, in terms which clearly reproduce the distinction between minority and mass cultures. For Eco, a closed text aimed 'at arousing a precise response on the part of more or less precise empirical readers' (Eco 1981: 8), as in Superman comic strips, for example, Ian Fleming's James Bond novels or Eugène Sue's *Les Mystères de Paris*. Eco insisted that, because such texts presuppose a sociologically 'average' reader, they are in fact 'immoderately open' to any possible 'aberrant' decoding by non-average readers. Open texts, by contrast, 'work at their peak revolutions per minute only when each interpretation is reechoed by the others, and vice versa', as in *Finnegans Wake*, for example, or *Ulysses*. Here 'the pragmatic process of interpretation is not an empirical accident independent of the text *qua* text, but is a structural element of its generative process' (ibid.: 9). Here, there are more or less competent readings, since an open text outlines a closed project of its model reader as a component of its own structure. But Eco clearly underestimated the sophistication of popular texts and popular readers. As Bennett and Woollacott observed, he construed popular reading as 'socially and culturally unorganized' only because he lacked familiarity 'with the determinations which mould and configure' it (Bennett and Woollacott 1987: 79). Such distinctions as these between readerly and writerly or closed and open texts might in themselves make good sense, especially were they to be considered positions on a continuum rather than binary oppositions, but in practice they have all too often allowed for a semiological refurbishment of the older distinctions between elite and popular, minority and mass.

For semiology, the literariness of literature could never be the effect of individual authorial 'genius'. A defining feature of the structuralist enterprise had been its resolute 'anti-humanism', its insistence that the intentions and actions of human subjects are irrelevant to the structural properties of systems. In this way, structuralism systematically 'decentred' the subject. In the 'Preface' to *The Order of Things*, for example, Foucault insists that 'man' is 'no more than a kind of rift in the order of things...only a recent invention, a figure not yet two centuries old, a wrinkle in our knowledge, and...he will disappear again as soon as that knowledge has discovered a new form' (Foucault 1970: xxiii). Foucault's own earlier work had constructed what he described as an 'archaeology' of discursive formations, or 'epistemes', that is, systematic conceptual frameworks which define their own truth criteria, according to which particular knowledge problems are to be resolved, and which are embedded in and imply particular institutional arrangements. In practice, he was concerned to establish the systematic, and in its own terms perfectly valid, nature of the dominant understandings of madness and illness in the seventeenth and early eighteenth centuries; and to contrast these with the new, equally systematic and equally internally valid, conceptions that emerged, very rapidly, in the late eighteenth century (Foucault 1965, 1973). For Foucault these 'epistemes' structurally determined the individuals subjected to them. This theoretical anti-humanism led Barthes to announce, and Foucault to endorse, the so-called 'death of the author'. This is the title of a much quoted essay in which Barthes had argued that literary texts should be understood in terms of intertextuality rather than supposed authorial intentions. In principle, he recognised the reader, rather than the author, as the '*someone* who holds together in a single field all the traces by which the written text is constituted'. This reader is 'without history, biography, psychology' (Barthes 1977: 148), nonetheless, and thus not so much an individual reading subject as a structural position. Barthes was concerned with the conventions that render the text intelligible to the reader, but this intelligibility is a function of the discourse itself, rather than of the individual reader's capacities and interests. The conclusion that 'the birth of the reader must be at the cost of the death of the Author' (ibid.: 148) is thus almost entirely rhetorical in function. When Foucault himself took up the theme, he too would decentre the individual subjectivity of both writers and readers, focusing instead on the various institutional uses of the discursive categories of authorship (Foucault 1977: 113–38).

As we have seen, semiology developed initially as an essentially 'structuralist' enterprise, aiming to discover the underlying structures which organise texts. But the central repressed problem in structuralism had always been that of how to guarantee the scientificity of a knowledge that was itself necessarily intra-discursive. Hence the move, initially anticipated by Derrida as early as 1966 (Derrida 1970), but only becoming more generally available during the 1970s, toward 'post-structuralism'. Where structuralism had aspired to scientific truth, post-structuralism would insist to the contrary that meaning is always necessarily plural. Felperin identified two main versions of post-structuralism, the 'textualist' and the 'contextualist', which he associated, respectively, with Derrida and Foucault (Felperin 1985: 71–2). Easthope points to two roughly parallel currents within British post-structuralism (Easthope 1988: 153). For Derrida, signification entails an indefinite referral of signifier to signifier 'which gives signified meaning no respite...so that it always signifies again' (Derrida 1978: 25). The analytical stress thus falls not on the underlying meaning of a text, but on its many possible meanings, and on 'difference', both within the text and within its contexts. In Foucault's later 'genealogy' (as distinct from the earlier structuralist 'archaeology') discourse is relativised by substituting relations of power for those of meaning. 'The history which bears and determines us', he argued, 'has the form of a war rather than that of a language' (Foucault 1980: 114). Perhaps the most telling example is in the first volume of the *History of Sexuality*, where he upturns the then widely accepted 'repression hypothesis', concerning Victorian sexuality, arguing to the contrary that new 'techniques of power exercised over sex' and a new 'will to knowledge...constituting...a science of sexuality' had in effect created the modern sexual subject, precisely through a 'putting into discourse of sex' (Foucault 1978: 12–13). Both Foucault and Derrida sought to identify the possibilities within discourse that discourse itself seeks to repress. The result is a cultural politics of demystification through relativisation, its aim the discovery, not so much of hidden truths, but of marginalised inconsistencies within the dominant discourses. As we shall see, such preoccupations have proven especially pertinent to the development of what we might term the new 'politics of difference'.

In its stress on the inextricable interconnectedness of institutional and discursive practices, Foucault's genealogy runs interestingly parallel to Williams's cultural materialism, Bourdieu's and Habermas's cultural sociology. And even Derrida insisted that deconstruction should interfere 'with solid structures, "material" institutions, and not only with discourses or signifying representations' (Derrida 1987: 19). This shift toward a more 'institutional' and hence less 'aesthetic' theory of culture almost seems to have become one of the characteristic moves in late twentieth-century 'Theory'. In post-structuralism, however, it led to a more radical relativism than in Williams, Bourdieu or Habermas. If there is no definitive textual meaning, as post-structuralism proposed, then it must follow that there can be no deep structure immanent within the text, whether it be one of Williams's 'structures of feeling', a Goldmannesque 'world vision' or even an Althusserian 'problematic'. Each of these would thus be seen to invent that which it professes to discover: merely one more reading amongst many, it would possess no special virtue, whether scientific or aesthetic. Moreover, if our current constructions of the past are as indelibly marked by their radical contemporaneity and radical indeterminacy, that is, their radical textuality, as post-structuralism also proposed, then there can be no determinate extratextual history to which such analyses might appeal for explanatory validation: history itself is only ever creative fiction, its findings not so much constitutive of as derivative from our contemporary preoccupations.

Neither of these propositions is devoid of insight, since our readings of literature and of history are indeed necessarily plural and contemporary. The second is more suspect than the first, however, for, as Jameson rightly insists, 'history is *not* a text, not a narrative', even though 'our approach to it...necessarily passes through its prior textualization' (Jameson 1981: 35). Insofar as history is indeed 'real', different historiographical narratives can give better or worse accounts of that reality. A history external to the literary or cultural text, though not to textuality itself, is thus still in principle available to cultural studies. Post-structuralism remains on much stronger ground when concerned with literature, as distinct from history, for there are, of course, many readings available for any particular literary text, from the hypothetical authorial original to the most recent of receptions, and each of these is as semiologically 'true' as any other. Nonetheless, even these readings are by no means equally 'true' sociologically. It may well be semiologically possible to read the Christian Bible as parody; sociologically, it would have been extremely ill advised within the city limits of Calvin's Geneva. The attempt to identify particular historically and socially influential readings still remains legitimate, then, but only so long as these are understood for what they are, not the aesthetic truth of the text itself but rather the sociological truth of the history of its production and consumption.

Psychoanalysis and post-structuralism

If structuralism's primary intellectual location was in semiology and linguistics, its influence also extended into anthropology by way of Lévi-Strauss and into psychoanalysis by way of Lacan. Given that our concerns are with the textual and the (post)modern, Lévi-Strauss need not detain us very long. Suffice it to note how central this work was to his own discipline (Lévi-Strauss 1963, 1976) and how much it engaged with, and in turn engaged, the wider theoretical debates in French intellectual life. Witness the critique of Sartrean humanism – or, for that matter, the widely cited and much borrowed comparison between 'primitive' science and the modern French *bricoleur* – in *The Savage Mind* (Lévi-Strauss 1966: 245–69, 16–22). Less absolutely central to his own field, Lacan's work nonetheless had a lasting impact on literary and cultural studies. Influenced, in turn, by Lévi-Strauss, Saussure and Jakobson, Lacan had used structural linguistics to recover what he viewed as the essential kernel of Freudian psychoanalysis. Hence his insistence that '*the unconscious is structured like a language*' (Lacan 1977a: 20). He developed a tripartite model of the pyscho-social world as comprising, respectively, the Imaginary, the Real and the Symbolic. The Imaginary here refers to the Freudian pre-Oedipal stage of infant development; the Symbolic to the world of language, social communication and culture; the Real to all that is inaccessible both to the Imaginary and to the Symbolic, but which nevertheless impinges on subjectivity and its functioning. According to Lacan, we become subjects, conscious both of ourselves and of the external world, only through entry into the Symbolic order. 'It is the world of words', he wrote, 'that creates the world of things' (Lacan 1977b: 65). But the Symbolic is masculine, it is the Law of the Father, entry into which is predicated upon the loss of Imaginary identity with the mother. The subject, thus constituted, is characterised above all by an originary lack, he argued, which can never be wholly 'sutured' over, and is thus driven by insatiable desires which are displaced from object to object in search of recognition and acceptance.

Lacanian psychoanalysis has been very widely influential, perhaps especially in feminist literary and cultural studies (cf. Grosz 1990). Kristeva famously renamed Lacan's 'Imaginary' the 'Semiotic', insisting that it persisted into adulthood as an alternative mode of signification. She borrowed from Plato the term '*chora*', meaning womb or enclosed space, to refer to the pre-Oedipal pulsions with which the Semiotic is linked:

> Our discourse – all discourse – moves with and against the *chora* in the sense that it simultaneously depends upon and refuses it.... The *chora*...is not a sign...it is not yet a signifier either...it is, however, generated in order to attain to this signifying position...the *chora* precedes and underlies figuration...and is analogous only to vocal or kinetic rhythm.
>
> (Kristeva 1984: 26)

Once the Symbolic is entered, she argued, the Semiotic is repressed, but not thereby superseded. Rather, it continues to constitute the heterogeneous and disruptive aspects of language. Where the Symbolic is masculine, the Semiotic is akin to, though not identical with, the feminine, that is, it is repressed and marginal. The Semiotic is thus culturally subversive, insofar as it deconstructs the binary oppositions fundamental to the structures of Symbolic language. For Kristeva, masculinity and femininity were essentially social constructs, then, and so it followed that biologically male poets could in fact be as marginal to, and as subversive of, the Symbolic as women. And, indeed, Kristeva's revolution in poetic language is a surprisingly male affair: witness the role of Mallarmé and Lautréamont (ibid.: 82–5). For feminist writers like Moi, this reworking of Lacan nonetheless held out the promise of a specifically 'feminist' deconstruction (Moi 1985: 172), even though Kristeva herself resisted the description. Feminists have also borrowed from Lacan the notion of the 'gaze' – derived from Freud's account of 'scopophilia', or the pleasure of looking – so as to analyse the specific functions of the male gaze. Where Freud had viewed the scopophilic drive as at the root of narcissism, voyeurism and masochism, Lacan saw it as entering into the formation of subjectivity itself, since we seek and find confirmation of self in the gaze of others. One of the more persuasive uses of this notion is in Mulvey, who argued that the general structure of conventional narrative cinema necessarily positions the male as active, the female as passive: 'WOMAN AS IMAGE, MAN AS BEARER OF THE LOOK' (Mulvey 1989: 19). Both in Lacan and in Mulvey the problem remains of how to explain conflictual, especially active and female, desires. As Grosz observed, the Lacanian model is unable to 'account for, to explain, or to acknowledge the existence of an active...explicitly female desire' (Grosz 1994: 275).

There was never anything explicitly or necessarily feminist, however, about Lacanian psychoanalysis: Slavoj Žižek, one of the best-known of contemporary Lacanians, has made something of a career out of offending feminist and other 'politically correct' sensibilities (Žižek 1997). A prolific writer, he moves readily between philosophy and politics, literature and film, in a startling blend of Hegel and Hitchcock, Lacan and Lukács (Žižek 1992, 2001). His early work had established, by turn, a Lacanian reconstruction of the theory of ideology (Žižek 1989) and a critical account of the politics of Lacan's return to Freud (Žižek 1991). Where neo-Marxian ideology critique had tended to view ideology as the effect of social structure, Žižek would insist that it was also and necessarily the effect of a Lacanian originary lack. Ideology can thus be understood as a fantasy attempt to suture such lack, 'basically a scenario filling out the empty space of a fundamental impossibility, a screen masking a void' (Žižek 1989: 126). Its 'pre-ideological kernel' takes the form of the spectre, he observes, which conceals '*not reality but its "primordially repressed", the irrepresentable X on whose "repression" reality itself is founded*' (Žižek 1994: 21). This 'traumatic kernel' of ideology, the fundamental antagonism unamenable to symbolisation, is thus the Lacanian Real masked by social structure (ibid.: 25–6). For Žižek, ideology entails the misrecognition, not of social reality itself, but of the illusions that structure this reality. People 'know very well how things really are', he writes:

> but still they are doing it as if they did not know. The illusion is therefore double: it consists in overlooking the illusion which is structuring our real, effective relationship to reality. And this overlooked, unconscious illusion may be called the *ideological fantasy*.
> (Žižek 1989: 32–3)

This attempt to rewrite the theory of ideology in Lacanian psychoanalytic terms has yielded strikingly original interpretations, most notably in film criticism. But, as with feminist borrowings from Lacan, it tends both to exaggerate the social system's capacity for dominative integration and to underestimate the possibilities for resistance and change. As Elliott notes:

> Whether one is in the grip of identity politics, reading Hegel, or simply watching Oprah Winfrey, these are for Žižek all instances of ideological fantasy aimed at effacing the sour taste of ontological lack, gap, and antagonism. Social differentiation and cultural discrimination are lost in this approach, as Žižek simply passes over the complex, contradictory ways in which people come to challenge or resist political ideologies.
> (Elliott 2003: 278)

The cultural politics of difference

Structuralism and post-structuralism theorised the human subject as necessarily 'encultured', that is, as existing only in and through cultural forms. On this view, identity is only ever constituted from out of cultural experience. If this is so, then it clearly suggests the essential arbitrariness of all identities that are culturally constructed as subordinate or inferior, not only 'working class', but also 'woman', 'black', 'immigrant', 'homosexual', 'colonial' and so on. If the first breach in the notion of a common culture had devolved upon the category of class, then the second very clearly devolved upon that of gender. There can be little doubt that feminism has radically redrawn the boundaries of academic knowledge in the human sciences over the past forty years. At one level, the reason is obvious: what had previously passed for knowledge of the human condition was very often simply knowledge of men. But to this general observation we should add the more specific point that culture was a central preoccupation for feminism, primarily because feminists were often committed to the view that women's oppression had cultural, rather than biological, roots. Initially most 'second wave' feminists were concerned above all to refute the kind of conservative argument which had insisted on the biological necessity of sexual difference. This led them to postulate an analytical distinction between biological sex and socially produced 'gender' (Millett 1977: 28–31). Unlike biological sexual characteristics, which are innate, gender was conceived as the product of a complex variety of sociocultural factors. This interest in the cultural production of social inequality would later be extended from gender to embrace most of Collini's 'grievances'. Feminists had read both high-culture and popular-culture texts as 'patriarchal', functioning in one way or another to position woman as subordinate. So Millett, for example, famously indicted Lawrence's *Lady Chatterley's Lover* for its 'transformation of masculine ascendancy into a mystical religion' (ibid.: 238). In roughly analogous fashion, Said's *Orientalism*, the founding text of what eventually became 'postcolonial theory', argued that British and French academic scholarship had constructed the 'Orient' as 'Other'. For Said, Orientalism was an 'enormously systematic discipline by which European culture was able to manage – and even produce – the Orient...during the post-Enlightenment period' (Said 1995: 3). In Britain, the Birmingham School of cultural studies explored the multiculturalism of its society through a similar critique of how white racism constituted blackness as 'Other' (Hall *et al.* 1978).

During the 1980s, feminist theory tended to move on from the earlier critique of patriarchal culture toward a more positive celebration of female difference. Theoretically, this often involved an invocation of post-structuralism, especially as refracted through Lacanian psychoanalysis and the so-called 'French feminism' of Kristeva, Irigaray, Cixous, Le Doeuff and others (Grosz 1989, 1990; Cixous and Clément 1986; Irigaray 1985; Kristeva 1984; Le Doeuff 1989, 1991). If the female was to be celebrated positively, then sexual difference became much less of a political and theoretical liability than hitherto: to celebrate female difference might mean to celebrate distinctly female pleasures of the text. Post-feminist 'queer theory' proceeded from a generally post-structuralist sense of the contingency of identity toward a radical deconstruction of the categories of 'gender' and 'sexuality' themselves. There 'is no gender identity behind the expressions of gender', wrote Butler, because 'identity is performatively constituted by the very "expressions" that are said to be its results' (J. Butler 1990: 25). ' "Homosexual", like "woman", is not a name that refers to a "natural kind" of thing', wrote Halperin: 'It's a discursive, and homophobic, construction that has come to be misrecognised as an object under the epistemological regime known as realism' (Halperin 1995: 45). Postcolonial and multicultural theory invoked a similarly post-structuralist rhetoric of 'difference' so as to 'decentre' the dominant culture – in this case, white, metropolitan, European culture. The colonial encounter could thus be read as self-deconstructing, insofar as it moved from 'mimicry' to 'menace', a 'difference that is almost total but not quite' (Bhabha 1994: 91); the multicultural as leading to a 'poetics of ethnicity', which swerves away from 'binary structures' to substitute 'irony' for 'authenticity' (Gunew 1994: 49). Hall's work of the 1990s increasingly gave pride of theoretical place to 'a *diaspora* experience' of 'unsettling, recombination, hybridization' (Hall 1996: 445). In North American 'black studies', West accorded a parallel significance to 'diversity, multiplicity and heterogeneity' and the need 'to historicize, contextualize and pluralize' (West 1999: 119).

At the level of practical politics, a critique of hegemonic misrepresentation might well suggest the need for a counter-assertion of some authentically 'subaltern' identity. That move was precluded, however, by the logic of post-structuralism, for if maleness and femaleness, whiteness and blackness were each constituted within and through discourse, then there could be no extra-discursively 'real' female, immigrant or postcolonial identity to which a feminist, multicultural or postcolonial cultural politics might appeal for validation. The dangers in the position should be apparent. As Showalter observed: 'Feminist criticism can't afford...to give up the idea of female subjectivity, even if we accept it as a constructed or metaphysical one' (Showalter 1989: 369). The dilemma was certainly apparent to Spivak, simultaneously a feminist, a 'Third World' intellectual and a 'deconstructionist', a translator of Derrida into English in fact. She suggested the need to adhere '*strategically*' to the 'essentialist notion of consciousness, that would fall prey to an anti-humanist critique, within a historiographic practice that draws many of its strengths from that very critique' (Spivak 1987: 206–7). This meant, in short, that whatever deconstruction's theoretical purchase when directed at European, white, male, bourgeois humanism, postcolonial feminists must nonetheless proceed *as if* humanism were still valid, *as if* the subject had still not been decentred, *as if* deconstruction had failed, if ever they were adequately to represent insurgent, or 'subaltern', consciousness itself. We might note that Spivak's 'strategic' humanism was taken up with some enthusiasm by Showalter (1989: 369).

The promise of difference theory, that culture be understood as radically in excess of both 'nation' and 'class', is as politically exciting as any in recent intellectual history. Its combination with identity politics has worked in and against the distinctive realities of late-capitalist culture, so that it sometimes attained a more fully contemporary relevance than any other kind of theorising. Indeed, Butler goes so far as to claim that a viable radical politics requires 'affiliation with poststructuralism', insofar as difference is 'constitutive of any struggle' (J. Butler 1999: 44). But deconstruction's relativising logic simultaneously threatens to undermine these politics as well as any other. What is so important, after all, about a critique of institutional oppression if what are oppressed are merely fictional identities? As Segal observes, 'deconstructive feminism...avoids the perils of generalizations about female subjectivity. But it courts the danger that its own interest in endlessly proliferating particularitics of difference...endorses a relativity and indeterminacy which works to undermine political projects' (Segal 1999: 32). Hence Barrett's concern that:

> If we replace the given self with a constructed, fragmented self, this poses...the obvious political question of who is the I that acts and on what basis,...who is the I that is so certain of its fragmented and discursively constructed nature.
>
> (Barrett 1999: 25)

Said canvassed a very different solution to Spivak's in his *Culture and Imperialism*:

> there seems no reason except fear and prejudice to keep insisting on...separation and distinctiveness, as if that was all human life was about...this...means not trying to rule over others, not trying to classify them or put them in hierarchies, above all, not constantly reiterating how 'our' culture or country is number one (or *not* number one, for that matter).
>
> (Said 1993: 408)

This isn't so much strategic essentialism as essentialism itself, a clear affirmation, in short, of the continuing political and intellectual relevance of a radicalised humanism. Yet this is a humanism as capable as any post-structuralism of undermining the Eurocentric certainties of Said's own academic discipline, which was comparative literature, and of the older liberal humanisms more generally. His reading of Austen's *Mansfield Park*, for example, as 'part of the structure of an expanding imperialist venture' is both powerfully demystifying and indisputably 'anti-imperialist'. But it also deliberately avoided the 'rhetoric of blame' in favour of what Said described as the 'intellectual and interpretive vocation to make connections...to see complementarity and interdependence' (ibid.: 114–15).

Postmodernism

Post-structuralism has often been represented as in some sense peculiarly 'postmodern'. And there is indeed a certain 'fit' between post-structuralist theoretical relativism and the kind of social and cultural pluralism many commentators find distinctive to our contemporary 'postmodern condition'. The institutionalised claims to authoritative cultural judgement characteristic of traditional literary studies were typically predicated on the prior assumption of white, European, middle-class masculinity. There was no theoretical space at all for the Islamic, the female, the proletarian, even 'the scientific', in Leavis's famous claim that culture is necessarily singular (F. R. Leavis 1972b: 93). By comparison, post-structuralism has held out the promise to theorise precisely all that is different. It is barely surprising, then, that postmodernism and post-structuralism should have been routinely assimilated to each other by both protagonists and antagonists of each. They are by no means synonymous, however: as Lash insisted, there is no necessary parallel between post-structuralism and postmodernism (Lash 1990: 153). French post-structuralism was generally far too preoccupied with the high modernist canon to accord any serious attention to a contemporary culture that had acquired an increasingly postmodern complexion: Barthes's writerly texts were modernist rather than postmodernist in character; so too was Kristeva's 'revolution in poetic language'; and insofar as Foucault's archaeology was able to envisage a 'post-modern' episteme, it is only that inaugurated by high structuralism itself (Foucault 1970: 385–6). As Callinicos noted with perverse approval, it is not at all clear that the major post-structuralist thinkers did in fact endorse the idea of the postmodern (Callinicos 1989: 5). That this is so was part of the failure of post-structuralism, however, for, as Huyssen argued, 'rather than offering a *theory of postmodernity* and developing an analysis of contemporary culture, French theory provides us primarily with an *archaeology of modernity*, a theory of modernism at the stage of its exhaustion' (Huyssen 1988: 209).

What, then, is postmodernism? The term was perhaps the most fashionable buzzword in the humanities during the 1980s and 1990s, used variously to refer to: the non-realist and non-traditional 'high' art of the post-Second World War period; art which radically accentuated certain key modernist characteristics; and aspects of a more generally 'late capitalist' culture (Hawthorn 1992: 110). I am concerned here mainly with the first and third usages and especially, but not only, with their implications for the high/low culture divide. As the prefix suggested, postmodernism came 'after' something else and, at the most obvious of levels, that something was 'modernism', meaning simply the kind of high art, characterised by a combination of aesthetic self-consciousness and formalist experimentalism, which emerged initially in late nineteenth-century Europe. Modernist culture developed through a series of avant-garde 'isms', almost all located in essentially adversarial relation, not only to aesthetic realism, but also to mass culture. High modernism thus typically ascribed a 'redemptive' function to art, which would at the very least 'save' itself, and possibly even humanity, from the philistinism of mass society. By contrast, postmodernist art typically attempted, or at least resulted from, the collapse of this antithesis between high and low, elite and popular. The obvious and nicely reciprocal example is Andy Warhol's use of Marilyn Monroe and Campbell's soup cans and David Bowie's or Lou Reed's use of Andy Warhol. Almost all the available theorisations of postmodernism agree on the centrality of this progressive deconstruction and dissolution of the high/low cultural distinction. Indeed, Huyssen went so far as to locate postmodernism quite specifically 'after the great divide' between modernism and mass culture.

There is a substantial theoretical literature on postmodernism, a great deal of it often uncritically celebratory (cf. Lyotard 1984; Baudrillard 1988, 1994; Eco 1986). Jeff Browitt and I have explored much of this elsewhere and I do not intend to repeat the exercise here (Milner and Browitt 2002: 164–202). Rather, I want to concentrate on one of the more important critical accounts, that developed by Jameson. Self-consciously postmodernist artistic movements were, for the main part, a product of the 1960s, 1970s and 1980s, rather than of the last fifteen years. Hence the recent tendency, especially amongst sociologists, to dismiss Jameson's work as in some sense outdated. But what Lash wrote of architecture is almost certainly true of the other arts: 'As a movement, postmodernism...is a thing of the past. As a presence at the end of the 1990s...it is ubiquitous' (Lash 1999: 56). In the dominant sociological theorisations there has also been a tendency to subsume the rupture between modernism and postmodernism into some more gradual process by which an earlier modernity evolved into a later. For Beck, this latest stage is the 'risk society', a 'reflexive modernization', which also represents a 'radicalization of modernity' (Beck 1994: 2–3; cf. Beck 1992). For Giddens, it is 'late modernity', a similarly reflexive 'post-traditional society', in which globalisation 'disembeds' the 'traditional contexts of action', so that 'lifestyle and taste' become 'as evident markers of social differentiation as position in the productive order' (Giddens 1994a: 95–6; 1994b: 143; cf. Giddens 1991). More interesting than either is Lash's own notion of aesthetic modernity as a 'second modernity', contemporaneous with the rationalism of the first, but based on reflexivity and difference rather than the rationality of the same (Lash 1999: 3–4).

The distinctively 'postmodern' moment – though this is no longer Lash's preferred term – arrived when both modernities were superseded, in the 'multimediatized cultural space' of the global information culture, by a new world order, at once post-national, post-human and even post-Western, in which human subjectivities become equal with 'animals, things, machines, nature and other objects' (ibid.: 11–14). The result is not so much difference as *in*difference. 'This is the scenario ever repeated in turn-of-the-twenty-first-century popular culture', he writes: 'there is no longer a constitutive outside', only 'a swirling vortex of microbes, genes, desire, death, onco-mice, semiconductors, holograms, semen, digitized images, electronic money and hyperspaces in a general economy of indifference' (ibid.: 344). As impressionistic description, this is suggestive, but as evaluation it is excessively melancholic, as explanation near-vacuous. We may readily concede to sociology that the crucial issues do indeed include mediatisation, globalisation, reflexivity and also, we might add, universal commodification. What it generally fails to recognise, however, is that the fate of the avant-garde, and the concomitant shift from modernist to postmodernist art, had functioned historically as key early warning signals of how these processes would eventually combine to threaten what most people in the West had previously understood, not only by 'culture', but also by 'society'. This is why the most persuasive and influential account of the deep structural roots of postmodernism remains Jameson's, which comes, not from sociology, but from literary and cultural studies. His various essays on the subject have become standard references (Jameson 1984, 1985, 1994, 1998) and his full-length study *Postmodernism, or the Cultural Logic of Late Capitalism* (1991) is for many the *locus classicus* of the postmodern debate. As Anderson rightly observed, Jameson's work has 'set the terms of subsequent debate' (P. Anderson 1998: 78).

Jameson's central argument is that there have been three main stages in the history of capitalism, each of which has its own characteristic 'cultural dominant'. Thus aesthetic realism was the cultural dominant of mid-nineteenth-century 'market capitalism'; modernism that of late nineteenth- and early twentieth-century imperialism or 'monopoly capitalism'; and postmodernism that of contemporary multinational 'late capitalism'. This late capitalism, he insisted, was in fact 'the purest form of capital yet to have emerged, a prodigious expansion of capital into hitherto uncommodified areas' (Jameson 1991: 35–6). Art itself is one of these hitherto largely uncommodified areas, postmodernism the form of its final and full commodification: 'aesthetic production today has become integrated into commodity production generally', wrote Jameson, 'the frantic economic urgency of producing fresh waves of ever more novel-seeming goods... now assigns an increasingly essential structural function and position to aesthetic innovation and experimentation' (ibid.: 4–5). Postmodernism is a commodity culture, then, in a double sense, both as a set of commodified artefacts actually available for sale in the culture market and as a set of texts the very textuality of which often affirms their own commodity status. As Jameson observed, 'the various postmodernisms...all at least share a resonant affirmation, when not an outright celebration, of the market as such' (ibid.: 305).

Like Huyssen, Jameson saw postmodernist culture as entailing a kind of 'aesthetic populism'. One of its most fundamental features, he argued, is:

> the effacement...of the older (essentially high-modernist) frontier between high culture and so-called mass or commercial culture, and the emergence of new kinds of texts infused with the forms, categories and contents of that very Culture Industry so passionately denounced by all ideologues of the Modern....
>
> (Jameson 1991: 2)

Postmodernist art is 'fascinated by this whole "degraded" landscape of schlock and kitsch, of TV series and Readers' Digest culture, of advertising and motels, of the late show and the grade-B Hollywood film' (ibid.: 2). As a thoroughgoing commodity culture, postmodernism can have no defining normative standards of its own: its value is what it will fetch in the market. It is thus a 'field of stylistic and discursive heterogeneity without a norm' (ibid.: 17). In consequence, parody, which assumes such norms, has been progressively effaced by pastiche, which does not. Both involve imitation, Jameson explained, but pastiche is a 'neutral practice of such mimicry, without any of parody's ulterior motives, amputated of satiric impulse, devoid of...any conviction that alongside the abnormal tongue you have momentarily borrowed, some healthy linguistic normality still exists' (ibid.: 17). In the absence of any truly distinct, contemporary style, postmodernism thus becomes 'the random cannibalization of all the styles of the past' (ibid.: 18). The result is a 'waning of...historicity', so that 'the past as "referent" finds itself gradually bracketed, and then effaced altogether, leaving us with nothing but texts' (ibid.: 21, 18). Discussing contemporary cinema's use of earlier novels and films, he argues that 'our awareness of the preexistence of other versions...is now a constitutive and essential part of the film's structure: we are now...in "intertextuality" as a deliberate, built-in feature of the aesthetic effect' (ibid.: 20). He also stressed the radically internationalising nature of socio-economic postmodernity, that is, late capitalism's peculiarly global character. There is now a world capitalist system, he argued, as distinct from the previous set of competing colonial empires. The new system and the new culture are thus simultaneously post-European, 'American' and global: 'it was the brief "American century" (1945–73)', he wrote, 'that constituted the hothouse, or forcing ground, of the new system, while the development of the cultural forms of postmodernism may be said to be the first specifically North American global style' (ibid.: x).

Moreover, Jameson was very clear that there is something 'progressive' about this 'original new global space', which is 'the "moment of truth" of postmodernism' (ibid.: 49). A fully contemporary version of what Western Marxism had meant by class consciousness would therefore need to apprehend precisely this truth. But the culture has now become so commodified as to structurally pre-empt such class consciousness, so that the capacity to map 'the system' either disappears or must temporarily lie elsewhere. That elsewhere is located somewhere between critical theory and a hypothetically postmodern political art. For this was Jameson's solution to the temporary absence of oppositional class consciousness from postmodern late capitalism: to posit the need for an 'aesthetic of cognitive mapping', through which to learn how to represent 'the world space of multinational capital' and so 'again begin to grasp our positioning as individual and collective subjects' (ibid.: 54). Cognitive mapping, he explained, is in reality a 'code word' for class consciousness 'of a new and hitherto undreamed of kind', which has not yet come into being. Hence the sense of his own work as the anticipation in theory of what may eventually become class consciousness, that is, as an experiment 'to see whether by systematizing something that is resolutely unsystematic, and historicizing something that is resolutely ahistorical, one couldn't outflank it and force a historical way at least of thinking about that' (ibid.: 418). At this point, Adorno's special significance for Jameson becomes apparent. For, despite its American idiom, this rhetorical and theoretical strategy is clearly reminiscent of the Frankfurt School. Adorno and Horkheimer had initially imagined their critical theory as aligned with a proletarian opposition to fascism. From at least the *Dialectic of Enlightenment*, such emancipatory potential inhered in the immanent logic of critical theory itself. As Jameson noted, this led Adorno to a kind of 'temperamental and cantankerous quietism' which proved a disabling liability at moments of popular politicisation. In the depoliticised 1990s, however, Adorno 'in the postmodern' had become 'a joyous counter-poison and a corrosive solvent to apply to the surface of "what is"' (Jameson 1990: 249). Like Adorno's, Jameson's critical theory functions by way of a great refusal, both of an increasingly totalised late-capitalist system and of the postmodernist ideologies that legitimate it. Hence the extraordinary grandeur of this intransigent resistance to the lures of commodity culture.

Hermeneutics, cultural materialism, new historicism, the sociology of culture, ideology critique, semiology, theories of difference – each of the theoretical approaches discussed in this chapter has carried with it the potential to sidestep, dissolve or transcend the older binary oppositions between high and low culture. And yet that potential was hardly ever realised, except perhaps in some of Williams's later writings. Postmodernism, by contrast, is not so much a theoretical perspective in its own right as the signifier of a far-reaching transformation in the culture and political economy of contemporary western societies. As Barrett observes: 'postmodernism is not something that you can be for or against: the reiteration of old knowledges will not make it vanish...it is a cultural climate as well as an intellectual position, a political reality as well as an academic fashion' (Barrett 1999: 156). And this is so whether we like it or not, whether we admit it or not. Part of what the term signifies is what Jameson meant by aesthetic populism. And insofar as this populist shift has occurred in the general culture, at least in its dominant forms, it is barely surprising that a parallel shift should have registered within the academy: as we noted in Chapter 1, the move from literary to cultural studies can in fact be read as one from a modernist to a postmodernist discourse about culture. This has never been simply a move from elitism to populism, from Milton to the movies as Bloom would have it, but rather a progressive and practical dissolution of the very notion of a radical distinction between elite and popular cultures. Whatever Bloom may fear, cultural studies will almost certainly continue to study Milton, but it will tend to do so only alongside and in connection with the study of movies, television, popular fiction and the rest. How exactly this might be done provides the subject matter for the chapters that follow.

Chapter 3

Mechanical reproduction

The forces of production

In Chapter 2 we observed how cultural studies emerged from an initial encounter between literary studies and sociology; we explored the contributions of each of these disciplines to contemporary analyses of culture; and we began to trace the impact of a set of theoretical notions deriving from ideology critique, semiology and the politics of difference. If cultural studies had been formed from out of a 'sociological turn' in literary studies, then it was subsequently re-formed from out of a 'linguistic turn' towards semiology and semiotics. The discipline's short history was thus characterised by a double movement: from the literary 'work' to its sociological 'context'; and from the sociological context to the cultural 'text', that is, to the work redefined and retheorised as bearing within its own textuality the mark of its contextual location. This latter move has been much more than a simple return to the 'work', since it retains much that had previously been understood as 'context' within its new sense of 'text'. Not everything, however. Many of the more specifically sociological aspects of context, that is, those pertaining directly to institutions rather than to their ideological impress within textuality, are typically elided in this movement away from a sociology of literature and towards a semiotics of culture. As Wolff observed of developments in feminist literary and cultural studies, 'what is still missing is an approach which investigates *both* texts *and* institutions' (1990: 106). In the next two chapters we turn to an examination of the central institutions of literary and cultural production, to what Eagleton termed 'the literary mode of production' (1976: 45) and the mode of cultural production more generally.

The literary mode of production

Eagleton first used the notion of a 'literary mode of production', at the height of his enthusiasm for Althusserian structural Marxism, in direct analogy with Marx's treatment of the economy proper. Althusser's uxoricide, structuralism's supersession into post-structuralism and the self-evident practical failure of Soviet Communism have each combined to render such enthusiasms radically suspect. We already have Derrida's post-structuralist warranty, however, for continuing to take Marx seriously, even after the failure of Communism (Derrida 1994). And, in any case, the notion of a literary mode of production remains an interesting one, quite apart from its intellectual ancestry. For Marx himself, human societies were classifiable, in what we can retrospectively recognise as a kind of comparative historical sociology, according to the predominant structural characteristics of their economic systems. He defined the 'economic structure' or 'mode of production' of a society as a combination of 'relations of production', that is, economic relations between groups of people, primarily forms of class structure, and 'forces of production', that is, forms of available productive technique, including technology and raw materials. He also identified four major modes of production, 'Asiatic, ancient, feudal and modern', though it is clear that these are not necessarily inclusive categories (Marx 1975: 425–6). No doubt there are many other modes in the historical record (cf. P. Anderson 1974: 218–28). But irrespective of the precise qualities of any particular mode, Marx was also insistent that the 'legal and political superstructure', on the one hand, and the 'forms of social consciousness', on the other (and these latter are explicitly formulated as including 'religious, artistic or philosophic' forms), should always be considered analytically distinct from economic production itself.

For all its declared pretensions to Marxist orthodoxy, then, Eagleton's notion of the 'literary mode of production' is in fact distinctly heterodox. But, of course, many of the more interesting contemporary uses of Marx are precisely thus. As McLennan has argued, citing by turn Mouzelis's 'mode of domination', Delphy's 'domestic mode of production' and Bourdieu's 'cultural capital', this kind of 'analogical borrowing' from Marxism 'in order to *develop* sociological theory' has often proven very fruitful (McLennan 1995: 124). Though McLennan paid it no attention, Eagleton's 'literary mode of production' is just such an analogical borrowing. Though the notion has excited only modest interest (cf. Barrett 1988: 101–2; Wolff 1990: 107–8), it still seems potentially fruitful in precisely this sense, most especially so for the development of a properly immodest cultural studies. What, then, did Eagleton mean by the term? Every literary mode of production, he wrote:

> is constituted by structures of production, distribution, exchange and consumption. Production presupposes a producer or set of producers, materials, instruments and techniques of production, and the product itself....The forces of literary production consist in the application of labour-power organised in certain 'relations of production'...to certain materials of production by means of certain determinate productive instruments.... Unified with these productive forces...are specific social relations of literary production.
>
> (Eagleton 1976: 47)

These are exactly Marx's terms, almost to the point of parody, but applied to a kind of 'production' he had carefully exempted from their purview. In fact, these are much less eccentric propositions than the terminology suggests: as Eagleton notes, they gesture toward forms already familiar to the academic 'sociology of literature' (ibid.: 47–8). But there was real novelty in Eagleton's argument, nonetheless, and for two main reasons. First, he insists that the literary mode of production 'is a significant constituent of the literary product itself...an internal constituent rather than merely an extrinsic limit of the character of the text' (ibid.: 48). This is not simply a matter of the impress of ideology within the text, which has become something of a theoretical commonplace in cultural studies, but of the literary production process on its products. The distinction, in the case of the nineteenth-century English novel for example, is between textualisations of Victorian 'bourgeois' ideology on the one hand (in George Eliot, high-minded moralism) and production geared towards Mudie's circulating library on the other (again in George Eliot, sufficiently circuitous plots as to sustain a 'three-decker' novel). Second, Eagleton warns that the social relations of literary production are not necessarily homologous with those of the 'general' mode of production (that is, the mode of production proper, in Marx's terms): the extent to which they 'reproduce the social relations of "general" production…is historically variable and determinate' (ibid.: 53). By this, Eagleton means, not that there is no connection between literary and general modes of production, but rather that the nature of these connections will vary according to the character of the general mode of production. Quite specifically, he suggests that modern capitalist relations of literary production are much less directly reproductive of more general social relations than was normal in most pre-capitalist systems.

In short, Eagleton argued both that cultural texts encode within themselves the mode of cultural production by which they have been produced, and that such modes of cultural production are never simply deducible from any comparative historical sociology of general modes of production. If this is indeed so, then the institutions of cultural production warrant much more determined attention than has become customary in cultural studies. Substantively, the central datum in any account of contemporary cultural production is the rise to dominance over the last five centuries of a distinctively 'capitalist' literary mode of production. Sociologists, historians and economists conventionally use the term 'capitalism' to describe an economy in which goods and services are produced primarily in order to be sold as commodities in a more or less competitive market. In such a system production is organised by an individual or collective 'capitalist' who advances the capital necessary for production, in the form either of machinery or of money, and whose activities are motivated in principle only by the pursuit of the maximum possible profit. In this system, the labour of others is also a commodity which the capitalist purchases at the price of salaries or wages. It is a truism that capitalism has become the dominant form of economic organisation in recent history. Less obvious but equally true is the fact that it also provides the dominant form of organisation for modern literary production. Indeed, the book trade was almost certainly the historical prototype for modern capitalist industry in general. As Febvre and Martin observe of fifteenth-century Europe, 'the printer and the bookseller worked above all and from the beginning for profit' (1976: 249).

The capitalist character of cultural production is at its most obvious in the kind of mass culture demonised by Leavisite English, which modest cultural studies has taken for its own. In all socially differentiated societies there have always been 'popular' as well as 'elite' cultures. But these earlier popular cultures were mainly oral in form, folk songs, folk ballads and so on. They typically entered into literary studies, moreover, not as demonised other, but as retrospectively valorised instances of popular virtue. Hence both the Leavisite myth of the pre-industrial 'organic community' and the early preoccupation with 'folklore' in comparative literature. What clearly is new is the kind of popular culture we now enjoy, predicated on the existence of cultural commodities offered for sale to a 'mass' audience. This kind of audience reached 'critical mass' only in the late nineteenth century and then only in Western Europe and the European colonies of settlement in North America and Australasia. This is a historically unique kind of culture, the most distinctive features of which include 'mechanical reproduction' at the level of forces of production and 'commodity production' at the level of relations of production. The first provides the central subject matter for this chapter, the second for the chapter that follows. But note that neither is the exclusive property of popular, as distinct from elite, cultures. Just as much as television, contemporary literature is both produced as a commodity and reproduced mechanically. The forces of literary production consist in material technologies on the one hand (printing, paper manufacture and so on), cultural forms on the other (the novel, the newspaper). The relations of production are constituted by the social relations between publishers, writers and readers (and various intermediary 'gatekeepers'). In each case, our main focus will fall on the distinctive features of contemporary cultural production itself, but that distinctiveness will be established in part by way of comparison with prior modes of cultural production.

Mechanical reproduction

The term 'mechanical reproduction' was coined by Benjamin, in his 1936 essay 'The work of art in the age of mechanical reproduction', which has been enormously influential in recent debates in cultural studies. He used it to refer to any form of cultural production characterised by the relatively large-scale, more or less exact, replication of cultural artefacts by means of machine technologies, in which each replica is neither any more nor any less the 'original' than any other. He gives the founding and stamping of bronzes, terra cottas and coins as the first historical examples of the process (Benjamin 1973b: 220). Later instances include woodcuts, printing, lithography, photography, film, radio, television, gramophone records, compact discs, audio and video tapes, and computer software. In passing, we should note how very many of these are in fact late nineteenth-century or twentieth-century inventions. For Benjamin, this was much more than a simple matter of technology, since mechanical reproduction transforms the nature of aesthetic experience itself. He argued that much of the aesthetic power of the traditional artwork derived from its status as a unique object, using the term 'aura' to refer to the uniqueness, authenticity and authority of the artwork, all of which he sees as inextricably interconnected. In Benjamin's view such aura derives from the artwork's embeddedness in cultural tradition, which in turn has its historical origins in the religious cult: the sacredness of art thus derives from the sacredness of magical and religious ritual (ibid.: 225). And it is this aura which 'withers in the age of mechanical reproduction' (ibid.: 223). The decline of aura thus becomes the characteristic feature of our 'age', the age of mechanical reproduction, which is, of course, both the age of popular culture and, we now know, the age of cultural studies.

The paradigmatic intellectual response to the decline of aura has been a deeply gloomy, cultural pessimism: Adorno came very close to this; the Leavises embodied it almost exactly. But for Benjamin mechanical reproduction and non-auratic art provided the initial preconditions, at least, for the creation of something that might become a 'cultural democracy'. 'It is inherent in the techniques of the film', he wrote, 'that everybody who witnesses its accomplishments is somewhat of an expert' (ibid.: 233). Consider a practical example from another medium. As is well known, J. S. Bach's *Brandenburg Concertos* of 1721 were supposedly written for Christian Ludwig, Margrave of Brandenburg, and in their original form could only have been performed for a patron able to maintain a sufficiently large orchestra. Even Christian Ludwig's house ensemble was in reality almost certainly too small for the *Concertos*, which were probably intended for Prince Leopold's court orchestra at Cöthen, where Bach served as Kapellmeister. Later, the technical development of the concert hall and the progressive commercialisation of musical relations of consumption enabled much larger middle-class audiences to purchase individual tickets to attend 'live' performances of the *Concertos*. Though much less exclusive, these were still 'unique' events, still in some sense strongly auratic. With the mechanical reproduction of sound, however, the *Concertos* were retrospectively rendered non-auratic. They are now available for consumption to anyone who owns a compact disc player and they are available, moreover, whenever and however those consumers may prefer (as background music, to be sampled in 'snatches', and so on). This almost certainly does represent the end of western civilisation as the Margrave of Brandenburg knew it, but that may not be an altogether bad thing. As Benjamin observed:

> The film makes the cult value recede into the background not only by putting the public in the position of critic, but also by the fact that at the movies this position requires no attention. The public is an examiner, but an absent-minded one.
>
> (Benjamin 1973b: 242–3)

The print media

Though Benjamin's own interests in mechanical reproduction were occasioned primarily by the cinema, he did describe printing as 'a special…particularly important, case' (ibid.: 221) of the process. This importance derives from its fundamental contribution to the making of modern, as distinct from medieval, culture. In medieval Europe, books had been handwritten, in manuscript (from the Latin *manus*, hand) and on parchment (which was made from animal skins). From the Fall of Rome in 410 AD until the twelfth century, the production of manuscript books had been effectively confined to the monasteries (M. Thomas 1976: 15). Organised large-scale copying along commercial lines began to develop during the thirteenth century, however, catering in particular for the new reading publics located around the new universities (ibid.: 19). This was a much larger and much more commercial book trade than is often supposed. As Thomas observes, 'the work of copyists and scriveners paved the way for the printers. On the eve of the appearance of the first printed texts a growing demand for books was obvious, particularly amongst the emergent social classes, the merchants and the bourgeoisie' (ibid.: 28). But there were obvious limits, nonetheless, to the development of an industry still dependent on pre-mechanical techniques of reproduction. The key technical precondition for printing was the development of paper, since animal skin takes ink relatively poorly and only calfskin, which was very expensive, could actually be used under press. Paper had been invented in China and was introduced into Europe by Arab merchants during the twelfth century, its use becoming general by the late fourteenth century (Febvre and Martin 1976: 30). The crucial technical development in printing itself was moveable type, that is, the design of individual letters or characters. This had been in use in China since the early eleventh century, and in Korea since the early thirteenth (ibid.: 75–6), but appears to have been developed quite independently in Europe in the mid-fifteenth century. The new industry was centred initially on the German city of Mainz, where several workshops were simultaneously in commercial operation by the 1450s (ibid.: 56).

The new technology transformed the book trade: in the mid-fifteenth century the average size of editions had been between 100 and 200; by 1500 the figure had reached 1,500 (ibid.: 217–18). Printing spread very rapidly, exported across Europe in the first place mainly by migrant German printers: it was introduced into England in 1476; into Russia by 1563; into North America in 1638 (ibid.: 182,

205, 209); into Australasia in 1788 (Goodwin 1986: 11). It resulted in an enormous expansion of reading (without printing it is difficult to see how the Protestants could ever have insisted on every man's – and even sometimes every woman's – right to read the Bible). But reading remained very much a minority practice until well into the nineteenth century: as late as the eighteenth century, and right across Europe, average print runs remained under 2,000 (Febvre and Martin 1976: 220). The breakthrough to mass production in fact comes only during the nineteenth century, partly as an effect of a series of technical innovations in printing, each of which had made for lower prices: the steam-powered press in the second decade of the century; the web press, printing on continuous rolls of paper, in the 1860s; type-setting machinery in the 1870s (Laurenson and Swingewood 1972: 129). 'Before the end of Napoleon's reign', wrote Escarpit, 'more sheets could be printed in an hour than had been possible in a day fifteen years earlier'. The 'period of large printings' began in Britain, he continues, 'in 1814, when 10,000 copies of [Byron's] *The Corsair* were sold on the day of publication. The wave reached France about 1830..., and by 1848 it had swept over the rest of Europe and America' (Escarpit 1966: 23). The annual issue of titles by English publishers increased from an average of 372 for the decade 1792–1802 to 580 in the 1820s, 2,600 in the 1850s, 6,044 in 1901, 12,379 in 1913, 12,690 in 1924, 17,137 in 1937 and 22,143 in 1958 (Williams 1965: 185, 187, 191–2). Though not strictly comparable, the roughly equivalent figures for France were an average of 3,774 titles for the years 1810–15, 6,399 for 1820–5, 7,892 for 1850–5, 13,053 in 1901, 14,460 in 1913, 8,864 in 1924 and 8,080 in 1937 (Allen 1991: 38). Whilst the overall trend was also one of growth, the obvious difference is in the relative stagnation during the late nineteenth century, later compounded by the structural effects of the First World War, which were not finally overcome until after 1945 (ibid.: 39).

Multi-volume titles were a characteristic publishing technique during the nineteenth century, especially in the earlier decades. The standard English version was the 'three-decker' library edition, a three-volume novel priced at 31 shillings and 6 pence, normally followed a few years later by a 6 shilling reprint (Sutherland 1976: 12). A random sample of 402 titles published in France in 1829 shows forty-five as comprising two or more volumes (Allen 1991: 41). These were the institutionalised centrepiece of what was in effect a high-price and low-volume book trade, aimed at wealthy patrons. The format notwithstanding, a number of alternative publishing techniques became available as the century proceeded. Sutherland identified four as major breaches in the English system, the combined effect of which was to make for a greatly expanded literary market: part publication, the circulating library, the prompt collective reissue and magazine serialisation (Sutherland 1976: 20–1). Comparing developments more generally across Europe and America, Escarpit stressed the significance of the circulating libraries (in French, *cabinets de lecture*) and serialisation, but also added the state-funded public library (Escarpit 1966: 24). Part publication in serial form began in England with Chapman & Hall's publication of Dickens's *Pickwick* in 1836, and continued until the early 1860s. Under this arrangement, the novel was published in 1 shilling monthly numbers, which were only subsequently consolidated into volumes. This made both for payment in easy instalments and for a lower final price, only £1.00 for *Pickwick*. Prompt cheap reissues of 'Collective Editions' in monthly or weekly parts, aimed especially at railway travellers, dated from the late 1840s. These included Colburn and Bentley's 'Standard Novels', which retailed at 2 shillings and 6 pence each, and Routledge's 'Railway Library', retailing at 1 shilling each. Magazine serialisation dated from the 1850s and 1860s. This was in effect the rebirth of serialisation, but through the medium of named magazines and weeklies, often established by the publishers as vehicles for 'quality' fiction. Dickens, Thackeray, Eliot, Trollope, Hardy and Conrad were all published in this fashion. The latter's *Heart of Darkness*, for example, originally appeared in three instalments in *Blackwood's Magazine*, beginning with the issue for February 1899, a mode of publication which is clearly encoded in the text itself, both in its form as a novella and in its use of the conventions of the nineteenth-century adventure story.

The circulating libraries in Britain, the *cabinets de lecture* in France, the *Leihbibliotheken* in Germany, were privately owned lending libraries, aimed at a much wider readership than that provided by outright purchase. In England, the most important was 'Mudie's Select

Library', founded by Charles Mudie in 1842 (Griest 1970). For an annual fee of 1 guinea, that is, 21 shillings, his customers could borrow one book at a time, but nonetheless change their books as often as they liked over the year. This represented a major expansion of the market: the first edition of Trollope's *Barchester Towers*, for example, sold 200 copies to Mudie and only 126 to bookshops. In France the *cabinets* often charged for each individual borrowing, but one could borrow a book for as little as ten centimes in parts of Paris during the first half of the century (Allen 1991: 45). Mudie's aside, other British circulating libraries included Lowndes, Bell's, Sael, Ebers' and the British Library, all in London, John Smith in Glasgow and James Sibbald in Edinburgh. Paris *cabinets* included Galignani, Houze, Janet et Cotelle, Renard, Garnier, Goullet, Hautecoeur, Gondar-Roblot, Ridan, Goujon, Rosier, Jocquinot, Galliot, Janotte, Piltan, Jeannot and Duverge et Josset. There were also extensive provincial networks in Britain, France and elsewhere (Moretti 1998: 154–5). But even as they expanded the market, so the circulating libraries seem also to have standardised its content. Comparing catalogues from 37 British libraries and 50 French *cabinets*, Moretti found that, over time, their content became restricted to a relatively well-defined and increasingly national canon, consisting almost exclusively of novels (ibid.: 154, 156). Such specialisation appears to have been even more marked in the case of provincial than metropolitan libraries: 'In households with only one book', he writes, 'we find religion; in libraries with only one bookcase, the canon; in towns with only one library, the novel' (ibid.: 160–1).

In the United States the pattern seems to have differed from that in Britain, France and Germany, so that nineteenth-century American small-town circulating libraries were actually less committed to canonical fiction, and correspondingly more so to religion and theology, than big-city libraries (ibid.: 161–2n.). In the nineteenth-century United States, publishing houses were normally much larger than in Europe: American editions were typically three or four times the size of those in England, prices only one-third or one-quarter of the English (Sutherland 1976: 70). This relative cheapness was in part a corollary of the widespread 'pirating' of editions prior to international copyright legislation in the 1890s (Coser *et al.* 1985: 22). But it also reflected the greater determination with which American publishing set out to establish a mass market for its products. As Coser, Kadushin and Powell note, the nineteenth century witnessed two successive attempts to launch a 'paperback revolution' in the United States: in the 1840s, as newspaper 'supplements' sold by newsboys and by mail order; and from the 1860s to the 1890s, very much in the form we know today. The Beadle Brothers, who pioneered the latter venture, established the prototype of the contemporary paperback novel during the American Civil War. Between 1860 and 1865 their titles sold more than 4 million copies, with sales of individual editions reaching as high as 80,000 (ibid.: 20–1). In Australia there was no domestic book-publishing industry to speak of for most of the nineteenth century, its booksellers dealing mainly in British books, its publishing concentrated on newspapers and magazines. At the very end of the century, however, the larger booksellers began to experiment with publishing. Angus and Robertson, for example, were appointed booksellers and publishers to the University of Sydney in 1888 and began publishing during the 1890s (Curtain 1993: 109).

What some have seen as an 'Americanisation' of British publishing began in the same decade. Certainly, these years witness a shift toward the American model of royalty payments to authors and lower prices to customers. The power of the circulating libraries was also increasingly challenged from three directions: by the development of free public libraries; by the increase in cheap railway reading; and by the publishers' decision to launch cheap one-volume editions of their three-decker novels (Laurenson and Swingewood 1972: 133). This latter development provoked a protracted dispute between British publishers and circulating libraries which eventually spelt the end of the three-decker, the annual output of which fell from 184 titles in 1894 to only four in 1897 (ibid.: 133). The new century witnessed a prodigious expansion in the book trade: by 1955 annual world book production had reached 269,000 titles, by 1970 521,000, by 1990 842,000 (UNESCO 1984: VI/11; 1993: 6/3). The twentieth century also witnessed a slow erosion of British hegemony over the Anglophone industry, and a corollary expansion in American publishing, though the shift in relative power was much less dramatic for print-capitalism than for the more general capitalist economy. British manufacturers long retained a stranglehold on Anglophone publishing outside North America: as late as 1961, 40 per cent of the books published in Britain were for export, one-quarter of these to Australia alone (Curtain 1993: 110). The US-dollar value of the British export trade in books and pamphlets increased from $552.7 million in 1980 to $1,854.7 million in 1997. Comparable figures for American exports were, respectively, $588.7 million in 1980 and $2,095.4 million in 1997 (UNESCO 1999: IV-140–9). Within a generally expanding industry, British publishing remained one of the key centres of international book production. In the 1960s only Britain, Russia, China, West Germany, Japan and the USA possessed national industries producing over 20,000 titles per annum (Laurenson and Swingewood 1972: 140). By 1996 the United Kingdom annual output of books had reached 107,263 titles, the US output 68,175 (UNESCO 1999: IV-82–9). By way of comparison, the aggregate figure for China was 100,951 titles in 1994, for Germany 75,515 in 1996, Russia 36,237 in 1996 and France 34,766 in 1995 (ibid.: IV-83, 86, 88).

The crucial technical developments in twentieth-century publishing were threefold: a relative shift away from fiction and toward non-fiction; the expansion of new 'non-bookshop' distribution networks; and a third, successful, 'paperback revolution'. The shift toward non-fiction, or to what Escarpit termed 'functional books' (1966: 36–41), especially textbooks, provides powerful testament to the commercial significance of the captive market delivered to the book trade by the systems of higher and secondary education. Out of well over 107,000 books published in the United Kingdom during 1996, only 21,686 were 'literary texts' (including popular fiction); of over 71,500 in Germany, 9,622; of over 35,200 in Italy, 8,539; of over 34,750 in France in 1995, 10,545, the highest rate in any of the four major Western European publishing industries, but nonetheless still less than one-third (UNESCO 1999: IV-86, 87, 89). In the United States, college text publishing has been one of the single most profitable sectors in the industry, commanding sales worth as much as $750 million in 1978 (Coser *et al.* 1985: 55). Mass-market publishing required mass-market distribution, in particular through retail outlets other than specialist bookshops, for example newsagents, supermarkets or department stores, and, especially in America, book clubs. By the early 1960s the latter accounted for up to one-fifth of total book sales both in the

United States and in West Germany (Escarpit 1966: 35). By 1969 'four general books out of five bought by or for individual American adults came to them through book-club or mass-market channels' (Lacy 1970: 421–2). A 1990 study of Australian readers found that of the 34 per cent who had bought books (66 per cent borrowed them) 18 per cent purchased from a bookshop and 16 per cent from other sources (newsagents, department stores, book clubs, etc.) (Guldberg 1990: 87).

Cheap paperbacks had been anticipated in a number of earlier publishing experiments: the Beadle Brothers in nineteenth-century America; Ferenczi's *Livre Moderne Illustré* series in France, which retailed at 3.50 francs between the two world wars (Escarpit 1966: 27). But the final and decisive 'paperback revolution' was launched in Britain by Penguin in 1935 and in the United States by Pocket Books in 1937 (Laurenson and Swingewood 1972: 142). Priced, respectively, at 6 pence and 25 cents, the two series transformed publishing into a true mass-market industry. The model was soon adopted elsewhere: the *Livre de Poche* in France, *Marabout* in Belgium, *Alcotan* in Catalonia, *Libri del Pavone* in Italy (Escarpit 1971: 70). Penguin's founder, Allen Lane, had combined commercial and pedagogical aspirations into a formula that made his company something close to a 'national institution': 'We...believed in the existence in this country of a vast reading public for *intelligent* books at a lower price, and staked everything upon it' (A. Lane 1978: 272). In 1937 Penguin launched the Pelican label for non-fiction titles, which lasted until 1990, and which quite decisively shaped the popular-intellectual culture of the 1960s (both Hoggart's *The Uses of Literacy* and Williams's *The Long Revolution* were published as Pelicans). Whatever the fate of Lane's pedagogical aspirations, the commercial achievement remains indisputable. Penguin was still in the last decade of the twentieth century the largest single 'quality' paperback publisher in Britain, with a backlist of 8,500 out of 12,000 titles. But where Lane's early books had been published at only one-fifteenth of the price of a hardback, by the early 1990s that differential had fallen to only half (*Sunday Times*, 11 June 1995).

If printing allowed for mechanical reproduction of the already existing form of the book, it also enabled the creation of an entirely new form, the newspaper. Early experiments with printed news had included the German *Zeitung*, in 1502, and *Avisa Relation oder Zeitung*, in 1609. But the first approximation to a 'national press' can be traced very precisely to the collapse of official censorship during the first years of the English Revolution. At the beginning of 1640 there were no news media of any kind in England and publication of home news was a punishable offence; by 1641, four newspapers had been founded; by 1642, 167; by 1645, 722 (Hill 1985a: 39). As Hill concluded: 'newspapers were of crucial importance in the struggle for men's minds' during the 1640s (ibid.: 40). The radical Levellers published a weekly newspaper, the *Moderate*, which ran for sixty-three weeks (Brailsford 1961: 570). From the restoration of the monarchy in 1660 until 1679, however, England had only one newspaper, the official government *Gazette* (Hill 1985a: 51). The first North American newspaper, *Publick Occurrences Both Foreign and Domestick*, began publication in Boston in 1690. But in general – and setting aside the important exceptional experience of the English Revolution – the public press is an eighteenth-century invention. The first daily newspaper in the world, the *Courant*, was founded in England in 1702; the first in France, the *Journal de Paris*, in 1777; the first in North America, the *Pennsylvania Packet*, in 1784. The periodical press also dates from the eighteenth century: Defoe's *Weekly Review* was founded in 1704, Steele's *Tatler* in 1709 and Addison's *Spectator* in 1711. In England further daily newspapers, the *Post*, the *Journal* and the *Advertiser*, followed in 1719, 1720 and 1730, respectively (Williams 1965: 203). Sustained by a broadly middle-class readership, this new press prospered even in the face of persistent attempts at state harassment and control: total annual sales of English daily newspapers increased from 2,250,000 in 1711 to 7,000,000 in 1753, 12,230,000 in 1776 and 24,422,000 in 1811. The first English regular evening paper, the *Star*, was launched in 1788, the first Sunday paper, the *Sunday Monitor*, in 1799 (ibid.: 206–7).

In England, France and the British North American colonies, Royal governments sought to impose severe restraints on the new medium. For much of the eighteenth century the London middle-class press was effectively regulated by a combination of taxes (the 'stamp duties') and bribes (or 'subsidies'). But in the early nineteenth century the first attempts were made to create an independent, 'unstamped' press, more

Radical in opinion, sold at lower prices, and increasingly aimed at a more working-class audience. Cobbett's *Political Register*, originally a Tory periodical, had swung to the Radical cause in 1804, and was then effectively relaunched in 1816, with its price cut to 2 pence and its content aimed quite deliberately at 'Journeymen and Labourers' (Thompson 1963: 452, 457, 234). T. J. Wooler's *Black Dwarf* followed in 1817, soon becoming the paper that 'commanded the largest Radical audience' (ibid.: 674). The weekly circulation of the *Register* reached a peak of something between 40,000 and 60,000, that of the *Black Dwarf* about 12,000 (ibid.: 718). The dominant technology was still that of the hand-press, almost certainly as socially egalitarian a technique of mechanical reproduction as any in history. As Thompson noted: 'The means of production were sufficiently cheap to mean that neither capital nor advertising revenue gave much advantage.... In favourable conditions...circulation...competed with, or greatly exceeded, all but a handful of the established journals' (ibid.: 674). By far the most important of these established journals was *The Times*, founded as a daily newspaper in 1785 to advertise the 'Logographic' press, and still at the forefront of technological innovation in the early nineteenth century. The most significant such innovation was clearly steam printing. Thompson records that the new technique had 'scarcely made headway' at the highpoint of the Radical press, but notes its introduction into *The Times* in 1814.

The long-term consequences of steam printing were complex, but one effect seems to have been to disadvantage would-be radical publications. *The Times*, by contrast, acquired a new pre-eminence as the voice of independent, but respectable, middle-class Reform. As Williams observed:

> alike in its commercial, political and technical elements, *The Times* was the perfect organ of the middle-class reading public which had created the newspaper press, and was now carrying it with it to a share in the government of the country.
>
> (Williams 1965: 211)

With no real competitor, its average circulation increased from 7,000 in 1820 to 10,000 in 1830, 30,000 in 1847 and 60,000 in 1855 (ibid.:

211, 213). In 1836 Émile de Girardin introduced steam printing into France for what would be his most successful newspaper, *La Presse*, itself quite deliberately modelled on *The Times*: within one year Paris newspaper subscriptions had increased from 70,000 to 200,000 (Escarpit 1966: 29; Chalaby 1997: 629). By 1840 *La Presse* had reached a circulation of well over 10,000, Armand Dutacq's *Le Siècle*, founded the same year, over 33,350 (Allen 1991: 326). Whilst *The Times* dominated the daily press in England, the Sunday newspapers were typically aimed at a more popular audience, occasionally flirting with more radical opinions and normally achieving much larger circulations: by 1850 the total circulation of the English Sunday press had reached 275,000, that of the daily newspapers only 60,000 (Williams 1965: 213–4). These more popular interests were finally translated into the daily press by the *Daily Telegraph*, founded in 1855, the year of the final repeal of the Stamp Tax. Thereafter, the *Telegraph* led the market, its circulation increasing to 141,000 in 1860, 200,000 in 1870, 250,000 in 1880 and 300,000 in 1890 (ibid.: 217). More popular and less respectably 'political' than *The Times*, the *Telegraph* was still very much a middle-class newspaper. Much the same might be said of *Petit Journal*, founded in 1863, which dominated the mid-century French market: its circulation reached 320,000 in 1870 and 583,820 in 1880 (Allen 1991: 326).

The mass-circulation newspaper, in the sense that we know it today, was a product of the last decade of the nineteenth century and the first of the twentieth. Important examples included Lord Northcliffe's *Daily Mail* and *Daily Mirror* in England, William Randolph Hearst's *San Francisco Examiner* and *New York Morning Journal* in the United States, Jean Dupuy's *Petit Parisien* in France. Two significant innovations in printing technology were introduced during the 1890s: the rotary press, which markedly improved the hourly printing rate; and the Linotype type-setter, which replaced the hand compositor. More efficient but also more expensive, Northcliffe used both on the *Daily Mail*, founded in 1896 as the first truly mass-circulation English newspaper, aimed as much at selling readers to advertisers as newspapers to readers. The *Mail* rapidly overtook the *Telegraph*, its circulation reaching 400,000 in 1898 and 989,000 in 1900 (Williams 1965: 226). In 1903 Northcliffe launched the *Daily Mirror*, the first picture-newspaper, which in 1911–12 reached a circulation of over a million (ibid.: 228). Hearst played a similar role in the United States, initially through the *Examiner*, acquired from his father in 1887, later the *Journal*, bought in 1895, then the *Evening Journal*, founded in 1896. Under Dupuy the daily *Petit Parisien* reached a circulation of 1,375,000 in 1910, 2,000,000 in 1916 (Allen 1991: 326; Chalaby 1997: 629). During the inter-war period the *Mail* was progressively supplanted in England by the *Daily Express*, founded in 1900 by Sir Arthur Pearson, Northcliffe's chief rival. It introduced larger headlines, more illustrations and new page designs, and by 1932 its circulation had clearly overtaken the *Mail* (Williams 1965: 230). *Paris-Soir*, founded in 1931 by Jean Prouvost and closely modelled on the British popular press, soon overtook *Petit Parisien* as the largest-circulation French daily newspaper, reaching a circulation of 1,000,000 in 1935 and nearly 1,740,000 in 1938–9 (Chalaby 1997: 629; Allen 1991: 325).

By the 1960s, newspaper reading had become as near-universal a habit in Western Europe as it ever would. In 1961 the circulation of British daily newspapers reached 609 per thousand inhabitants, the highest in the world (Williams 1965: 232). From the 1940s until the 1960s, the English market was dominated by the *Daily Mirror* and the *Daily Express*, each with circulations of around 4 million (ibid.: 231–2; Williams 1976b: 29–30). Thereafter, however, the figures tended to decline. For the United Kingdom, the daily circulation per thousand inhabitants fell to 453 in 1970, 417 in 1980, 388 in 1990 and 331 in 1996 (UNESCO 1999: IV-131). Much the same pattern can be observed in other affluent liberal democracies: in the United States the figure declined from 296 in 1970 to 212 in 1996; in France from 238 in 1970 to 218 in 1996; in Italy from 144 in 1970 to 104 in 1996; in Australia from 321 in 1970 to 296 in 1996 (ibid.: IV-117, 127, 128, 131). There are no strictly comparable figures for Germany, given the very different structures in East and West prior to reunification, but parallel trends were clearly at work. Indeed, there appears to have been a general decline in newspaper circulation throughout North America, Europe and Australasia: across the whole of Europe, circulation per thousand inhabitants fell from 304 in 1975 to 261 in 1996. This is not to suggest that the press had become a spent force. Increasingly, however, even the most successful newspapers tended to be incorporated into much larger and often multinational media conglomerates.

The largest-circulation newspaper in Britain at the turn of the twentieth and twenty-first centuries was *The Sun*. Originally founded as a relaunch of the ailing left-wing *Daily Herald*, it had been acquired by the Australian-based News Limited in 1969 and recast in much more popular guise, its circulation rapidly expanding to reach nearly 3 million in 1973 (Williams 1976b: 31). It became the financial linchpin of a much wider operation, however, extending to include other newspapers, book publishing and satellite television. Axel Springer Verlag (ASV) in Germany and Centre Presse in France both followed a similar pattern. But this growth and extension occurred within the context of a remorselessly downward pressure on the overall newspaper market: when its founder, Robert Hersant, died in 1996, Centre Presse was deeply in debt (Chalaby 1997: 629). Globally, this decline in the western newspaper market was very nearly offset by a roughly commensurate increase in Africa, Asia and Latin America: across Asia the circulation rate rose from 54 to 66 per thousand inhabitants between 1970 and 1996. The overall effect, according to the United Nations Educational, Scientific and Cultural Organisation (UNESCO), was that the total number of daily newspapers across the planet increased from 7,300 in 1975 to 8,391 in 1996, their estimated total circulation from 448 million to 548 million copies, thus giving only a very slow overall decline in the rate per thousand inhabitants, from 110 in 1975 to 96 in 1996 (UNESCO 1999: IV-3). The decline in 'the West' remained very real, nonetheless, and suggests something of the competitive power of the newer technologies of mechanical reproduction deployed in the audio-visual media.

The audio-visual media

Our main concern here is with literature, which is still in its most widespread forms both written and printed. But the new audio-visual media also make extensive use of writers and writing: both Dylan Thomas's *Under Milkwood* and T. S. Eliot's *Murder in the Cathedral* were originally written for radio; and, as Williams rightly observed, the 'largest audience for drama, in our own world, is in the cinema and on television' (Williams 1973a: 399). So let us take a cursory glance at the historical development of these newer technologies of mechanical reproduction. The oldest of the new media is the cinema, the invention of which is generally credited to Louis and Auguste Lumière, who organised the first film projections before a paying public in December 1895. A comparatively recent filmography of the Lumières' work has catalogued 1,425 separate titles, each lasting about forty-five seconds, the vast majority of which were filmed between 1895 and 1902 (*Le Monde*, 5 May 1995). Film excited widespread public enthusiasm across the western world and motion-picture shows very rapidly found a place in popular entertainment as part of music-hall programmes. These early film shows were designed to demonstrate the technology itself rather than to serve any narrative effect. To become cinema, in the sense that we now know it, two further developments were required: at the level of production, some idea of film narrative; at that of consumption, some form of motion-picture theatre. Cinemas were relatively simple, functional buildings until luxury picture palaces were inaugurated in the United States with Roxy Rothapfel's 1913 New York Regent (D. Collins 1982: 62). Whether simple or luxurious, the cinema was organised around much the same principle as the live theatre, whereby consumers are assembled together away from their homes, for a particular, delimited period of time, to enjoy a show collectively. Mechanical reproduction allowed exactly the same film to be shown in many theatres simultaneously, thus stripping cinema of the 'aura' of theatre, but the cinema remained 'special', insofar as it was outside the home, unlike television. Typically, the architecture of the picture palace worked precisely so as to enhance this quasi-auratic quality.

From the mid-1890s until the First World War, a series of relatively autonomous 'national' cinemas developed right across Europe, North America and Australasia, each with its own relatively autonomous production centres. The first full-length feature film was arguably Australian, *The Story of the Kelly Gang*, produced in 1905 (Jacka 1997: 72). Many of these smaller national cinemas went into decline after the First World War, very much as an effect of the increasing penetration and control of their domestic markets by Hollywood. This was partly, no doubt, the result of a 'better' American product, but partly also Hollywood's developing control over exhibition and distribution circuits. American predominance over the international industry was further enhanced by the coming of sound, a much more expensive technology, requiring substantial investment to convert both production and exhibition. The cinema occupied a central position in popular culture for much of the twentieth century, but during the post-Second World War years its position tended to remain static or even to decline. According to UNESCO, estimated annual world output of 'long films', excluding China, reached 4,170 in 1970, 3,630 in 1980 and, including China, 4,615 in 1989 (UNESCO 1993: 6/7). By 1970 there were 268,000 permanent cinemas outside China, in 1980 256,000, in 1989 252,000. World cinema seating capacity, again excluding China, had reached 31 per thousand inhabitants by 1970, but fell thereafter to 24 per thousand in 1980, and 18 per thousand in 1989 (ibid.: 6/8). World cinema attendances, excluding China, reached 13,300 million in 1970, but fell to 12,750 million in 1980 and 12,700 million in 1989 (ibid.: 6/9). In 1995 the United Kingdom's 2,019 cinemas recorded estimated total attendances of about 114.6 million, an annual attendance rate of 2.0 visits per inhabitant and gross box office receipts of £384 million. Figures for the United States in 1994 were, respectively, 26,586 cinemas, 1,210.0 million attendances, 4.6 visits per inhabitant and $5,250 million in gross receipts; for France in 1995, 4,365 cinemas, 130.1 million attendances, 2.2 visits and 452 million francs; for Germany in 1995, 3,861 cinemas, 124.5 million attendances, 1.5 visits and DM1,183 million; for Australia in 1995, 1,137 cinemas, 69.0 million attendances, 4.6 visits and $A502 million in gross receipts (UNESCO 1999: IV-196, 200, 201, 203).

Of all the popular media, the cinema is the most traditional in its social form, a public art just as the theatre had always been. By contrast, the more recent media technologies located in the overlapping complexes of radio, television and the home computer are much more privatised and domestic in character. Historically, the first to develop was, of course, radio. A general system of electric telegraphy, transmitting messages by wire, had been established by the 1870s and, in its early stages, radio was conceived essentially as an advanced form of telegraphy, with the great advantage that it would be 'wireless'. Indeed, the original BBC state monopoly over radio broadcasting arose from a conviction that the technology would be of value primarily as a means of military communication. The shift to imagining and constructing radio as a new kind of mass medium dates only from the mid-1920s, when the decisive technical innovations were made both in the United States and in Europe. Radio then became 'broadcasting', that is, casting the signal broadly to many receivers, rather than narrowly to a single receiver as part of a two-way transmission. Broadcasting proper began in 1923 more or less simultaneously in Europe, North America and Australasia. Here there was a marked shift away from the theatre/cinema model to a system characterised by the combination of one transmitter per station and many receivers, very often (and indeed invariably in the earlier stages) located in the home. This was what Adorno and Horkheimer would describe as 'the rationale of domination itself...the coercive nature of society alienated from itself' (1979: 121). Coercive or not, it was a thoroughly domestic and domesticated entertainment, mechanical reproduction absolutely stripped of aura. Williams linked it to what he called 'mobile privatisation' (1974: 26), that is, an at once mobile and home-centred way of life. 'The new homes might appear private and "self-sufficient" ', he wrote, 'but could be maintained only...from external sources.... This relationship created both the need and the form of a new kind of "communication": news from "outside", from otherwise inaccessible sources' (ibid.: 27). In Britain the BBC retained its monopoly over radio broadcasting until the 1960s; in the United States, by contrast, radio broadcasting was pioneered by private companies. Most European countries tended to follow the British model, at least initially, though in some government and private companies both became involved. This kind of mixed model was also adopted in Australia and Canada.

So far as contemporary commercial broadcasting is concerned, radio is now overwhelmingly popular music and chat. The format was developed in the 1960s, substantially in response to the success of television, which had severely dented radio audiences. The radio as a central item of furniture, around which the family had gathered in the evening, was thus succeeded by the portable transistor and the car radio. This is radio to accompany other activities, requiring an even more 'distracted' form of attention than Benjamin could ever have imagined. But it has remained a much more stable component in popular cultural technology than the immediate challenge from television seemed to threaten. The number of radio sets in use across the planet has steadily increased from a total of 906 million in 1970 to 1,384 million in 1980, 2,075 million in 1990 and 2,432 million in 1997; the rate per thousand inhabitants from 245 in 1970 to 312 in 1980, 394 in 1990 and 418 in 1997 (UNESCO 1999: IV-8). More detailed figures for eleven selected UNESCO member states are given in Tables 3.1 and 3.2.

The success of radio broadcasting clearly provided the inspiration for television, which was imagined as an improved form, not so much of cinema as of radio, in short, as a kind of broadcasting. Pictures had been successfully transmitted by wire, that is, by a kind of telegraphy, as early as 1862. But it was only in the 1920s that the major technical advances were made in the basic design of television. As with radio, we find the one transmitter/many receivers pattern. As with radio, the technology seems peculiarly compatible with 'mobile privatisation'. As with radio, the

Table 3.1 Number of radio receivers in use, selected UNESCO member states, 1970–97

	Radio receivers (thousands)			
	1970	*1980*	*1990*	*1997*
Australia	12,000	16,000	21,600	25,500
Brazil	20,000	38,000	57,000	71,000
China*	65,000	95,000	372,000	417,000
France	25,000	39,900	50,370	55,300
Germany**	50,000	55,000	69,650	77,800
India	17,000	26,000	67,000	116,000
Japan	23,250	79,200	111,000	120,500
Russia†	94,600	130,000	55,000	61,500
South Africa	4,000	8,000	11,450	13,750
UK	45,000	53,500	80,000	84,500
USA	290,000	454,000	529,440	575,000

Source: UNESCO Statistical Yearbook 1999: IV-211, 219, 220, 223, 224, 230, 234, 236; UNESCO Statistical Yearbook 1993: 9/5–9/8; UNESCO Statistical Yearbook 1989: 10–18.

* Chinese figures exclude Hong Kong throughout.

** 1970 and 1980 figures are for West Germany only, 1990 and 1997 figures for the whole of Germany.

† 1970 and 1980 figures are for the whole of the Soviet Union, 1990 and 1997 figures for the Russian Federation only.

Table 3.2 Radio receivers per thousand inhabitants, selected UNESCO member states, 1970–97

	Radio receivers per thousand inhabitants			
	1970	*1980*	*1990*	*1997*
Australia	957	1,098	1,279	1,391
Brazil	208	312	385	434
China*	78	95	323	335
France	492	741	888	946
Germany**	824	893	878	948
India	31	38	79	120
Japan	223	678	899	956
Russia†	389	490	371	417
South Africa	181	290	337	355
UK	809	950	1,390	1,443
USA	1,380	1,973	2,084	2,116

Source: UNESCO Statistical Yearbook 1999: IV-211, 219, 220, 223, 224, 230, 234, 236; UNESCO Statistical Yearbook 1993: 9/5–9/8; UNESCO Statistical Yearbook 1989: 10–18.

* Chinese figures exclude Hong Kong throughout.

** 1970 and 1980 figures are for West Germany only, 1990 and 1997 figures for the whole of Germany.

† 1970 and 1980 figures are for the whole of the Soviet Union, 1990 and 1997 figures for the Russian Federation only.

British government established a state monopoly, although this lasted only until the 1950s. The BBC launched its broadcasts around the coronation of King George VI in 1936. The United States followed in 1939, with the lead taken, as with radio, by private companies (public-sector television, PBS, didn't begin until the 1960s and still remains very small). In both cases television was developed as an essentially domestic appliance. Only Nazi Germany experimented with the obvious alternative model, in which the mode of reception for *Fernsehen* (literally, 'distance seeing') was collectivised and public, rather than individualised and private. There were no television services elsewhere until after the Second World War (the BBC discontinued them during the war) and, in all three cases, the initial reach of the service was very small. In the 1950s, however, the new medium spread very rapidly through Europe and thence to the wider world. Whereas British television was launched with a coronation, the Australian industry chose a sporting event, the 1956 Melbourne Olympics (which suggests much about the differences between the two cultures). By 1970 the world total for television sets in use had reached 299 million, that is, a rate of 81 sets per thousand inhabitants. Total figures increased to 563 million in 1980, 1,092 million in 1990 and 1,396 million in 1997, rates per thousand inhabitants to 127 in 1980, 208 in 1990 and 240 in 1997 (ibid.: IV-8). The respective figures for our eleven selected states are given in Tables 3.3 and 3.4.

If printing was the decisive technological innovation in the development of cultural modernity, then these audio-visual media, television in particular, have just as surely marked cultural postmodernity. In its capacity for intertextuality as much as its technical sophistication, in its form, that is, as much as its technology, television is the most distinctively postmodern of media (J. Collins 1992:

Table 3.3 Number of television receivers in use, selected UNESCO member states, 1970–97

	Television receivers (thousands)			
	1970	*1980*	*1990*	*1997*
Australia	2,758	5,600	8,200	10,150
Brazil	6,100	15,000	30,800	36,500
China*	660	9,020	309,001	400,000
France	12,000	19,000	22,800	34,800
Germany**	22,000	27,000	44,400	46,500
India	28	3,000	27,000	63,000
Japan	35,100	62,976	75,500	86,500
Russia†	34,000	76,500	53,978	60,500
South Africa	70	2,010	3,700	5,200
UK	18,000	22,600	24,900	30,500
USA	84,600	155,800	203,500	219,300

Source: UNESCO Statistical Yearbook 1999: IV-211, 219, 220, 223, 224, 230, 234, 236; UNESCO Statistical Yearbook 1993: 9/12–9/15; UNESCO Statistical Yearbook 1990: 10–14.

* Chinese figures exclude Hong Kong throughout.

** 1970 and 1980 figures are for West Germany only, 1990 and 1997 figures for the whole of Germany.

† 1970 and 1980 figures are for the whole of the Soviet Union, 1990 and 1997 figures for the Russian Federation only.

Table 3.4 Television receivers per thousand inhabitants, selected UNESCO member states, 1970–97

	Television receivers per thousand inhabitants			
	1970	*1980*	*1990*	*1997*
Australia	220	384	486	554
Brazil	64	123	208	223
China*	0.8	9.0	267	321
France	236	353	402	595
Germany**	363	439	554	567
India	0.1	4.4	32	65
Japan	335	539	611	686
Russia†	143	288	364	410
South Africa	3.2	73	109	134
UK	324	401	433	521
USA	403	676	799	806

Source: UNESCO Statistical Yearbook 1999: IV-211, 219, 220, 223, 224, 230, 234, 236; UNESCO Statistical Yearbook 1993: 9/12–9/15; UNESCO Statistical Yearbook 1990: 10–14.

* Chinese figures exclude Hong Kong throughout.

** 1970 and 1980 figures are for West Germany only, 1990 and 1997 figures for the whole of Germany.

† 1970 and 1980 figures are for the whole of the Soviet Union, 1990 and 1997 figures for the Russian Federation only.

333–8). It was Williams who first suggested that television programming could be better understood as a total 'flow' of broadcasting than as a sequence of discrete, individual programmes. Viewing, he observed, is 'planned, by providers and then by viewers, *as a whole*'; the 'central television experience', he argued, is 'the fact of flow' (Williams 1974: 93, 95). Following Williams, Jameson has argued that this 'situation of total flow' tends to render both memory itself and critical distance obsolete: 'memory seems to play no role in television, commercial or otherwise (or...in postmodernism generally): nothing here haunts the mind or leaves its afterimages' (Jameson 1991: 70–1). Using the term 'video' to denote both 'video art' and commercial television, he concludes that these are 'the art form par excellence of late capitalism' (ibid.: 76). In a discussion directed toward the art video, but intended as relevant to commercial television, Jameson argues that, where modernism had problematised the connection between sign and referent previously assumed by realism, postmodernism now problematises that between signifier and signified. The outcome is contemporary televisual culture, he concludes, a random play of signifiers, continuously reshuffling the fragments of pre-existent texts: 'metabooks which cannibalize other books, metatexts which collate bits of other texts – such is the logic of postmodernism' (ibid.: 96). The VCR and Pay TV have transformed film from a theatrical into an increasingly televisual medium. Together they also open up the prospect of a continuing detachment of audiences from networked television, so that it is now possible to imagine some equivalent to the computer monitor as a fully privatised 'on-line' point of entry into a world of non-networked private entertainment. Furthermore, digital television will permit the delivery of up to five or six hundred channels and will thus make the medium even more decentred than ever.

The developments we have been charting are overwhelmingly in the forces of production, quite specifically in the technologies of mechanical reproduction. Such has been their impact that it is tempting to define our cultural world as technologically driven. Williams contrasted such 'technological determinism', that is, the argument that technology simply causes cultural effects, with what he termed the 'symptomatic technology' explanation, the argument that technology is symptomatic of other socio-cultural developments (Williams 1974: 13). Interestingly, he concluded that neither view was entirely adequate: because technologies are sought with intent, rather than just simply developing as an autonomous dynamic in their own right; and because they meet known social needs, to which they are central, not marginal. His conclusion warrants repetition:

> When there has been such heavy investment in a particular model of social communications, there is a restraining complex of financial institutions, of cultural expectations and of specific technical developments, which though it can be seen, superficially, as the effect of a technology is in fact a social complex of a new and central kind.
>
> (Williams 1974: 31)

Rehearsing the argument much later, in circumstances increasingly perceived as fraught with intellectual and political danger, he would insist that:

> a technical invention as such has comparatively little social significance. It is only when it is selected for investment toward production, and when it is consciously developed for particular social uses – that is, when it moves from being a technical invention to what can properly be called an available *technology* – that the general significance begins.
>
> (Williams 1989b: 120)

Such selections are made all the time and, as we shall see in the chapter that follows, they are made for us increasingly by the great transnational media corporations.

Cultural form

Printing, film, radio, television and the various techniques of mechanical reproduction are each 'forces of production' in the most obviously 'material' of senses. In comparison, literary and cultural 'form' seems much less properly so. By form I will mean, for the moment at least, no more than the rules and conventions specific to particular 'kinds' of art. If such conventions are always necessarily constraining, then they are simultaneously also enabling: they typically entail a complex combination of prohibitions on what may not be done, recommendations as to what can be done and prescriptions as to what should be done. In this latter respect, they can be considered forces of production, that is, cultural technologies for the production of art. If forms are, in this sense, forces of production, then the question arises as to whether they too, like the more obviously material forces, might reasonably be considered essentially social products. In conventionally literary-critical terms, notions of 'form' or 'genre' (we shall attempt to untangle the terms shortly) are used precisely to classify literature and literary history 'not by time or place...but by specifically literary types of organisation or structure' (Wellek and Warren 1976: 226). They are thus deemed to possess an essential immutability, which renders their character fundamentally ahistorical. Confronted by the possibility of 'a sociology of form', Wellek and Warren remain unconvinced that 'the social determination of genres...could be shown conclusively' (ibid.: 109). The weight of their conclusion is borne, of course, by the term 'conclusively'. We can readily concede that no comprehensive sociology of genre has ever existed, nor is even ever likely. But it is difficult, nonetheless, to imagine how form could be constructed other than by people in interaction with other people, that is, socially. The obvious alternative hypothesis, that form is a product of innate human nature, seems even more difficult to establish 'conclusively' and is surely belied by the almost self-evident historical variability of genres.

Despite Wellek and Warren's reservations, it is in this area that some of the most impressive – albeit controversial – examples of sociologically inspired research have actually been conducted. Indeed, there is a plausible case to be made that it is at this level of form that the social enters most profoundly into the constitutive nature of art itself. Much 'sociology of art and literature' has sought direct parallels between the aesthetic 'content' of particular cultural texts and the social content of their particular contexts. But, as the young Lukács insisted, 'in literature what is truly social is form' (cited in Moretti 1988: 10). Following Lukács, Moretti argued that the history of literature should be rewritten 'as a sociology of symbolic forms, a history of cultural conventions' (ibid.: 19). The best results of historical-sociological criticism, he concluded, were those 'aimed at defining the internal laws and historical range of a specific genre', citing as instances Lukács on the novel, Benjamin on baroque drama, Goldmann on French classical tragedy and Adorno on the twelve-note system (ibid.: 9; cf. Lukács 1962, 1971; Benjamin 1977; Goldmann 1964; Adorno 1973). To this, we might well add Moretti's own work on the *Bildungsroman* (Moretti 1987). His more recent work has taken a quantitative turn, combining Wallerstein's world-system theory with a sociology of literature apparently more akin to Escarpit than Lukács or Goldmann. But this would be a misreading, since for Moretti these quantitative pressures also have their effect '*within literary form itself*' (Moretti 2003: 80).

Clearly, the whole question of literary form is intimately bound up with the idea of non-mechanical 'reproduction': if two literary texts are examples of a form, then this is so only because they in some sense 'reproduce' the features of that form. Williams distinguished two main kinds of meaning attaching to the term 'reproduction': on the one hand uniform copying by processes of mechanical reproduction; on the other genetic reproduction, 'where typically forms – species – are prolonged, but in intrinsically variable individual examples' (Williams 1981: 185). The reproduction of literary and cultural form is analogous to reproduction in this second sense of the term. As we observed in Chapter 2, Williams identified three distinct levels of form, termed respectively 'modes', 'genres' and 'types'. He reserved the term 'mode' for what he identified as the deepest level of form, as in the distinction between the 'dramatic mode', in which the action is performed before an audience, the 'lyrical mode', that is, the non-mimetic composition of a single voice, and the 'narrative mode', where action is recounted as a tale told to an audience by a teller. Historically, these modes persist through quite different social orders: 'the level of relations involved...can be more accurately referred to an anthropological or societal dimension than to the sociological in the ordinary sense...they are very general, and their reproduction is at least relatively autonomous' (ibid.: 194).

Williams nominated the term 'genre' for relatively persistent instances of each mode, as for example in the distinction between tragedy and comedy within the dramatic mode or epic and romance within the narrative mode. Such genres are 'significantly more subject to variation between different epochs and different social orders', he observes, noting that neither the epic nor romance survived into the modern, bourgeois epoch 'at least without radical redefinition' (ibid.: 195). Still more variable and still more dependent on particular social relations are what Williams termed 'types', that is, 'radical distributions, redistributions and innovations of interest, corresponding to the specific and changed social character of an epoch' (ibid.: 196). Examples would include 'bourgeois drama' or the 'realist novel'. Defined in relation to a classificatory schema such as this, form might well appear essentially static: an interest in reproduction could easily translate into a preoccupation with continuity as distinct from change. Neither Williams nor Moretti was so inclined, however. Indeed, the latter recognises the force of the objection, conceding that a sociology of forms will provide a necessarily slower history than a study of great authors or great books. He is insistent, nonetheless, that innovation can be properly understood only against the background of convention (Moretti 1988: 15). For Williams, too, a proper attention to the typical, the modal, the characteristic would also enable us to recognise 'innovation in process...one of the very few elements of cultural production to which the stock adjective, "creative", is wholly appropriate' (Williams 1981: 200).

For both Williams and Moretti, form is essentially an aspect of textuality, which inheres within a designated group of texts as their common textual property. However, as we saw in Chapter 2, much post-structuralist theory has evinced a thoroughgoing scepticism as to the possibility of discovering any definitive meaning inherent within a text, preferring rather to focus on the indefinite plurality of possible readings to which a text might give rise. And what applies to a text in particular might well apply also to the form in general. This line of argument can be prosecuted by way of either Derridean deconstruction or Foucauldian discourse analysis. If the former, as with Freadman for example, then the problem becomes that of how to deconstruct the intrication of the text 'in the systems deployed to classify it' (Freadman 1988: 95); if the latter, as with Frow, then that of how to understand such systems as institutional arrangements through which networks of intertextuality are socially 'constructed...maintained or shifted' (Frow 1986: 187). On either view a sociology of form, such as Williams and Moretti had envisaged, becomes simply inoperable. As Bennett – yet another Foucauldian – put it, 'the concept of genre is more usefully interpreted when used as a means for analysing historically and culturally variable systems for the regulation of reading and writing practices than as a kind of writing amenable to socio-genetic explanation' (Bennett 1990: 81). Like Williams and Moretti, Bennett and Frow freely acknowledge the necessarily social nature of literary relations. Like Williams and Moretti, they each set out to sidestep such ontological dualisms as those between 'real' history and 'less real' literature, base and superstructure, 'real' content and 'less real' form. This may be achieved in one of two ways, however, either by historicising literature, as do Williams and Moretti, or by narrativising history, as do Bennett and Frow.

Frow and Bennett are much more interested in the socio-discursive institutionalisation of 'literary history', as a contemporary academic discipline, than in literary 'history', in the sense of 'the past' as real object. Thus Frow:

> The gestural appeal to the 'materiality' of history, and its definition as 'the real'...are indicative of the theological function the

> concept plays.... The absolute existence of the referent outside any semiotic framework is the tautological guarantee of a truth which transcends ideology.
>
> (Frow 1986: 27–8)

And Bennett: 'history...is most appropriately regarded as a specific discursive regime, governed by distinctive procedures, through which the maintenance/transformation of the past as a set of currently existing realities is regulated' (Bennett 1990: 50). When followed through to their logical conclusions, such conceptions point toward an epistemological relativism such as could effectively free literary-historical research from almost any (extra-discursive) empirical controls. Bennett himself resists the relativist implications of his own Foucauldianism: 'the past', he writes, functions not as an extra-discursive real, 'but *as if it were* such a referent in the sense that it constitutes the last court of appeal for historical disputes' (ibid.: 50). But this reads suspiciously like a case of having one's theoretical post-structuralist cake and eating it. The fundamental problem here is a radical overemphasis on reading as against writing, consumption as against production, the present as against the past, in short, almost the obverse of the vices characteristic to traditional literary humanism.

No doubt the past can only ever be understood in the present. No doubt texts and forms (or genres) repeatedly acquire new meanings, which often function, in turn, so as to systematically organise and reorganise present understandings both of the present and of the past, both of those texts and forms and of others. Williams's recognition that the literary tradition is necessarily a 'selective tradition' can, of course, be generalised to include all forms of cultural tradition, including literary historiography. Bennett tellingly cites his own findings on how quite different generic conventions for detective fiction differently structured the American and British receptions of the James Bond novels (ibid.: 101. cf. Bennett and Woollacott 1987: 76–90). But none of this need imply that the historical past is in principle either unknowable or unrecoverable. And insofar as the past is indeed recoverable there is nothing to preclude an at least proximate understanding of the generic conventions operative at the time when a text was written or composed, as also those governing later moments in the subsequent histories of its reception. Nor is there any good reason to suppose that such conventions are never transmitted through time and space. And, in the absence of any such reason, the possibility remains that certain forms might recur, in some at least of their significant aspects, in geo-historical contexts quite different from those of their origin. At one point, Bennett quoted Bakhtin's argument to the effect that the novel is an unfinished form, a 'genre of becoming' (Bakhtin 1981: 22, cited in Bennett 1990: 96). But Bakhtin is a much less helpful source than Bennett supposed. For Bakhtin, the novel was not so much a genre as a process, by which the canonical fixity of all prior genres was progressively undermined through 'novelisation'. Substantively, this anticipates much of what Bennett had to say about 'the sociology of the novel'. Theoretically, its implied premise, that previously dominant literary cultures had indeed been organised around such relatively well-defined genres, stands in direct contradiction to Bennett's more general argument against the 'sociology of genres'.

I have laboured the point here because I want to insist that form is not simply a matter of retrospective academic classification, as post-structuralism seemed to suggest, but also a prospectively productive force within the literary mode of production. The work of art, wrote Barthes, 'is what man wrests from chance' (1972: 152). But it is also, as Barthes himself made clear, what form produces from chance. Formal expectations, formal conventions, whether of a sonnet or of a student essay, enter into the writing of any particular sonnet, any particular essay, as forces of production. This is so even for as open a form as the novel or, for that matter, the newspaper. For all Bennett's scepticism concerning genre, it is clear that both possess a certain formal durability, which is why, in practice, we find no difficulty in distinguishing the one from the other and both or either from poetry or drama. I have linked the novel and the newspaper at this point because these are the most distinctively 'modern' of written forms, each in its own way unusually consonant with print-capitalism and print culture. In principle, of course, all written literature can be printed and indeed it normally is. But drama is written to be performed rather than to be read; and poetry has a characteristic brevity (even epic poetry) and an often quasi-oral character (especially epic poetry) which mark it as having no special affinity with print. Novels and newspapers, by contrast, are almost unimaginable without mechanical reproduction.

These are the two forms first carried to mass markets by means of mass production during the nineteenth century.

Anderson argued that these forms – the novel and the newspaper – provided the technical preconditions for a distinctly modern type of imagining, that of the nation. Unlike such pre-national formations as the religious community and the dynastic monarchy, he observed, the 'imagined community' of the nation is understood as passing through what Benjamin had termed 'homogeneous, empty time' (1973a: 263), where simultaneity is indicated only by temporal coincidence measured in terms of clock and calendar. The newspaper, Anderson wrote, has a 'novelistic format': it 'is merely an "extreme form" of the book, a book sold on a colossal scale, but of ephemeral popularity. Might we say: one-day bestsellers?' (B. Anderson 1991: 33, 34–5). The evidence for this thesis has been quantified, but the argument qualified, by Moretti, who concludes that:

> The novel didn't simply find the nation as an obvious, pre-formed fictional space: it had to wrest it from other geographical matrixes that were just as capable of generating narrative – and that indeed clashed with each other throughout the eighteenth century.
>
> (Moretti 1998: 53)

Supra-national genres, like the Robinsonade, and local narratives, like the love story, clearly persisted through the century, he notes, so that the predominance of the national novel is not finally consolidated until 'the very end of the century' in what was in fact a 'contraction of narrative space' (ibid.: 55). But if nation, novel and newspaper did indeed become connected in nineteenth-century Europe, and I think they did, then the 'sociology of form' becomes a matter of greater import than Bennett would have had us believe. I want to conclude this chapter, then, with an examination of some of the debates over the so-called 'sociology of the novel'.

The sociology of the novel

Bennett's primary concern was with the novel, rather than with form *per se*, though he was careful to present this as a merely 'convenient' instance of a more general argument (Bennett 1990: 86). Reviewing a substantial body of 'sociological' speculation about the novel, as represented paradigmatically by Watt's *The Rise of the Novel* (1963) and Goldmann's *Towards a Sociology of the Novel* (1975), Bennett concluded that:

> It is difficult to see how the respective strengths and weaknesses of such contrastive accounts of the novel's positivity might ever be adjudicated. In each case, the definition of the novel carries with it a set of already-determined rules for reading the relations between text and social structure.... When the deployment of the same method results in irreconcilable theories whose competing claims cannot be meaningfully assessed, there are good reasons for thinking the method is inherently flawed.
>
> (Bennett 1990: 95)

To anticipate the argument a little, Bennett seems to me mistaken here on three main counts. In the first place, I doubt that either Watt's or Goldmann's definition necessarily carries with it any already determined rules for reading text/society relations. Second, though their respective definitions are certainly different, and in some respects incompatible, these differences arise, not from any predisposition to prejudge the evidence, but from a set of inherited differences between two already established traditions of speculation about the novel. Third, though their competing claims almost certainly cannot be directly assessed against each other, they are each assessable nonetheless against alternative accounts using similar definitions, which clearly suggests that in each case the central propositions are more meaningful than Bennett allows.

Before turning to Watt and Goldmann, it might be as well to begin with some attempt at brief preliminary definitions both of the 'novel' and of the 'epic' (since this last figures prominently in some accounts of the novel). Bennett finds such definitions guilty of harbouring determinedly preconceived notions as to the nature of the connections between text and context, literature and society. My hope here is to be able to construct 'definitions' that do in fact leave such questions deliberately open. Definition may not be quite the right term, however:

these are not so much formal definitions as what Weber meant by an 'ideal type'. Weber defined the ideal type thus:

> An ideal type is formed by a one-sided *accentuation* of one or more points of view and by the synthesis of a great many diffuse, discrete, more or less present and occasionally absent *concrete individual* phenomena which are engaged according to those one-sidedly emphasized viewpoints into a unified *analytical* construct (*Gedankenbild*). In its conceptual purity, this mental construct (*Gedankenbild*) cannot be found empirically anywhere in reality.
>
> (Weber 1949: 90)

In short, it is an abstraction, a model, the purpose of which is to cast light on social reality. 'It has the significance', writes Weber, 'of a purely *limiting* concept with which the real situation or action is *compared* and surveyed for the explication of certain of its significant components' (ibid.: 93).

An epic can be defined ideal-typically as a long verse narrative. The earliest extant example is the Babylonian *Epic of Gilgamesh*, composed in Akkadian during the eighteenth or nineteenth century BC, but based on earlier Sumerian texts probably dating from the twenty-first. These, in turn, were written-down versions of Sumerian or Akkadian oral poetry composed in the twenty-third century BC or earlier. More familiar to most western readers are the Greek epics the *Iliad* and the *Odyssey*, both again originally oral in form and later written down, probably during the sixth or seventh century BC. Such epics typically recorded the collective history, magic, religion and lore of a people and, as an effect precisely of their orality, were often highly repetitive (a familiar instance is the *Odyssey*'s 'wine-dark sea'). We now know that Sîn-liqe-unninni, whom the Babylonians regarded as the author of *Gilgamesh*, in fact edited pre-existing texts into the standard version, *Sha naqba imuru*, or 'He who saw the Deep' (George 1999: xxiv–xxv). As to the Greek epics, there has been much debate over whether there ever was an individual 'Homer': Thomson concluded that 'Homer is not one but many hereditary poets' (Thomson 1978: 577); Ong that Homeric language was 'generated over the years by epic poets using old set expressions which they preserved and/or reworked largely for metrical purposes', a language 'specially contoured through use of poets learning from one another generation after generation' (Ong 1988: 23). *Beowulf*, composed before 850 AD, but not written down, in its extant form, until about 1010 (Alexander 2001: xiv), is the obvious example from Old English of a roughly analogous form. Virgil's *Aeneid* is rather different. Though modelled on the earlier Greek oral epics, it was both individually authored and deliberately written, in the years between 30 BC and Virgil's death in 19 BC. Virgil chose a great 'national' legend, that of the Romans as the descendents of Trojans, for the subject matter of his epic. This, in turn, provided the model for many later written epic poems, the most famous of which in English is almost certainly Milton's *Paradise Lost*, first published in 1667. These six poems were composed in very different ways, in different languages, in different times and places. And yet there is a sense in which we can meaningfully speak of their possessing a certain commonality of form, if only ideal-typically. That this commonality might be a matter simply of retrospective academic classification seems arguable for *Gilgamesh* and *Beowulf* (though not decisively so). Elsewhere it is clearly implausible: Milton had read both Virgil and Homer, Virgil had read Homer, and so both the Roman and the English poet were able to *use* the conventions governing the earlier texts so as to *produce* their own.

An equivalently simple definition of the novel would be that it is a long, continuous prose narrative, but we need also to add that it is a written and printed form and that its narratives are fictions. Neither Watt nor Goldmann makes very much of printing, both tending to treat the technology as merely a material means to an aesthetic end. Watt did note in passing that 'the novel is perhaps the only literary genre which is essentially connected with the medium of print', but the remark serves mainly as the occasion for a discussion of Richardson's role in the trade (Watt 1963: 204). In fact, cultural technology invariably enters into the nature of the form itself. Ong distinguishes between 'primary oral cultures', which know no writing, 'chirographic cultures', which know writing but not print, and print cultures. 'In the west', he writes:

> the epic is basically and irremediably an oral art form. Written and printed epics...are self-conscious, archaizing imitations of

> procedures demanded by the psychodynamics of oral story-telling.... Romances are the product of chirographic culture, creations in a new written genre heavily reliant on oral modes...but not consciously imitating earlier oral forms.... The novel is clearly a print genre, deeply interior, de-heroicized, and tending strongly to irony.
>
> (Ong 1988: 158–9)

The point has been made elsewhere (Couturier 1991) and it is surely right. Unfamiliar with post-structuralism as they often were, many early novelists were fascinated by the novelty of their form and part of this fascination was with the technology itself. Already in the 'Prologue' to the Second Part of *Don Quixote*, Cervantes had admitted to knowing that one of the greatest of the Devil's temptations 'is to put into a man's head that he can write and print a book, and gain both money and fame by it' (1950: 468). Precisely because the novel is printed it can be lengthier, more interiorised and more prosaic than any previous literary form. Precisely because it is self-consciously fictive, heroic national myths and histories, which are at the very centre of the epic, can only ever occupy a peripheral place in its action.

The earliest examples of the novel are more difficult to define than the epic. There are in fact many rival claimants to the title: *Don Quixote* itself, the Second Part of which was completed in 1614; Madame de La Fayette's *La Princesse de Clèves*, which dates from 1678; Grimmelshausen's *Der abentheurliche Simplicissimus*, from 1669; Defoe's *Robinson Crusoe*, from 1719. Some of this disagreement is simply a matter of retrospective cultural nationalism. But it also depends on what exactly we mean by 'the novel'. As Bennett noted, there is even an argument that the form dates from classical antiquity (1990: 83–4; cf. Perry 1967). As Spearman insisted in her quarrel with the 'theory of the middle class novel', the first European prose 'romances', in the sense of linked sets of relatively discrete, self-contained episodes, date from as early as the thirteenth century; continuous prose narratives date from the fifteenth century; and something akin to the novel can be found in eleventh-century Japan and sixteenth-century China (Spearman 1966: 85, 89, 118–43). We might well concede this last point about the Asian novel, clearly the product of an older print culture. But neither the classical 'novel' nor the earliest of the European 'romances' were print forms and nor were the latter fictions, in the contemporary sense of the term, since their subject matter typically inhabited the quasi-truth of myth and legend. If the novel is different from the romance, then this difference is a matter of its printed form on the one hand, its fictive subject matter on the other. Whatever the historical origins of the European novel, and whatever its classical and non-European prehistories, there is no doubting the form's centrality to nineteenth-century European culture or the international predominance of its British and French variants. As Moretti observes:

> the novel closes European literature to all external influences: it strengthens, and perhaps it even establishes its *Europeanness*. But then this most European of forms proceeds to deprive most of Europe of all creative autonomy: two cities, London and Paris, rule the entire continent for over a century, publishing half (if not more) of all European novels.
>
> (Moretti 1998: 186)

How, then, did Goldmann and Watt proceed with their respectively French and British sociologies of the novel? In Goldmann's case, much of the 'sociological' speculation to which Bennett takes exception had derived from Hegel's *Philosophy of Fine Art*. For Hegel, the central aesthetic distinction had been between tragic or dramatic form, on the one hand, and epic form, on the other. He traced their origins to ancient Greece, arguing that both give form to the supposedly harmonious 'totality' of classical Greek social life, respectively an 'intensive' totality of movement in the drama and an 'extensive' totality of objects in the epic. In this schema, literary-historical development since antiquity is simultaneously judged as aesthetically inferior and explained as the sociological effect of the 'alienation' of post-classical 'man' from post-classical society. The novel is thus for Hegel an inferior kind of epic, a degraded form: 'What fails us here is the...world-condition... which is the source of the genuine Epos. The...novel...presupposes a basis of reality already organized in its *prosaic form*' (Hegel 1975: 171). This schema was transmitted into twentieth-century sociological aesthetics primarily by way of Lukács's *The Theory of the Novel*. For Lukács, the epic had given form to a totality of life, a totality pre-given in reality by the social integration of the civilisations of classical antiquity. The novel, by contrast, 'is the epic of an age in which the extensive totality of life is no longer directly given...yet which still thinks in terms of totality' (Lukács 1971: 56). Where the epic poem had been organised around the hero as representative of a community, moving within a world of immanent values, the novel is built around the unrepresentative 'problematic hero', moving in search of authentic values. The central problem in the novel is thus 'the incommensurability of soul and work, of interiority and adventure' (ibid.: 97), which takes three ideal-typical forms: where the soul is too narrow for reality, as in *Don Quixote*; where reality is too narrow for the soul, as in Flaubert's *L'Éducation sentimentale*; and where this incommensurability is resolved through an education in self-imposed limitations, as in the *Bildungsroman* (here Lukács's paradigmatic instance is Goethe's *Wilhelm Meister*).

The novel as a form is thus for Lukács centrally organised around the problematic hero in pursuit of problematic values within a problematic world. This conception clearly provided Goldmann with the theoretical starting point for his *Towards a Sociology of the Novel*: here, too, the novel revolves around the problematic hero's search for authentic values in a degraded society. But where Lukács, following Hegel, had defined such degradation in relation to 'post-classical' social disintegration, Goldmann, following Marx, would postulate a 'rigorous homology' between the literary form of the novel and the economic form of the commodity. In short, for Goldmann the novel develops as a function of what Marx had meant by 'commodity fetishism': it 'seems to express...a search for values that no social group defends effectively and that the economic life tends to make implicit in all members of society' (Goldmann 1975: 10). All of this is true only of the early novel, however, the novel of individual biography. As the social structure evolves from competitive into monopoly capitalism, then, so this process generates a progressive disappearance from the novel of the individual subject as problematic hero. The inter-war years provide the occasion for a temporary experiment with the community as collective hero: here Goldmann's main interest is in Malraux (ibid.:

18–131). But the main line of development thereafter, Goldmann concludes, is characterised 'by the effort to write the novel of the absence of subjects' (ibid.: 13). Paradoxically, in a world of reification, a world truly without subjects, the *nouveau roman* of Robbe-Grillet and Sarraute itself becomes 'radically realistic' (ibid.: 149).

In Watt's *The Rise of the Novel*, the new form had been a much later and more exclusively English affair than for Goldmann or Lukács. Watt located the 'novelty' of the novel in what he described as its 'formal realism', that is, 'the narrative embodiment of...the premise...that the novel is a full and authentic report of human experience' (Watt 1963: 32). Here, the paradigmatic instances are Defoe's *Robinson Crusoe* and *Moll Flanders*, Richardson's *Pamela* and *Clarissa*, Fielding's *Joseph Andrews* and *Tom Jones*. Watt stressed the crucial importance of the growth of a new individualistic social order in the period after the Glorious Revolution of 1688. The novel's realism, its concern with 'realistically' described relations between 'ordinary' individuals, runs parallel to the more general development of philosophical realism, middle-class economic individualism and Puritan individualism. The result is a 'change in outlook' away from the objective, social and public orientation of earlier forms and toward the more subjective, individualist and private orientations both of the novel itself and of cultural modernity in general (ibid.: 182). More specifically, Watt argued that the form also addressed the interests and capacities of the new middle-class reading public and the new book trade evolving in response to those interests and capacities. As middle-class tradesmen themselves, Defoe and Richardson

> had only to consult their own standards of form and content to be sure that what they wrote would appeal to a large audience. This is probably the supremely important effect of the changed composition of the reading public and the new dominance of the booksellers upon the rise of the novel.
>
> (Watt 1963: 61)

As we have seen, Bennett holds that both Watt's and Goldmann's definitions of the novel necessarily carry with them already determined rules for reading text/society relations. Watt's analysis is governed by Weber's *The Protestant Ethic and the Spirit of Capitalism* as the 'master-text' of capitalism, Bennett argued, Goldmann's by Marx's *Capital*, and the deployment of both 'is conditioned by a prior delimitation of the novel's positivity derived from the system of generic contrasts which governs the process of generic definition' (Bennett 1990: 95). In short, Watt defines the social order as individualistic because he already understands the novel form as realistic (and *vice versa*); Goldmann defines the social order as commodified because he already understands the novel form as problematic (and *vice versa*). Now clearly Watt and Goldmann do indeed subscribe to different accounts of capitalism, taken from Weber and Marx, respectively. In itself, this is unobjectionable, however, since all analyses must begin somewhere, with some assumed pre-givens. The definitions of the form are, in any case, nothing like so intimately connected to the master-texts as Bennett believes. Quite the contrary, each seems logically compatible with quite different accounts of text/society relations. That this is so can be readily demonstrated, moreover, from the existence of alternative accounts that do in fact combine form and 'master-text' quite differently.

To cite an obvious contra-instance, Kettle's *An Introduction to the English Novel* was clearly Marxist in inspiration (unlike Goldmann, Kettle was actually a Communist) and yet equally clearly subscribed to a definition of the novel in terms of its formal realism. For Kettle, the novel was 'a realistic prose fiction', which 'arose as a realistic reaction to the medieval romance.... Romance was the non-realistic, aristocratic literature of feudalism' (Kettle 1967: 26, 28–9). Conversely, Fehér, a one-time student of Lukács, combined a broadly Marxian reading of capitalism with a largely 'Weberian' theory of the novel (albeit of a very different kind to that in Watt). The novel is the art form of the first 'purely social' (as opposed to natural) society, Fehér wrote, and is thus centred around freedom, the freedom of action of the hero, their ability to change their circumstances: 'in all its non-fetishistic exemplars, the novel imparts to the reader the knowledge of the maximum possibilities of humanization of which this society is capable' (Fehér 1986: 58). Indeed, it isn't obvious that even Goldmann's analysis actually required *Capital* as its 'master-text'. As we have noted (and as Bennett notes), its main inspiration was *The Theory of the Novel*, written during the First World War, at a time when Lukács was both personally and intellectually very close to the circle around Weber, and when he presumably would have been more likely to cite *The Protestant Ethic* than *Capital* as his model (though, in fact, he cites neither).

Watt's and Goldmann's respective definitions of the form are, of course, very different, perhaps even in some respects incompatible. Their differences arise, however, not from a determination to prejudge the evidence, but from a set of inherited differences between two already established 'national' traditions of speculation about the novel, respectively the English and the 'German'. Lukács was Hungarian, of course, and Goldmann French (to be precise, Franco-Rumanian), but both defined their own intellectual formation mainly in relation to this German tradition. Hegel's prejudice against the novel is but one instance in a long tradition of 'the tyranny of Greece over Germany' (cf. E. M. Butler 1935), which embraced Goethe and Schiller, Hegel and Nietzsche, and had acquired a certain taken-for-grantedness long before Goldmann's reworking of Lukács. Much the same might be said in respect of Watt's 'Englishness'. The 'great tradition' of the English novel was essentially realistic even for the Leavisites. Thus Leavis on Austen: 'The principle of organization…is an intense moral interest…in life that is in the first place a preoccupation with certain problems that life compels on her as personal ones' (F. R. Leavis 1962b: 15). As late as *The Long Revolution* even Williams would continue to define the central problems of the contemporary English novel primarily in relation to realism (Williams 1965: 300–16). Even the *Concise Oxford English Dictionary* defined the novel as 'Fictitious prose narrative of book length portraying characters and actions credibly representative of real life in continuous plot' (Sykes 1976: 746). Spender and Lovell have each taken Watt to task for his exclusive preoccupation with the novel's patrilineal rather than matrilineal inheritance, arguing persuasively for the significance of female writers and fantastic motifs in the earlier history of the form (Spender 1986: 115–18, 137; Lovell 1987: 44–5). But Lovell was obliged to concede that Watt merely 'echoed conventional wisdom in identifying the innovators as Defoe, Fielding and Richardson.... He simply took as given established literary judgements' (ibid.: 20). In short, neither Watt nor Goldmann constructed his own 'definitions' of the novel. Rather, they each subscribed to already current, widely accepted definitions readily available from within the dominant intellectual traditions of their respective 'national' cultures.

Though the competing claims advanced by Watt and Goldmann probably cannot be assessed directly against each other, they are each assessable nonetheless against other, more strictly comparable, accounts. For example, Goldmann's thesis that the novel is a fundamentally problematic form can be tested (and found wanting) against Fehér's that it is merely ambivalent (Fehér 1986: 57). Watt's that the realist novel functions so as to articulate middle-class values can be tested (and found wanting) against Swingewood's that, in Fielding, realist conventions are deployed in the service of 'the virtues of...traditional rural England' (Laurenson and Swingewood 1972: 203). Indeed, both Lovell's and Spender's work clearly tests and invalidates certain central theses advanced by Watt, requiring at the very least that we reformulate his argument as applying only to an early bourgeois, male preference for formal realism. All this suggests that in each case the central propositions are more meaningful than Bennett allows. Moreover, insofar as Goldmann's and Watt's arguments are incommensurable (or incomparable), this is so primarily because they are addressed to what are clearly, in Williams's terms, different 'levels of form'. Goldmann – and before him both Hegel and the Lukács of *The Theory of the Novel* – were interested in what Williams termed the narrative 'mode' and the novel 'genre'. By contrast, Watt's researches were directed toward what Williams would recognise as the 'type' of the realist novel. Even the older Lukács had conceded in passing, without ever intending any serious qualification to his own more generally Hegelian framework, that a 'broad, realistic portrayal of the present' developed initially in the eighteenth-century English novel (Lukács 1962: 16). Sometimes, even such inveterate 'totalisers' can achieve a specificity and precision lost on the most Foucauldian of 'specific intellectuals'.

If it is difficult to see how Goldmann's and Watt's respective strengths and weaknesses can ever be adjudicated; this is so because they are not actually under dispute, because the sociology of the narrative mode, the novel genre and the realist type are separable enterprises, both logically and empirically. This is not to suggest that either version inhabits the best of all possible theoretical worlds, merely that the game is worth the candle and should not therefore be closed down by post-structuralist fiat, especially not so as to move into something like cultural policy studies. That said, both Goldmann's approach and Watt's do indeed remain disfigured by a remorseless selectivity, their fixation with the canonical foreground to the exclusion of what Moretti, after Cohen, terms 'the great unread' (Moretti 2000: 55). Their kind of sociology needs itself to be situated and contextualised by Moretti's own 'history of norms...a less innovative, much "flatter" configuration...repetitive, slow – boring, even'. Malraux and Robbe-Grillet, Defoe, Richardson and Fielding would thus become not so much exemplary as instantial, not so much a paradigm as a case study. 'But...are we so sure that boredom is boring?', Moretti continues:

> Once we learn to confront it, the flatness of literary conventions will appear the genuine enigma it is. How does a new narrative form crystallize out of a collection of haphazard, half-baked, often horrendous attempts? How does a convention change, or, better: *does* it ever change? Or does it remain stable in a thousand disguises – until the day it suddenly disintegrates? And why does it remain stable so long? And why does it then collapse? And how on earth can the *same* convention work in such *different* places...?
>
> (Moretti 1998: 150)

These are the kinds of question any adequate sociology of form must surely learn to pose.

The Moretti thesis: core, periphery and literary form

We have noted Moretti's interest in world-system theory. The idea first surfaced in his work as a way to understand how a relatively small number of exceptional works – Goethe's *Faust*, Melville's *Moby-Dick*, Wagner's *Der Ring des Nibelungen*, Joyce's *Ulysses*, Pound's *The Cantos*, Eliot's *The Waste Land*, Musil's *Der Mann ohne Eigenschaften*, García Márquez's *Cien años de soledad* – might belong to a single field he termed the 'modern epic' (Moretti 1996: 1–2). He argued that, unlike their canonical equivalents in French or English literature, these were 'all *world* texts, whose geographical frame of reference is no longer the nation-state, but a broader entity – a continent, or the world-system as a whole'. They were also each a product of the system's 'semi-periphery', sites of 'combined development', where 'historically non-homogeneous social and symbolic forms, often originating in quite disparate places, coexist in a confined space' (ibid.: 50). Here the analysis is primarily textual, its purposes at times oddly reminiscent of Bloom and other would-be canonists. Nonetheless, this canon is relocated geographically and culturally away from the core and towards the periphery. In the *Atlas of the European Novel* the argument resurfaces, but in quantitative and sociological guise. Expressed thus, it becomes more pessimistic, a map of how Franco-English cultural hegemony pre-empted the development of other literatures. Yet even here he also points to the positive possibilities simultaneously opened up in the periphery. Citing Schwarz on Brazil, Moretti writes of how 'peripheral' literatures can in fact be 'sustained' by 'historical backwardness' (Moretti 1998: 195; Schwarz 1992: 29). 'It is *extremely* unlikely for backwardness to be a "support"', he continues:

> but if, for whatever strange reason, this unlikely conjunction occurs, the horizon does indeed open up…*the new model is the product of a new space*: the semi-periphery of Europe, the semi-periphery of the world-system.… A new space encourages paradigm shifts…because it poses new questions – and so asks for new answers.… The outcome of a new geographical space, these forms then produce *a new fictional space*.… A new space that gives rise to a new form – that gives rise to a new space. Literary geography.
>
> (Moretti 1998: 195–7)

More recently, he has expanded on this analysis, textual and quantitative, to advance an extremely ambitious map of how comparative literature might be refigured as a discipline. We referred to this very briefly in Chapter 1, but let me conclude this chapter with an account of what we might term the 'Moretti thesis'.

Moretti argues that comparative literature – or more properly the study of *Weltliteratur* – can no longer be conceived simply as national literature writ large, 'literature, bigger', in his phrase, but must, rather, be reorganised around entirely different categories and conceptual problems. It 'is not an object', he continues, 'it's a *problem*, and a problem that asks for a new critical method: and no one has ever found a method by just reading more texts'. The model he proposes, adapted from Wallerstein, is that of a 'world literary system', simultaneously '*one*, and *unequal*: with a core, and a periphery...bound together in a relationship of growing inequality'. If this is how the system itself functions, then the appropriate mode of analysis will become 'distant reading', he concludes, where distance '*is a condition of knowledge*', permitting the analyst 'to focus on units...much smaller or much larger than the text: devices, themes, tropes – or genres and systems' (Moretti 2000: 55–7). This combination of distant reading and world literature allows him to treat the history of the modern novel as a 'system *of variations*', in which pressure from the Anglo-French core tended towards uniformity, but variable local reality in the periphery and semi-periphery tended towards difference. The result is a series of localised structural 'compromises', between foreign plot, local characters and local narrative voice, in which the 'one-and-unequal literary system' becomes embedded into the form itself (ibid.: 58–66). He offered this analysis as an example, not a model, of how comparative literature might proceed, but clearly believes in the wider applicability of sociological formalisms of this kind (ibid.: 58, 66). Hence the concluding insistence that comparatists 'have always been too shy in the presence of national literatures, too diplomatic'. These are not parallel universes, he insists:

> No; the universe is the same, the literatures are the same, we just look at them from a different viewpoint; and you become a comparatist for a very simple reason: *because you are convinced that...viewpoint is better*. It has greater explanatory power; it's conceptually more elegant; it avoids that ugly 'one-sidedness and narrow-mindedness'.... 'Don't delude yourself', writes Stendhal of his favourite character: 'for you, there is no middle road'. The same is true for us.
>
> (Moretti 2000: 68)

Moretti's conjectures have excited much controversy, both in the radical review which published it (Prendergast 2001; Orsini 2002; Kristal 2002; Arac 2002) and in scholarly comparatism more generally (Apter 2003: 253–6; Spivak 2003: 107–9n.; Parla 2004). In response, he has conceded to Prendergast that other kinds of literature may well follow different patterns from the novel; and to Parla and Arac that even the English novel was itself originally a peripheral development in relation to an earlier Spanish core (Moretti 2003: 75, 79). But he refuses to retreat from the world-systems perspective itself, conceding very little indeed to Kristal's objection that the approach is occidentalist or, perhaps, 'occidento-centric'. Though Moretti makes no mention of it, this was also Spivak's objection: 'this *is* nationalism', she writes, 'U.S. nationalism masquerading as globalism' (Spivak 2003: 108n.). Moretti's response is salutary: 'Theories will never abolish inequality: they can only hope to explain it' (Moretti 2003: 77). Proceeding to an explicit discussion of the politics of the encounter, moreover, he becomes even more insistent. If '*the way we imagine comparative literature is a mirror of how we see the world*', he writes, then his conjectures are intended as a mirror to 'the unprecedented possibility that the entire world may be subject to a single centre of power...which has long exerted an equally unprecedented symbolic hegemony' (ibid.: 81). Gesturing toward the immediate political context in 2003, he cautions that, if the global campaign against the American invasion of Iraq had given cause to rejoice, it nonetheless also gave cause for cultural historians to reflect. Such reflection will be directed toward the world-system, presumably, as well as to the movements and forms it calls forth in opposition to itself.

Couched in these general terms, the combination of world-systems theory, distant reading and the sociology of literary form has real purchase. It is unclear, however, why exactly it should become *the* method of comparative literary studies, as distinct from one amongst many. Here, Spivak is surely right to insist that:

> the real problem with this identification, between writing good reference tools for the novel form...and for the entire discipline... is a denial of collectivity.... Why should the...whole world as our object of investigation be the task of every comparativist...?
>
> (Spivak 2003: 108n.)

Why, indeed? She continues:

> In fact, most close reading comparativists do not only read a few texts. They spread out and rely on good reference instruments such as Moretti will provide. They consult secondary texts based on other people's close readings, as Moretti will. Where they *can* closely read, they see the 'criticism' provided by the encyclopedist as necessarily superficial and unsatisfactory.
>
> (Spivak 2003: 108n.)

This defence of close reading is warranted and, in fact, overlaps with our own earlier argument for cultural critique as against cultural engineering. But there is more to Moretti than the provision of reference tools; and sociological analysis need be neither superficial nor unsatisfactory. The point, surely, is that these are different levels of analysis, defining different objects of study and requiring different kinds of theory and method. That both are comparativist in scope, with the potential to resist both brute Eurocentrism and, more pertinently, brute Americanism, is surely at least as significant as that either or both are practised primarily in the Euro-American university system.

Let me conclude this chapter with a few brief suggestions as to how world-systems theory might be applied to a field that previously attracted both Moretti's and Spivak's attentions: the post-Gothic genre, or 'type', in Williams's terms, we have since come to know as 'science fiction', but which was inaugurated – according to the dominant accounts at least – by Mary Shelley's *Frankenstein* (cf. Moretti 1988: 83–108; Spivak 1999: 132–40). The cultural geography of 'SF', as it is known to its devotees, has followed a fairly clear pattern. Conceived in England and France, at the very core of the nineteenth-century world literary system (Shelley initially, but above all Verne and Wells), it continued in both throughout the twentieth and into the twenty-first century (through Huxley, Orwell, Lewis, Wyndham, Hoyle, Clarke, Moorcock, Ballard, Banks, Macleod and Miéville in Britain; Rosny, Anatole France, Renard, Spitz, Boulle, Merle, Walther, Brussolo, Arnaud and Houellebecq in France). Its frontiers expanded to include the Weimar Republic (Gail, von Harbou and Lang, von Hanstein), early Soviet Russia (Belyaev, Bogdanov,

Bulgakov, Mayakovsky, Platonov, Alexei Tolstoy, Zamyatin) and inter-war Czechoslovakia (Karel Čapek, Troska). Exported to Japan in the post-Second World War period (Abé, Hoshi, Komatsu, Murakami), it also flourished in Communist Poland (Fialkowski, Lem, Wisniewski-Snerg) and, more significantly, in late-Communist Russia (Altov, Bilenkin, Bulychev, Emtsev and Parnov, the Strugatski brothers, Tarkovsky). But the United States became absolutely central and near-hegemonic, nonetheless, from the inter-war period (Gernsback, Campbell, Asimov, Heinlein and 'the pulps') through the New Wave (Delany, Dick, Ellison, Spinrad, Tiptree, Zelazny) and on to the present (Gibson, Sterling and post-cyberpunk; Le Guin, Russ, Piercy and feminism; Kim Stanley Robinson). Moreover, this American hegemony extended from print to film (Whale, Kubrick, Lucas, Spielberg, Scott, Cameron, Burton and Verhoeven) and television (Roddenberry, Straczynski, Carter and Whedon).

The late nineteenth- and early twentieth-century pattern more or less exactly replicates the general Anglo-French hegemony which Moretti sketched in his *Atlas of the European Novel*. Just as the earlier decades had been dominated, both in terms of sales and translations, by the historical novels of Scott and Dumas, so were the later by Verne's *voyages extraordinaires* and Wells's 'scientific romances'. In itself this is unsurprising: Jameson's quasi-Lukácsian argument for SF as a functional near-equivalent to the historical novel has long been a commonplace of academic science fiction studies (Jameson 1982; cf. Lukács 1962). But the type's more recent geographical trajectory is less predictable. Csicsery-Ronay has argued that this cultural geography is best understood as a correlate of imperialism: 'The dominant sf nations are precisely those that attempted to expand beyond their national borders in imperialist projects' (Csicsery-Ronay 2003: 231). Citing Hardt and Negri's *Empire*, which he plausibly reads as itself a quasi-science fictional text, Csicsery-Ronay writes that SF was 'driven by a desire for the imaginary transformation of imperialism into Empire' (ibid.: 232; cf. M. Hardt and Negri 2000). There is something to be said for this view of the sub-form's internal space as systematically imbued with the myth of Empire, understood as a 'technoscientific' regime. But it seems much more obviously applicable to American SF – Asimov's *Foundation* trilogy is the exemplary instance – than to its European precursors. To generalise thus from the part to the whole seems unwarranted. Moreover, the extrinsic history underpinning the account is clearly suspect, as Csicsery-Ronay almost admits when he hazards the improbable suggestion that Čapek and Lem be considered late products of the Austro-Hungarian Empire (Csicsery-Ronay 2003: 243n.). Čapek perhaps, but Lem was born in Lvov, now in the Ukraine and never a Habsburg city, three years after the collapse of the dual monarchy. True, he eventually moved to Krakow, which had indeed been a Habsburg march, but only in 1946, by which time the city was both Polish and Communist. The connection seems tenuous, to say the least. Moretti's approach, by contrast, suggests a more plausible explanation: that what each of the non-Anglo-French 'SF nations' have in common, Poland and Czechoslovakia as much as the USSR, the Weimar Republic and the inter-war United States, is their semi-peripheral status in relation to the cultural core of the world-system.

Furthermore, this extrinsic pattern is matched by an epistemic rupture within the form. Their darker undercurrents notwithstanding – one thinks of Nemo and of the Morlocks – Verne and Wells had generally written from within a self-confidently optimistic positivism, often bordering on the utopian. SF in Germany, Russia and *Mitteleuropa* abandoned this liberal futurology, opting either for an explicitly communist utopianism or, more interestingly, for dystopia, whether communist or capitalist, a theme later reimported into England by Orwell, that most unEnglish of English icons. Positivistic SF would be resumed in inter-war America, however, where Gernsback coined the term 'scientifiction' – later converted into 'science fiction' by Campbell – and traced its origins retrospectively to Verne and Wells (and also Poe), though not, significantly, to the Eastern and Central Europeans or to Shelley (Clute and Nicholls 1993: 311). But this was positivism in a very different register, nonetheless, an escapist response to the Great Depression rather than the easy celebration of scientific triumphalism: hence the quasi-Marxian character of Asimov's early 'Futurianism'. This second epistemic shift is vital and it was, of course, a distinctly American achievement. But the United States was still then much nearer to the periphery than the core of the world literary system. At one point, Moretti asks why, in comparably 'peripheral' circumstances, the US had failed to produce a paradigm shift akin to that in Latin American magic realism. His answer is that:

> success and failure are highly *contingent* results...the United States *could* indeed have produced a paradigm shift in the history of the novel in the mid nineteenth century.... On the other hand...paradigm shifts are extremely rare events, and therefore what needs to be explained is not...their absence..., but rather their occurrence.
>
> (Moretti 1998: 196n.)

No doubt this is so. But there is an alternative possibility: that North American 'backwardness' *did* indeed produce precisely such a shift, not at the level of the modern epic, but in a marginal sub-form which would later generalise itself across the entire field of popular culture, from novel to film to television, so as to become the nearest we may ever have to a postmodern epic. We will return to this matter in Chapter 6.

Chapter 4

Commodity culture

The relations of production

As we noted in Chapter 3, the trade in printed books was from its very inception a mainly capitalist industry, in which books were produced to be sold for profit, and where the primary relations of production between publishers, writers and readers were essentially commodity relations. Publishers bought manuscripts from writers in order to sell printed books to readers. The book trade is thus one instance among many of what Bürger termed the social 'institution' of 'bourgeois art'. He proposed a historical typology of aesthetic social relations, measured along three main axes, respectively the function of the artwork, its mode of production and its mode of reception (Bürger 1984: 48–9). This gave him three main kinds of art: sacral, courtly and bourgeois (see Table 4.1).

Table 4.1 A historical typology of art

	Sacral art	*Courtly art*	*Bourgeois art*
Function	cult object	representational object	portrayal of bourgeois self-understanding
Production	collective craft	individual	individual
Reception	collective (sacral)	collective (sociable)	individual

Source: P. Bürger (1984: 48).

In themselves, sacral and courtly art are insufficiently internally differentiated as categories to be of much real analytical purchase: the former is defined so broadly as to embrace, for example, both an aboriginal corroboree and a Catholic mass. Their primary function in Bürger's analysis is not, however, as elements in a comparative sociology of aesthetics, but rather as heuristic devices by which to establish the specificity of bourgeois art itself. And here the analysis clearly works: commodity production has indeed entailed historically unprecedented forms of highly individualised cultural production and consumption. Such relations are very recent: most earlier patronage systems required neither publishing nor commodity exchange as mediations between writer and reader. Even where books had been published and occasionally sold, as in ancient Rome, these relations remained marginal to the primary relationship between writer and patron. As Auerbach observed:

> The concern of the ancients for the welfare of poets and writers never went beyond the institution of patronage. The *bibliopola*, to whom the writer turned over his manuscript for production and 'publication', seems to have paid him nothing for it. And I know of no instance of a writer complaining about this state of affairs.
>
> (Auerbach 1965: 242)

As we also noted in Chapter 3, capitalist relations of literary production pre-date printing itself: workshops employing copyists to produce vernacular manuscript books for commercial sale had existed from as early as the end of the twelfth century in France, the early fourteenth in England (M. Thomas 1976: 25). But in fifteenth-century Europe the new technology fused with these already existing commodity relations in an explosive combination that would produce what Benedict Anderson nicely termed 'print-capitalism' (1991: 36).

Print-capitalism

Semiology has tended to analyse literature through a communications model, centred around the writer as addresser and the reader as addressee (cf. Jakobson 1960: 353), where publishing merely became part of the text's context. In the academic 'sociology of literature', by contrast, publishers were normally more visible, but typically represented, in terms deriving from the sociology of mass communications, as 'gatekeepers', that is, 'people who, by virtue of their position in an organization, operate sluice gates for ideas, deciding which will be offered and what will be excluded' (Coser *et al.* 1985: 4). If this was an improvement on semiology, it still radically underestimated the extent to which publishers as capitalists predominate over and often actually initiate capitalist literary production. The first of these print-capitalists were generally master printers, often also acting as publishers and booksellers, although some specialist publishers did not in fact have their own presses, for example Sebastien Cramoisy, who published a tenth of the books produced in Paris between 1625 and 1660 (Febvre and Martin 1976: 136, 127). The vast majority of the early printers owned only relatively small establishments, so that as late as the eighteenth century most books came from workshops containing only two or three presses and employing around ten journeymen and apprentices – the minimum number required to keep a press in production was five people (ibid.: 137).

The master printers were organised into their own guilds, in France the Guild of St John the Evangelist, founded in 1401; the journeymen into their brotherhoods or chapels, precursors of the modern trade unions. Industrial relations in the new industry were often hard fought: between 1569 and 1573 there were three main strikes at the Antwerp workshops of Christophe Plantin, then the most powerful book manufacturer in Europe and one of the largest at any time before the nineteenth century (ibid.: 140, 133–4, 125–6). During the mid-sixteenth century the master printers and booksellers campaigned, in the main part successfully, for state-enforced powers to regulate the trade against both journeymen and potential newcomers. The resulting 'Companies of Stationers' were granted charters of incorporation and corollary regulatory powers in England in 1557 and in France in 1570 (ibid.: 141). Febvre and Martin summarise the general history of early modern publishing thus: in the sixteenth century the great 'humanist printers' were enlightened publishers, prosperous and successful men of culture and refinement, the confidants and protectors of writers, in the first rank of the struggle to spread new, often Protestant, ideas; in the seventeenth century a prolonged crisis of overproduction, which depressed earnings across the industry, and the political authoritarianism of the Counter-Reformation combined to reduce publishing to a newly subordinate status, with publishers as merely the servants of writers, rather than their equals or protectors; in the eighteenth century the Enlightenment and the struggle against royal absolutism occasioned new alliances between writers and the new philosopher-publishers, and a new material affluence and intellectual adventurousness (ibid.: 143–59).

In one important respect, developments in England varied from this more general European pattern. In England, as elsewhere, the industry seems to have steadily expanded from a very small base during the sixteenth century and contracted a little during the seventeenth, only to expand again in the eighteenth: in London, there were only two or three printers at the beginning of the sixteenth century, 13 in 1558, 34 in 1563, 40 in 1577, 97 in 1595, 60 in 1660, 75 by 1724, and well over 150 in 1757 (Williams 1965: 181–2). But the revolutionary crisis of the mid-seventeenth century, which had no direct equivalent on the European mainland, seems to have been accompanied by a very substantial expansion in publishing. In 1637 the pre-revolutionary autocracy had cut the number of authorised London printers to twenty and provided for unlicensed printers to be pilloried and whipped (Hill 1985a: 37). With the collapse of censorship in 1640, however, the trade expanded very rapidly: George Tomason counted twenty-two titles published in 1640, 1,966 in 1642; by 1649 there were at least sixty printers in London (ibid.: 40; Williams 1965: 181). In England during the seventeenth century, France and Germany in the sixteenth, all three in the eighteenth, publishing was often simultaneously a capitalist enterprise in pursuit of profit and a politico-religious crusade in pursuit of liberty. As Febvre and Martin observed of the alliance between printing and Protestantism in sixteenth-century Germany: 'they refused to print Catholic pamphlets but devoted painstaking care to printing the works of Luther…even if it was not always from conviction that they behaved like this it was at least from self-interest…. Luther…made the fortunes of his printers' (Febvre and Martin 1976: 292).

Throughout Europe, the printing industries flourished in the eighteenth century, their expansion carried forward by the new forms of middle-class reading, the newspaper, the periodical and the novel. Both book and newspaper publishing were typically organised into relatively small family businesses, often the creation of one man, competing in relatively free markets. Publishing began as a highly competitive 'cottage industry', then, and continued as such for an unusually long period mainly because of 'low capital entry costs' (Coser *et al.* 1985: 25). Habermas viewed these developments as part of the socio-historical emergence, during the seventeenth and eighteenth centuries, of a distinctly middle-class, or 'bourgeois', public opinion. This 'public sphere', as he termed it, was 'the sphere of private people come together as a public', a public made up of formally free and equal rational individuals. As such, it was an entirely novel phenomenon: these bourgeois would-be citizens, he wrote, 'soon claimed the public sphere...against the public authorities themselves.... The medium of political confrontation was peculiar and without historical precedent: people's use of their reason' (Habermas 1989: 27). The public sphere was centred on institutions such as the *salons* in France, the learned societies (or *Tischgesellschaften*) and literary societies (or *Sprachgesellschaften*) in Germany, and the coffee houses in England. These sustained both the early novel and the early newspaper and periodical press. This bourgeois public sphere was gradually undermined during the nineteenth century, in part as a result of the further industrialisation of printing, in part because of the eruption into it of social interests opposed to its apparently 'rational' norms: the working class, political Radicalism, feminism and, in England, religious Dissent (Eagleton 1996b: 35–6). We should note, however, that these challenges were themselves made possible by the relatively open and small-scale nature of the relations of literary production. As Thompson observed: 'the successful Radical periodical provided a living...for the editor,... for regional agents, booksellers, and itinerant hawkers, thereby making of Radicalism...a profession which could maintain its own full-time agitators' (Thompson 1963: 674). This would be as true for France in the 1830s and 1840s as of England during the making of its working class (Graff 1987: 281).

If the print media in the core capitalist economies remained highly competitive domestically throughout the nineteenth century, they were nonetheless also able to expand into and in some respects dominate other foreign markets. Hence the international predominance of English and French novels noted in the previous chapter. Moretti describes the nineteenth-century literary economy as comprising 'three Europes. With France and Britain always in the core; most other countries always in the periphery; and in between a variable group, that changes from case to case' (Moretti 1998: 174). French novelists were more successful in the Catholic South, British in the Protestant North, but the whole continent read Scott, Bulwer-Lytton and Dickens, Dumas, Sue and Hugo (ibid.: 178–9). Moretti's empirical indicators here are the volume of translations recorded in the various national bibliographies. These tell us nothing about foreign ownership of print-capital *per se*, though we may surmise it was generally minimal; nor necessarily about profit flows, at least not until after the development of reliable systems of international copyright enforcement. But they do provide powerful evidence of patterns of cultural influence, nonetheless, which in turn suggest the likelihood of corollary financial returns. Moretti also shows how the 'long and bitter rivalry between the continent's two narrative superpowers' was eventually won by France, rather than Britain, 'making Paris...the Hollywood of the nineteenth century'. By the mid-nineteenth century translations of French novels into Italian outnumbered British by a ratio of eight to one, whilst those into Danish were running roughly even (ibid.: 184).

More monopolistic forms of large-scale capitalism only became significant within the core capitalist economies at the end of the nineteenth century, in the first instance in newspaper rather than book publishing. The Northcliffe and Hearst revolutions in England and the United States thus marked the beginning a new phase in the ownership and control of the print media. Thereafter, the pattern in both countries would increasingly be that of the great newspaper 'publishing empire' led by the 'press baron'. By 1908 Northcliffe owned the *Daily Mail*, the *Daily Mirror*, *The Times*, two Sunday papers and an evening paper; Pearson the *Daily Express*, the *Standard* and the *Evening Standard* (Williams 1965: 229). By 1922 Hearst owned a network of twenty-one daily and eleven Sunday newspapers extending across eleven cities (Chalaby 1997: 625). Interestingly, neither Dupuy's *Petit Parisien* nor Prouvost's *Paris-Soir* developed along these lines. Indeed, Chalaby goes so far as to argue that, for the first half of the twentieth century, press baronage remained an almost exclusively 'Anglo-American phenomenon': 'Before the Second World War', he writes, '...the nation-wide press conglomerate was unknown in France' (ibid.: 629). The impact of totalitarianism, Communist, Fascist or both, tended to obstruct such developments in Eastern and Central Europe: by 1945 over 80 per cent of the German press was under the direct control of the Nazi Party (H. Hardt 1988: 137). But in France, where a (heavily censored) free-market press persisted even during the German occupation, the absence of press baronage needs to be explained. Chalaby points to five major factors: substantially lower levels of advertising revenue; much less heavily concentrated urban populations; a less homogenous market structure and, hence, a relatively smaller available market; the greater significance of non-commercial motives, Catholicism for *La Croix*, Communism for *L'Humanité*, in a more politicised and ideologically polarised culture; and, finally, a much closer association between the literary and journalistic fields (Chalaby 1997: 631–9). The latter point is interesting: Balzac, Lamartine, Dumas and Hugo all owned and edited newspapers; the sole equivalent in England is Dickens, who edited the *Daily News* for a sum total of three weeks (ibid.: 637–8).

Press monopolisation continued as a long-term structural trend in Britain throughout the twentieth century. By 1995 the three largest British newspaper groups controlled 74 per cent of the circulation of national daily newspapers and 84 per cent of national Sundays (Curran 1997: 78). But from the Second World War onwards, a parallel pattern appears throughout Western Europe. By 1968 Axel Springer's ASV controlled over 39 per cent of the circulation of Germany daily newspapers and 17 per cent of the circulation of German magazines (H. Hardt 1988: 142). Its titles included both the tabloids *Bild-Zeitung* and *Bild am Sonntag* and the broadsheets *Die Welt* and *Welt am Sonntag*. In France, Hersant's Centre Presse became the first group 'to attain proportions comparable to British or American conglomerates' (Chalaby 1997: 629). It bought *Le Figaro* and *L'Aurore*, a chain of provincial newspapers, including *Le Progrès de Lyon*, and newspapers in Belgium, New Caledonia, Poland and Hungary. Moreover, what had begun as a press phenomenon extended into book publishing during the second half of the century.

Coser, Kadushin and Powell date the move away from the cottage industry model in the American book trade to as late as the 1960s, when Houghton Mifflin and Random House first became public stock companies. The annual rate of American publishing industry mergers peaked at forty-seven and forty-four in 1968 and 1969, respectively (Coser *et al.* 1985: 25–6). This trend toward monopolisation was increasingly associated with the development of multimedia corporations, with interests in both newspaper and book publishing, and increasingly also in other media. A second wave of American publishing mergers during the mid-1970s was marked by 'the growth and proliferation of multimedia conglomerates, with interests in film, television, cable TV, newspapers, magazines, home video equipment, and book publishing' (ibid.: 29). In Germany, ASV moved into books, radio and television; in France, Centre Presse launched La Cinq television network. In Italy, Silvio Berlusconi's Fininvest had interests in books (its Mondadori is the country's largest publisher), television (its Mediaset owned three commercial networks) and the press (*Il Giornale*). In the early 1980s Rupert Murdoch's News Corporation acquired two major publishing houses, Collins in Britain and Harper & Row in the United States, merging them to form HarperCollins (Feather 1993: 169). During the 1980s and 1990s many of these conglomerates acquired an increasingly international and global character. By the last decade of the twentieth century the British book trade was dominated by four publishing groups: Random Century, News Corporation's HarperCollins, the Pearson Group and Reed International. All four had extensive international operations and two originated outside the United Kingdom, Random in the United States, News in Australia (ibid.: 169–70).

The most significant shift under post-war late capitalism was thus that from national publishing empires to international media conglomerates. Murdoch's News Corporation is in some respects very close to the paradigm of a 'postmodern publisher'. Beginning in South Australia in the 1920s, with Keith Murdoch's Adelaide *News*, the company expanded to acquire the national *Australian*, the Melbourne *Herald-Sun* and the Sydney *Daily Telegraph-Mirror*, so that by 1995 it commanded something like two-thirds of total Australian daily newspaper circulation (Schultz 1997: 35–6). Moving offshore, it acquired newspaper, publishing, television and film interests in Britain and in the United States. In Britain it bought *The Times* and *The Sun*, the *Sunday Times* and the *News of the World*; in America the *New York Post*. News acquired Twentieth Century Fox film studios and successfully launched Fox as an embryonic fourth national television network in the US. It owns the television rights to American Football, English Premier League soccer and Rugby League. It is now the second-largest book publisher in the United Kingdom, with an annual turnover of about £160 million. In addition to HarperCollins, its publishing imprints include: Collins Crime, Flamingo, Fourth Estate, Jane's, Voyager, Thorsons and Times Books in the United Kingdom; Beech Tree, Greenwillow, Hearst, Mulberry, William Morrow and Zondervan in the United States (Turner 2002: 46, 469). In 1989 News launched the first British satellite channel, Sky TV, deliberately pre-empting the officially approved BSB, which it effectively took over the following year. In 1993 News Corporation bought a majority holding in Star TV, a pan-Asian satellite network which broadcast to more than fifty countries, including India and China, thereby giving it control over BBC World's South Asia and Middle East television broadcasts. In 1995 Murdoch sold a 13.5 per cent stake in News to MCI Communications, the second largest long-distance telecommunications company in the world, thus establishing a direct link with British Telecom. This is as big and as globalised a media empire as they come. The English television playwright Dennis Potter famously named his cancer 'Rupert' after Murdoch. The point about terminal cancers, however, is that they eventually take over the entire body.

As Curran has argued, the conjunction of a commodified press with commercial advertising and highly unequal distributions of income tends to produce a 'polarized' market for newspapers: on the one hand, a 'quality' press, with relatively small readerships and relatively high advertising revenues; on the other, a 'popular' press, with much larger readerships and relatively high sales receipts (Curran 1997: 97–100). As Williams summed it up: ' "the masses" – crime, sex, sport, personalities, entertainment, pictures; "the minority" – traditional politics, traditional arts, briefings on popular trends' (Williams 1976b: 103). For media conglomerates such as News Corporation, 'high' and 'low' cultures are merely different niche markets: like Northcliffe before him, Murdoch determinedly acquired both 'quality' and 'popular' outlets, both in Australia and elsewhere (the *Australian* is a quality paper, the *Telegraph-Mirror* a popular). Book publishing typically exhibits a roughly analogous dual-market structure. 'There are now two pronounced segments of the book trade', explain Coser, Kadushin and Powell:

> one in which books are media properties and part of a high-risk speculative mass market characterized by a winner-take-all system of huge windfalls and disastrous failures; and the rest of the industry...[whose] audience is not large, nor are their successes or failures grand.
>
> (Coser *et al.* 1985: 41)

In book publishing, however, there is no direct equivalent to the advertising revenues secured by quality newspapers. Why, then, we might well ask, are there 'quality' publishers at all?

Lane distinguished ideal-typically between publishers motivated by some kind of 'cultural goal' and those motivated by the 'economic goal' of profit. The 'general publisher', at one extreme, carries a normally unprofitable current list, but maintains a backlist that is important as a proportion both of total titles and of total income; the 'genre publisher', at the other, combines a high turnover with low unit profit and makes high profits, but at high risk. General publishers fund the current losers in 'quality' fiction through their backlists, Lane explains, partly because these losers will become the backlist of the future, but partly also because the publishers subscribe to culturally 'elitist' beliefs in the value of good literature. British publishers of this kind were an elite group historically, enjoying high social status, higher education and a high rate of self-recruitment. 'Where the great publishers of the past saw their role as the creation of public taste', Lane concluded, 'publishers today generally tend to respond to the cross pressures either by directing their attentions to fulfilling market demands, or by trying to sustain or recreate what they believe to be the consensual values of the past'. The myth of the Golden Age thus served both to explain and legitimate 'the passive, but nevertheless, positive, role that publishers exert' (M. Lane 1970: 251). There was perhaps a certain disingenuousness to Lane's treatment of publishing 'values'. The central point, however, is that the backlist performs much the same function for 'quality' book publishing as does advertising for the 'quality' press. Escarpit made much the same point, when he distinguished between the 'cultured' and 'popular' circuits in French publishing (Escarpit 1971: 60–9). And Coser, Kadushin and Powell applied a similar model to the United States, drawing the parallel between these two kinds of publishing and, respectively, the 'core' and 'peripheral' industries of the wider American economy, where the former are oligopolistic and dominated by large corporations, the latter competitive and including many smaller firms (Coser *et al.* 1985: 41–2).

Bourdieu developed a roughly analogous, but theoretically more sophisticated, approach to French publishing, distinguishing between 'commercial' firms, which aimed at short-term profit, and 'cultural' businesses, which aimed to accumulate symbolic capital, which would nonetheless be transformed into material capital, but only in the much longer term (Bourdieu 1993: 97–101). Comparing two publishing houses drawn from each end of the spectrum, respectively Robert Laffont and Éditions de Minuit, he showed how their different 'temporal structures correspond to two very different economic structures'. Founded in 1941, Laffont owns Julliard, Nil, Seghers and Fixot and publishes a whole series of best-selling authors, covering 'fiction' and 'literature', but also 'self-help', 'general science' and 'psychology'. Founded a year later, initially as a Resistance press, Minuit specialised in 'essays, literature, literary criticism, philosophy, social science, sociology' (Turner 2002: 449). Its authors included Sarraute, Duras and Robbe-Grillet (who was actually a reader for Minuit) and also Samuel Beckett. At the time of Bourdieu's study, Laffont was already a large publicly listed company, owned in part by Time-Life, employing 700 people and publishing about 200 titles a year, many of them bestsellers (in the year surveyed one-quarter had print runs of over 20,000); Minuit a small private company, employing twelve people and publishing twenty titles a year, few with print runs over 3,000, many selling less than 500 copies. Minuit's profitability depended entirely on its backlist, including Beckett's *Godot*, 'which sold fewer than 200 copies in 1952 and twenty-five years later had sold more than

500,000' (ibid.: 99). Bourdieu's point, however, is that such long-term investments make sense only in relation to the 'economy of cultural production', in which 'investments are recompensed only if they are in a sense thrown away, like a gift, which can only achieve the most precious return gift, recognition..., so long as it is experienced as a one-way transaction'. As with the gift – the reference to Mauss is surely intentional – 'the intervening time...provides a screen and disguises the profit awaiting the most disinterested investors' (ibid.: 101; cf. Mauss 1989).

At one level, the distinction between the two kinds of publishing is merely a matter of different strategies directed toward different markets. But there is more to it than this: whether viewed cynically as 'cultural capital' or idealistically as 'quality publishing', the cultured circuit has clearly performed functions that are irreducible to the commercial, even in the longest of long terms. These appear to be 'ideological' or 'hegemonic'. As Williams pointed out, there are varying degrees of symmetry between cultural production and social reproduction. He identified three main types of asymmetry, each evident in a different area of cultural conflict: the organisation of censorship, the organisation of the market, and the relations between reproduced and popular culture (Williams 1981: 98–100). The central point here is that, as a profit-motivated industry, the capitalist book trade meets the ideological and political needs of the socially dominant groups much less directly and much less immediately than had earlier forms of the organisation of literacy. Hence the repeated conflict between the trade and both the church and the state. But these conflicts find a parallel within the publishing industry, in those between 'core' and 'peripheral' sectors. This is, in fact, a fourth type of asymmetry: in Weberian terms, that between the publisher as member of a particular class and as member of a particular status group (the 'learned' or the 'educated'); in Marxist terms, between the publisher as capitalist and as purveyor and guarantor of the dominant ideology. In the longer term the economic imperative may well be determining. But in the short and medium term there has often been room for tension, conflict and struggle between the claims of profit and principle, class and status, economics and ideology.

If all this seems rather abstract, let us illustrate the point with a specific example. George Orwell was one of the central cultural icons of Cold War western anti-Communism during the 1950s and 1960s, his dystopian novel *Nineteen Eighty-Four* not only a bestseller but also part of Bloom's Western Canon (Bloom 1994: 555). Orwell was well known for his angry denunciations of the intellectual dishonesty of British intellectuals, their lack of commitment to intellectual freedom. Overstated though these sometimes seem, they become more readily understandable when one considers the intriguing story of the struggle to find a publisher for *Animal Farm*, his Swiftian satire on the history of Soviet Communism. He offered the manuscript initially to Victor Gollancz, the leading left-wing publisher in the country. Perhaps predictably, Gollancz turned it down, writing thus to Orwell's agent on 4 April 1944: 'I am highly critical of many aspects of internal and external Soviet policy: but I could not possibly publish...a general attack of this nature' (Crick 1980: 312). Orwell then sent the manuscript to Jonathan Cape, whose initial expressions of interest soon cooled. Cape explained his reasons in a letter to their chief literary adviser on 19 June:

> I mentioned the reaction that I had had from an important official in the Ministry of Information with regard to ANIMAL FARM. I must confess that this expression of opinion has given me seriously to think.... I can see now that it might be regarded as something which it was highly ill-advised to publish at the present time.
>
> (Crick 1980: 313)

Orwell moved on to Faber, whose most distinguished and very probably most right-wing editor, T. S. Eliot, replied on 13 July: 'We agree that it is a distinguished piece of writing.... On the other hand, we have no conviction...that this is the right point of view from which to criticise the political situation at the present time' (ibid.: 315). The point, of course, is that the Soviet Union was at the time still Britain's ally in war against Germany. Germany surrendered in May 1945 and Warburg published *Animal Farm* in August.

Such considerations are by no means confined to matters of high politics, but they probably operate most powerfully at this level. A more recent example was occasioned by the Al-Qaeda attack on the New York World Trade Center on 11 September 2001. The first 50,000 copies of *Stupid White Men*, Michael Moore's comically serious polemic against the President George W. Bush, had been printed on 10 September and were scheduled for distribution on the day of the attack. The publisher, ReganBooks, an American subsidiary of Murdoch's HarperCollins, refused to release them, asked Moore to rewrite up to half the book, threatened to charge him $US100,000 to cover reprinting costs and, when he considered taking the manuscript elsewhere, insisted they owned exclusive rights both to publish and not to publish. A campaign of letter writing by librarians and others eventually pushed HarperCollins into a reluctant release, but with no publicity in the press, radio or television and a clear instruction that there would be no second printing (Moore 2002: xi–xviii). The book proved such an overwhelming commercial success, however, that News were unable to resist reprinting, though they held firm on the pledge not to advertise. As Moore observed in the 'Introduction' to the 2002 Penguin edition:

> *Stupid White Men* is in its fifth month on the bestseller list as I write, and still #1 this week in the *New York Times*. There has still not been a single ad taken out for the book and I have appeared on only TWO broadcast network TV shows.... That's it. A virtual media blackout.
>
> (Moore 2002: xix)

Such treatment is by no means confined to left-wing writers. The same publisher, HarperCollins, had a few years previously refused to publish *East and West*, a book it commissioned from Chris Patten, the last British Governor of Hong Kong and also a former Conservative government minister, for fear that it might compromise Star TV's increasingly close relationship with the Chinese government (Page 2003: 474, 476–7). Nor is self-censorship confined to book publishing. The inappropriately named Clear Channel Communications, which then owned around 1,170 radio stations across the US, responded to the same Al-Qaeda attack by immediately circulating a list of 150 songs to be taken off the air, including quite literally everything by the recently disbanded radical rap-rock band Rage Against the Machine (*New York Times*, 19 September 2001). Early in 2003 Clear Channel Communications imposed a similar ban on the Dixie Chicks for their opposition to the Anglo-American invasion of Iraq. It seems likely that these relatively public actions are merely the tip of a veritable iceberg of corporate censorship. Clearly, publishers and their counterparts in other media are by no means passive conduits for the transmission of cultural products from producers to consumers. Clearly, they are affected by factors other than profit: by ideology, or values if we prefer, as in Gollancz's opposition to any general attack on the USSR; or by reasons of state, as in Cape's discussions with the important official from the wartime Ministry of Information. We will return to this matter of the state in the concluding sections of the chapter.

Writers and writing

As anyone who ever attempted to write an essay, let alone a novel, can readily attest, writing is at once extremely time-consuming and, in the short-term at least, highly 'unproductive'. In the language of economic theory, it is a kind of investment with an unusually long lead-time. Writing is only possible, then, on the condition that some extra-literary social institution fund writers through this lead-time. As Escarpit had it: 'even the most ethereal of poets eats and sleeps each day' (1971: 37). Williams distinguished four main types of 'authorial' relations of production, each of which provides its own distinctive 'solution' to the sociological problem of the writer: respectively, those of the 'instituted artist', 'patronage', the 'market' and, finally, what he termed 'post-market institutions' (Williams 1981: 36–56). Market relations are, of course, the distinguishing feature of a capitalist literary mode of production and these will be our prime concern here. But it might be as well to begin by situating these in relation to a comparison with earlier forms of 'institutedness' and patronage.

By the first, Williams refers to the kind of communally sponsored, particular social role, typically that of the prophet-seer, which is often found in tribal societies, both pre-literate and literate. Here the role of the 'artist' – who would not, of course, be a writer, in any strict sense of the term, in a pre-literate culture – is 'instituted' as such, as an official part of the central organisation of the society. Extant examples of this kind of relationship can be found amongst the tribal Aboriginal communities of northern Australia, where 'the body of culturally significant texts is distributed among tribal members according to individuals' custodianship of particular places in the country, associated laws and ritual objects' (Muecke *et al.* 1988: 31). Williams's own example, however, is that of the Celtic bards. We could just as easily add the authors of *Gilgamesh* and the *Iliad* or *Beowulf*. As we have seen, epic verse such as this was originally oral and only later written down; it typically recorded the collective history of a people; and as an effect precisely of this orality it was often highly repetitive. It is sometimes tempting to imagine these as the cultural products of relatively egalitarian, undifferentiated societies, classless if not pre-patriarchal, such as can indeed be found in tribal Australia. But, as Williams's own discussion of the Celtic bards makes clear, 'instituted artists' are also present in tribal societies with elaborated systems of social stratification. The Celtic bards themselves were a particular privileged 'order' within what Weber could easily have recognised as an 'estate' system of inequalities based on 'status' (Weber 1948: 186–7).

Patronage, too, is essentially a relation of status, but one where the writer's role is not actually instituted as such. Rather, the potential 'patron', whether individual or institutional, is able to exercise a choice as to whether or not to sponsor a particular writer or artist. As Escarpit defined it, patronage is 'the support of a writer by a person or institution that protects him but that, in return, expects satisfaction of the cultural need' (Escarpit 1971: 38). Williams identified five different kinds of patronage, though only three of these seem especially important, those he terms, respectively, 'retainer and commission', 'protection and support' and 'sponsorship' (Williams 1981: 39–43). In the first, the court or the aristocratic household officially recognises and retains the individual writer in a relatively close and permanent relationship with the patron. Such retainers were characteristic of high feudalism (Chaucer, for example), but also of imperial Rome (Virgil and Augustus). In the second, an enduring but less intimate relationship is established between patron and writer: Williams's example is that of the Elizabethan theatre companies. These two can be conflated, as for example in Laurenson and Swingewood, as 'old' patronage (1972: 108). The third kind, sponsorship, or 'late patronage' as it is sometimes termed, describes a situation where artworks are commodities for general sale, but where a particular sponsor nonetheless provides initial financial support so as to make their production possible. In England, the practice dates from the Elizabethan period and is best represented by the dedication fee. In return for a fee, the writer publicly dedicated his writing to the sponsor, at a standard going rate for an Elizabethan drama of about 40 shillings. Such fees were tied only to the particular text and implied no continuing relation of patronage: the playwright and pamphleteer Robert Greene, for example, had sixteen patrons for seventeen books (ibid.: 107).

Market institutions proper are those in which artworks are produced as a commodity to be sold for money on the market. The seventeenth and eighteenth centuries witnessed the cumulative development of market institutions both in Europe and North America. A useful legislative indicator of cultural commodification is copyright, since full commodification almost certainly requires the development of enforceable systems of recognised cultural property. The first effective such legislation dates from the English Copyright Act of 1710, France followed suit during 1777–8 (Febvre and Martin 1976: 164–5) and international regulation came with the Berne Convention in 1891. Williams identified four main types of market production: 'artisanal', where the individual writer sells the artwork directly in the market; 'post-artisanal', where the writer sells to a bookseller; 'market professional', where increasingly professionalised writers sell their literary properties to increasingly capitalised publishers; and 'corporate professional', where the writer works as a salaried employee of large media corporations, in television, radio, journalism and advertising, for example (Williams 1981: 44–54). The heyday of the author as market professional was almost certainly in Europe during the nineteenth century. Typically, European publishers bought the author's copyright outright for cash. Such payments could provide the basis for a considerable fortune: Disraeli was paid £10,000 for *Endymion*, George Eliot £7,000 for *Romola*; Dickens's estate was worth £93,000 at his death (Sutherland 1976: 5, 105; Laurenson and Swingewood 1972: 120). Balzac's contract for the *Comédie humaine* provided for a cash payment of 15,000 francs on publication and a further 15,000 francs once two-thirds of the edition had been sold; Hugo was paid more than 250,000 francs for *Les Misérables* (Escarpit 1971: 42–3; Allen 1991: 36).

From the turn of the century, however, the 'royalty' system, pioneered in the United States, became much more general. Here, the writer is paid an initial 'advance' of some kind and thereafter a percentage of the receipts from sales. Substantial sums can still be paid as advances under the royalty system: Truman Capote received $500,000 for *In Cold Blood*, Tom Wolfe $600,000 for *The Right Stuff* and a further $500,000 for the movie rights (Laurenson and Swingewood 1972: 165; Coser *et al.* 1985: 43), Martin Amis £500,000 for *The Information*; and in 1995 Murdoch's HarperCollins agreed to pay the largest ever advance in British publishing history, £35 million, to Jeffrey Archer for the print, television and film rights to his next three novels. An exceptionally popular commercial writer can even become rich from royalties: immediately prior to the release of *Harry Potter and the Order of the Phoenix*, J. K. Rowling was reported by *The Times* to have earnt some £280 million from the sale of an estimated 200 million copies of her books worldwide combined with royalties from the films based on them (*The Times*, 20 June 2003). The general effect of the royalty system, however, has been greater financial insecurity and declining average real incomes. The result is a 'star system', in some ways analogous to that in professional sport, where a few wealthy writers coexist alongside a great many who barely earn a living.

A 1957 survey of about one-fifth of the membership of the British Society of Authors found that only 82 of over 600 respondents earnt £1,500 or more per annum, whilst 40 per cent earnt less than £5 per week, that is, £260 per annum (Findlater 1978: 283). In 1961 a majority of British writers earnt less than the national average wage from their writing. Much the same pattern occurred in the United States: a survey of members of the American Authors Guild found a median income from writing for 1979 of less than $5,000 per annum for all writers and only $11,000 per annum for 'committed full-time' writers (Coser *et al.* 1985: 231, 233). A 1983 survey of Australian authors found an average gross income from writing for the year

1981–2 of $A6,700, as compared with average earnings for the same year of over $A20,000 for professional, technical, administrative and executive occupations (Australia Council 1983: 20, 1). What we have been tracing here is a progressive movement, by turn, towards the commercialisation of writing, and thence towards what Elmer Rice provocatively termed the 'industrialistion of the writer' (Rice 1978: 313–16). Nineteenth-century market professionals clearly wrote for the market, but on terms which provided some degree of financial security, at least in Britain and France. In the twentieth century, by contrast, the market professional increasingly fell hostage to the vagaries of the star system, whilst financial security became more available to the corporate professional, writing not only for the market, but also as a salaried employee. In practice, these latter need not always be formally employed by a corporation, since supposedly 'freelance' commissions are actually common. The central matter at issue here is not so much the employment contract as the point of origin of the production. As Williams noted, the corporate structure is increasingly characterised by 'a highly organized and fully capitalized market in which the direct commissioning of planned saleable products has become a normal mode' (Williams 1981: 52).

As we noted above, Williams also identified 'post-market institutions' as a fourth set of authorial relations of production. By this he referred to direct or indirect forms of government funding of the arts, or 'public patronage' as it is sometimes described. There is no doubt that the middle decades of the twentieth century witnessed considerable state patronage of writing. This was most obviously true of the so-called 'Eastern bloc' countries during the Communist period, although subsidies were also often operative in the West, albeit normally on a smaller scale. Williams himself thought of such relations as 'post-market' in part because he imagined Communist societies to be in some sense 'post-capitalist'. It isn't at all obvious, however, that there was ever anything particularly *post*-capitalist about them. Eastern Germany and Czechoslovakia aside, the Communist bloc had never really experienced anything even remotely approximating a full-blown private capitalism, and it is difficult to see how something can become post-capitalist without first having been capitalist. Though often represented thus by both its champions and detractors, the old

Soviet Union was surely never a post-capitalist society, not even in embryo. In retrospect, the pure form of Soviet-style regime, that is, the endogenously developed variant rather than that imposed from without by military invasion, seems to have been a kind of transitional society, but transitional to capitalism rather than to anything western radicals like Williams might have recognised as 'socialism'. As such, Communist society is best understood, it seems to me, in the terms proposed by Kautsky, one of its early left-wing critics, that is, as a form of 'state capitalism' (Kautsky 1983: 146). State capitalism was an essentially primitive form of capitalism, we can now see, which tended over time to develop towards more fully evolved forms of private capitalism.

Communist relations of literary production might better be understood, then, as analogous to 'pre-capitalist' or 'early capitalist' forms of patronage. As in earlier patronage systems, officially sponsored writers often enjoyed considerable material security. As in earlier patronage systems, the price of such security was normally a general subservience to the cultural needs of those in authority, a subservience powerfully satirised in the Soviet case by Bulgakov (1967). As in earlier patronage systems, an element of direct personal sponsorship was sometimes involved, for example in Khrushchev's early support for Solzhenitsyn. State patronage in the West often followed a similar pattern, so that during the Cold War successive United States governments determinedly sponsored anti-Communist writers through such 'front organisations' as the Congress for Cultural Freedom. Almost invariably, state sponsorship has been the reward for patriotism, loyalty and respectability: the poets laureate of England are celebrated neither for their literary daring nor their social unconventionality nor their political radicalism. Such public patronage thus tends to reproduce and complement the socio-cultural effects of the market itself. It seems unhelpful, then, to attempt to analyse its operation through the notion of a distinctively 'post-market' set of relations of literary production. This is not to suggest that such relations are unimaginable or that they can never come into existence. But to be able to identify 'post-market' institutions of cultural production will require that we first know what a post-capitalist society would actually look like. I doubt we are in any position to do so at present. In the meantime, state sponsorship is surely better analysed in terms of the more general problem of state regulation of the market. We shall return to this matter below.

We have observed how capitalist authorial relations of production generally superseded earlier forms of institutedness and patronage. This has entailed a corollary transformation in the forms of organisation and self-organisation of writers, that is, in authorial organisations, or 'formations' as Williams (1981: 57) termed them. Williams himself identified three main kinds of pre-capitalist formation: 'bardic orders', that is, organisations of instituted artists; 'craft guilds', which were common in late-medieval cultural production; and 'academies', which eventually separated out from the guilds as 'art' began to distinguish itself from 'craft' (ibid.: 58–61). Successor institutions to both guilds and academies persist into modernity: respectively, the craft union and the academy as educational institution. But Williams also specifies two further kinds of formation as distinctive to the capitalist mode of cultural production: the 'professional society' and the artistic 'movement'. Professional societies are organisations of market professionals, sometimes augmented by corporate professionals, which aim to further their collective economic interests in the cultural marketplace. As such, they are of only historically recent provenance: the French Société des Gens de Lettres was founded in 1838, the British Society of Authors in 1888, the Authors League of America in 1912, the Australian Society of Authors as late as 1963. Movements, by contrast, are organised around essentially non-economic objectives; this is 'a quite different type of cultural formation, in which artists come together in pursuit of some specific artistic aim' (ibid.: 62). As Williams notes, movements of this type – circles, schools, 'isms' of various kinds – have been of central importance to the recent history of the arts. He develops a relatively sophisticated theoretical framework for their analysis and applies it to three concrete instances, the circle around William Godwin, the Pre-Raphaelite Brotherhood and the Bloomsbury Group. The detail need not detain us here, but we should note his conclusion that:

> no sociological analysis of formations can replace either general history or more specific individual studies. Yet it is still an

> indispensable kind of analysis, since there is normally a very wide gap between, on the one hand, general history and the associated general history of particular arts, and, on the other hand, individual studies.
>
> (Williams 1981: 86)

Perhaps the most distinctive feature of artistic movements in the modern period has been their recurrent aspiration to the status of 'avant-garde', a term most readily translatable into English as 'vanguard', but more commonly rendered in the French. Insofar as we can speak of 'aesthetic modernism' as a generic category, it is clear that such modernisms entailed 'a distinguishable group of assumptions, founded on a broadly symbolist aesthetics, an *avant-garde* view of the artist, and a notion of a relationship of crisis between art and history' (Bradbury and McFarlane 1976: 29). In the avant-garde conception, the role of the intellectual is understood as that of cultural leader, much like the revolutionary vanguard in the Leninist view of politics. There is no doubting the novelty of such formations. As Poggioli observed: 'It is evident that such a concept...is present in the Western historical consciousness only in our epoch, with the most remote temporal limits being the various preludes to the romantic experience' (Poggioli 1968: 15). Other observers are even more insistent on the phenomenon's historical recency: like Bradbury and McFarlane, Williams sees the avant-garde as distinctive to the period between 1890 and 1930 (Williams 1981: 83); for Bürger, who seeks to establish a very clear distinction between high modernist 'Aestheticism' and the 'historical avant-garde' proper, the focus falls even more decisively on the 1920s (Bürger 1984: 22). Jameson toys with the idea that the postmodern condition has rendered such avant-garde formations obsolete: 'we are beyond the avant-gardes', he writes, 'the collaborative...eschews the organization of a movement or a school, ignores the vocation of style, and omits the trappings of the manifesto or program' (Jameson 1991: 167). There is much truth in this, no doubt, but the obvious contra-instance, ironically enough, is one Jameson knows well: cyberpunk science fiction, which Lewis Shiner even described as 'the Movement' (Shiner 1992: 25).

In most pre-capitalist literary modes of production, there is a close 'fit' between the social status of the authorial role and that of the particular people who happen to inhabit it. This is much less true of the capitalist literary mode of production. As Eagleton put it:

> The specificity of the articulation between 'general' and literary social relations in capitalist formations is to be found in the fact that...the literary social relations...do not necessarily reproduce these [general] social relations as they hold between the *particular individual agents of the literary productive process*.... An aristocratic novelist may be consumed by proletarian readers, or *vice versa*, but these 'general' social relations of the particular agents are 'cancelled' by the market relations of literary commodity production.
>
> (Eagleton 1976: 53)

Novelists are almost invariably either market or corporate professionals in Williams's terms, 'petty-bourgeoisie' in the more Marxian terms Eagleton would have deployed; writers for television and the press are more likely to be 'corporate professionals', or in Marxian terms 'new petty bourgeoisie' (cf. Wright 1978: 61–83). But insofar as writers also occupy 'non-literary' class positions, then in principle these may be quite varied. Just how varied is, of course, a matter for empirical investigation. For France, the best-known work is that by Escarpit; for England, that by Williams and by Altick.

Escarpit's main interests were in the geographical distribution of writers between Paris and the provinces and in the effects of generation and age on literary productivity. He did, however, attempt an account of their class backgrounds, though interestingly not their gender balance. Comparing the occupations of a sample of nineteenth-century canonical French authors with those of their parents, Escarpit found that 8 per cent of the writers came from aristocratic family backgrounds, 84 per cent from the middle classes, 8 per cent from the manual working class and peasantry; and that 91 per cent were themselves middle-class professionals, 52 per cent professional writers or artists. The details are given in Table 4.2. Escarpit contrasts these findings with figures for the sixteenth, seventeenth and eighteenth centuries, which pointed to a wider range of social origins, with writers more likely to come, not only from the nobility (28 per cent),

Table 4.2 The social origins of nineteenth-century French writers and their parents (percentage distribution)

Social origin	*Parents*	*Writers*
Leisure aristocracy	8	9
Clergy	0	4
Army, navy	24	4
Liberal professions and universities	16	8
Industries, businesses and banks	20	0
Diplomatic and administrative posts	4	16
Lesser administrative posts and employees	8	8
Writers and artists	8	52
Politicians	4	8
Technicians	0	0
Manual workers and peasants	8	0

Source: Escarpit (1971: 36).

as might be expected, but also from the working class and peasantry (10 per cent). Moreover, this embourgeoisement of writing appeared to persist from the nineteenth into the twentieth century: of 128 French novels published in 1954, 57 per cent were written by professional writers or academics, 17 per cent by lawyers or civil servants and 7 per cent by engineers or doctors of medicine (Escarpit 1971: 36–7). Escarpit's conclusion is clear:

> from one generation to another, a concentration occurs around a middle zone of the social scale which constitutes what we should call the 'literary milieu'.... This phenomenon...is characteristic of the nineteenth and twentieth centuries. It did not always exist.
>
> (Escarpit 1971: 37)

In *The Long Revolution* Williams conducted a long-range study of 350 canonical writers, drawn from the *Oxford Introduction to English Literature*, for the period 1470–1920. Though he chose not to represent the findings in tabular form, I have compiled Tables 4.3 and 4.4 from this data. Comparison of the educational and social-class backgrounds of these writers over nine sub-periods led Williams to four main conclusions: that the relative popularity of Elizabethan

Table 4.3 The social origins (father's occupation) of English writers, 1480–1930

Social origin	*Period (assigned on the basis of the tenth year after the particular writer's birth)*								
	1480–1530	*1530–80*	*1580–1630*	*1630–80*	*1680–1730*	*1730–80*	*1780–1830*	*1830–80*	*1880–1930*
Nobility	3	3	0	2	} 2	2	1	0	1
Gentry	8	12	9	7		0	8	7	7
Professional	4	9	13	7	13	11	25	31	30
Merchants	0	4	1	0	1	1	9	6	2
Tradesmen	0	3	4	3	2	4	5	} 9	5
Craftsmen	1	5	1	2	1	3	5		4
Farmers	2	0	2	0	0	4	2	0	2
Labourers	0	0	0	0	0	0	1	0	2
Uncertain	3	2	3	1	0	0	1	0	0
TOTAL	21	38	33	22	19	25	57	53	53

Source: derived from Williams (1965: 255–63).

Table 4.4 The educational backgrounds of English writers, 1480–1930

Educational background	*Period (assigned on the basis of the tenth year after the particular writer's birth)*								
	1480–1530	*1530–80*	*1580–1630*	*1630–80*	*1680–1730*	*1730–80*	*1780–1830*	*1830–80*	*1880–1930*
National grammar schools	4	8	12	6	6	4	18	19	32
Local grammar schools	5	9	9	7	9	8	14	16	8
Scottish/Irish local schools	0	0	0	0	0	5	4	7	0
Private schools	0	0	0	0	0	0	0	0	2
Elementary education only	0	0	0	0	0	0	0	0	4
Dissenting academies	0	0	0	1	0	0	0	2	0
Home or private tuition	5	2	3	4	2	3	16	7	4
Uncertain	7	19	9	4	2	5	5	2	3
Oxford or Cambridge University	17	27	28	13	8	8	24	24	32
Other university	2	2	0	4	0	4	9	15	5
Not university or uncertain	2	9	5	5	11	13	24	14	16
TOTAL	21	38	33	22	19	25	57	53	53

Source: derived from Williams (1965: 255–63).

drama is correlated with the relatively diverse class background of its writers; that the more socially limited drama of the period 1580–1680 and the class-based Restoration theatre are correlated with a corresponding narrowing of social-class backgrounds; that, in the eighteenth century, there is an apparent correlation between the new middle-class literature and new middle-class writers; and that the late nineteenth century witnesses a social and imaginative narrowing of the literary mainstream, partly offset by the special importance of 'minority' groups, such as women and foreigners (Williams 1965: 264–5).

Altick's 1962 study of 1,100 British writers over the period 1800–1935 provided more detail than Williams, but generally confirmed the earlier study's findings on class and education. As Tables 4.5 and 4.6 clearly show, the great majority of nineteenth- and twentieth-century writers were both middle class (83.9 per cent for the period 1800–35, 84.2 per cent for 1900–35) and university educated (52.5 per cent for 1800–35, 72.3 per cent for 1900–35). Altick also specifically charted the progressive professionalisation of writing: 17 out of the 282 writers in the 1800–35 sample were professional journalists, 37 out of 363 in the 1900–35 sample (Altick 1978: 58–9). Like Escarpit, both Williams and Altick detected the paradox that, as the book trade cultivated its new mass market, a largely middle-class profession wrote for an increasingly working-class audience. Similar patterns have also been found elsewhere. Coser, Kadushin and Powell's survey of 219 American writers found them overwhelmingly middle class and well educated: many were professors (40 per cent of even the general 'trade' authors), about half the remainder were other kinds of professional, the rest editors and journalists (Coser *et al.* 1985: 232–3). A survey of 183 Australian writers found that 56 per cent were university educated, 21 per cent to a level resulting in postgraduate academic qualifications (Australia Council 1983: 15).

The lack of any necessary fit between literary and general social relations under capitalism is in fact more readily observable for gender than for class. Where the overlap between general and social relations is more or less exact, as in bardic orders of instituted artists, patriarchal relations simply precluded the possibility of a female bard. By contrast, the anonymity and autonomy of authorship under capitalist

Table 4.5 The social origins of British writers, 1800–1935: class

Class (father's occupation)	*Period (according to the date when writers begin to produce their significant work)*							
	1800–35		*1835–70*		*1870–1900*		*1900–35*	
	No.	%	No.	%	No.	%	No.	%
Upper class (nobility, gentry)	26	12.7	26	11.3	13	7.9	24	10.0
Upper middle class (bankers, merchants, etc.)	36		25		20		10	
Middle middle class:								
Arts and professions	74		128		83		137	
Other	34		32		27		49	
Lower middle class (tradesmen, artisans, etc.)	28		18		18		6	
Total middle class	172	83.9	203	87.8	148	90.3	202	84.2
Labourers	7	3.4	2	0.9	3	1.8	14	5.8
TOTAL	205	100	231	100	164	100	240	100

Source: derived from Altick (1978: 51–2).

Table 4.6 The educational backgrounds of British writers, 1800–1935

Educational background	*Period (according to the date when writers begin to produce their significant work)*							
	1800–35		*1835–70*		*1870–1900*		*1900–35*	
	No.	%	No.	%	No.	%	No.	%
Little or no schooling	20	11.3	13	5.9	7	4.1	19	7.2
Education ended at secondary level	64	36.2	62	27.9	43	25.0	54	20.5
University or comparable institution	93	52.5	147	66.2	122	70.9	191	72.3
TOTAL	177	100	222	100	172	100	264	100

Source: Altick (1978: 53).

Table 4.7 The social origins of British writers, 1800–1935: gender

Gender	*Period (according to the date when writers begin to produce their significant work)*							
	1800–35		*1835–70*		*1870–1900*		*1900–35*	
	No.	%	No.	%	No.	%	No.	%
Females	59	20.9	49	16.1	56	21.4	80	22.0
Males	223	79.1	256	83.9	206	78.6	283	78.0
TOTAL	282	100	305	100	262	100	363	100

Source: Altick (1978: 50).

relations of literary production clearly permits women writers, even in the presence of more generally patriarchal gender relations. The prevalence of male pseudonyms during what Showalter termed the first 'feminine' phase in the development of the English 'female tradition' (1978: 19) is evidence of precisely such lack of fit between literary and social relations. Both Williams (1965: 260) and Altick pointed to the significance of women writers in nineteenth-century England. In Table 4.7, again taken from Altick's survey, women make up about 20 per cent of the sample in all four periods.

Coser, Kadushin and Powell report exactly the same figure for the proportion of women in their sample of contemporary American writers (1985: 233). By contrast, the Australia Council's survey of contemporary Australian writers suggests a very different pattern: 45 per cent of the writers in its sample were women, as compared to only 9 per cent of composers, 15 per cent of musicians and 38 per cent of visual artists (Australia Council 1983: 13). As Moers concluded: 'Literature is the only intellectual field to which women, over a long period of time, have made an indispensable contribution.... Here, in the history of literature alone, women have been both central and female' (Moers 1978: ix). The obvious weakness in Escarpit, Williams and Altick is their shared dependence on retrospective canonisation for the definition of their samples. The total number of published writers was clearly very much larger than this: from a comparison between census data and the number of new titles, Cross calculates that 'there were about 20,000 persistent nineteenth-century writers' in England (1985: 3). If canonisation is the effect of a tradition as selective as Williams believed, then there is good reason to question whether such small samples can be considered socially representative. Spender's 'by no means definitive' list of 568 novels by 106 eighteenth-century women novelists certainly suggested that this problem might be particularly acute in the case of gender (Spender 1986: 119–37). That said, Lovell was surely right to insist that Altick's 'figure of 20 per cent...is still very high for a middle-class profession'. She was right, too, to add that 'It would be high even today in a profession which is not feminized' (Lovell 1987: 82).

As we noted in Chapter 2, traditional humanist literary criticism understood its task essentially as that of 'interpreting' the 'work' so as to discover its authoritative meaning, that is, the meaning intended by the author. Structuralist and post-structuralist semiology, by contrast, has revelled in the theoretical implications of the 'death of the author' as announced by Barthes and subsequently endorsed by Foucault. By this Barthes didn't mean to suggest that no one writes books, or that books somehow write themselves, but rather that literary meaning is always much more than the meaning intended by the writer, the writer therefore much less than the sole 'author' of such meaning. No doubt Barthes overstated his case. But, as Wolff observed, all art is indeed collectively produced; the values expressed in art are ideological and, hence, systematically related to wider socio-economic structures; the materials of literary technique and form are also collective constructs; and the reader does play an active role in the construction of literary meaning (Wolff 1993: 118–21). Wolff herself was distinctly cautious, nonetheless, in the face of the more extreme implications of Barthesian and post-Barthesian anti-humanism. The 'author' retains a 'central relevance', she concluded, if 'understood as constituted in language, ideology, and social relations' (ibid.: 136). For Wolff, at least, there was still a more than residual 'role of the writer'.

Such caution has become unfashionable in our postmodernist intellectual climate. And there are indeed good reasons to be sceptical of socially authoritative (that is, canonical) accounts of authorial intention. The past can only ever be reconstructed in the present, as part of Williams's 'selective tradition', and such tradition will be powerfully shaped by contemporary interests that are as much 'social' and ideological as disinterestedly 'scholarly'. But when the selection of tradition ceases to be the prerogative of relatively autonomous institutions of canon formation, whether academic or religious, it by no means follows that the process of selection is thereby itself superseded. Quite the contrary, social pressure is then merely much more likely to be exerted either directly through the state or through the market. Consider as an example the strange fate of Orwell's *Nineteen Eighty-Four*. As we have seen, he had considerable difficulty in finding a publisher for *Animal Farm*. Once published, however, the book proved a great success: the first impression of 4,500 copies sold out very quickly in August 1945; a second impression of 10,000 followed in November and the book has been continuously in print ever since;

Harcourt Brace published it in the United States in 1946, where it was selected as a Book-of-the-Month Club choice; subsequently, it has been translated into virtually every major language. Orwell's British and American publishers were thus only too happy to take on *Nineteen Eighty-Four*, first published in June 1949. Warburg sold nearly 50,000 copies in Britain and Harcourt Brace 170,000 in the United States during the first year of publication alone. This too was selected as a Book-of-the-Month Club choice, selling a further 190,000 copies during this first year. Like *Animal Farm*, it has never since been out of print (Crick 1980: 336, 393).

Both *Animal Farm* and *Nineteen Eighty-Four* became key Cold War texts, central elements in an emergent ideology insisting that socialism necessarily led to tyranny. This reading began to be developed in the United States almost as soon as the books had been published, that is, at a time when Eric Blair, the individual human being who wrote under the pseudonym George Orwell, was still as a matter of biological fact a not quite yet dead author. In 1949 Orwell, unlike Shakespeare or Milton, was still available for comment on the meaning of his own text. Confronted and confounded by the American reception, Orwell insisted that Warburg issue a press release including the following statement:

> the danger lies in the structure imposed...by the necessity to prepare for total war...if such societies...come into being there will be several super states.... These...will...be in opposition to each other or...will pretend to be much more in opposition than in fact they are. Two of the principal super states will obviously be the Anglo-American world and Eurasia. If these two great blocks line up as mortal enemies it is obvious that the Anglo-Americans will not take the name of their opponents and will not dramatise themselves on the scene of history as Communists. Thus they will have to find a new name for themselves. The name suggested in NINETEEN EIGHTY-FOUR is of course Ingsoc, but in practice a wide range of choices is open. In the U.S.A. the phrase 'Americanism' or 'hundred per cent Americanism' is suitable and the qualifying adjective is as totalitarian as anyone could wish.
>
> (quoted in Crick 1980: 395)

Still troubled by his new American readership, Orwell wrote to the American United Auto Workers Union (UAW) on 16 June 1949:

> My recent novel in NOT intended as an attack on Socialism or on the British Labour Party (of which I am a supporter) but as a show-up of the perversions to which a centralised economy is liable and which have been partly realised in Communism and Fascism.
>
> (Orwell 1970b: 564)

Crick deduced from this correspondence that:

> *Nineteen Eighty-Four* is a long premeditated, rational warning against totalitarian tendencies in societies like our own rather than a sick and sudden prophecy about a Soviet or neo-Nazi takeover, still less a scream of despair and recantation of his democratic Socialism.
>
> (Crick 1980: 397)

No doubt, this is only one amongst many possible readings of the Orwell text. Its author is still, after all, a deeply controversial figure, whose politics continue to excite the most partisan of responses, from Hitchens's (2002) almost uncritical enthusiasm to Lucas's (2003) barely disguised hostility. For the latter, Orwell had no real socialism to recant; for the former, he is the very model of what a socialist should have been. Crick's reading was more dispassionate, perhaps, but justified nonetheless on what are quite clearly humanist grounds: that it is indeed possible to recover something of an author's original intentions, especially if he should have made fairly determined, even desperate, attempts to explain them; and that such intentions can indeed provide the key to a privileged, if not necessarily the absolutely privileged, reading of a text. Neither of these propositions seems obviously unreasonable.

On 21 January 1950 Orwell died at University College Hospital in London (he had in fact written his letter to the UAW from a sanitorium). Now really dead, the author was finally unable to insist on his own or any other reading of the text. The dominant Cold War readings of *Nineteen Eighty-Four* and *Animal Farm* were constructed and sustained not by some abstract 'reader', as Barthes's account might lead us to suppose, but by precisely those institutionalised, politically and economically dominant, vested interests, both in the West and in the Soviet bloc, that Orwell himself had so cordially detested. There are other Orwell texts, of course, *Homage to Catalonia* for example, his memoirs of fighting on the Republican side during the Spanish Civil War. This was much less successful than either *Nineteen Eighty-Four* or *Animal Farm*: published in 1938, the first edition of 1,500 copies still hadn't sold out thirteen years later; there was no second edition in Orwell's lifetime; and when one finally appeared it was only as a necessary component in a Uniform Edition of Orwell's works (Crick 1980: 245). Yet this text is surely the key to an understanding of Orwell's own peculiar political position as an anti-capitalist, anti-Communist, libertarian socialist, in short, someone quite unamenable to either Soviet or western variants of Cold War ideology. Postmodern scepticism often professes as much indifference to the question of 'politics' as to that of authorial intention: never mind the principles, feel the textuality, as it were. But it is surely a matter of some consequence, for our understanding of both the texts and their subsequent receptions, that the Orwell who wrote both *Animal Farm* and *Nineteen Eighty-Four* was also the same individual human being who explained in 1946 that:

> The Spanish war and other events in 1936–7 turned the scale and thereafter I knew where I stood. Every line of serious work that I have written since 1936 has been written, directly or indirectly, *against* totalitarianism and *for* democratic Socialism.... What I have most wanted to do throughout the past ten years is to make political writing into an art.
>
> (Orwell 1970c: 28)

Readers and reading

In most societies literacy has been the prerogative of a very few, in many it has been altogether unknown. Writing was invented in Mesopotamia around 3500 BC, the first phonetic alphabet of consonants by Semitic peoples around 1500 BC, the first with vowels by the

Greeks around 720–700 BC (Ong 1988: 85, 89, 24). Near-universal literacy has become such a commonplace of contemporary western culture as to acquire a certain taken-for-grantedness. But it is, in fact, an entirely 'artificial technology', in Ong's words, 'the technology which has shaped and powered the intellectual activity of modern man' (ibid.: 83). As Williams insisted, reading is a highly specialised form of cultural reception, requiring extensive cultural training:

> while anyone in the world...can watch dance or look at sculpture or listen to music,...some forty per cent of the world's present inhabitants can make no contact whatever with a piece of writing, and in earlier periods this percentage was very much larger. Writing as a cultural technique is wholly dependent on forms of specialized training, not only...for producers but also, and crucially, for receivers.
>
> (Williams 1981: 93)

Auerbach estimated that, at its height, the total reading public of the Roman Empire could have numbered 'no more than a few tens of thousands' (Auerbach 1965: 239), sharing a relatively undifferentiated literary culture written in the distinctly 'literary' languages of 'High Latin' and Greek (as distinct from vernacular Latin and the various 'barbarian' vernaculars). The last fragments of this imperial reading public must have disappeared from the former Western Empire by the beginning of the sixth century, he concluded. Thereafter, Latin continued as a purely written language – the *only* written language in the West – effectively monopolised by an isolated, geographically dispersed, clerical intelligentsia of scholars, teachers and students within the Catholic Church. Medieval Latin was thus a sacred language, the common property of a small trans-European bilingual intelligentsia, mediating between spoken and profane vernaculars on the one hand and the written truth-language on the other. This configuration, though strange to contemporary sensibility, is by no means peculiar to medieval Catholic Christendom. As Anderson points out, analogous structures recur in both the Chinese Middle Kingdom and the Ummah Islam (B. Anderson 1991: 12–13). A secular vernacular literature begins to develop in Western Europe only in the twelfth century: the first 'literary' vernacular manuscripts appear around 1200 AD; a courtly public emerges during the thirteenth century in France, Provence, Germany and, most importantly, in Italy; in Bologna and in the Tuscan cities, more or less simultaneously, there are the beginnings of a modern reading public, organised around the great urban patrician families for whom Dante wrote (Auerbach 1965: 293–4, 296). During the fourteenth century, initially in Italy, but later elsewhere, a small vernacular reading public emerges, as Italian and then later other European vernaculars evolve into literary languages.

The scale and significance of this vernacular reading public were enormously expanded by the impact of printing. As Febvre and Martin concluded: 'by the 16th century the printed book had been produced in sufficient quantities to make it accessible to anyone who could read' (1976: 262). In France calendars, lives of the saints, almanacs and Books of Hours, in England popular ballads and chapbooks (or joke books) all sold to a relatively wide general public (ibid.: 264; Williams 1965: 178). Williams suggests that, in late-medieval England, books were bought by a small professional reading public, concentrated in the clergy, law and medicine, and by a small general audience (ibid.: 178). For France, a guide to the social composition of the more affluent sections at least of this public is provided by the catalogues of private libraries drawn up before solicitors as part of inheritance proceedings. Lawyers of various kinds owned 126 out of 377 such libraries dating from the late fifteenth and the sixteenth centuries, non-academic clergy owned 87, university teachers and students 18, merchants, tradesmen and artisans 66 (Febvre and Martin 1976: 263). In England, in particular, very high levels of literacy seem to have been attained by the mid-seventeenth century. As Altick concluded: 'it seems likely that in the Tudor and Stuart eras the ability to read was more democratically distributed among the English people than it would again be until at least the end of the eighteenth century' (Altick 1998: 18). Milton's *Paradise Lost* sold 1,300 copies within two years of publication; chapbooks could sell as many as 20,000 (Williams 1965: 181). Both the Protestant Reformation and the English Revolution clearly have some direct bearing on the expansion of reading during the seventeenth century. Altick and Williams agree that popular literacy rates almost certainly declined after the Restoration in 1660, but that a middle-class reading public persisted nonetheless. It was this public which expanded once more during the latter half of the eighteenth century: London publishers were producing an average of 372 books per annum in the decade 1792–1802, as compared with about 150 per annum in the decades immediately prior to the Revolution (ibid.: 185, 181).

During the eighteenth century, literacy seems to have increased in France, England and its North American colonies and probably also in Scandinavia and Germany (Graff 1987: 182). In France literacy rates virtually doubled during the eighteenth century, although they were consistently much higher in the northern and south-western provinces and departments and amongst men as compared to women (ibid.: 192–3). The percentage of men able to sign the marriage register increased from an average of 40 per cent for the decade 1740–9 to 46 per cent for the immediate pre-Revolutionary decade, 1780–9, and 49 per cent for the revolutionary decade, 1790–9; the percentage of women from 19 per cent to 25 per cent and 30 per cent respectively (ibid.: 195). The reading public expanded proportionately, but it seems to have been surprisingly conservative in taste. As Graff concludes: 'the trend of the evidence...indicates a greater weight of tradition, "inertia," than change or modernity in the distribution of public materials' (ibid.: 218). In England the expansion was less genuinely popular in the eighteenth than in the seventeenth century. Watt judged it overwhelmingly middle class and urban in character and argued it was essentially a result of the increase in the total size of this particular class. 'The price of a novel', he wrote, 'would feed a family for a week or two.... The novel in the eighteenth century was closer to the economic capacity of the middle-class additions to the reading public...but it was not...a popular literary form' (Watt 1963: 43). He also stressed the growing significance of female readers within the middle class. The century witnessed a new 'literary balance of power', he concluded, tilting toward the new middle class, and thereby favouring ease of entertainment over more traditional critical standards. Hence the development of the new realism in Defoe and Richardson.

By comparison, the late nineteenth-century expansion really does seem to mark the inauguration of a mass reading public. In part, this is a direct result of a general increase in literacy rates, itself an effect of the expansion of popular education. Marked increases in literacy are observable throughout North America and much of Europe during the nineteenth century. In the United States the national illiteracy rate declined from 20 per cent in 1870 to 10.7 per cent in 1900 (Graff 1987: 376). In England and Wales the percentage able to sign the marriage register increased from 58.4 per cent in 1839 to 94.65 per cent in 1893 (Williams 1965: 187). In France the percentage of men able to sign the marriage register increased from 68.4 per cent for the years 1851–5 to 93.0 per cent for 1891–5, the percentage of women from 52.6 per cent to 88.6 per cent (Allen 1991: 59). For Britain, Williams also stresses the importance of a number of other factors: the expansion of the railway system (and hence of railway bookshops); the dramatic fall in book prices after the introduction of yellow-back books in 1851; a general rise in disposable incomes; and the development of free public libraries (Williams 1965: 189–91). As Altick observed:

> the democratizing of reading led to a far-reaching revolution in English culture. No longer were books and periodicals written chiefly for the comfortable few; more and more, as the century progressed, it was the ill-educated mass audience...that called the tune to which writers and editors danced.
>
> (Altick 1998: 5)

By the beginning of the twentieth century, a mass market for both novels and newspapers had been securely established in England, France, the United States and much of Western Europe. Writing in the 1950s, Altick concluded that: ‘By 1900 the...reading public had attained substantially the size and character it possesses today...the major tendencies in the past half-century were, for the most part, continuations of those already in existence’ (ibid.: 365). For Altick, as for most other mid-century Western European commentators, the ‘problem’ of functional literacy had been effectively superseded by that of cultural literacy: ‘Nearly everybody reads something nowadays, but only a small minority read wisely or well’ (ibid.: 375). Altick’s original study coincided with the beginnings of British commercial television, however, and at one point he noted in passing the theoretical possibility that other mass media might eventually render printing obsolete. A half-century later, we are in a much better position to judge the effects of this and other developments in the audio-visual and printed media. How much do people read? Who reads? What do they read? And what do they get out of it?

It seems clear that reading is still very widespread: 45 per cent of respondents to a 1980 British survey were 'currently' reading a book; 48.5 per cent of a 1994 Australian survey had read a book during the previous seven days (Mann 1982: 147; Australia Council 1995: 13). Tables 4.8, 4.9 and 4.10 chart the social composition, measured by class, gender and age, of Mann's pioneering 1968–9 sample survey of English bookshop customers and library borrowers. Mann's readers seemed to be overwhelmingly, but not exclusively, middle class: at a time when managerial and professional groups made up only 15 per cent of the United Kingdom working population, they accounted for some 66 per cent of non-student London bookshop customers and 12 per cent of non-student library borrowers; by contrast, manual workers made up 60 per cent of the working population, but only 3 per cent of London bookshop customers and 18 per cent of library borrowers (Mann 1971: 105, 127). In this survey both library borrowers and bookshop customers turned out to be disproportionately male; and both library borrowing and book purchasing appeared to decline with age (ibid.: 101–2, 123–4). More recent British studies have tended to confirm Mann's findings. Annual surveys from the early to mid-1980s discovered a clear positive correlation between class and reading, for example, but nonetheless found that well over one-third of the respondents from social classes D and E claimed to be currently reading (Euromonitor 1989: 122–3). A 1994 Australian survey found clear positive correlations between income, education and reading, a clear negative correlation between age and reading, and a significantly higher rate of reading amongst females than amongst males (Australia Council 1995: 15). These figures were for books in general, of course, rather than for 'literature' in particular. But literature, or 'fiction' at any rate, is still apparently of central importance to contemporary reading habits, especially as indicated by library borrowings. Mann found that 'literature, poetry, drama', 'general

Table 4.8 Social composition of English bookshop customers and library borrowers, 1968–9 survey: class*

Class (occupational background)	*London customers*		*Provincial customer*		*Provincial borrowers*		*% of population*
	No.	%	No.	%	No.	%	
Higher managerial, administrative and professional	43	13	23	10	11	3	3
Intermediate managerial, administrative and professional	172	53	43	20	36	9	12
Supervisory, clerical, junior managerial	83	26	92	42	196	51	17
Skilled manual	5	2	27	12	53	14	34
Semi- and unskilled manual	3	1	5	2	14	4	26
Casual workers	–	–	–	–	2	1	} 8
Pensioners	–	–	–	–	34	9	}
Housewives	11	3	20	9	38	10	
Unemployed	1	–	–	–	–	–	
No answer	6	2	9	4	4	1	
TOTAL	324	100	219	99	388	102	100

Source: derived from Mann (1971: 105, 127).

Table 4.9 Social composition of English bookshop customers and library borrowers, 1968–9 survey: gender

Gender	*London customers*		*Provincial customers*		*Provincial borrowers*	
	No.	%	No.	%	No.	%
Male	415	66	209	61	278	55
Female	218	34	131	39	232	45
Not recorded	13	–	–	–	–	–
TOTAL	646	100	340	100	510	100

Source: derived from Mann (1971: 101–2, 123–4).

Table 4.10 Social composition of English bookshop customers and library borrowers, 1968–9 survey: age

Age	*London customers*		*Provincial customers*		*Provincial borrowers*	
	No.	%	No.	%	No.	%
Under 16 16–20	} 113	} 18	10 85	3 25	21 118	4 23
21–24	176	27	73	21	75	15
25–34	190	29	56	16	78	15
35–44	93	14	51	15	69	14
45–54	46	7	28	8	52	10
55–64	22	2	22	6	52	10
65	5	1	15	4	45	9
No answer	1	–	0	–	–	–
TOTAL	646	98	340	98	510	100

Source: derived from Mann (1971: 101–2, 123–4).

fiction' and 'light fiction' together accounted for 26 per cent of books bought and 60 per cent of books borrowed (Mann 1971: 115, 131). More recently, 69 per cent of the readers sampled in a 1988 survey claimed to be 'currently' reading 'fiction' (Euromonitor 1989: 125). The 1994 Australia Council survey found that 30 per cent of the books bought and 61 per cent of books borrowed were 'fiction'; by comparison, 'poetry and plays' accounted for only 2 per cent of books bought and close to 0 per cent of those borrowed (Australia Council 1995: 143, 157). To the extent that ours is still a print culture, the novel is still its preferred literary form.

There is also evidence to suggest that different literary genres are differentially preferred by different social classes. Bourdieu's study of the social distribution of French cultural tastes and practices in the 1960s asked its respondents to identify the three kinds of book they most preferred. The class distribution of preferences for eight genres is shown in Table 4.11. The most striking feature here is probably the clear antipathy to classics, poetry and philosophical essays in the working classes, to philosophy in the middle classes and to love stories in the upper. It is interesting and understandable that readers likely to be the least travelled were the most interested in travel writing. More generally, there were clear positive correlations between higher class position and a preference for modern authors, classics, poetry and philosophy, clear negative correlations for love stories, travel and thrillers. But despite these variations, there was evidence of a general preference across the classes both for prose as a medium and the novel as a form. It is curious, then, but not at all surprising, that historical novels should have been popular with all social classes. We might note in passing, however, that this particular preference was not shared by one class fraction within the upper class, that is, 'teachers in higher and secondary education and artistic producers', whose class position is based on very strong claims to cultural distinction (Bourdieu 1984: 530).

A recent Australian study, inspired in part by Bourdieu and based on a very large national survey of the cultural practices and preferences of over 2,750 adults, attempted to provide a 'social cartography' of everything that counts as 'culture', from 'home-based leisure activities' to book reading and the 'use of libraries, museums and art galleries' (Bennett *et al.* 1999: 1–2). Whilst its general findings need not detain us here, the evidence on reading is interesting. Bennett, Emmison and Frow found substantial evidence of gender and class differentials in reading habits. The women in their sample were significantly more predisposed towards reading than men: whereas 69.7 per cent of women claimed to read often and only 4 per cent hardly ever, 48.9 per cent of men read often and 12.8 per cent hardly ever (ibid.: 148).

Table 4.11 Distribution of preferences for different types of book by different classes in France, 1963/1967–8 (%)

Class	*Type of book (respondents were asked to choose the three they most preferred)*							
	Love stories	*Travel*	*Thrillers*	*Historical novels*	*Modern authors*	*Classics*	*Poetry*	*Philosophical essays*
Working classes	36	61	57	40	19	10	8	2
Middle classes	23	45	43	45	40	28	21	12
Upper classes	6	33	38	41	42	35	25	25

Source: Bourdieu (1984: 530–1).

Moreover, they tended to read different types of book: whilst 26.2 per cent of the women preferred romances and only 1.8 per cent of the men, 22.0 per cent of the men preferred books on 'sport and leisure', only 2.7 per cent of the women (ibid.: 150). Class differences were also marked, despite the supposedly 'classless' nature of Australian society: the strongest class preference for poetry, for example, was amongst employers (5.2 per cent), that for crime and mystery amongst managers (34.3 per cent), for sport and leisure amongst manual workers (19.1 per cent) (ibid.: 165). In Chapters 5 and 6 we will explore something of how Gothic and science fictional systems of intertextuality are connected to Mary Shelley's novel *Frankenstein*. It is interesting, then, to note what Bennett, Emmison and Frow found about the contemporary Australian readerships for these sub-forms. SF was significantly more popular than horror, they discovered, but also very much more gendered as masculine: whereas 5.0 per cent of women and 6.3 per cent of men preferred 'horror' to other genres, 5.2 per cent of women and 14.5 per cent of men preferred SF (ibid.: 150). Turning to class, they found the highest preference for horror amongst manual workers (7.2 per cent), for SF among supervisors (13.3 per cent) (ibid.: 165).

We know that people read and we know that they read novels. What seems much less clear, however, is what exactly it is that they make of the books they read. As we saw in Chapter 2, literary and cultural theory has very often represented the experience of reading as differing substantially according to whether what is read is 'high' or 'low' culture. High culture had almost invariably been understood as requiring the active engagement of the reader, popular culture their merely passive acquiescence, and this had been so whether the distinction was theorised as between literary and culinary works or minority culture and mass civilisation, the avant-garde and the culture industries or authentic art and ideology, the text of *jouissance* and the text of *plaisir*, open and closed texts, *écriture féminine* and patriarchal discourse. This distinction is much less obviously present in Williams, where the opposition between innovation and reproduction is not intended as analogous to that between minority and mass cultures. And in the more postmodern versions of post-structuralist semiology, the reader is so constructed as to be able to read almost any text virtually as they please, conformingly, resistingly, negotiatedly, or whatever.

Each of these last two moves seems necessary, especially given the sheer tenacity of the high/low and active/passive tropes. We need to acknowledge that the elite/popular opposition provides far too undifferentiated a sense of what different texts are actually like. As Williams insisted: 'all kinds of writing produce meaning and value...we have to accept it as a true range, without any categorical division between what is done on one side of a line and what is done on the other' (Williams 1979b: 326). And we also need to acknowledge the plurality of possible readers' responses to any given text.

That said, reading is not so much a set of random responses as a definable social practice organised within identifiable socio-discursive spaces: for even the most resisting reader, it is actually quite difficult to laugh at *Schindler's Ark*. Theoretically, what is required is some concept akin to Bennett's notion of the 'reading formation', by which he meant a 'set of intersecting discourses which productively activate a given body of texts and the relations between them in a specific way' (Bennett 1983: 216). Bourdieu's three zones of taste are probably best understood as reading formations of this kind. In practice, however, such formations are almost certainly structured by other socio-demographic factors, gender, ethnicity, generation, sexuality, and so on, as well as by class. Empirically, we need to know a great deal more about how people read. Ironically, the first research in this area was probably Richards's *Practical Criticism* (1929), simultaneously a defining moment in literary-critical cultural elitism and an empirical investigation into reader response. Richards's famous 'experiment' confronted a sample of readers, the majority Cambridge undergraduates studying for an honours degree in English, with poems marked by neither a title nor the name of an author. His findings were very clear:

> Without further clues (authorship, period, school, the sanction of an anthology, or the hint of a context) the task of 'making up their minds about it'...was felt to be really beyond their powers. The extraordinary variety of views put forward, and the reckless, desperate character of so many...indicate...how unprepared for such a testing encounter the majority of the readers were.
>
> (Richards 1929: 315)

For Richards, this served to demonstrate the inadequacy of the readers. Much more productively, his findings can be seen as powerful testimony to the practical importance of reading formations. If even these highly educated students no longer knew 'how' to read once cut loose from any appropriate socio-discursive context, then it seems more than likely that nor does anyone else. The point, of course, is that we are not normally bereft of such socio-discursive context, in short, reading is an irreparably social process.

If Richards's undergraduates were positioned in relation to a highly elite reading formation, its counterpart, at the other extreme of the socio-cultural hierarchy, may well be the 'fan' sub-culture. Especially important in sport, popular music and such literary and film genres as science fiction, 'fan' readers – literally, fanatics – approach their preferred texts with a kind of activist enthusiasm that almost beggars description. The most famous example from SF are the *Star Trek* fans, or 'Trekkers', whose conventions can involve thousands of people, dressing up in Star Fleet uniforms, 'filking' (singing songs, originally folk songs in particular, to especially adapted SF lyrics), trading memorabilia and so on. For structuralism, and to a large extent for semiology more generally, fans such as these appeared the most subjected of subjects, the most readerly of readers, near-slaves to the objects of their fanaticism. But recent quasi-ethnographic research has increasingly tended to suggest otherwise. Fan reading seems not only not passive, but also positively creative, to the point of stimulating cultural production, in the full sense of the active making of new artworks. Hence Jenkins's definition of 'fans' as:

> consumers who also produce, readers who also write, spectators who also participate.... Fans produce meanings and interpretations; fans produce art-works; fans produce communities; fans produce alternative identities. In each case, fans are drawing on materials from the dominant media and employing them in ways that serve their own interests and facilitate their own pleasures.
>
> (Jenkins 1992a: 214)

The essay on filking, from which this quotation is taken, forms part of a larger investigation into SF fandom, which includes Jenkins's *Textual*

Poachers (1992b) and the co-authored *Science Fiction Audiences* (Tulloch and Jenkins 1995). The term 'textual poaching', which appears in both the essay and the books, is borrowed from de Certeau, who used it to describe how subordinate sub-cultures appropriate materials from the dominant media so as to rework them in their own interests (Jenkins 1992b: 24–7; Tulloch and Jenkins 1995: 38–41; de Certeau 1984: 174). The analogy is with poaching from a gamekeeper (*braconner*), rather than poaching eggs (*pocher*). The filker, who borrows melodies from other established musicians and ideas for lyrics from *Star Trek* scripts, is thus precisely what de Certeau had meant by a *braconnier*.

Another interesting example of textual poaching, again from SF, is 'slash fiction'. The Jenkins essay mentions this in passing, when it refers to fan writers who may explore the 'erotic aspects of the texts', including even 'homoerotic romance between Kirk and Spock' (Jenkins 1992a: 215), the two male lead characters in the first of the *Star Trek* television series. But, as Jenkins knew well, and as he explores in *Textual Poachers* (Jenkins 1992b: 185–222), there is in fact a very large body of 'fanzine' – that is, fan-authored magazine – fiction devoted precisely to the theme of a gay relationship between Kirk and Spock. The 'slash' in slash fiction refers to that in 'K/S', a code indicating that the stories, artwork, etc. in the fanzine will be concerned with same-sex relationships. There are other slashed couples, but K/S pornography/erotica was the first and is still by far the most extensive and prolific. As Penley observes of *The 25th Year*, a collaborative K/S novel, published in 1991 and including the work of over thirty fan writers, poets and artists: 'Nothing better exemplifies the way slash writers have developed…a model of equality and individuality' (Penley 1997: 143). Perhaps the most striking finding to emerge from both Jenkins and Penley is that K/S fiction was overwhelmingly written, not by gay men, but by heterosexual women. Apparently, it is easier to imagine a genuinely egalitarian but sexual relationship between men 300 years into the future than between men and women in the present. As Penley concludes, these 'amateur women writers' are writing their own 'sexual and social utopias' (ibid.: 145) through the materials to hand, in short, they are poaching – actively, creatively and subversively.

The state, ideology and the market

As we noted earlier, the relations of literary production intersect, not only with the more general social relations of production, but also, and quite specifically, with the social relations of political power operating in and around the state. Paradoxically, the unprecedented commercialisation of cultural production inaugurated by print-capitalism precipitated, in turn, an enormous expansion of state intervention into the cultural process, in the form both of subsidy and of censorship. Subsidy need not detain us very long, since literary production, unlike some other forms of artistic production, has not normally been heavily subsidised in private-capitalist societies. In Britain, for example, the most important form of cultural subsidy is that dispensed by the English Arts Council, which planned to spend something like £2 billion during the period 2003–6. But this is directed overwhelmingly toward 'high' culture of the kind that can be performed by national 'flagship' companies such as the Royal Shakespeare Company, the National Theatre, Covent Garden and the English National Opera. There is no doubt that government funding can be used as a form of political control. The early attempts to tax the English Radical press out of existence, which we noted in Chapter 3, had as their obverse direct government subsidies to conservative newspapers: Walpole spent over £50,000 on these over a ten-year period; between 1789 and 1793 nine newspapers were in receipt of direct government funding; in addition, the government also made direct payments to individual journalists amounting to over £1,600 in 1792–3 (Williams 1965: 206, 208).

Censorship has been of much more direct importance to the literary process. From the fifteenth century until the eighteenth, the European book trade experienced repeated attempts by both church and state to control printing through 'licensing' systems. Exclusive rights to publish books were granted as early as the late fifteenth century in Italy, the early sixteenth century in France and Germany (Febvre and Martin 1976: 241). Licensing guaranteed the publisher exclusive rights over a book and thereby functioned as a primitive form of copyright (indeed, the first demands for such rights appear to have come from Milanese publishers themselves). However, by according the state the power to license these rights, it also functioned as a primitive form of pre-publication censorship. As Febvre and Martin observe: 'Under cover of copyright regulations the King [of France], and those other European monarchs who also adopted this system, kept a close watch on book production' (ibid.: 246). Licensing was first introduced in England in 1531 and continued until 1695 (Williams 1981: 100), interrupted only by a temporary breakdown during the Revolution. Conflict between freedom of expression and state policy is probably as old as state power itself. But, as Williams points out, there was real novelty in the attempt at prevention rather than retribution, a novelty clearly occasioned by printing, since the rapid and extensive mechanical reproduction of texts had meant these could reach an audience before ever retribution could be attempted. By and large, early modern licensing systems proved ultimately ineffective. As Febvre and Martin observed of their operation in France: 'the prime outcome of the policy...was the establishment, around the French borders...of a series of printing businesses producing pirated editions and editions of banned books in complete freedom' (Febvre and Martin 1976: 247). Eventually, the sheer size of the book trade compelled a shift to post-publication censorship by prosecution in both France and England.

Early modern censorship was directed against blasphemy on the one hand, sedition on the other, and the two were inextricably interconnected in societies where the dominant political discourse was itself in part religious. An English royal proclamation of 5 June 1558 nicely defined the aims of the censorship as the prevention of books 'whereby not onely God is dishonored, but also an encouragement geuen to disobey laweful princes and gouernors' (D. Thomas 1969: 9). As Charles I would later insist: 'No bishop, no king'. Such censorship is readily analysable as a form of political oppression, an operation of Althusser's repressive state apparatus both in its own defence and in that of the central ideological state apparatus, the church. The move to post-publication censorship seems to have been intended as a more efficient way of handling essentially the same problems. Significantly, the English Blasphemy Act dates from 1698, that is, from only three years after the end of licensing. Moreover, censorship by prosecution could also be supplemented by prohibitive levels of taxation: the first newspaper duties, imposed by the Stamp Acts of 1712, were explicitly designed, not to raise revenue, but as a 'way of suppressing libels'; the Newspaper Stamp Duties Act of 1819 deployed these taxes quite deliberately as a weapon against the Radical 'pauper press'. This fiscal censorship was seriously undermined by the 'War of the Unstamped Press' of 1831–6, which led to hundreds of prosecutions, but only finally ended with the repeal of the last Stamp Tax in 1855 (Williams 1965: 203, 209, 215; Altick 1998: 48, 327–8, 339–40). For all the tenacity with which the European dynastic states had resisted the development of a 'free press', Thomas concluded that, in England at least, 'from the end of the seventeenth century until the middle of the nineteenth there had been a growing freedom of expression on political and religious issues' (D. Thomas 1969: 6).

Developments thereafter are less easily summarised. Prosecution for blasphemy has indeed effectively fallen into disuse, at least in Western Europe. The issue remains alive in more overtly religious societies, especially in the Islamic world: the obvious example is the death sentence directed at Salman Rushdie by the Iranian Ayatollah Khomeini in 1989 for the publication of *The Satanic Verses* (cf. Spivak 1993). Overt political censorship for reasons of state has been augmented in most western societies, by such measures as the British Official Secrets Act of 1889 and by the extension of wider systems of state regulation, including those informal contacts between Jonathan Cape and the Ministry of Information. The nineteenth century also witnessed the emergence of much stricter sexual taboos: the first British Obscene Publications Act was passed in 1857; the second, which introduced a defence on grounds of literary merit, in 1959. In France the official reasons given for censorship reveal a long-run decline over time in anxieties about a possible threat to political and social authority, but a corresponding increase in concern to defend the moral order, especially in sexual matters (Allen 1991: 94). The details are given in Table 4.12. 'The relevant question', Thomas argued, 'is not "Does censorship exist?" but rather, "Under what sort of censorship do we now live?" ' (D. Thomas 1969: 7). He was absolutely right, of course: if all states censor, as indeed they do, then the interesting question becomes what they censor and why. But his own predisposition to view censorship as inherently undesirable deflected him from any consideration of its more creative possibilities. Hence the distinctly pessimistic conclusion:

> it is open to the Crown to take action against literature under the law of seditious libel, to say nothing of the Official Secrets Act; the Race Relations Act, and even such an unlikely piece of legislation as the Prices and Incomes Act of 1966.... If literary censorship is less strict...this may be just as much a reflection of the diminished status of literature as a token of liberal attitudes in government.... The technology of the late twentieth century offers the means of silencing men...by the most effective method of all, by ignoring them.
>
> (D. Thomas 1969: 315–16, 318)

Both the reference to the British Race Relations Act and the quite unconscious sexism of the language point toward what many would later see as exactly such creative possibilities. For, of course, one of the key issues in censorship since the late 1960s, when Thomas published this research, has been precisely the (largely unsuccessful) attempt by feminists to silence the pornography of *men*. Moreover, this has often been linked to an argument for other kinds of censorship, to be exercised by, or on behalf of, other oppressed or subordinate social groups. Until as late as the early 1970s, western political radicalism had been overwhelmingly opposed to censorship. The failure of the first British prosecution under the 1959 Act, against Penguin in 1960 for the paperback edition of Lawrence's *Lady Chatterley's Lover*, was widely applauded as a victory for progress and enlightenment

Table 4.12 Official reasons for the interdiction or modification of sampled censorship cases in France, 1814/15–1940 (%)

Period	*Political/social authority*	*Moral order*	*Other reasons*
1814/15–30	66	34	0
1830–48	65	35	0
1848–51	67	33	0
1851–70	47	50	3
1870–1940	17	62	21

Source: adapted from Allen (1991: 94).

(Hoggart himself had been a key witness for the defence). But only a decade later, Millett would denounce Lawrence as 'the evangelist of... "phallic consciousness"' and his novel as 'the transformation of masculine ascendancy into a mystical religion' (Millett 1977: 238). The argument was stated even more forcefully by Dworkin: 'We will know that we are free when the pornography no longer exists' (1981: 224). Dworkin and MacKinnon went on to draft a model anti-pornography ordinance, one version of which was eventually adopted by the city of Indianapolis. Like the censorship provisions of the British Race Relations Act, these American feminists were part of what Sutherland termed 'the censorship of enlightenment' (1982: 191–8). This reversal in enlightened sensibilities has occurred with extraordinary rapidity: 'The idea that pornography constitutes a "social harm" and is hence eligible for legal suppression – the very idea that the 1960s liberals and libertarians sought to laugh out of court as a Victorian prejudice – is once again gaining ground' (Hunter *et al.* 1993: 4).

Hunter, Saunders and Williamson took this very rapidity as the starting point for their own, generally Foucauldian, account of the development of the obscenity laws. As we observed in Chapter 2, Foucault had rejected the 'repression hypothesis', insisting that, since the end of the sixteenth century, the 'putting into discourse of sex' had been subjected to 'a mechanism of increasing excitement' (Foucault 1978: 12). His conclusion, directed against both Freud and Lawrence, is striking. Distinguishing between the 'idea' of 'sex' and the social organisation of 'sexuality', he wrote that:

> what we now perceive as the chronicle of a censorship and the difficult struggle to remove it will be seen rather as the centuries-long rise of a complex deployment for compelling sex to speak, for fastening our attention and concern upon sex, for getting us to believe in the sovereignty of its law when in fact we were moved by the power mechanisms of sexuality.
>
> (Foucault 1978: 158)

Seen in this light, pornography can be understood as 'a definite apparatus for transmitting norms of sexual conduct and feeling relayed in certain techniques and practices' (Hunter *et al.* 1993: 5); and obscenity legislation as part of this same complex of techniques and practices. From this perspective, Hunter, Saunders and Williamson are led to an account of the regulation of pornography, at once both more and less sympathetic than those suggested by the repression hypothesis: less so insofar as they see the censors as necessarily complicit with, indeed productive of, that which they seek to censor; but more so insofar as they identify Victorian censorship as in some respects analogous to our own contemporary 'censorship of enlightenment'. Discussing the 'Hicklin' judgement of 1868, which first defined obscenity as tending to deprave and corrupt, they show how the definition was necessarily relative to 'a classification of vulnerable populations and dangerous places'. This was an effect neither of hypocrisy nor of paternalism, they conclude, but rather a 'straightforward outcome of the manner in which erotic representations crossed the thresholds of the new institutions whose management of problem populations extended to the policing and welfare of their sexuality' (ibid.: 189). If nothing else, their analysis serves to remind us that much of what literary critics have meant by Literature, its capacity for allusion and elusion, has also been, in part, the effect of censorship (Patterson 1984: 4). The shift from Soviet to post-Soviet modes of literary production can be read as evidence of an analogous process (cf. Pavlyshyn 1994). As to their critique of liberal anti-censorship campaigns, this is interestingly cognate with some recent feminist arguments against pornography, although they judge the Dworkin–MacKinnon position unrealistically utopian (Hunter *et al.* 1993: 245–6). In their stress on the sociality of sexuality, Foucauldians and radical feminists alike have in fact developed much fuller responses than Thomas to his earlier question concerning the *sort* of censorship under which we live.

As we noted above, state intervention in the market arises as a result of what Williams termed 'the most significant modern form of asymmetry' between cultural production and social reproduction. 'Simple Marxist versions of social and cultural reproduction', he wrote:

> often elide the bourgeois market with the 'ideological apparatus' of the bourgeois state. Yet it is clear that there is significant and sustained conflict, over some crucial cultural issues, between the

> state in its simplest form (as in legislation on obscenity or on official information) or the 'apparatus' in its more complex form (as in religious or educational campaigns against 'sex-and-violence' or 'materialism'), and the actual profitable operations of the capitalist market.
>
> (Williams 1981: 102)

The cultural politics of this asymmetry are complex and variable and it seems unreasonable to suppose they are amenable to any definitive resolution. But two relatively clear, albeit potentially contradictory, lines of inquiry seem pertinent. Insofar as the state, especially in its executive prerogatives, remains substantially undemocratic, and insofar as publishing remains a relatively open and competitive industry, censorship will probably be better analysed as a form of repression. But insofar as the state, especially in its legislative procedures, has become more accountable to an at least quasi-democratic public sphere, and insofar as publishing has become increasingly monopolised and globalised, censorship might well be analysed as an attempt at community control over the irresponsibilities of corporate commerce. The former seems more likely to be the case in relation to sedition and blasphemy, the latter to obscenity. But these are only ideal-typical constructs, located at some remove from the practicalities of political life. In practice, the choice between the pulpit and the pornographer appears both unavoidable and yet distinctly unsatisfactory. That this is so is in no small measure an effect of the collapse of what was once the 'socialist project'. For, as it became increasingly difficult to imagine a future beyond capitalism, so there seemed little left to say against commercially profitable industry, except perhaps that it is immoral.

Chapter 5

Texts and contexts

From Genesis *to* Frankenstein

As we have seen, literary studies defined 'literature' as a 'canon' of writing possessed of so high a value that it takes on a qualitatively different character from such non-canonical writing as mere 'fiction', journalism and so on. As Bloom explained it: 'One breaks into the canon only by aesthetic strength, which is constituted primarily of an amalgam: mastery of figurative language, originality, cognitive power, knowledge, exuberance of diction' (1994: 29). For Bloom, as for Eliot and Leavis – or for Auerbach (1953) and Curtius (1953) in comparative literature – literary studies is the study of this canon. For cultural studies, by contrast, the 'literary' is a sub-system of the 'cultural', its texts cognate with those of fiction and the audio-visual media, analysable according to roughly similar procedures. The distinction between literature and non-literature is thus only one of degree and not of kind. Such is the cultural studies view, and such is my own. In this chapter and the next, I want to suggest something of the intellectual purchase of this approach through an exploration of some of the intertextual connections between *Genesis*, John Milton's *Paradise Lost*, Mary Shelley's *Frankenstein*, a number of 'Frankenstein' films, Karel Čapek's *R.U.R.*, Fritz Lang's *Metropolis*, Ridley Scott's *Blade Runner*, one episode from Chris Carter's *The X-Files* and a number of related episodes in Joss Whedon's *Buffy the Vampire Slayer*. Each of these texts can be read as dealing with the problem of an abortive creation and a 'fall' from an earlier perfection, either anticipated or realised. I propose to analyse their various accounts of the fall by way of a series of, respectively, contextual and textual considerations.

Genesis

The Bible is *the* central text of European high culture: at the risk of stating the obvious, there can be nothing more 'canonical' than the original canon itself. Its first five books, the 'Pentateuch' as they are known to Christians, the 'Sefer Torah' to Jews, were reputedly written down by the prophet Moses in the thirteenth century BC. They are extended narratives, recounting the history, religion and law of the Jewish people; their initial and often subsequent mode of reception was both collective and sacral; they derive in part from earlier oral forms, but are nonetheless themselves written; they seem likely to have been collectively composed by what Williams might have termed priestly 'instituted artists'; and they would have been written in Hebrew, either on clay tablets or papyrus scrolls. The first of the five books is called *Bereshith* in Hebrew transliterated into Roman characters, *Genesis* in English. It includes the story of Adam and Eve, which would become the creation myth for three great world religions and is still today perhaps the best known of all Biblical tales. Weber suggests that it dates from much later than Moses: its abstract, 'unplastic' imagery 'is an accomplishment typical of priests', he argues, which 'originated in Exile times in deliberate opposition to the Babylonian environment' (Weber 1952: 226). This would make it a written rather than an oral text, dating from the sixth or fifth century BC. But the Sefer Torah clearly bears the impress of a prior oral culture, so that it is probably best considered an example of what Ong meant by 'chirographic culture', that is, written texts still heavily dependent on prior oral modes.

Primary oral cultures make extensive use of mnemonic devices, or memory aids, one of the most important of which is the 'additive' oral style, where new elements in the narrative are added on by the repeated use of 'and', in Hebrew *we* or *wa*. So *Bereshith* begins:

> Bereshith bara' 'elohim 'eth hashamayim w'eth ha'arets. Weha'arets hayetah tohu wabohu wehoshek 'al-peney tehom weruah 'elohim merahepheth 'al-peney hamayim. wayo'mer 'elohim yehi 'or wayehi or. wayar' 'elohim 'et-ha'or ki-tov wayavdel 'elohim beyn ha'or uveyn hahoshek. wayiqra' 'elohim la'or yom welahoshek qara' layelah wayehi 'erev wayehi-voqer yom 'ehad.
>
> (*Bereshith*: I, 1–5)

The English translation in the so-called 'Authorized version' of 1611 reads thus:

> In the beginning God created the heaven and the earth. And the earth was without form, and void; and darkness was upon the face of the deep. And the Spirit of God moved upon the face of the waters. And God said, Let there be light: and there was light. And God saw the light, that it was good: and God divided the light from the darkness. And God called the light Day, and the darkness he called Night. And the evening and the morning were the first day.
>
> (*Genesis*: I, 1–5)

The nine introductory 'ands', like those in the Douay version of 1610 discussed by Ong, are translations of *we* or *wa* and therefore instances of 'recognizable oral patterning' (Ong 1988: 37). Ong adds that the Douay translation kept so close to the Hebrew in part because it was itself 'produced in a culture with a still massive oral residue'. This was also true for the Authorized version. Elsewhere, Ong observes that the sacral in general has a special affinity with the 'interiorizing force of the oral word', so that in the Bible the 'orality of the mindset…is overwhelming' (ibid.: 74–5). If *Bereshith* is not an oral form in quite the same sense as *Gilgamesh* or the *Iliad*, it nonetheless shares in much of the same orality, even in translations as late as the seventeenth century. The Authorized version of *Genesis* is quite specifically English, Christian and Protestant, intended in part for private reading and individual interpretation. We cannot assume that it simply 'reproduces' the Hebrew, since all translation is necessarily both an interpretation and a rewriting. As Bassnett observes: 'the process of translating texts from one cultural system into another is not a neutral, innocent, transparent activity' (1993: 160). But we can almost certainly assume that it bears a much closer relation to the Hebrew than do more recent English translations. It is also the version most familiar to Milton, Shelley and Scott alike, and thus the most relevant to our own subsequent analyses.

With the cautionary reminder that this text is in part the product of Hebrew antiquity, in part of English Protestantism, in part other intervening Greek, Latin and English translations, we can proceed to a preliminary analysis of *Genesis*. As we have seen, it begins with an account of the creation of the world, but it proceeds very quickly to the story of the creation of man and woman, to that of the interdiction imposed on them by God, of their breaking that interdiction, and of the punishment subsequently inflicted upon them. The main characters in this narrative are God, the creator; his creations, Adam, Eve and the serpent; and the anonymous narrator, conventionally assumed to be Moses. About the essential God, as a being in itself, there is not much to say: both scriptwriter and lead actor in a drama of his own making, he is not much given to self-analysis. Like the linguistic sign, God is better understood by way of his relations to the other elements in the theological system theoretically centred on him. Almost all theologies attempt some account of the relationship between God and humanity, as also between God and goodness, and *Genesis* is no exception. It is very clear on both counts: as to the first, the proper relationship is one of unquestioning obedience such as obtained prior to Eve's beguilement by the serpent; as to the second, goodness is quite simply that which God wills. We will return to the matter of obedience shortly. For the moment note only that it requires no justification: the text is written in an imperative voice that precludes the possibility of questioning. As to the matter of goodness, this is a much less obvious affair than it might at first appear. In polytheistic religions the various gods very often share in a whole range of human emotions and motivations, from the most base to the most noble. In monotheistic religion, however, the one God is invariably understood as willing the good, if only because the contrary proposition, that of a singular, omnipotent and malevolent deity, is so dreadful as to be beyond belief.

But even if we already know that what God wills must be good, the problem still remains as to whether this is so because that which God wills is necessarily right (that is, goodness is defined arbitrarily by divine decree) or whether it is so because God wills only that which is right (that is, God, being good, wills only good things, goodness being understood as independent of and antecedent to any divine decree). *Genesis* clearly takes the former option: the world is good because God made it and because he saw that it was so (*Genesis*: I, 31). Indeed, some of God's actions in the story would surely not be good were they to be judged according to Moses's (and God's) own ten commandments (*Exodus*: XX). To take the obvious example, when God forbids Adam to eat from the tree of knowledge he warns him that 'in the day that thou eatest thereof thou shalt surely die' (*Genesis*: II, 17). Now this is in fact quite untrue and therefore, in human terms, a lie: when they finally do eat from the tree, neither Adam nor Eve dies, though both are certainly punished in other ways. Later, when God punishes the serpent 'Because thou hast done this' (ibid.: III, 14), what the serpent has done is in fact to tell Eve the simple truth that she will not die when she eats from the tree.

Nor are God's lies true by metaphorical extension from death as an individual experience to mortality as a general condition. The narrative is clear that Adam and Eve's mortality is in no way an effect of their eating from the tree of knowledge. There is in fact no suggestion either that these first humans have ever been immortal or that they have as yet ever contemplated any such possibility. It is only God himself, seeing that Adam and Eve now possess the knowledge of good and evil, who fears that they might also reach for immortality:

> And the LORD GOD said, Behold, the man is become as one of us, to know good and evil: and now, lest he put forth his hand, and take also of the tree of life, and eat, and live for ever: therefore the LORD GOD sent him forth from the Garden of Eden.
>
> (*Genesis*: III, 22–3)

This tree of life is a second tree, from which Adam and Eve neither eat nor even attempt to eat. This God is a truly jealous God, who would expel humanity from Eden merely on the suspicion that they might attempt to become as immortal as he and the angels already are. God may not actually have borne false witness against Adam and Eve, but nor has he exactly given them the benefit of the doubt.

The serpent is God's creation, but only by inference from a more general creation of 'every beast of the field, and every fowl of the air' (ibid.: II, 19). Since the serpent is indeed such a beast, the inference seems warranted nonetheless. We are told very little else about the serpent, except that he is 'more subtil than any beast of the field' (ibid.: III, 1). At no point, however, is there any suggestion that the serpent might be something other than a beast: there is no reference at all in the *Genesis* narrative either to Satan or to any other fallen angel. A fallen Lucifer makes a very a brief appearance in the *Book of the Prophet Isaiah*, but this can more plausibly be read as referring to the rulers of Babylon than to the Prince of Darkness (*Isaiah*: XIV, 12–15). In anything like its developed form, the myth of the fallen angels seems to be of an entirely Christian provenance. In the Gospel according to St Luke, Christ is quoted as telling the seventy evangelists that he had witnessed Satan's fall from heaven; in his Second Epistle, Simon Peter likens false prophets to the angels that had sinned and were cast into hell; in his General Epistle, Jude compares the angels who 'kept not their first estate' with the Jews who had worshipped the Golden Calf and with the cities of Sodom and Gomorrah; and in the Revelation, St John the Divine tells both of a war in heaven between Michael and Satan and their respective angels and of Satan's imprisonment for a thousand years in a bottomless pit (*St Luke*: X, 18–19; *II Peter*: II, 4; *Jude*: 6; *The Revelation*: XII, 7–9; XX, 1–3). None of this, however, is anticipated in *Genesis*. As Weber explains, the myth of the fall was much less central to ancient Judaism than to Christianity: 'The rabbis...considered the worship of the golden calf an incomparably greater offence than Adam's disobedience' (Weber 1952: 227). If the serpent is not Satan, neither a fallen angel nor a devil in disguise, as subsequent readings would later infer, then we are confronted by an obvious lacuna in the narrative: what exactly is the serpent's motivation? Why does he incite Eve to eat from the tree of knowledge? The text has no answer other than that of the serpent's subtlety. Where Adam is persuaded to eat by Eve, and Eve to eat by the serpent, the serpent needs no persuasion, but merely chooses to tell Eve the truth about the tree of knowledge for no obvious reason. His is an apparently unmotivated and disinterested intervention. But this is an answer, of course: to seek knowledge or to persuade others to do so, to disobey the divine commandment to ignorance or to persuade others to do so, these are themselves evidence of malevolent intent. The sin is in the knowing.

If there are no fallen angels in *Genesis*, this is because the human characters are themselves almost as god-like as any angel could wish to be. We are told quite explicitly that the God of *Genesis*, who is of course male, has created both Adam and Eve, Adam in his own image, Eve less so:

> So God created man in his own image, in the image of God created he him; male and female created he them.
>
> (*Genesis*: I, 27)

These humans are distinguishable from gods and from angels only by virtue of their ignorance of good and evil, on the one hand, and their mortality, on the other. In every other respect, we are told, God has made them 'after our likeness' (ibid.: I, 26). The world is theirs to command, they have 'dominion over the fish of the sea, and over the fowl of the air, and over every living thing that moveth upon the earth' (ibid.: I, 28). Of the two humans, Adam is made first from out of a combination of dust and the breath of God; Eve second, from out of Adam's rib, which makes her in part Adam's creation also (ibid.: II, 7, 21–2). Writing from a feminist position, Gilbert and Gubar famously described the *Genesis* narrative as 'Western patriarchy's central culture myth' (1984: 201). Certainly, this story of the masculine origins of procreation effects an ideological inversion of the biological truth that women give birth to men. The power to reproduce has for much of human history been one of the things men have most envied about women, and the aspiration to such power seems a recurring topos in patriarchal myth. So just as Athena was born from the head of Zeus (Aeschylus 1989: 103), Eve is born from Adam's rib.

Neither Adam nor Eve is an individualised character of the kind familiar to us from the contemporary novel and cinema: they are social archetypes, the first man and the first woman, representative of all the men and all the women yet to come. Their fall is thus 'our' fall, their punishment 'our' punishment, where 'we' are the sacred community to which the text is addressed, as also all those other sacred communities to which it will later be readdressed. If Adam and Eve are archetypal, then so too is their transgression. Their 'fall' has a dual aspect: it is in the first place disobedience, and in the second the search for forbidden knowledge. God has commanded that Adam and Eve should never eat from the 'tree of the knowledge of good and evil' (*Genesis*: II, 16–17) and, once they have so eaten, he directly rebukes them for their disobedience:

> Hast thou eaten of the tree, whereof I commanded thee that thou shouldest not eat?
>
> (*Genesis*: III, 11)

Later Adam, though not Eve, is individually reproached for having 'eaten of the tree, of which I commanded thee, saying, Thou shalt not eat of it' (ibid.: III, 17). The text thus repeatedly identifies the tree quite specifically as that which God has commanded them not to eat from, thereby defining their sin as that of disobedience.

The fall is not simply disobedience, however, but also the search for and acquisition of forbidden knowledge, that is, knowledge of good and of evil. Logically, the question of obedience has no necessary bearing on forbidden knowledge: the divine injunction retains its force, precisely because it is divine, irrespective of whether the tree yields knowledge or mulberries. But the *Genesis* story insists that the tree really did confer knowledge. The suggestion to this effect is first introduced into the narrative by the serpent:

> Ye shall not surely die: for God doth know that in the day ye eat thereof, then your eyes shall be opened, and ye shall be as gods, knowing good and evil.
>
> (*Genesis*: III, 5)

Though much subsequent interpretation might consider him a dubious source, the serpent in fact speaks the truth. Eve herself recognises that the tree is 'a tree to be desired to make one wise' (ibid.: III, 6) and her expectations are confirmed in practice, once she and Adam have eaten, when 'the eyes of them both were opened' (ibid.: III, 7). More importantly, the one truly authoritative voice in the text apart from the narrator, that of God himself, also clearly confirms the serpent's account: 'the man is become as one of us, to know good and evil' (ibid.: III, 22).

Adam has been led to disobedience by Eve, Eve by the serpent, and all three will be punished by God. The serpent is condemned to crawl 'upon thy belly' and to eat dust; Eve to 'bring forth children' in sorrow and to be ruled over by Adam; Adam to labour in sorrow and to eat bread only 'in the sweat of thy face' (ibid.: III, 14, 16–19). As many feminists have noted, Eve's punishment will provide a powerful rationale for the immutability of patriarchy. But, just as powerfully, Adam's preordains an equally immutable class hierarchy amongst men. The punishment God metes out to Adam and Eve thus provides both a narrative solution to the textual problem of transgression and an ideological justification for the social problem of inequality: women are doomed to be ruled over by men, and (most) men doomed to hard labour in the fields, by virtue of their own ancestral sinfulness. Moreover, the original sins of disobedience, on the one hand, and the search for forbidden knowledge, on the other, clearly enjoin upon humanity a more general commandment to obedience and ignorance. This fall and all the falls to come are very definitely humanity's own fault. The serpent had been the occasion for disobedience and it is indeed a peculiarly subtle beast of the field. But its sin is its own, for which it continues to be punished; humanity's sins humanity's, for which they too will continue to be punished. *Genesis* is thus at once both theologically authoritative and socially authoritarian. It is the last word as well as the first, not the prolegomenon to a later narrative of salvation, but rather a definitive explanation for the way things are. As Weber concludes: 'Adam and Eve's fall is an etiological myth for death, the toil of labor, and the labor of birth, hostility to the snake and later, to all animals. This exhausts its significance' (1952: 227).

Paradise Lost

John Milton's *Paradise Lost* was composed during the late 1650s and early 1660s and finally completed in 1665. The first edition in ten books was published by Peter Parker in 1667, at a price of 3 shillings, the second in twelve books by Samuel Simmons in 1674. It is an epic poem, but very much a written 'art epic', intended both for mechanical reproduction through print and for sale as a literary commodity to an aggregate of individual consumers, rather than to a single patron. Milton provides us with a very early example of the writer as market professional, albeit one whose writing was sustained by a very direct dependence on the patriarchal division of domestic labour. He had worked as a senior public servant for the revolutionary government under the Commonwealth and as a private school teacher, but also as something close to a professional writer. Milton's contract provided for an initial payment of £5 for the manuscript, a further £5 when the first edition of 1,300 copies had sold out, and further payments of the same amount were the second and third editions to sell out. In 1680, six years after Milton's death, his widow sold all rights to the poem for £8 (Febvre and Martin 1976: 164; Milton 1966: 201). These are relatively sophisticated terms, in many respects analogous to later copyright arrangements. As French once remarked in a slightly different context, 'Milton had a range of vision which included both God and the main chance' (1938: 73).

Bloom has no doubt as to Milton's place in the canon, nor that it is secured essentially by this great epic poem. 'There are', he observes, 'only a few works that seem even more essential to the Western Canon than *Paradise Lost*' (Bloom 1994: 26). This is less self-evidently so than Bloom allows, however. Characteristically, Bloom himself dismissively registers contemporary feminist 'resentment' against Milton (ibid.: 169). But, since the School of Resentment exhibits a scepticism toward canon formation *per se*, these particular resentments remain beside the point. Much more significant are the objections levelled at Milton by those who might normally be expected to share Bloom's more general canonical allegiances. The obvious instances are Eliot and Leavis. Eliot notoriously dismissed Milton's poetic language as merely '*artificial* and *conventional*', his imagery as general rather than particular, his style as so essentially rhetorical in character as to result in a dislocation between the poem's auditory and intellectual meanings (Eliot 1968: 12). Moreover, this intellectual meaning was itself reprehensible: 'A theology that I find in large part repellent, expressed through a mythology which would have been better left in the book of *Genesis*' (ibid.: 19). For Leavis, Milton's verse exhibited a 'feeling *for* words rather than a capacity for feeling *through* words', deploying a peculiarly latinised English, remote from the spoken language, which suggests a deeper, general, sensuous impoverishment (F. R. Leavis 1972b: 53). The poet himself has 'character', Leavis surmises, but is, 'for the purpose of his undertaking, disastrously single-minded and simple-minded. He reveals everywhere a dominating sense of righteousness and a complete incapacity to question or explore its significance and conditions' (ibid.: 60).

In short, Bloom's judgement that 'Milton's place in the canon is permanent' (1994: 169) is simply inaccurate as a description of what the actual custodians of the canon have actually done with Milton, in England if not in the United States. This difference between the English and American institutionalised receptions is in itself culturally significant. Like William Blake and Percy Shelley, Milton is a poet whose ideas have been a source of more or less perpetual embarrassment to respectable English opinion. He supported the abolition of the monarchy and the House of Lords; he wanted to disestablish the Church of England; he was in favour of a radical liberalisation of censorship; he argued for the introduction of cheap and easy divorce; he even insisted that the Belfast Presbyterians not be allowed to dictate policy in Ireland. All of this is no doubt utterly uncontroversial, even conventionally conservative, in the United States, but hardly so in England. An obvious way to avoid this political nastiness is to submerge it into an expanded religiosity, so that Milton becomes a religious as distinct from a political poet (a distinction almost all seventeenth-century Englishmen would have found incomprehensible). Even then there are problems, for Milton's religion was a sectarian Protestantism of the more extreme kind. No doubt this too is quite uncontroversial in many of the United States. In England, however, where respectable opinion tends to vacillate between straightforward indifference to religion, on the one hand, and the polite niceties of a state church, at once theologically Catholic and politically national, on the other, even Milton's religion is still something of an embarrassment. In truth, Raleigh's response, to pronounce the poetry a magnificent 'monument to dead ideas', is about the best that English canonical authority could ever manage (Raleigh 1900: 88). In general, American literary critics, whether cultural conservatives like Bloom or cultural radicals like Gilbert and Gubar, seem to have no idea just how anomalous a figure Milton is for the English, if not perhaps for 'English'.

Milton was one of the most prominent republican intellectuals during the revolutionary crisis of the 1640s and 1650s, when an English king was tried and executed and a first English republic temporarily established. As a relatively senior civil servant to Cromwell's Council of State, he had written the main semi-official justifications both for republicanism and for regicide. Acting essentially on his own initiative, Milton published *The Tenure of Kings and Magistrates* on 13 February 1649, only two weeks after the execution of Charles Stuart. He was appointed 'Latin secretary' to the Council of State in March of that year and *Eikonoklastes*, his officially commissioned reply to the Royalist *Eikon Basilike* (purportedly Charles's own posthumously published reflections), was published on 6 October of the same year. *Pro Populo Anglicano Defensio*, published in February 1651, and *Defensio Secunda*, published in May 1654, were also official commissions. As late as 1660, when the Restoration was already imminent, he had rallied to the intellectual defence of the republic in his last published political pamphlet, *The Ready and Easy Way to Establish a Free Commonwealth*. But the ready and easy way proved elusive, the City of London closed its coffers to the revolutionary government and General George Monck handed the army over to the Restoration. Milton himself went into hiding, his major political tracts were burned by order of the restored monarchy, he was arrested and imprisoned and his name canvassed as a possible candidate for exclusion from the Act of Pardon. At one level, *Paradise Lost* clearly functions as a reflection on the problems of tyranny, revolution and counter-revolution. During the revolutionary wars and in the years of republican triumph, the 'Independents', as Cromwell's party were known, had seen their repeated victories as in themselves evidence both of their own moral rectitude and of divine justice. As Milton had argued, 'certainly in a good cause success is a good confirmation' (1848a: 494). The Restoration confronted the former Independents with an entirely new problem, that of defeat. Both for Milton personally and for the ex-Independents more generally, this would entail two main responses: the one *personal* and individualist; the other *political* and historical. *Paradise Lost* has as its central object this problem of defeat, whether actual or potential, and each of these responses is in fact canvassed within the poem.

As Bloom rightly observes, Milton was 'a Protestant poet, indeed *the* Protestant poet' (1994: 171). Bloom is much less clear, however, as to what exactly this Protestantism might have entailed. From our own twenty-first-century vantage point, informed as it unavoidably is by the experience of Northern Irish Presbyterianism, the South African Dutch Reformed Church and North American evangelical fundamentalism, it has become increasingly difficult to imagine a Protestantism that was neither intellectually obscurantist nor politically reactionary. And yet such was Milton's. In both prose and poetry, Milton's writing attests to an intellectual and political rationalism of a kind which importantly anticipated both the Enlightenment and the radical-democratic politics of the American and French Revolutions. The Protestant Reformation of the sixteenth century was begun, in large part, as a rationalist critique of the transparent irrationalities, both intellectual and institutional, of established Catholicism, a critique which aimed in the first place at reform rather than schism. Thereafter, Protestantism performed a quite decisive role in the early stages of politico-cultural modernisation, both in Europe and North America. Indeed, the association between Protestantism, capitalism and revolution has become something of a commonplace for historical sociologists. This argument has been most commonly identified with Weber, but even Engels (1970: 384–5) noted a roughly analogous correlation. Weber famously argued that Protestant theology demanded of its adherents 'a systematic self-control' (1930: 115) of such a kind that their everyday conduct became thoroughly rationalised. According to Weber, this rationalisation in turn gave rise to an ethic, essential to the 'spirit of capitalism', in which accumulation, devoid of hedonism, became an end in itself.

Early Protestantism was thus peculiarly 'rationalist' in character. In the specific case of Revolutionary Independency, this rationalism can usefully be conceptualised as something akin to what Goldmann meant by a 'world vision'. As we noted in Chapter 2, Goldmann privileged the criterion of 'coherence', both as a literary-critical value in its own right and as a characteristic feature of social-class world visions. In retrospect, this notion seems clearly inappropriate as a universalist criterion, whether for aesthetics or for sociology. But, as I also argued in Chapter 2, it might still retain a residual, local relevance to the very specific circumstances represented by a Sartrean 'fused group'. In the English Revolution, Cromwell and the Revolutionary Independents can plausibly be analysed as such a group. During the mid-seventeenth-century revolutionary crisis, significant sections of the English bourgeoisie attempted a revolutionary transformation of the English feudal state into a fully fledged bourgeois republic. The conflict gave rise to a rationalist 'world vision' which sought to contrast the irrational present with the rational institutions, modes of behaviour, etc. to which the revolutionaries aspired. Protestant rationalism was in the first place a form of moral *individualism*, organised around the absolute centrality of the radically free, non-determined, discrete, rational individual. Protestantism asserted this doctrine centrally and primarily in its insistence on individual interpretation of the Bible. The demand for an English translation of the Bible was thus one of the first posed by English Protestantism. But Revolutionary Independency went much further than previous Protestants, by insisting that the state should also endorse religious toleration. The theoretical basis for tolerationism was provided by a sustained belief in the capacity of the individual, free from the tyranny of a state church, to distinguish truth from error.

Politically, such individualism implied a thoroughgoing opposition to privilege and tradition; ontologically, it implied a conception of the self based on a radical dualism between reason and passion; and, ethically, it implied a stern opposition to the claims of passion. Milton's own explanation for popular resistance to republicanism is thus characteristically Independent: 'being slaves within doors, no wonder that they strive so much to have the public state conformably governed to the inward vicious rules by which they govern themselves' (Milton 1848b: 2). Rationalisms are very often logically atheistic, although atheism is a very strange charge to level at men such as Cromwell, Vane, Ireton, Harrison or Milton. Theirs was nonetheless a very different God from that of *Genesis*, a God whose presence in the world would be effected only through his 'Elect', that is, via the medium of discrete individuals. Divine plans were thus to be achieved through the exercise of the rational free wills of human beings and not through any direct intervention of God into the world. In revolutionary Protestantism much of the separation between God and man characteristic of traditional religion was thus effectively abolished. Opposed both to bishops and kings, this prototypical version of new bourgeois man could take nothing on trust, and would be guided only by 'that intellectual ray which God hath planted in us' (Milton 1848c: 387).

Milton's account of the moral purpose of *Paradise Lost* is given in the poem's opening invocation of the muse:

> That to the highth of this great argument
> I may assert Eternal Providence,
> And justify the ways of God to men.
> (*Paradise Lost*: I, 24–6)

This is already very different from *Genesis*: where the Judaic text is accusatory and imperative in tone, Milton's is justificatory and apologetic. For Jewish and most later Christian and Islamic theologies, it is men, rather than God, whose ways require justification. But in Milton the polarities have been reversed: humanity questions and accuses; God must justify himself. The reasons are not too difficult to discern. When Milton attempted a proof of the existence of God, in his heretical and unpublished *De Doctrina Christiana*, he specifically argued from the evidence of the world as orderly and from the notion that the ordering principle in question must be morally beneficent (Milton 1848d: 14–15). The Restoration had unavoidably thrown into doubt the moral benevolence of the universal order. For Milton, it had become imperative to seek out a new justification and to explain the specific problem of the defeat of the 'godly party'. As Hill quite rightly insisted, all three of Milton's great poems, *Paradise Lost*, *Paradise Regained* and *Samson Agonistes*, 'deal with intensely topical problems set by the defeat of God's Cause' (Hill 1985b: 310). And it is precisely this concrete social and political problem which poses the more general moral problem *Paradise Lost* takes as its theme.

This theme is, of course, that of the fall. In *Paradise Lost*, unlike *Genesis*, there is a twofold fall, that of the angels and that of the first humans, each as it were a 'case study' of a wider problem, that of the fall-in-general. What kind of beings inhabit Milton's epic universe? As in *Genesis*, the main characters are God, the creator, and his various creations. In *Paradise Lost*, however, the creations are all either angels or humans, since the serpent is recast as Satan, the leader of the fallen angels. For Milton, both people and angels, whether fallen or unfallen, partake of the same essential nature: as Raphael tells Adam, they differ 'but in degree, of kind the same' (*Paradise Lost*: V, 490). The highest common factor in this underlying affinity is *individuality of personality*. Milton's constructed epic is thus quite unlike both *Genesis* and the classical Homeric epic in that it permits a substantial development of character and of individuality. The most obvious example is Satan, whose famously soliloquy at the beginning of Book IX, a deliberate revelation of his state of mind, is much more reminiscent of Shakespeare than of 'Moses' or 'Homer' (ibid.: IX, 99–178). But Adam, Eve, and to a lesser extent the Son of God and the leading angels and devils, all provide examples of similarly individualised and interiorised personality. The Council in Hell in Book II, for example, is constructed as a real debate between different individualised characters, Moloch, Belial, Mammon and Beelzebub. On God's side, both Raphael and Michael are similarly individualised. And in the confrontations with Satan, at the end of Book V and the beginning of Book VI, the angel Abdiel comes fully equipped with the individual psychology of one of Cromwell's Ironsides.

If both angels and humans possess individuality, then they are both thereby 'creatures rational' (ibid.: II, 498). For Milton, individuality implies a corresponding rationality and free will. As in *Genesis*, so too in *Paradise Lost* God is the one character in the text whose voice is definitively authoritative. And it is God who, referring by turn to men and to fallen angels, explains to the Son that:

> ...I made him just and right
> Sufficient to have stood, though free to fall.
> Such I created all th'ethereal Powers
> And spirits, both them who stood and them who failed;
> Freely they stood who stood, and fell who fell.
> (*Paradise Lost*: III, 98–102)

All rational creatures are in possession of free will because, as God says, 'reason also is choice' (ibid.: III, 108). Thus the moral destinies of the poem's protagonists are the outcome of processes that are internal and volitional rather than external and deterministic. As in *Genesis*, the moral responsibility for the fall itself, and for all the falls to come, will rest with man rather than with God. But whereas in *Genesis* this provides evidence only of humanity's innate sinfulness, in *Paradise Lost* it becomes evidence of their innate capacity for rational choice. For Milton, the choice whether or not to fall is one that will remain permanently and perennially available.

Milton's moral individualism gives rise to an essentially meritocratic epic cosmos: his Heaven and Hell are each organised according to thoroughly bourgeois principles. Indeed, Milton goes to quite implausible lengths to insist that Sonship is an achieved, rather than ascribed, status. Again, it is God who explains that the Son is:

> By merit more than birthright Son of God,
> Found worthiest to be so by being good,
> Far more than great or high; ...
> (*Paradise Lost*: III, 309–11)

By a nice conceit, even Satan is

> ...by merit raised
> To that bad eminence; ...
> (*Paradise Lost*: II, 5)

Such meritocratic inclinations run directly contrary to much of the sense of the *Genesis* narrative. But Milton himself repeatedly attempts to recast the myth into this new meritocratic mould, at one point going so far as to suggest that the pursuit of virtue might eventually lead even humans to angelic status (ibid.: V, 493–503).

The world of *Paradise Lost* is thus a world of discrete rational individuals, each in possession of free will, hierarchically ordered according to the principle of promotion according to merit. The only exception is the creator as distinct from the creations. Theologically, Milton's God functions not so much as a particular person standing by merit at the top of the cosmological hierarchy, but as an abstract principle transcending hierarchy altogether. For Milton, God is in effect identical to reason. When Milton had sought to justify the trial of Charles Stuart, he had argued, not that kings are subject to the will of God, but that 'justice is the true sovereign and supreme majesty' (Milton 1848b: 34). Similarly, he had dismissed the Royalist argument that political government is subject to a special divine dispensation, on the grounds that God's intervention is 'visible only in the people, and depending merely upon justice and demerit' (ibid.: 17). And when he argued for the execution of tyrants on the grounds that God so commanded, Milton was careful to add, writing in Latin for an international audience:

> Non tamen tyrannum perimi, quia Deus iussit, idcirco bonum erat et licitum, sed quia bonum et licitum erat, idcirco Deus iussit.
>
> (Milton 1651: 123)

> It was not therefore lawful to kill a tyrant because God commanded it; but God commanded it, because, antecedently to his command, it was a justifiable and a lawful action.
>
> (Milton 1848e: 96)

The God in which Milton believed was not so much a person as an abstract principle. He is law, he is reason, he is the first cause, and in all these respects he is necessarily impersonal. Hence what is almost certainly the poem's central weakness, its anthropomorphic rendering of the deity.

In general, God's appearances in the narrative are necessitated by the demand for some authoritative exposition of the poem's theology, the general effect of which is to render him obsessively preoccupied with self-justification. Lines which might work as summaries of an abstract law become unacceptable as the spoken words of a particular omnipotent person. Consider the point at which God forbids Adam to eat from the tree of knowledge:

> The day thou eat'st thereof, my sole command
> Transgressed, inevitably thou shalt die.
>
> (*Paradise Lost*: VIII, 329–30)

Note the use of the word 'inevitably' (the equivalent in *Genesis* is 'surely'). In the mouth of a personal God, these lines appear the product of an arbitrary tyranny of the most brutal and unsympathetic kind. For if God is an omnipotent person, then this inevitability follows on only as a consequence of his own arbitrary decision. But Milton contrives to imply quite the contrary: the inevitability of Adam's death follows precisely from the impersonality of the laws of reason and nature rather than from any merely personal whim. Why, then, did Milton so personalise his own impersonal God? The answer lies in the original Biblical myth itself. For whatever rationalised theology Milton may have subscribed to, the God of the Old Testament stubbornly remains a person rather than a principle, a king rather than a law. As a result, the God of *Paradise Lost* becomes an unfortunate hybrid: a Biblical personage mouthing sentiments which do justice to Milton's theology, that is, to his conception of the ways of God, but which nonetheless fail to justify the person of God to men.

If Milton's God is impersonal reason, and God's creations discrete rational individuals, then what exactly does it mean for such creatures to fall? In *Genesis*, as we have seen, the fall is twofold: it is, first, disobedience *per se*; and, second, and more specifically, the search for hidden knowledge. Milton attempts to reconstruct the myth, however, so that its central theme becomes that of the conflict between reason and passion. The rationalism of Milton's re-reading of the Biblical myth is at its most clear in his account of the fall of the angels. The exchange between Abdiel and Satan at the beginning of Book VI is here extremely significant. In response to Satan's claim to stand for liberty as opposed to servility, Abdiel replies:

> Unjustly thou deprav'st it with the name
> Of servitude to serve whom God ordains,
> Or nature; God and Nature bid the same,
> When he who rules is worthiest, and excels
> Them whom he governs. This is servitude,
> To serve th'unwise, or him who hath rebelled
> Against his worthier, as thine now serve thee,
> Thyself not free, but to thyself enthralled; …
>
> (*Paradise Lost*: VI, 174–81)

Here we have almost the whole of Milton's theory of politics: the doctrine that God and Nature are essentially one and that divine commands thereby conform to the laws of nature and reason; a meritocratic theory of government in which just government is seen as that of the worthy over the unworthy, servitude obedience to the tyranny of the unworthy; finally, and most significantly, the recognition that the tyrant Satan is himself un-free insofar as he remains enthralled to his passions. In Milton's version, the fall of the angels arises from the subordination of their reason to the dictates of the passion of pride.

The fall of humankind is similarly restructured. It is neither disobedience *per se* nor, still less, the search for forbidden knowledge which precipitates this second fall: unlike *Genesis*, *Paradise Lost* explicitly rejects the notion that the tree actually yielded knowledge. Thus Adam to Eve:

> ...we know
> Both good and evil, good lost and evil got,
> Bad fruit of knowledge, if this be to know.
> (*Paradise Lost*: IX, 1,071–3)

For Milton, the second fall is in fact a second triumph of passion over reason. Raphael's final warning to Adam at the end of Book VIII thus contains, by implication, something very close to a summary of the Miltonic theory of the fall:

> ...take heed lest passion sway
> Thy judgement to do aught which else free will
> Would not admit; ...
> (*Paradise Lost*: VIII, 635–7)

In the attempt to recast this second fall Milton confronted much more serious obstacles than with the angels. For, of course, *Genesis* is very specific on the subject. Milton's version is clearly asserted both in Raphael's earlier warnings and in Michael's subsequent commentary, which perform the functions of, respectively, a prescript and postscript to the main body of the action. The action itself, however, remains problematic. Saurat's suggestion (1924: 152–5) that the fall is essentially a product of sensuality almost certainly captured the substance of Milton's intention, the form of the myth the poet would prefer to have found in *Genesis*. But the Biblical account contains not the slightest hint that this is the case. Given Milton's commitment to the sequence of events presented there, it is barely surprising that a 'close reading' of Book IX, in isolation from the rest of the poem, leads to the kind of exasperated bewilderment evident in Peter's comment that 'God alone knows why they've fallen' (1960: 137). But this is disingenuous. Milton tells us repeatedly that they have fallen because they have allowed their passions, specifically their sensuality, to subordinate their reasons. Against the weight of the initial Biblical story, Milton manages to sustain this notion that the fall of humankind is the product of the triumph of passion over reason.

Interestingly, Milton's version renders the myth less explicitly patriarchal than in *Genesis*. For in *Paradise Lost* Adam and Eve commit essentially the same sin: they each allow their passions to overtake their reason. As Bloom noted, feminist criticism has been overwhelmingly hostile to Milton and his epic. Whatever the poet is 'to the male imagination', wrote Gilbert and Gubar, 'to the female imagination Milton and the inhibiting Father – the Patriarch of patriarchs – are one' (1984: 192). That *Paradise Lost* is indeed a patriarchal text, both in general conception and in much of the detail, seems indisputable. But a great deal of this misogyny derives directly from *Genesis*, nonetheless, and it is Milton who attempts to rewrite the myth in significantly less misogynist – or at least significantly more universal – a form. For Milton, the fundamental opposition runs between reason and passion, rather than between man and woman, and he was quite capable of imagining woman as reason. He had written as much in the divorce pamphlets:

> particular exceptions may have place, if she exceed her husband in prudence and dexterity, and he contentedly yield: for then a superior and more natural law comes in, that the wiser should govern the less wise, whether male or female.
>
> (Milton 1848f: 325)

More to the point, *Comus* is organised around exactly the same categories as *Paradise Lost* – reason, passion, the fall – but here the Lady embodies reason, her brothers fail at least temporarily and Comus himself is the slave to sensuality. Belsey concedes most of this, only to add: 'in case this should appear to be an effect of Milton's deliberate intention...*Samson Agonistes* offers a useful corrective' (1988: 53). But it does no such thing. When Milton represents Dálila as sensuality, or Eve as reason seduced, how can this possibly detract from the prior representation of the Lady as reason triumphant? Quite the contrary, it suggests, rather, that these categories are much less gendered than many feminist critics argued. Of course, Milton wasn't a feminist. But he almost certainly was a bourgeois humanist, whose notions of chastity (applying to men as much as to women) and married love were significantly less patriarchal than the Cavalier alternatives on offer at the time.

During the Archangel Michael's account to Adam of the future course of human history, Milton deliberately poses the problem of the fall as a general problem with overtly political implications. The treatment of Nimrod, the world's first tyrant, is particularly telling (*Paradise Lost*: XII, 82–101). Here we learn that those who will fail in the government of themselves will necessarily fall prey to tyrannical government from without. Milton's central conclusion is clear: the defeat of the godly and the triumph of unreason over reason, whether acted out in the Garden of Eden or in the England of 1660, is always determined ultimately by the moral failure of the godly themselves. This, then, is Milton's initial explanation for the problem of defeat, though the explanation is not as yet a solution. In the last two books of *Paradise Lost*, however, and especially in Book XII, Milton finally proposes the solution. Here Adam receives from Michael the double promise of a future time when the earth will be a 'far happier place' than Eden and of a 'paradise within thee, happier far', permanently available to the truly good (ibid.: XII, 464, 587). Here, then, is Milton's reaction to the problem of defeat: a personal defence of reason against unreason combined with the conviction that history will ultimately secure the triumph of reason. The poem's conclusion is thus essentially optimistic: where the *Genesis* narrative had functioned so as to confirm humanity's irreparably fallen state, *Paradise Lost* holds out the prospect precisely of reparation. As Adam himself concludes:

> O goodness infinite, goodness immense!
> That all this good of evil shall produce,
> And evil turn to good; ...
> (*Paradise Lost*: XII, 469–471)

This is the optimism of a bourgeois humanism that can still imagine a perfected humanity, even in the face of catastrophic political defeat. During the early 1640s, Milton had hoped for the imminent establishment in England of the kingdom of the saints; by the early 1660s, that prospect had been relegated to a distant future, but had not been abandoned.

Frankenstein

Mary Shelley's novel *Frankenstein* was begun in June 1816, completed in May 1817 and published anonymously by Lackington, Hughes, Harding, Mavor & Jones as a 'three-decker' novel in March 1818. This anonymity was neither accident nor affectation, but arose very directly from the concrete circumstances of Shelley's 'scandalous' parentage and equally 'scandalous' elopement (Gilbert and Gubar 1984: 241–2; Maclean 1994a: 28–9; cf. Maclean 1994b). The immediate occasion of its composition has become the stuff of legend. Early in 1816 Lord Byron had invited Mary Godwin, as she then still was, her lover Percy Shelley and her half-sister, Clare Clairmont, to join him on vacation that summer in Geneva. Clairmont had herself been Byron's lover and it was she who had first introduced him to Mary and Percy. The Byron and Shelley parties met late in May and, at Byron's suggestion, one evening in June they each agreed to write 'a ghost story' (M. Shelley 1980: 7). Both Byron's own unfinished vampire story and a short novel, *The Vampyre*, by his physician and secretary, Dr John Polidori, were eventually published. It is for Mary Shelley's novel, however, that the evening is remembered today. Though critical reaction was mixed, the novel proved an immediate commercial success. A second two-volume edition appeared in 1823, by which time its authorship was already public knowledge. In 1831 Colburn and Bentley published a fully revised third edition as No. 9 in their series of 'Standard Novels'. *Frankenstein* was the product of a much more developed print-capitalism than *Paradise Lost*; its audience the enlarged literary market of the early nineteenth century; and its author, her gender notwithstanding, eventually a much more successful market professional than Milton could ever have been. Though only *Frankenstein* of her novels still commands public attention, she in fact made a career as a professional author. Widowed by Percy Shelley's drowning in 1822, and struggling to give their surviving second son an education at Harrow and later at Cambridge, often in the face of determined hostility from Percy's father, she turned to professional writing as one of the few middle-class careers open to a single mother. Her other books included five novels, *Valperga* (1823), *The Last Man* (1826), *Perkin Warbeck* (1830), *Lodore* (1835) and *Falkner* (1837).

Until comparatively recently, *Frankenstein* had been very definitely excluded from the canon of English Literature. Neither F. R. Leavis's *The Great Tradition* (1962b), for many years the most influential account of the English novel, nor even Q. D. Leavis's attack on the corrupting effects of popular fiction, *Fiction and the Reading Public* (1979), bother so much as to mention it. Volume 5 of *The Pelican Guide to English Literature*, an important Leavisite project in its time, judged the novel 'second-rate' and 'simple' (Harding 1957: 45). The *Dictionary of National Biography* – a magnificent monument simultaneously to turn-of-the-nineteenth-century scholarship and prejudice – dismissed Mary Shelley thus:

> Possessing in full measure the defects of her qualities, she had not the insight to discern the prophetic character of Shelley's genius; and, although she admired his poetry, her inner sympathy was not sufficiently warm to console him for the indifference of the world.
>
> (Stephen and Lee 1921: 29)

Against much of the weight of previous canonical judgement, Bloom managed to include both Mary Shelley and her novel in his version of the Western Canon (1994: 542). But it is difficult not to read this as a grudging and unadmitted concession to the feminist branch of the School of Resentment. Had it not been for Hollywood cinema and feminist literary criticism, she would easily have been lost to contemporary historical memory.

A sociological variable of special relevance to Shelley's novel is the kind of authorial 'formation' Williams termed a 'movement'. Her parents, Mary Wollstonecraft and William Godwin, had been key figures in the very movement Williams himself cites as an early example of this kind of formation, the circle of pro-French English Radicals loosely grouped around Godwin during the late 1780s and the 1790s (Williams 1981: 75–7). Godwin's *Enquiry Concerning Political Justice* (1971) was one of the central texts of English philosophical anarchism, Wollstonecraft's *A Vindication of the Rights of Women* (1975) a founding text for English feminism. Whilst the British Government had determinedly opposed the French Revolution of 1789, many English Radicals, including both Wollstonecraft and Godwin, remained actively in sympathy with it. When in 1790 Burke had published his counter-revolutionary *Reflections on the Revolution in France*, Wollstonecraft was the first to reply on behalf of English Radicalism: 'Man preys on man; and you mourn for the idle tapestry that decorates a gothic pile', she wrote in her *A Vindication of the Rights of Men* (Wollstonecraft 1977: 82). During the early 1790s Radical opinions had been fairly widespread in the English middle classes. But after 1793, when Britain joined Austria and Prussia in counter-revolutionary war against France, Radicalism had increasingly become identified with pro-French treason. The French Revolution thus occasioned a crisis within English Radicalism that transformed the Godwinians from 'an alternative tendency within the general social order, and in some respects a central tendency within the rising industrial bourgeoisie', into a much more clearly 'oppositional tendency' (Williams 1981: 75). Godwin and Wollstonecraft themselves became lovers, she became pregnant, and they were married in 1797, despite their shared opposition to the institution, so as to legitimate the still unborn child who would become Mary Shelley. Wollstonecraft died ten days after giving birth to this daughter. Godwin himself became an increasingly isolated figure, but nonetheless exercised real influence over a later Radical intellectual formation, which formed around Mary's eventual husband, Percy Shelley.

Along with Byron, Percy Shelley occupies a peculiar position in early nineteenth-century English history, at the point of intersection between political Radicalism and literary Romanticism. Beginning with the German *Sturm und Drang* writing of the 1770s, Romanticism had been above all an intellectual reaction against the hyper-rationalism of the European Enlightenment. Though elsewhere often deeply reactionary in its political implications, in England Romanticism was quite commonly aligned with the political 'left'. The British war effort against France had been sustained by political and industrial repression, on the one hand, and rapid industrialisation and technological innovation, on the other. As Thompson observed: 'England, in 1792, had been governed by consent and deference.... In 1816 the English people were held down by force' (1963: 605). The effect had been to depress working-class living standards very dramatically. As a result, a new Radicalism emerged, increasingly centred on illegal trade unionism and the machine-breaking tactics of the so-called 'Luddites'. Both Byron and Percy Shelley publicly opposed the bloody repression directed by the Government at these Luddites (cf. Byron 1991; P. B. Shelley 1993). The latter was an admirer of both Wollstonecraft's and Godwin's political writings. Early in 1811, shortly before his expulsion from Oxford, he had written to Godwin to express his enthusiasm for *Political Justice*. He met Godwin in London late the following year and Mary herself in the spring of 1814. Percy was still married, his first wife Harriet already pregnant with their second child, when in July of that year he and Mary 'eloped' to France, accompanied by Clairmont. They were disowned by most of 'polite' society, by Shelley's family and even by the erstwhile exponent of free love, William Godwin himself. In February 1815 their first child, a daughter, was born prematurely and died after only a few days.

As it turned out, *Frankenstein* would be the first surviving fruit of their marriage, the 'hideous progeny', much encouraged by Percy's 'incitement', which Mary would bid 'go forth and prosper' in her 'Introduction' to the 1831 edition (M. Shelley 1980: 10). The novel is structured around three distinct narrative levels. The first, the novel's 'frame narrative', consists of the letters to his sister, Margaret Saville, from Robert Walton, an English explorer whose ship rescues Frankenstein from the arctic wastes. Walton's letters enclose a second narrative, that of Victor Frankenstein, a Genevan scientist who tells Walton of his creation of a monster and of the terrible tragedies that have befallen his family as a result. This in turn encloses a third narrative, the unnamed creature's own story, as told to Frankenstein in chapters XI–XVI. The novel thus works by way of a series of narrative shifts, in which the reader is progressively taken further into the realm of the monstrous and then returned back to the realm of 'normality'. Much of its narrative effect derives from the manner in which the reader's sympathies are attached, by turn, to each of the three narrators, including even – and perhaps especially – the monster himself. Moreover, all three narratives tell the story of a fall from an earlier actual or presumed innocence into actual or potential disaster.

The 'Preface' to the first edition of the novel, ostensibly by its author, but actually written by Percy, pointedly compares *Frankenstein* to a series of canonical texts, 'most especially Milton, in *Paradise Lost*' (ibid.: 13). Like *Paradise Lost*, *Frankenstein* is a reworking of the *Genesis* myth. Though God never actually appears as a character in the novel, Walton, Frankenstein and the other humans are clearly his creations and the creature's novelty consists precisely in the fact that he alone is man-made rather than God-made. In the 1831 'Introduction', Mary would recall her initial sense of the story thus: 'Frightful must it be; for supremely frightful would be the effect of any human endeavour to mock the stupendous mechanism of the Creator of the world' (ibid.: 9). The novel thus assumes the 'fact' of God's creation of humanity, whilst broaching the possibility that humanity might be able to create the non-human, or the 'post-human' as we might well say today. From the title page on, the novel repeatedly refers both to *Genesis* and to *Paradise Lost*. Its epigraph is taken from Book X of Milton's poem, where Adam asks of God what will eventually be the monster's question to Frankenstein:

> Did I request thee, Maker, from my clay
> To mold me Man? did I solicit thee
> From darkness to promote me…?
> (Paradise Lost: X, 743–5)

The creature is thus a new Adam and Frankenstein a new 'Maker'. But in creating life Frankenstein has usurped a power that properly belongs only to God. Hence the description of his creature as 'the living monument of presumption' (M. Shelley 1980: 80). Like Adam and Eve in *Genesis*, Frankenstein aspires to forbidden knowledge. But, unlike Adam and Eve, he also self-consciously aspires to a truly god-like power, that of creation itself. Such presumption is what the Greeks had meant by *hubris*, and its punishment what they had termed *nemesis*. This, then, is the structure of Frankenstein's fall: the sin of hubris followed by the punishment of nemesis.

What kind of creature is Mary Shelley's monster? According to Frankenstein's account, he had intended to create 'a being like myself...an animal as complex and wonderful as man' (ibid.: 53), but succeeded only in producing 'a thing such as even Dante could not have conceived' (ibid.: 58). Yet it is not quite so simple: Frankenstein's monster is in fact much more truly 'like himself' than he will allow. The book's central narrative, and by far the most familiar to later cinema audiences, is the creature's own story, told in the first person. But, unlike many film monsters, Shelley's daemon learns both to speak and to read: the creature's nicely canonical literary education consists in Goethe's *Sorrows of Werter*, Plutarch's *Lives* and, of course, Milton's *Paradise Lost* (ibid.: 127–9; Bloom 1994: 532, 537, 539). The effect of this autodidactic education suggests a clear affinity between creator and creature in their shared predilection for forbidden knowledge. Prior to the discovery of this library, the monster had learnt from the cottagers only 'to admire their virtues, and to deprecate the vices of mankind' (M. Shelley 1980: 127). But through his reading, especially of *Paradise Lost*, the creature is forced into the 'lowest dejection':

> Like Adam, I was apparently united by no link to any other being in existence; but his state was far different from mine in every other aspect.... Many times I considered Satan as the fitter emblem of my condition; for often, like him, when I viewed the bliss of my protectors, the bitter gall of envy rose within me.
>
> (M. Shelley 1980: 129)

Romantic readings of *Paradise Lost* had tended to see Milton as romanticising the devil. This was certainly both Blake's view (1927: 6) and Percy Shelley's (1970: 205); and it is shared by Gilbert and Gubar (1984: 201), for example, and by Bloom (1994: 172–3). It is thus tempting to read Mary Shelley's sympathy for her monster as in some respects a development from this reading. There is indeed warrant for this in the text. In its closing pages, when the monster confesses to Walton, 'Evil thenceforth became my good' (M. Shelley 1980: 220), he clearly 'quotes' from Milton's Satan:

> ...All good to me is lost;
> Evil, be thou my good; ...
> (*Paradise Lost*: IV, 109–10)

And shortly thereafter he even describes himself as 'the fallen angel' who 'becomes a malignant devil' (M. Shelley 1980: 221). But the novel's sympathy for this particular devil also functions to remind us just how ungod-like Frankenstein's behaviour actually is. For Frankenstein has betrayed his creation, in the first instance at least without just cause. Hence the underlying 'truth' in the monster's critique delivered when they meet on Mont Blanc:

> Remember, that I am thy creature; I ought to be thy Adam; but I am rather the fallen angel, whom thou drivest from joy for no misdeed. Every where I see bliss, from which I alone am irrevocably excluded. I was benevolent and good; misery made me a fiend. Make me happy, and I shall again be virtuous.
>
> (M. Shelley 1980: 100)

The monster's own fall consists in the sin of murder, but the source of this sin lies not so much with the creature himself as with the creator who has abandoned him.

Moreover, the novel gestures toward the possibility that in companionship a solution might have been available for this particular fall. An Adam without an Eve, abandoned by his God, the creature curses his creator:

> 'Hateful day when I received life!' I exclaimed in agony. 'Accursed creator! Why did you ever form a monster so hideous that even *you* turned from me in disgust?.... Satan had his companions, fellow-devils, to admire and encourage him; but I am solitary and abhorred.'
>
> (M. Shelley 1980: 130)

If the monster's fallen condition has indeed arisen primarily from this solitariness, then the power to effect a solution clearly rests with Frankenstein. Like Adam in *Paradise Lost* (though not in *Genesis*, where the initiative is taken by God), the monster asks his creator for a mate. Frankenstein at first refuses (ibid.: 144) but is eventually persuaded around by what are, by conventionally human standards, clearly reasonable arguments:

> My vices are the children of a forced solitude that I abhor; and my virtues will necessarily arise when I live in communion with an equal. I shall feel the affections of a sensitive being, and become linked to the chain of existence and events, from which I am now excluded.
>
> (M. Shelley 1980: 147)

Frankenstein has already very nearly completed this second monster, when he suddenly determines to break his word and to destroy it, as it turns out in full view of the despairing creature. Frankenstein's reasons are interesting:

> one of the first results of those sympathies for which the daemon thirsted would be children, and a race of devils would be propagated upon the earth.... Had I the right...to inflict this curse upon everlasting generations?
>
> (M. Shelley 1980: 165)

For Spivak, this is the 'language of racism' (1999: 134), but she is mistaken, surely, since race is used here as a synonym for species, as in the 'human race', rather than as a racist category for distinguishing between humans. For Shelley herself, Frankenstein's bad faith seems to require no rational justification; certainly none is given in the novel. Species-loyalty, 'speciesism' as contemporary animal rights activists might describe it, is sufficient in itself. This is humanism in the sense, not of a generously inclusive insistence on 'our' common humanity, but of an exclusive insistence on 'their' inhumanity and non-humanity, worse yet their possible 'post-humanity'. Slusser suggests that Shelley here established what would in fact become the central problem in subsequent science fictional approaches to the 'posthuman', a problem he nicely terms 'the Frankenstein barrier':

> What is at stake with Victor Frankenstein...is...the sin against the second chance modern science offers humanity by remaking its fallen body and directing it toward further things to come. Victor opens the way to the future only to betray that openness.
>
> (Slusser 1992: 51)

We will return to Slusser's 'Frankenstein barrier' very shortly. For the moment, however, consider briefly the structure of the fall as it appears in the third major narrative, that of the explorer Walton. In all respects other than outcome, this structure is more or less homologous with that in the Frankenstein narrative. The theme of 'the Modern Prometheus', the novel's subtitle, is established in Walton's letters well before we actually meet Frankenstein. Like Prometheus, both Walton and Frankenstein aspire to forbidden knowledge, at whatever cost to themselves, in the interests, as they imagine it, of the greater good of the human race. It is Walton who explains to Frankenstein that 'One man's life or death were but a small price to pay for the acquirement of the knowledge which I sought' (M. Shelley 1980: 28). Like Frankenstein, Walton commits the sin of hubris and, left to his own accords, it is clear he will persist in his relentless search for the warm waters at the Pole, where 'snow and frost are banished' (ibid.: 15). There, presumably, he will eventually encounter nemesis, as death, somewhere in the Arctic wastes. But in the Walton narrative the fall remains a potential that is never fully realised. Where Frankenstein had laboured alone in his 'workshop of filthy creation', 'a solitary chamber, or rather cell, at the top of the house' (ibid.: 55), Walton's explorations require the active co-operation of an entire ship's crew. And it is they who save him from the effects of his own hubris by the exercise of a kind of collective social control.

With their ship trapped in the ice and in imminent danger of destruction, a delegation of six sailors demands that Walton agree to sail southward once the ship is free. Neither Frankenstein nor Walton ever shares their fears: Frankenstein insists that the expedition is a glorious venture precisely 'because danger and death surrounded it' and he urges them on to 'be men, or be more than men' (ibid.: 214–15); Walton accedes to their demands but only reluctantly, 'my hopes blasted by cowardice and indecision; I come back ignorant and disappointed' (ibid.: 215). The point, however, is that the sailors are absolutely right: this way lie madness and death. For Frankenstein only nemesis can 'solve' hubris; for his creature the one mooted alternative is in effect dismissed as unthinkable; but for Walton the hubris of science can be contained – and in that sense 'solved' – if rendered socially accountable. Poovey (1984: 131–3) read this as an essentially 'conservative' solution to the problem of individual ambition, O'Flinn (1986: 202) as radical, even socialistic. In a sense, both are right, for such assertions of the claims of community and sociality against those of individuality and egotism have been key elements in the political rhetorics of conservatism and socialism alike. There is no doubting Mary Shelley's own later conservatism. And yet the young girl Poovey sees as traumatised by the scandal of her own literary aspirations did indeed persist in the profession of English letters; and she was indeed Godwin's and Wollstonecraft's daughter, Shelley's lover, Byron's friend.

The Walton frame narrative is generally omitted from film and stage adaptations of the novel and this is in itself hardly surprising: its main function, to underline and underscore the two primary narratives, becomes more or less redundant in these other more economical media. There is at least one important difference, however, between the primary and frame narratives that warrants some further comment: there is nothing at all in the Walton story even remotely equivalent to Slusser's Frankenstein barrier. Where Victor Frankenstein (and Mary Shelley) deliberately refuses a solution plausibly available to the monster's (and thus Frankenstein's) problems, Walton's sailors refuse only the problem itself. The Frankenstein barrier arises precisely because Shelley's novel, and with it much of subsequent science fiction, contrives to elicit the reader's sympathies for a resolution it nonetheless cannot and will not deliver. If the Walton and Frankenstein narratives were directly homologous, then the creature would never have been brought to life. This is perhaps the ethically necessary outcome – what 'should' have happened – the outcome to which the Walton narrative directs us. But it is belied by the core narrative, the monster's as distinct from Frankenstein's, which insists that the daemon is both pitiful and pitiable, in short, that he warrants at the very least our sympathy, at most perhaps even a mate.

The creature outlives his creator to put his own case directly to Walton:

> while I destroyed his hopes, I did not satisfy my own desires. They were for ever ardent and craving; still I desired love and fellowship, and I was still spurned. Was there no injustice in this? Am I to be thought the only criminal, when all human kind sinned against me?.... Even now my blood boils at the recollection of this injustice.
>
> (M. Shelley 1980: 221–2)

Why this sympathy for the monster? A literary-critical answer might be that it works so as to make the novel more interestingly complex, both ethically and narratologically (as indeed it does). But a cultural studies approach could refigure the question as one of ideology, connecting it to the two intellectual 'formations' intersecting in Mary Shelley's early biography, the Godwin and Shelley circles. Both were deeply critical of the repressive policies of successive British governments, whether directed toward middle-class dissent or working-class rebellion, both also loosely feminist. This, in turn, suggests the possibility of reading the text itself through the categories of 'class' and 'gender'.

Frankenstein was written at a time of great class conflict, by a writer whose close circle of friends and relatives had been acutely aware of and concerned about precisely those conflicts. Her monster knows of 'the division of property, of immense wealth and squalid poverty'; he knows too that a man with neither 'high descent' nor riches becomes 'a vagabond and a slave, doomed to waste his powers for the profits of the chosen few!' (ibid.: 120). He also clearly exhibits some of the more obvious characteristics of the people/Mob, as represented by Byron in his maiden speech to the House of Lords. Byron had chastised the Tory Government thus:

> even a mob may be better reduced to reason by a mixture of conciliation & firmness, than by additional irritation and

> redoubled penalties...the Mob...can also defy you, when Neglect and Calamity have driven them to despair.
>
> (Byron 1991: 25)

Like these Luddites, the monster warrants our sympathy; like them, his plight is an effect of the unregulated application of modern science; like them, he is also dangerous and threatening. At one level, then, *Frankenstein* readily invites a reading in which the fate of the poor daemon becomes an allegory for that of the poor working-class 'Mob'.

This line of argument was developed very powerfully, if not altogether persuasively, by Moretti. In his reading, the analogy runs between Frankenstein and the monster, on the one hand, and modern industrial capitalism and the modern working class, on the other. It is not so much nineteenth-century English Luddism, however, as contemporary Italian (and American) car factories that attract Moretti's attention: 'Like the proletariat, the monster is denied a name and an individuality. He is the Frankenstein monster; he belongs wholly to his creator (just as one can speak of a "Ford worker")' (Moretti 1988: 85). When Moretti makes explicit reference to the novel's nineteenth-century historical context, it is to Chartism, which was in fact a much later political movement, rather than to Luddism. Such anachronism sits uneasily beside his own declared commitment to rewriting literary history 'in the context of a total history of society' (ibid.: 19) and clearly undermines the analysis at the level of detailed application, though not necessarily that of the original more general conception. Much more persuasive, at least in its stronger sense of the immediate historical context, is O'Flinn's view of the novel as suggesting, 'in the imaginative terms of fiction, that Luddite violence was not the result of some brute characteristics of the nascent English working class but an understandable response to intolerable treatment' (O'Flinn 1986: 211).

Though conceding the possibility of class analyses such as these, Spivak reads the novel as a critique of 'the axiomatics of imperialism', both 'in substance and rhetoric' (1999: 137, 115). The monster thus becomes a version of the 'native informant', subjected to a civilising education, who nonetheless cannot finally be contained by the master–slave relationship (ibid.: 135, 137–8, 139). There is clear force to this reading and good extratextual reason, never actually cited by Spivak, to suppose that Shelley herself had direct acquaintance with, and was opposed to, the conditions of 'black' colonial slavery. In 1815 she had spent some weeks at Clifton near Bristol, one of the centres of the Atlantic slave trade. As Seymour plausibly speculates:

> Mary could see black men being worked on Bristol Quay; she could hear the callously pragmatic views of those who had owned and now technically employed them. Surrounded by troubling evidence that abolition had brought little change of attitude..., Mary was provided with a new element of the story she began to write the following summer.
>
> (Seymour 2001: 139)

But the evidence she cites from the novel, that the monster had 'yellow skin, black hair and giant limbs', is less than persuasive. Monsters do tend to be monstrous, after all, and these particular monstrosities are as attributable to Yorkshire weavers as to African slaves. At the level of textual analysis, then, there is actually very little to suggest that this particular master–slave dialectic is primarily colonial rather than classed in its character. Indeed, the few direct references to imperialism quoted by Spivak (1999: 136–8) are clearly extraneous to the creator–creature relationship. This leads me to persist in a class reading, whilst conceding, nonetheless, that it be framed by the wider context of European imperialism.

Frankenstein was also, however, the work of the daughter of a famous feminist mother. At one level, the gratuitous deaths of the servant, Justine Moritz, and of Frankenstein's fiancée and eventual bride, Elizabeth Lavenza, can be read as writing Wollstonecraft's 'wrongs of woman' directly into her daughter's text (Maclean 1994a: 34). Written by a man, the story of Justine's false condemnation and execution for William's murder might merely seem casually brutal; written by a woman, it becomes a protest against the patriarchal order under which such injustice remained possible. The novel is also a critique of patriarchy in the most literal of senses, that is, as the rule of fathers. Mary Shelley's famous feminist mother had died giving birth, leaving her to be brought up and, as it turned out, eventually disowned by her famous anarchist father. When Frankenstein creates new life, in yet another inversion of the biological truth that only women give birth, we recognise the familiar patriarchal trope of male procreation. Here, however, it is parodied and subverted. Though Frankenstein certainly creates life, he neither can nor will nurture this creation: 'No father had watched my infant days, no mother had blessed me with smiles and caresses' (M. Shelley 1980: 121). In truth, Frankenstein disowns this 'son', just as Godwin had disowned his daughter. We cannot know whether the irony in the novel's dedication to Godwin – set page to page against the epigraphical quotation from *Paradise Lost* – is intentional or not. But Shelley's ideal of parenthood is clear from her representation of Frankenstein's parents (ibid.: 34) and it is clear that her own father had fallen very far short of it. As Maclean observed, in Shelley's *Frankenstein* three 'fathers' are inextricably interwoven: God the heavenly Father, Frankenstein the fictional father, and Godwin the real father (Maclean 1994a: 31).

Maclean reads *Frankenstein* as addressing a specifically feminist or at least female 'politics of procreation' (ibid.: 34), devolving in part on childbirth and death in childbirth, both that of mothers and of children. This was, of course, how Mary Shelley lost both her mother and her daughter. In one of the pioneering studies of the female literary tradition, Moers analysed Shelley's novel as a study in maternal revulsion, 'a birth myth…lodged in the novelist's imagination…by the fact that she was herself a mother' (1978: 92). Gilbert and Gubar also located the novel's composition very precisely in years when Shelley was almost continuously pregnant, 'confined', or nursing, so that her developing sense of herself as literary creator seems to have been inseparable from that as 'daughter, mistress, wife, and mother'. The result, they concluded, is 'a female fantasy of sex and reading' (Gilbert and Gubar 1984: 224). Johnson even argued that *Frankenstein* could be read as a kind of autobiography, a story of maternal rejection, on the one hand, and the elimination of the mother, on the other (Johnson 1982: 6–7, 8–9). This last, she wrote, is the meaning of the monster's promise to be with Frankenstein on his wedding night: 'Mary herself was in fact the unwitting murderous intruder present on her own parents' wedding night' (ibid.: 9; cf. M. Shelley 1980: 168). Whatever we make of these particular arguments, the more general significance of *Frankenstein*'s status as a woman's novel seems unavoidable. But to acknowledge the gendering of its writing in this way need not imply any necessary commitment to psychoanalytic and metaphorical, as opposed to socio-historical, modes of analysis, as Lovell (1987: 63–7) almost seems to suggest. Death in childbirth, both that of mothers and that of children, was a central aspect of nineteenth-century English socio-historical reality, its differential impact on male and female experience in part the effect of biology, to be sure, but also and substantially the effect of a more generally patriarchal social structure. The wonder is not so much that Shelley wrote this reality into her text, but that so few writers would follow her example.

Frankenstein in the cinema

Whether or not Mary Shelley's novel is judged canonical, there can be no doubting its subsequent success within popular culture. *Frankenstein* became the founding text of a modern myth that has been enormously influential across a whole range of forms and genres. Its appeal became apparent very shortly after publication: the first theatrical adaptation, Richard Brinsley Peake's melodrama *Presumption, or the Fate of Frankenstein*, was a huge success at the English Opera House in 1823; the same year also witnessed four other London theatre versions, respectively another melodrama and three comic burlesques. From the very beginning, then, stage Frankensteins played with the comic possibilities of parody and pastiche, as well as those for gothic horror. Such theatrical adaptations were also successful in France. The first was a melodrama, *Le Monstre et le magicien* by Jean Touissant Merle and Antoine Nicolas Béraud, performed at the Théâtre de la Porte Saint-Martin in 1826. It too was a great success, in part because of its reportedly spectacular special effects. From 1823 to 1887, eighteen different stage adaptations were performed in the British and French commercial theatre. Special effects, or what During calls 'secular magic', were as important to the popular theatre in the nineteenth century as to the cinema today, and then, as now, *Frankenstein* seemed tailor-made for their use (During 2002: 252–8). Forry lists 96 different known dramatisations during the period 1821–1986 (Forry 1990: 121–6). Between 1931 and 1986, there were well over 80 new English and foreign-language editions of the novel, over 70 stage adaptations and over 190 films (ibid.: 108, 127). A cursory survey early in 2004 of the electronic archives of a number of leading daily newspapers showed that the *Washington Post* had carried 879 articles referring to Frankenstein since 1987 and 154 in the previous two years; the London *Guardian* (combined with the Sunday *Observer*), 612 since 1998; the Paris *Le Monde*, 350 since 1987 and 17 in the previous year; the *Frankfurter Allgemeine Zeitung*, 143 since 1993, 12 in the previous year; the Melbourne *Age*, 166 since 1994, 32 in the previous year. No doubt, many of these references were to film, stage, television or radio versions, or to such matters as the controversy over genetically modified crops, rather than to the novel. But the sheer volume of reference and adaptation is itself testimony to the power of the myth.

The first American silent film version appeared as early as 1910, a second in 1915, an Italian silent film version in 1920. But it was the first sound film which provided perhaps the most enduring image of 'the monster': Universal's 1931 *Frankenstein*, directed by James Whale, and starring Colin Clive as Frankenstein and Boris Karloff (billed as '?') as the monster. This practice of not naming the actor playing the creature dated from the earliest stage versions of *Frankenstein*. Apparently, the novel's anonymous author had herself judged this 'nameless mode of naming the unnameable rather good' (Gilbert and Gubar 1984: 241). Whale's film launched a whole series of Universal 'Frankenstein' movies: *The Bride of Frankenstein* (1935), *Son of Frankenstein* (1939), *The Ghost of Frankenstein* (1942), *Frankenstein Meets the Wolf Man* (1943), *House of Frankenstein* (1944) and even *Abbott and Costello Meet Frankenstein* (1948). The first colour version was Terence Fisher's *The Curse of Frankenstein*, directed for the British Hammer Films in 1957, and starring Christopher Lee as the monster and Peter Cushing as 'Baron' Frankenstein. This is almost certainly, after Whale's, the other best-known Frankenstein film. Like Universal, Hammer went on to produce its own series of sequels, *The Revenge of Frankenstein* (1958), *The Evil of Frankenstein* (1964), *Frankenstein Created Woman* (1966), *Frankenstein Must Be Destroyed* (1969), *The Horror of Frankenstein* (1970) and *Frankenstein and the Monster from Hell*

(1973). Fisher directed all but two of the films and Cushing played Frankenstein in all but one. Both the Universal and Hammer series were products of what Williams termed 'corporate professional' relations of cultural production. The production process was initiated by the film company, in each case, and combined an extensive apparatus of complex technologies with a large number of salaried and commissioned employees, including scriptwriters. The screenplay for Whale's *Frankenstein*, for example, was by Garrett Fort and Francis Edwards Faragoh, with John L. Balderston also credited as having adapted it from Peggy Webling's play, based on the novel by 'Mrs Percy B. Shelley'. Authorship is thus by no means the easiest of categories to use to analyse artworks such as this. The films were mechanically reproducible marketable commodities, sold to distributors, so as eventually to be consumed collectively and distractedly in the darkness of the cinema theatre. Though today available on video, none was originally devised as such. Both series were also the products of a still recognisably 'national' cinema, the one American, the other British (indeed, Hammer Horror may well turn out to be the last great commercial achievement of a national British cinema).

Most film and stage versions dispense with the Walton frame narrative: in Whale's *Frankenstein*, the story is told 'straight' by the camera as omniscient observer; in Fisher's *The Curse of Frankenstein*, Frankenstein himself narrates the story from the death cell where he is about to go to the guillotine. Generally, film versions have tended to relocate audience sympathy away from the monster and often also away from Frankenstein. In Whale's film, Frankenstein himself provides a fairly conventional representation of middle-class decency, a bloodless, unRomantic and modernised version of the over-enthusiastic student scientist of the novel. The creature, however, is nasty, brutish and tall, if not positively evil: he attacks Frankenstein, he murders a young girl, he terrifies Elizabeth. In Fisher's film, by contrast, Frankenstein is transformed into something very close to an embodiment of evil itself. A middle-aged baron rather than a student, a philanderer who even gets Justine pregnant, 'a lethal nutter, an archetypal mad scientist' (O'Flinn 1986: 216), this Frankenstein murders 'Professor Bernstein' for no better reason than to secure the poor man's brain for his monster. In both films, the creature is incapable of speech, let alone quotation from *Paradise Lost*, and in the Hammer version he becomes merely incidental, in effect little more than an occasional vehicle for Frankenstein's malevolence.

Though both films inherit their central characters and many of the central incidents from Shelley's novel, neither is addressed to what we have been calling the problem of the fall. If there is a residual echo of Mary Shelley's fallen angel in Whale's film, then it is to be heard when Frankenstein attempts to justify his scientific ambitions:

> Have you never wanted to do anything that was dangerous? Where should we be if nobody tried to find out what lies beyond? Have you never wanted to look beyond the clouds and the stars or to know what causes the trees to bud and what changes a darkness into light? But if you talk like that people call you crazy. Well if I could discover just one of these things, what eternity is for example, I wouldn't care if they did think I was crazy.

This angel never quite falls, however: he has merely made a mistake. Indeed, the mistake isn't even his own, but rather that of the laboratory assistant, Fritz, who accidentally supplies the monster with an 'abnormal brain', thereby suggesting the odd inference that in different conditions the experiment might actually have 'worked'. In any case, the creature is destroyed, Elizabeth survives with nothing worse than an unusually severe case of prenuptial fright, and she and Frankenstein presumably live happily ever after. There is no such happy ending in Fisher's *The Curse of Frankenstein*, but nor for that matter is there much of a happy beginning. Baron Frankenstein is no fallen angel for the simple reason that he betrays no sign whatsoever of ever having been anything other than irreparably wicked. The film offers no explanation as to why this should be so: as the title suggests, Frankenstein is merely cursed that way. For O'Flinn these different intertextual uses of the Frankenstein story can be articulated to changes in the dominant ideology. Comparing the two films to the novel, he concludes that:

> The possibility of working-class insurrection that had concerned Mary Shelley and terrified Universal was no longer a prime source

> of anxiety in 1956.... But...the development of atomic and hydrogen bombs created a new and dire nightmare of the risk of world destruction flowing from a single, deranged individual.
>
> (O'Flinn 1986: 217)

One of the more recent film adaptations was Tristar's 1994 *Mary Shelley's Frankenstein*, directed by Kenneth Branagh, who also played Frankenstein, and co-starring Robert De Niro as the monster and Helena Bonham Carter as Elizabeth. This too was a product of corporate professional relations of production, but of a much more developed kind than in the earlier film series. Its credits were positively Byzantine in their complexity: it was produced by Francis Ford Coppola, James V. Hart and John Veitch; Fred Fuchs is listed as executive producer and Kenneth Branagh and David Parfitt as co-producers; the screenplay was by Steph Lady and Frank Darabont. It was the product of a transnational rather than national industry, largely financed in the United States, produced in association with Japan Satellite Broadcasting, filmed at Shepperton Studios in England and on location in the Swiss Alps. Like the earlier movies, it was produced for cinema release, but unlike them it was also produced to be recycled thereafter as video, to be sold or rented to individual consumers in the mobile privatisation of their own home entertainment systems. The video release in 1995 was by Columbia Tristar and very deliberately marketed as not yet available on either pay or free-to-air television stations. Unlike the earlier films, this version reinstated the Walton frame narrative and also clearly attempted to establish some sympathy both for Frankenstein and the creature. Frankenstein's scientific ambitions were plausibly Promethean, as in the novel, and his creature speaks, reads and has real cause for complaint, again as in the novel. The promise of a much greater fidelity to the sense of the novel is clearly affirmed in the film's title (itself simultaneously an intertextual and marketing reference to Coppola's 1992 movie *Bram Stoker's Dracula*). At more than one level, it did in fact deliver on the promise: the pastiche of Romantic music in Patrick Doyle's score, Branagh's own strenuously overacted performance, the use of startlingly dramatic Alpine location shots as backdrop, all provided powerful and peculiarly filmic allusion to the culture of early nineteenth-century

Romanticism. But this was still Branagh's rather than Shelley's *Frankenstein* and there are at least two interesting respects in which the film can be read as a distinctly postmodern rewriting of the Frankenstein myth.

At the level of form, the film mobilised a whole range of the most sophisticated technical resources of late twentieth-century film-making to manufacture a knowing allusion to, rather than the illusion of, historical fidelity to the early nineteenth century. For all the apparent accuracy of costume detail, for example, the film actually made hardly any use of the authentically nineteenth-century dialogue readily available in Shelley's novel, preferring to replace it with almost entirely new, anachronistically contemporary, speech. At one point, the script even knowingly quotes what must be the most famous of all Colin Clive's lines from the 1931 version: 'It's alive, IT'S ALIVE!' This is a very good example of what Jameson meant by the 'waning of historicity' in postmodernism. Thematically, the film also broaches the distinctly postmodern notion of the 'posthuman'. As we noted in Chapter 2, structuralist and post-structuralist theories, on the one hand, and a range of new technologies for re-embodiment and disembodiment, on the other, have all combined so as to decentre earlier humanist notions of the human. As Hassan observed more than a quarter of a century ago: 'five hundred years of humanism may be coming to and end, as humanism transforms itself into something that we must helplessly call posthumanism' (1977: 212). This has become an increasingly pressing theme in recent speculation located in the various theoretical spaces between post-cyberpunk and cyborgs, virtual reality and the internet. Citing the practical success of post-war scientific and cultural theory in deconstructing the hierarchical dualisms of western thought, Haraway famously insisted that: 'They have been cannibalized...or..."techno-digested". The dichotomies between mind and body, animal and human, organism and machine, public and private, nature and culture, men and women, primitive and civilized are all in question ideologically'. For Haraway, this required the development of a new kind of posthuman cultural politics, that of the 'cyborg', a 'kind of disassembled and reassembled, postmodern collective and personal self...the self feminists must code' (1991: 163).

The film's formal and thematic postmodernisms are nicely combined when Branagh's Frankenstein explains his vision of the radical potential of modern science to Clerval, played by Tom Hulce, and Waldman, played by John Cleese. The conversation takes place over dinner and it is everyday in tone, albeit most certainly not lighthearted:

> VICTOR: ...sooner or later the best way to cheat death will be to create life.
>
> HENRY: Oh, now you have gone too far. There's only one God, Victor.
>
> VICTOR: Leave God out of this. Listen, if you love someone and they have a sick heart, wouldn't you give them a healthy one?
>
> HENRY: Impossible...
>
> VICTOR: No. It's not impossible. We can do it. We're steps away from it.... And if we can replace one part of a man, we can replace every part. And if we can do that, we can...design a life, a being that will not grow old or sicken, one that will be stronger than us, better than us, one that will be more intelligent than us, more civilized than us...
>
> (Branagh 1994: 65)

This is late twentieth- rather than early nineteenth-century speech and the reference to heart transplant technology, in particular, is radically anachronistic. But so too is the vision of a stronger, better being, which so very firmly gestures in the direction of the postmodern, posthuman cyborg.

As we have noted, Slusser argued that, although Shelley's *Frankenstein* clearly opened up the first posthuman possibilities, it also just as clearly closed them off. In Branagh's film, the 'Frankenstein barrier' seems much less secure. The precise point at which the novel reaches its outer limit, where Frankenstein refuses to create a mate for the creature, and hence to create a race of devils, is exactly where Branagh departs most dramatically from the Shelley narrative. In what is perhaps the most horrifying sequence in the film, Frankenstein resurrects the murdered Elizabeth to create a second, female, monster; the creature appears to claim her as his bride; he and Frankenstein contest for her love; and finally, apparently appalled by her condition, she breaks an oil lamp over her head and kills herself in the flames. Branagh's Frankenstein had, in fact, taken the step Shelley's could not. When Elizabeth destroys herself the narrative is able to proceed toward a resolution that more or less replicates that in the novel. But the original taboo on the creation of reproducible posthuman life has been broken nonetheless. This is possible, in part, because the taboo itself retains an only residual effect in a culture like ours, where genetic engineering and prosthetics, artificial intelligence and virtual reality, nuclear weaponry and space travel, have all become commonplace subjects for everyday discourse. The film may even owe something to recent theoretical debates about the posthuman itself. McHale pointed to the 'feed-back loop' between 'high' postmodernist fiction and 'low' science fiction: 'Popular-art models are assimilated by high art (and vice versa) more quickly now than ever before', he writes, 'this has the...consequence of producing an even more intimate interaction, an ever-tighter feedback loop, between high and low' (McHale 1992: 227). There are other feedback loops, however, between high fiction and popular film, for example, or between high theory and science fiction. So William Gibson's *Virtual Light* readily acknowledges a debt to a work of theory, Mike Davis's *City of Quartz* (Gibson 1994: 334; Davis 1990). It is difficult to resist the speculation that, like many other contemporary science fiction writers, Branagh and his scriptwriters might themselves have been would-be cyborgs.

Chapter 6

Texts and contexts

From Rossum's Universal Robots *to* Buffy the Vampire Slayer

When Bloom wrote of *Paradise Lost* that it 'now reads like the most powerful science fiction' (1994: 171) he was absolutely right, but right in a way that clearly threatened to subvert the notions of canonicity he claimed to defend. For if there is one thing we can safely say about SF, it is that it most definitely isn't canonical. The term 'science fiction' and its associated generic self-consciousness were derived, not from literature, in any sense that a literary critic would recognise, but from the 'pulp fiction' magazines of the inter-war United States. Hugo Gernsback (after whom the annual 'Hugo Awards' are named) had coined the word 'scientification' in 1926 in the first issue of *Amazing Stories*; 'science fiction' itself became common only after 1938, when John W. Campbell Jr changed the name of a rival 'pulp' from *Astounding Stories* to *Astounding Science-Fiction* (Clute and Nicholls 1993: 25, 64). This was a 'low' genre, then, lower than literature, lower than film, perhaps even lower than television. Bloom might well dispute this: SF novels are included in his version of the canon, Ursula Le Guin's *The Left Hand of Darkness*, for example, and Russell Hoban's *Riddley Walker* (Bloom 1994: 564–5). Certainly, there is no disputing the older tradition, from well before the pulps, of literary and quasi-literary writing about 'science', which Gernsback traced to

Verne, Wells and Poe. But, as with Bloom's enthusiasm for Freud, attempts to canonise whatever the keeper of the canon happens to like, irrespective of their more general socio-cultural location, result in something close to theoretical incoherence. Whatever Bloom may prefer, just as Freud remains the arch-theorist for the anti-canonists, so SF remains resolutely popular and 'low', at least in some of its most significant aspects. If Bloom admires them, nonetheless, then this is his problem, but it is neither theirs nor ours.

Mary Shelley's *Frankenstein* reads even more like powerful science fiction than *Paradise Lost*. Indeed, there is a good case to be made that it was itself the first real SF novel. The founding text of recent scholarly work in science fiction studies is taken, by general consensus, to be Suvin's *Metamorphoses of Science Fiction* (Hollinger 1999: 233), which famously defined the genre as a '*literature of cognitive estrangement*' distinguished by '*the narrative dominance or hegemony of a fictional "novum"...validated by cognitive logic*' (Suvin 1979: 4, 63). There was a clear prescriptive intent here, to exclude myth, folktale and fantasy (ibid.: 20, 68–9). This insistence on the cognitive functions of the form and on an attendant opposition to fantasy has been called into question on more than one occasion. Indeed, even Suvin later conceded that: 'Novum is as novum does: it does not supply justification, it demands justification. Where is the progress progressing to?' (2000: 1). But his definition in relation to a cognitive novum is defensible, surely, at least insofar as its focus falls on knowledge as enlightenment in general, rather than on science in particular. Interestingly, this was precisely the distinction Percy Shelley had made in his preface to the first edition of *Frankenstein*:

> The event on which the interest of the story depends is exempt from the disadvantages of a mere tale of spectres or enchantment. It was recommended by the novelty of the situations which it develops; and, however impossible as a physical fact, affords a point of view to the imagination for the delineating of human passions more comprehensive and commanding than any which the ordinary relations of existing events can yield.
>
> (M. Shelley 1980: 13)

In short, the novel is concerned, not with ghosts, but with the possible consequences and ethical implications of a hypothetical scientific development. The significance of this shift has been registered by many subsequent commentators: both Aldiss's history and Clute and Nicholls's encyclopaedia take *Frankenstein* as their starting point (Aldiss 1975: 7; Clute and Nicholls 1993: 568); Kadrey and McCaffery judged it 'a veritable source book for SF motifs and clichés' (1991: 17); even the chief ideologue of cyberpunk, Bruce Sterling, regarded it as 'a wellspring of science fiction as a genre', albeit perhaps only of '"Humanist" SF' (Sterling 1990: 39–41).

When Frankenstein refuses the monster's demand for a mate, the creature warns: 'You are my creator, but I am your master; – obey!' (M. Shelley 1980: 167). This inversion, whereby the creation threatens to acquire power over its creator, has become a staple of modern SF. When set in either the present or the past, such rebellion remains the stuff of 'scientific romance', to borrow Wells's borrowing from Verne's English translator (cf. James 1994: 9), in which the scientific invention as novum appears within a social world still recognisably our own. If set in the future, however, it very easily becomes the stuff of 'utopia' or 'dystopia'. Though utopia as a form clearly preceded SF chronologically, Suvin argued that it had been transformed retrospectively into '*the socio-political subgenre of science fiction*', that is, social-science-fiction (Suvin 1979: 61). By utopia he meant not so much a perfect society as an '*imaginary community...in which human relations are organized more perfectly than in the author's community*' (ibid.: 45). This insistence on the comparative – 'more perfectly' rather than 'perfect' – allowed him to accommodate Saint-Simon, Wells and Morris as well as Bacon and Fénelon. Perfect utopias are thus only a limit case, a sub-class of the wider species of merely better worlds. Moreover, as we move from utopia to its obverse, dystopia, there are only ever comparatives, since absolute imperfection appears to beggar both description and articulation. For Williams, as for Suvin, SF was the distinctly modern form of utopia and dystopia. There are four characteristic types of each, Williams argued, the paradise or hell, the positively or negatively externally altered world, the positive or negative willed transformation and the positive or negative technological transformation. The latter two are the more characteristically utopian/dystopian modes, he concluded, especially in SF, because transformation is normally more important than mere otherness (Williams 1980: 196–9). Artificial beings inhabit both the utopias and the dystopias of SF: the former would include the sentient ships of Banks's 'The Culture', Asimov's famous positronic robots and even Commander Data in *Star Trek: The Next Generation* (Banks 1987, 2000; Asimov 1970). But here I want to focus initially on the dystopian variant, as represented by three proto-canonical SF texts, one play and two films: Karel Čapek's *Rossum's Universal Robots*, Fritz Lang's *Metropolis* and Ridley Scott's *Blade Runner*. Thereafter, we will turn from film to television, from the future to the present, to examine two 'postmodern' retellings of the Frankenstein story, each with its own artificial beings, though each closer to scientific romance than either utopia or dystopia.

Rossum's Universal Robots

We concluded Chapter 5 with a brief account of three Frankenstein films. Much as each moved away from Shelley's original story, all remained loyal to her conception of man-made intelligent life as a surgically produced 'monster'. But in twentieth- and twenty-first-century SF, the monster has been reworked as the mechanical 'robot', the artificially human 'android' (literally 'manlike') and the half human, half machine 'cyborg'. Fictional human-like machines can be traced back at least to E. T. A. Hoffmann's *Der Sandmann* of 1816. But the word 'robot' is an early twentieth-century coinage, not, as might be imagined, from American English, but from Czech. Derived from *robotá*, meaning hard labour, it first appeared in Karel Čapek's 1920 play *R.U.R. (Rossum's Universal Robots)*. The play's title is given in English even in the Czech original, with 'Rossum' intended as an English-sounding proper name, which nonetheless also connotes the Czech common noun *rozum*, meaning 'reason'. Čapek's robots – *Robot* in the masculine, *Robotka* in the feminine, *Roboti* in the plural – are human in form, that is, what we now term 'androids'. But they are mechanically manufactured, nonetheless:

> Pak je montovna, kde se to dává dohromady, víte, jako automobily.
>
> (Čapek 1966: 22)

> [there's the fitting shed, where all the parts are put together, like motor-cars.]
>
> (Čapek 1961: 15)

First suggested to Čapek by his brother, Josef, the new word rapidly acquired its more familiarly metallic connotations. The Čapek brothers were key figures in the literary life of the ill-fated first Czechoslovak Republic, founded in 1918 from the ruins of the Austro-Hungarian Hapsburg Empire and conquered by Nazi Germany in 1939, only months before the Second World War. Karel had died late in 1938, but Josef was interned in the concentration camp at Bergen-Belsen, where he survived until early 1945. Both had made professional, quasi-polymathic careers in the arts, Josef as painter, novelist, essayist and critic, Karel primarily as a playwright, but also a journalist, stage manager, novelist, essayist and – like Mary Shelley – travel writer (including writings on England). The brothers were, in Williams's terms, market professionals, the new men of letters of the doomed liberal republic.

The Czech script for *R.U.R.* was published in book form in 1920, the play first performed in Prague on 2 and 3 January 1921 (Čapek 1966: 117). A German translation by Otto Pick, probably intended for the German-speaking Sudetenland, was published in Prague in 1922 under the title *W.U.R. Werstands Universal Robots* (Čapek 1922). This is the first appearance in German of what would become the word *Roboter*. Interestingly, whereas most subsequent translations retained Čapek's title, Pick Germanicised the pseudo-English 'Rossum' as 'Werstand', a proper name connoting the German word *Verstand*, meaning intelligence, mind or reason. An American English-language version was performed in 1922 by the New York Theatre Guild, a British version by the Reandean Company at St Martin's Theatre in London in 1923. Distinct British and American translations followed in book form later that year. A Japanese translation appeared in 1923, French and Russian in 1924, Rumanian and Turkish in 1927, Italian in 1929, Bulgarian in 1931, Swedish in 1934 (Čapek 1966: 204–5). The play and its keyword 'robot' were thus already internationally well known by the time Lang released *Metropolis*. Reviewing the latter shortly after its Australian premiere in 1928, the *Sydney Morning Herald* (16 April 1928) expressly compared the film to *R.U.R.* A product of the 1920s, when theatre still retained much of its nineteenth-century popularity, and film – still black and white, still silent – had fewer obvious comparative advantages, it reached a much larger audience than is now normal for non-mechanically reproducible drama and is still almost certainly the Czech play best known outside the Czech Republic. There are today four main English translations: two by Paul Selver, one for the original American stage production, the other for the original British, both probably based on the 1920 Czech script (Čapek 1923, 1961); Novack-Jones's 1989 translation, based on the 1921 Czech script (Čapek 1990); and the most recent, by Majer and Porter, which controversially translates 'Rossum' into 'Reason' (Čapek 1999). There has been much controversy over which is preferable, but given Čapek's own declared admiration for Selver and Philmus's more recent scholarly defence of the latter's work (Philmus 2001), I have decided to use his translation, in its British version, except where this seems completely inappropriate.

R.U.R. is organised into four acts, the first a prologue, the last sometimes treated as an epilogue. All are set in the future on an anonymous island housing the offices and factory of the eponymous 'Rossum's Universal Robots', an English (or American) sounding corporation which has acquired a global monopoly on the manufacture of artificial workers. In the prologue we are introduced to the key figures in its operation: the plant director, Harry Domin, and the chief engineer, Fabry; the two head scientists, Doctors Gall and Hallemeier; the head of marketing, Konzul Busman, and the head of construction, Stavitel Alquist; and also to two robots, the female Sulla and the male Marius. We also meet the company president's daughter, Helena Gloryová, when she interrupts Domin and Sulla at their work. In the British translation, Domin is rendered as Domain, Hallemeier as Helman, Busman as Berman, the visitor as Helena Glory, daughter of an Oxbridge professor. Middle class and quasi-feminist in character, we learn she has come to the island as a representative of the 'Liga humanity', or Humanity League, which aims to liberate Robots from human oppression (Čapek 1966: 28; 1961: 21–2). Her reforming zeal is soon deflected, however, by Domin's romantic attentions, so that at the opening of the second act, set ten years later (five in the British translation), they are already long married.

If the prologue is comic, vaguely reminiscent of Shaw's *Major Barbara*, then the two acts that follow are written in a distinctly dystopian register, much closer to Chekhov or Ibsen. The second traces the initial human responses to the beginnings of a Robot Revolution, hints that Gall has been experimenting to produce a small number of near-human Robots and, in a key exchange between Helena and the upstart Robot, Radius, allows the latter both to denounce humanity and to articulate his own will to power (Čapek 1966: 49–50; 1961: 44–5). The third shows the besieged humans organising in defence of Domin's house, debating the morality of their situation – including Gall's admission that he has indeed attempted to make Robots into humans – and finally being attacked and overwhelmed by Radius and his followers. In the fourth and last act Alquist alone survives of all humankind, retained by the Robots in an apparently futile effort to find ways to reproduce themselves in the absence of their human creators. In the Czech original three Robots, Radius, Primus and Damon, in effect debate the morality of their own situation, but the latter character is omitted from the British translation. This is unfortunate, given the intensely philosophical nature of the debate: as Kinyon (1999) astutely argues, Radius is the Hegelian master in search of recognition, Damon, initially at least, the Kantian categorical imperative incarnate, Primus an embodiment of Christian self-sacrificial love.

Like *Paradise Lost* and *Frankenstein*, *R.U.R.* deliberately reworks the *Genesis* story. In the Czech original, though not in the British translation, the nurse, Nana, actually warns Helena thus:

> Já říkám, to je proti Pánubohu, to je d'áblovo vňuknuti, dělat ty maškary mašinou. Rouháni je to proti Svořiteli,..., je to urážka Pána, kterej nás stvořil k vobrazu Svýmu.
>
> (Čapek 1966: 38)

> [I'm telling you, churning out these machine-made dummies is against the will of God. It's the devil's own doing. Such blasphemy

> is against the will of the Creator,...it's an insult to the Lord who created us in His image.]
>
> (Čapek 1990: 57)

Like Shelley, Čapek was interested, not so much in angels and devils, however, as in the creation of posthuman intelligent life. Although it makes no direct reference to *Frankenstein*, the play clearly borrows from *The Island of Doctor Moreau*, Wells's own reworking of Shelley's novel (Wells 1996). When Domin recalls old Rossum's unsuccessful pioneering work in robotics to the recently arrived Helena, he describes a presumption closely akin to Frankenstein and Moreau:

> Víte, chtěl jaksi vědecky sesadit Boha.... Nešlo mu o nic víc než podat dukaz, že nebylo žádného Pánaboha zapotřebí. Proto si umanul udělat člověka navlas, jako jsme my.
>
> (Čapek 1966: 16)

> [He wanted to become a sort of scientific substitute for God, you know.... His sole purpose was nothing more or less than to supply proof that Providence was no longer necessary. So he took it into his head to make people exactly like us.]
>
> (Čapek 1961: 7)

But, Domin continues, the old atheist 'neměl drobet pochopení pro industrii' (Čapek 1966: 17) ['hadn't the slightest conception of industrial matters'] (Čapek 1961: 8). So, despite the company's mythologising accounts of its origins, it turns out to be an engineer, the old man's nephew, who successfully completed the project. Engineering is, of course, an applied science and, as Domin explains, young Rossum's success was as much a matter of commercial as scientific acumen:

> A teprve mladý Rossum měl nápad udělat z toho živé a inteligentní pracovní stroje...Mladý Rossum vynalezl dělníka s nejmenším počtem potřeb. Musel ho zjednodušit. Vyhodil všechno, co neslouží přímo práci. Tím vlastně vyhodil člověka a udělal Robota.
>
> (Čapek 1966: 17–18)

> [But it was young Rossum who had the idea of making living and intelligent working machines.... Young Rossum invented a worker with the minimum amount of requirements. He had to simplify him. He rejected everything that did not contribute directly to the progress of the work. In this way he rejected everything that makes man more expensive. In fact, he rejected man and made the Robot.]
>
> (Čapek 1961: 8–9)

These are machines, then, made and sold for profit, more intelligent than humans, but soulless:

> Jsou mechanicky dokonalejší než my, mají úžasnou rozumovou inteligenci, ale nemají duši.
>
> (Čapek 1966: 18)

> [Mechanically they are more perfect than we are, they have an enormously developed intelligence, but they have no soul.]
>
> (Čapek 1961: 9)

Much secondary commentary on *R.U.R.* reads its reworking of the hubris topos quite specifically as fear of 'the menace of science' (Klaić 1991: 80–4), expressed here in this opposition between machine and soul. But there is more to Čapek than technophobia, for, unlike Frankenstein's invention, young Rossum's has been geared to the demands of the capitalist commercial market, which secures its distribution on a global scale. Hence, Domin's busy absorption in commercial routine, in the play's opening scene, and the trade route maps and marketing slogans specified for its set:

> Nejlacinější práce: Rossumovi Roboti...
> Tropičtí Roboti, nový vynález. Kus 150 d....
> Každý si kup svého Robota!...
> Chcete zlevnit svoje výrobky? Objednejte Rossumovy Roboty.
>
> (Čapek 1966: 11)

> [CHEAP LABOUR. ROSSUM'S ROBOTS...
> ROBOTS FOR THE TROPICS. 150 DOLLARS EACH...

> EVERY ONE SHOULD BUY HIS OWN ROBOT...
> DO YOU WANT TO CHEAPEN YOUR OUTPUT? ORDER ROSSUM'S ROBOTS.]
>
> (Čapek 1961: 1)

Even when disaster is imminent, after the human birth-rate has fallen precipitately, when Robots employed as soldiers on a mass scale have risen up in rebellion against humankind, R.U.R. still persists with business, driven on, not simply by hubris, it is clear, but above all by profit. Faced with catastrophe, Domin justifies the project retrospectively as a noble attempt to triumph over the servitude of labour. But Alquist, and with him Čapek, will have none of it:

> Starý Rossum myslel na své bezbožné kejkle a mladý na miliardy. A není to sen vašich R.U.R. akcionářu. Jejich sen jsou dividendy. A na jejich dividendy lidstvo zahyne.
>
> (Čapek 1966: 67)

> [Old Rossum only thought of his godless tricks, and the young one of his millions. And that's not what your R.U.R. shareholders dream of either. They dream of dividends. And their dividends are the ruin of mankind.]
>
> (Čapek 1961: 66)

On first encounter, such explicit anti-capitalism is surprising in a writer well known for his sympathy with Anglo-American liberalism. Čapek's Charles University doctoral thesis had unfavourably compared German philosophical idealism with the pragmatism of James, Dewey and Peirce (Čapek 1925a); he would later write affectionately about England, Scotland and the British (Čapek 1934, 1925b); he was a close friend and admirer of Thomas Masaryk, first President of the Czechoslovak Republic and the most Anglophile of Czech liberals (Čapek 1969). As Klaić observes, Čapek was 'a democrat, a political moderate, an authoritative spokesman for the republican virtues of Masaryk's Czechoslovakia' (1991: 80). In short, he was no Marxist. Like many other continental European liberals, however, he had recognised the potential contradiction between liberal politics, on the one hand, and capitalist economics, on the other, so firmly repressed in early twenty-first-century Anglo-American liberalism.

In *R.U.R.* the unregulated pursuit of corporate profit, through the global marketing of high technology, leads to absolute disaster, the destruction of the human race itself, an outcome anticipated and sought by no individual or corporation, but produced nonetheless by the logic of capitalist competition. With this theme, Čapek introduced into twentieth-century SF one of its two major dystopian topoi. The other, of course, was the overweeningly intrusive totalitarian state, introduced into Russian by Zamiatin in his 1920–1 *My* (*We* in English, *Nous autres* in French) and into English by Orwell (who had read *Nous autres*) in *Nineteen Eighty-Four* (Zamiatin 1970; Orwell 1970d: 95–9; 1954). For the most obvious of contextual reasons – Stalinism in Russia, Fascism in Italy, Nazism in Germany – the dystopian imaginings of the middle decades of the twentieth century were preoccupied with the problem of totalitarianism. Indeed, Čapek himself would address this theme, through the figure of the Marshall, in his 1937 SF play *Bílá Nemoc* (Čapek 1937, 1938). But in *R.U.R.* he had also, and perhaps more interestingly, confronted the problem of a globalising, corporate-capitalist, scientific-industrial complex, which acquired renewed urgency only in the science fictions of the late twentieth and early twenty-first centuries.

In *R.U.R.*, as in *Paradise Lost*, the *Genesis* story is retold as a double fall: first, that of humankind into extinction, through a combination of hubris, technological excess and unbridled capitalism; and, second, that of the Robots into a parallel near-extinction, through their cruelty in disposing of their one-time human masters. If the former is an explicit commentary on corporate capitalism, the latter can be read as an allegory of the fate of the Bolshevik Revolution. The references are at times unmistakeable. The Robots are armed and driven to revolution by wars between and within capitalist states. Their rising is initiated in the first instance by a national union of Robots at Le Havre, claiming to speak on behalf of the Robots of the world:

> Roboti světa! My, první organizace Rossumových Univerzálních Robotu, prohlašujeme člověka nepřítelem a psancem ve vesmíru…

Nešetřte mužu. Nešetřte žen. Uchovejte továrny, dráhy, stroje, doly a suroviny. Ostatní zničte. Pak se vrat'te do práce. Práce se nesmí zastavit.

(Čapek 1966: 61)

[Robots throughout the world. We, the first national organization of Rossum's Universal Robots, proclaim man as an enemy and an outlaw in the Universe.... Spare no men. Spare no women. Save factories, railways, machinery, mines, and raw materials. Destroy the rest. Then return to work. Work must not be stopped.]

(Čapek 1961: 59)

Both this manifesto and the post-revolutionary state that ensues are as obsessed with production as their human predecessors. In the Czech original, though not in the British translation, the new society is even governed by a Robot Central Committee, the 'Ústřední Výbor Robotu' (Čapek 1966: 88). Its leader, Radius, claims to act for the collective, but is clearly in pursuit of individual power and thus, no doubt, close to what might be Čapek's understanding of Lenin:

Nechci žádného pána...Chci být pánem jiných...Já chci být pánem lidí.

(Čapek 1966: 49)

[I don't want any master. I want to be master over others.... I want to be master over people.]

(Čapek 1961: 45)

In Čapek's dystopia the world is radically transformed for the worse, first by humans, then by Robots, through both will and technology, very much in the manner described by Williams. Moreover, the logics both of will and of technology are sketched out in such detail as to produce a powerful socio-political warning. The problem remains that here all such logic, whether human or Robot, tends remorselessly to self-destruction. Indeed, the play might plausibly have ended in what Marx and Engels called the mutual ruin of the contending classes. Its actual conclusion, however, is that life will continue even though humanity may not, which is more optimistic, but nonetheless obviously belied by what precedes it and therefore distinctly improbable. Where no politics will work, the only alternative, it seems, is unconditional romantic love, of a distinctly human, patriarchal and even bourgeois variety, which Milton might have found familiar. In ways both unexplained and inexplicable to commonsense materialism, whether capitalist or communist, the play insists that mutually reciprocal, self-sacrificial, romantic, heterosexual love between the Robot Primus and the Robotess Helena – named after her human predecessor – will yield the promise of new life. Alquist, the sole surviving human, is thus given the last speech, in which to pronounce them the new Adam and Eve:

> Heleno, ved' ho.... Jdi, Ademe. Jdi, Evo; budeš mu ženou. Bud' jí mužem, Prime.
>
> (Čapek 1966: 101)

> [Helena, lead him. Go, Adam – Go, Eve. You shall be his wife. Be her husband, Primus.]
>
> (Čapek 1961: 104)

Opening the Bible, Alquist quotes directly from *Genesis* (Čapek 1966: 101; 1961: 104; *Genesis*: I, 27–8, 31). He and the play then conclude by citing the song of Simeon from the Christian Gospel according to St Luke (*St Luke*: II, 29–30). This is rendered slightly misleadingly in Selver's British translation, but with more dramatic effect for an English audience, as a direct quotation from the 'Nunc Dimittis' in the form given by the Anglican *Book of Common Prayer*, then still recited daily in the Church of England's 'Order for Evening Prayer'. The reference is rendered more accurately, however, that is, as an allusion rather than a quotation, by Novack-Jones:

> Nyní propustíš, Pane, služebníka svého v pokoji; nebot' uzřely oči mé – uzřely – spasení tvé skrze lásku, a život nezahyne!... Nezahyne!... Nezahyne!
>
> (Čapek 1966: 102)

> [Now, Lord, lettest Thou Thy servant depart in peace, according to Thy will, for mine eyes have seen Thy salvation.]
>
> (Čapek 1961: 104)

> [Now let Thy servant depart in peace, O Lord, for my eyes have beheld – beheld Thy deliverance through love, and life shall not perish!.... It shall not perish!...Not perish!]
>
> (Čapek 1990: 109)

Whichever translation we adopt, the conclusion is clear: no matter what the sterilities of capitalist robotics and communist Robots, love and life will finally survive. Christian rhetoric thus serves to underwrite what is a prehumanist, rather than humanist or posthumanist, solution: that God's will can indeed be done, whatever might result from the free wills of humans and their creations. By comparison with *Genesis* and *Paradise Lost*, the novelty here is in the possibility that God might choose to do his will without benefit of humans. This is neither Hebraic and tribal nor Protestant and bourgeois, but closer to a kind of pantheism, which in some ways anticipates recent debate about the posthuman and deep-ecological speculation about the planet's capacity to survive the depredations of our species. But for Čapek it was surely the way to square a circle, to produce an optimistic resolution where none was readily available. History would be less kind to the Czechoslovak Republic than Čapek to his Alquist.

Metropolis

In the previous chapter we observed some of the complexities involved in 'adapting' Shelley's novel to film. In this chapter, as we move from the theatre to the cinema to television, we need to say more about the differential possibilities and limitations of these media. Film theorists have often taken understandable exception to Adorno and Horkheimer's thesis that:

> The development of the culture industry has led to the predominance of the effect, the obvious touch, and the technical detail over

> the work itself – which once expressed an idea, but was liquidated together with the idea.
>
> (Adorno and Horkheimer 1979: 125)

But if this was clearly overstatement as a comment on film in general, it nonetheless retains a peculiar pertinence to SF cinema in particular. For in this sub-form, where the literary novum is indeed typically an 'idea' and the central cinematic device typically an 'effect', there is likely to be a real tension between the novum and its representation as spectacle. Insofar as this is so, it will only ever be as a 'law of tendency', towards the conceptualisation of the novum as idea in the written medium, towards its specularisation as effect in the cinematic, with the theatre positioned somewhere in between, but with all three understood as points on a continuum, rather than as permanent structural properties of the respective media.

The central preoccupation in *Metropolis* is, as its title suggests, not the robot, but rather the city. As Williams stressed, the megalopolis has been a crucial site of recent utopian and dystopian imaginings: 'Out of an experience of the cities came an experience of the future' (Williams 1973b: 272). He traced this transformation in the first instance to late nineteenth-century London, citing as examples Morris's *News from Nowhere* and Wells's *A Story of the Days to Come*. But he was clear that the argument applied to film as well as to the novel and he traced a line of descent from Wells to Lang (ibid.: 274). This will also be our understanding of the connections between utopia, dystopia and the city. Whatever else it might be, however, Williams's *The Country and the City* was in no sense 'postmodern': both its SF and its cities were very clearly 'modern'. But the hyperurban experience that so interested him has in fact become characteristic of postmodern 'hyperreality'. I use the terms modernism and postmodernism here as instances of what Williams had meant by a 'structure of feeling'. But their empirical substance has been better addressed by Baudrillard and Jameson than by Williams. To summarise and compound their accounts: in the late twentieth century, western culture and society entered into a third 'post-industrial' or 'multinational' stage, founded on electronics rather than electricity, information and 'hyperreality' rather than production and productivism (Jameson 1991: 35; Baudrillard 1994: 121); these transformations were the effect of mutations in the nature of capital (Jameson 1991: 35–6; Baudrillard 1993: 8); this 'late capitalism' was increasingly mass-mediated, asocial and transnational rather than national in scope (Jameson 1991: 49; Baudrillard 1983: 19); the resultant postmodern media culture became so 'imprinted on human subjectivity and existential experience' (Jameson 1992: 131) that identity came increasingly to be understood as constructed and hence indeterminate; referentiality thus became so attenuated that the signifier became its own referent, the real was superseded by the hyperreal, and intertextuality *per se* emerged as the characteristically postmodern aesthetic effect (Baudrillard 1975: 127–8; 1993: 3; Jameson 1991: 20). To all this we can add the further proposition, widely canvassed in contemporary debate from Haraway (1991) to Hayles (1999) to Fukuyama (2002), that the posthuman has become a characteristically postmodern thematic. I want to use this set of propositions as a way into a reading of *Metropolis* and *Blade Runner*, designed to chart the shift from modern to postmodern structures of feeling and relations of cultural production.

Metropolis was nearly two years in the making, had its first theatre release in January 1927 and is still, by some counts, one of the most expensive films ever made in Germany. It was directed by Fritz Lang, an Austrian rather than a German, who had earlier made *Dr Mabuse, der Spieler* (1922), the quasi-science fictional film about an evil criminal genius which triggered a series of sequels and the six-hour fantasy *Die Niebelungen* (1923–4). *Metropolis* featured Bridgette Helm as Maria, a childcare worker for working-class children and would-be social reformer and 'moderate' agitator to their parents. Alfred Abel played Joh Fredersen, the tyrannical master of Metropolis, and Gustav Fröhlich his son, Freder, who falls in love with Maria. Rudolph Klein-Rogge played Rotwang, the mad scientist, who designs and builds the first screen robot and, on Fredersen's instructions, turns it into a duplicate Maria. Interestingly, Lang used the term *Mensch-Maschine* or, in the plural, *Maschinen-Menschen*, rather than 'robot', even though the latter was already available from the Čapeks. This was a black and white silent film, a mechanically reproducible marketable commodity, sold to distributors to be consumed collectively, and, in Benjamin's phrase, 'in a state of distraction' (1973b: 242), in the darkness of the cinema theatre. Though film theorists often insist that cinema is consumed much less 'distractedly' than television or radio, Benjamin's implicit comparison was with the printed book and here he was surely right. Like much filmically ambitious SF, *Metropolis* was prohibitively expensive, costing some DM5 million, which nearly bankrupted the state-sponsored Universum Film Aktiengesellschaft. It was the product of a still recognisably national German cinema, but acquired speedy distribution in Britain and the US, in part thanks to the absence of sound, since the translation of intertitles was much cheaper than either subtitling or dubbing. The initial three-hour version no longer exists: it was cut to 128 minutes for the 1927 UK print, seventy-five minutes for the 1927 US print and ninety minutes for the 1928 German re-release. A near-complete restoration, including a soundtrack based on the score for the 1927 Berlin premiere, was released by the Murnau Foundation in 2002, however, and this is the version I have used here.

In *Metropolis* the architecture of the dystopian cityscape functions as a synecdoche for the wider catastrophe that has overcome its population: the city *is* the dystopian novum, catastrophe encoded in all its social and architectural forms. This catastrophe is not exactly a fall, however, in the sense we observed in *Genesis*, *Paradise Lost*, *Frankenstein* and *R.U.R.*, since the film offers no account of any prior processes which brought it about. Though the city must logically be the product of some combination of human will or technology, to borrow Williams's terms, Lang makes no attempt to explain how: the dystopia obeys no logic of process; it merely is. The catastrophe therefore functions primarily by way of extrapolation from existing social relations of class and gender. Although not explicitly identified with Berlin or any other particular location, this science fictional future city is clearly organised around the conflict between capital and labour that dominated the German cities of the 1920s. It is a class-divided city, vertically stratified between the darkest proletarian depths where the workers live, the intermediary levels where they work in conditions of extreme alienation – illustrated at length in one of the film's best-known sequences – and the high city of light inhabited by the privileged classes. Gesturing towards the sunlit heights of this hypermodernist cityscape, Freder demands of his father:

> ...und wo sind die Menschen...deren Hände Deine Stadt erbauten—?
>
> [...and where are the people...whose hands built your city—?]

The camera cuts to a shot of the next shift of workers descending by lift to the subterranean factories, as Fredersen retorts:

> Wo sie hingehören...in die Tiefe
>
> [Where they belong...in the depths].

Interestingly, this vertical social stratification – which would become a standard trope in SF cinema – has no equivalent in reality, where cities still tend to be stratified horizontally. The film's strikes, crowds, riots and even the false Maria as female agitator all echo something of the German Revolution of 1918, in which Rosa Luxemburg, for example, had played a key role. Importantly, there is still hope in this city, both the false hope of revolution, as Lang saw it, and the real hope of social reconciliation, attained in its closing scenes. The extraordinarily ambitious architecture of the high city, which much preoccupied Lang in its making, signifies this hope at least as much as it does Fredersen's hubris.

Like many other urban dystopias, *Metropolis* exhibits a fundamentally masculinist view of gender, in which the 'otherness of woman' is represented, to borrow Huyssen's description, by 'two traditional images of femininity – the virgin and the vamp,...both focused on sexuality' (Huyssen 1988: 72). Here, the roles are played, respectively, by the two Marias, human and robot. The film uses the nightclub and the female performer as signifiers of urban life, so that when the false Maria performs before the audience at Yoshiwara's, she does so simultaneously for the voyeurism of the 'cinematic gaze'. For Mulvey, as we have seen, the spectator position in narrative cinema prescribes a masculine point of view. So the film-goer comes to occupy a position of voyeuristic dominance over woman as the sexualised object of the cinematic gaze. This has become a distinctly unfashionable view in cinema studies and one

Mulvey herself had occasion to question (Mulvey 1989: 29–37). Nonetheless, the robot Maria functions exactly thus. Interestingly, however, the film self-reflexively draws attention to the process, by inserting a montage of gazing male eyes into the frame, and thereby threatens to undermine it. As Huyssen observes, 'by thematizing male gaze and vision...the film lays open a fundamental filmic convention usually covered up by narrative cinema' (1988: 75). But it still proceeds to punish its 'bad woman' for inviting the gaze: the false Maria, a flesh-covered robot found raucously celebrating amidst the bourgeois revellers at Yoshiwara's, is seized by the angry working-class insurrectionists, led by Grot, Fredersen's foreman and on occasion his company spy. Played by Heinrich George, Grot urges the mob to vengeance on 'die Hexe', the ubiquitous 'witch' of misogynist fantasy:

> Verbrennt die Hexe. – Auf den Scheiterhaufen mit ihr!!!
>
> [Burn the witch. – To the stake with her!!!]

And this is, indeed, her fate, even if the sudden exposure of a metallic body beneath the burning flesh somehow absolves all concerned – Freder included – of the barbarism entailed in such summary justice.

If intertextuality is a built-in feature of the aesthetic effect in post-modernism, as Jameson argues, then *Metropolis* is clearly a modern rather than postmodern text, original in precisely an avant-gardist sense. The Expressionist sets, by Otto Hunte, Eric Kettelhut and Karl Vollbrecht, bespeak the style of a very particular time and place. Whilst the film has functioned as an intertext for much subsequent SF cinema, its own central effect is nonetheless novelty rather than inter-textuality. If the posthuman is one of postmodernism's characteristic thematics, then in this respect, too, *Metropolis* is modern rather than postmodern. Indeed, Rotwang and his *Mensch-Maschine* are even more obviously reworkings of Frankenstein and his monster than were the Rossums and their robots. When Rotwang unveils his robot to Fredersen, in a scene that would establish the basic template for screen robots from the 1920s through to George Lucas's C3P0, the scientist is as obsessively hubristic as any in SF:

> Noch 24 Stunden Arbeit – , und kein Mensch...wird den Maschinen-Menschen von einem Erdgeborenen unterscheiden können—!
>
> [Give me another 24 hours – , and no one...will be able to tell a robot from a mortal—!]

But this improbable promise is met when Rotwang later clothes his *Mensch-Maschine* in the appearance of flesh borrowed from the kidnapped Maria. The mechanics of this process – the dials, the bubbling liquids, the decisive moment when the decisive lever is pulled, the bolts of electricity directed at the prone body – established another screen template, loyally adhered to by subsequent Frankensteins, from Whale through to Branagh.

Metropolis is rich in Biblical references, from Babel to the crucifixion and the Apocalypse, but interestingly there is no reference to *Genesis*. Indeed, the film is much less concerned with either the fall or the ethics of creation than with problems of individual identity and subterfuge. Rotwang's motive for creating the robot is above all to recreate Hel, his doubly lost lover, lost to Fredersen in sexual competition, to death in giving birth to Freder. Fredersen's reason for substituting a false Maria for the false Hel seems simply to discredit the true Maria. And Rotwang obliges, we learn, only to be avenged on Fredersen:

> Du Narr! Nun sollst Du auch das Letzte verlieren, das Du von Hel noch hattest...Deinen Sohn...
>
> [You fool! Now you will lose the one thing you still have from Hel...your son...]

This is a tangled web of deception and counter-deception, then, leading to mutual ruin. But if the film invokes the threat of the robot Maria as a man-made substitute for woman, we are nonetheless in little doubt that Freder, at least, can distinguish the true from the false. Almost at a glance, he sees that:

> Du bist nicht Maria –!!!

[You are not Maria –!!!]

The line is repeated:

DU BIST NICHT MARIA –! Maria redet zum Friden, nicht zum Mord –! Das ist nicht Maria – !!'

[YOU ARE NOT MARIA –! Maria speaks of peace, not killing –! This is not Maria –!!]

'Du bist nicht Maria', Freder insists, and he is right. There is no fundamental uncertainty here as to the nature of individual identity: a true man can readily spot a true woman.

The robot's destruction by fire replicates the classically humanist solution to the problem of the posthuman, as it appeared in *Frankenstein*. The true Maria then inspires Freder to unite capital and labour, Fredersen and Grot, in a moment that simultaneously endorses the division of labour by class and by gender, assuring him that:

Hirn und Hände wollen zusammenkommen

[Head and hands want to join together.]

As the film concludes, she continues:

aber es fehlt ihnen das Herz dazu... Mittler Du, zeige ihnen, den Weg zueinander... MITTLER ZWISCHEN HIRN UND HÄNDEN MUSS DAS HERZ SEIN!

[but they don't have the heart to do it... Oh mediator, show them the way to each other... THE MEDIATOR BETWEEN HEAD AND HANDS MUST BE THE HEART!]

Apparently, a good man needs a good supportive woman at his side, rather than a spitefully subversive *Mensch-Maschine*.

This denouement is 'a lingering residue of expressionism', Huyssen observes, '...which covers up the persisting domination of labor by capital and high technology, the persisting domination of woman by the male gaze and the reestablished repression of...sexuality' (Huyssen 1988: 81). 'Covering up' is the key phrase here. For the film's ending can be read as nicely social-democratic or horribly fascist, according to taste, and is quite possibly both, if only because neither could ever have been achieved so cheaply in any imaginable historical reality. A social-democratic solution would actually require active structures of co-partnership like those designed in the post-war *Bundesrepublik*, a fascist solution, the active suppression of working-class resistance like that secured in the concentration camps of the Third Reich. But *Metropolis* simply avoids the serious issues it raises, in much the same way as most contemporary Hollywood cinema, by substituting effect for idea, both the histrionic affects of the Freder/Maria relationship and the elaborate special effects characteristic of SF cinema. And this is what finally excites our admiration in the film: not its ideas, which are rarely better than trite by comparison with *R.U.R.*, but rather the spectacular effects used to create the city and the robot. Serious issues do not cease to be serious, however, merely by being avoided. The screenplay for *Metropolis* was co-written by Lang and his then wife, Thea von Harbou. She joined the Nazi Party in 1932, whilst he fled into exile in the USA. In 1926 the contradiction between readings had been nothing like so readily apparent.

Blade Runner

Blade Runner was first released in 1982, a second 'director's cut' in 1992. The film was produced for Warner Brothers by the 'Blade Runner Partnership' at a reported cost of $27 million (Kolb 1991: 146n.). Directed by the English film-maker Ridley Scott, who had earlier directed *Alien*, and loosely based on Philip K. Dick's 1968 novel *Do Androids Dream of Electric Sheep?*, it featured Harrison Ford as Rick Deckard, the 'blade runner' of the title, whose job it is to 'retire' escaped 'replicants' or androids. Rutger Hauer and Daryl Hannah played Roy Batty and Pris, two fugitive replicants; Sean Young, Rachael, the replicant with whom Deckard eventually falls in love; William Sanderson, J. F. Sebastian, designer of the replicants; and Joe Turkell, Eldon Tyrell, head of the Tyrell Corporation, which manufactures them. Like Branagh's *Mary Shelley's Frankenstein*, *Blade Runner* was a product of highly developed corporate professional relations of production, a marketable commodity to be initially consumed in the cinema theatre and subsequently recycled as video. For all its later cult reputation, Scott had clearly aimed at commercial as much as critical success, even though the film's first release turned out to be a box-office disaster, losing some $12 million (ibid.: 132). He regards himself as the film's author: hence the 'director's cut'. But there is an obvious incongruity, nonetheless, in insisting on the authentic authorial voice and authentically authorised text of a film the central theme of which is precisely the inauthenticity, or at least the indeterminacy, of identity and memory.

In any case, as Landon observes: 'the adaptation of *Blade Runner* involved a large number of people and factors over a considerable period of time – to the extent that credit or blame for any particular aspect of the adaptation may be impossible to assign with any certainty' (Landon 1991: 93–4). The first draft for the film script was in one sense Dick's novel. But thereafter a series of scripts were written and rewritten, initially by Hampton Fancher and later by David Peoples (neither of whom wrote the voice-over narration included in the 1982 version but not in the director's cut). Whilst the film was in production, Dick had become increasingly hostile to the project: he had disliked *Alien* and told Scott as much; and he disliked Fancher's screenplay (Rickman 1991: 103–5, 107–8). But he was much more enthusiastic about the footage he was eventually shown (ibid.: 106–7). Dick's novel had been concerned with what it meant to be human, with how inhuman behaviour dehumanises humans to the level of androids, and was thus predicated on an essentially humanist notion of the radical difference between humans and non-humans. Like *Mary Shelley's Frankenstein*, *Blade Runner* is much less secure in its humanism. As Dick noted, Peoples's screenplay introduced an entirely new 'reciprocal motion', in which the replicants became progressively humanised as Deckard became progressively dehumanised. Dick insisted on reading the amendment as entirely complementary with his own preoccupations: 'this fusion of Deckard and the replicants is a *tragedy*.... This is horrifying because he is now as they are, so the theme of the novel is completely and essentially retained' (Van Hise 1982: 22).

Whatever Dick's own intentions in *Do Androids Dream of Electric Sheep?*, this reading of *Blade Runner* remains unconvincing, if only because the film's 1982 closing sequence, where Deckard and Rachael successfully escape from Los Angeles, has been commonly read as an unambiguously happy ending. This was how it was read by Scott, for example, who actively disliked it on precisely those grounds. Moreover, there is one very particular condition which would entirely undermine a Dickian humanist reading of *Blade Runner*, that Deckard should turn out not to be human at all, but to be yet another replicant. This view has been widely canvassed by critics and audiences alike, and apparently it is Scott's own: 'Within the context of the overall story, whether it's true or not in the book, having Deckard be a replicant is the *only* reasonable solution' (Kolb 1991: 177n.). Certainly, this seems to be the import of the famous 'unicorn scene' reinserted into the director's cut. Whether or not he is a replicant, there can be little doubt that Deckard himself and the replicant characters, Rachael on the one hand, the four surviving Nexus 6 escapees on the other, are all recognisably fallen angels. The film makes repeated intertextual use of earlier angelic sources, most obviously perhaps at the point where Batty misquotes Blake to the eye-maker Chew. The original is from *America: A Prophecy* and runs thus:

> Fiery the Angels rose, & as they rose
> deep thunder roll'd
> Around their shores: indignant
> burning with the fires of Orc...
>
> (Blake 1977: 216)

But Batty has it as 'Fiery the angels fell, deep thunder rolled around their shores, burning with the fires of Orc'. This certainly isn't Milton's Satan and his crew, but by turning Blake's risen into fallen angels the misquotation pointedly gestures towards *Paradise Lost*.

Like most of our earlier texts, *Blade Runner* is a story of the fall: each of the three main protagonists, Deckard, Rachael and Batty, either has already fallen at the outset or will fall in the course of the narrative. How, then, is this problem of the fall structured in Scott's film? We can begin by noting that, if Deckard is indeed a replicant, then all three of the central characters are creations of the same creator, Dr Eldon Tyrell. In the post-catastrophic dystopia that is the Los Angeles of November 2019, a city soaked in acid rain and choking on pollution, where animal life has already become virtually extinct and most healthy humans have already moved 'off-world', in this city Tyrell is, in Batty's phrase, 'the God of bio-mechanics'. The Los Angelean cityscape is dominated by the Tyrell Corporation building, a gleaming glass pyramid reaching so far above street level as to be lit by natural sunlight. Neither Milton's Paradise nor yet Shelley's workshop of filthy creation, this is a recognisable extrapolation from the great corporate towers that cluster at the centre of most contemporary cities. And its purpose is much the same: 'Commerce is our goal here at Tyrell'. In *Blade Runner*, as in *R.U.R.*, it is commerce, then, that has finally driven humankind to an impasse. Neither a god nor even a Frankenstein, Tyrell himself is demonstrably amoral, almost banally so. Nowhere is this more apparent than in the central confrontation between Tyrell and Batty, creator and creature, the film's equivalent to the encounter between Frankenstein and his monster on Mont Blanc. 'I have done questionable things', Batty confesses to the man he has already described as his 'maker'. 'Also extraordinary things – revel in your times', replies Tyrell. The only ethical judgement suggested in this scene is that implied by the replicant's own comment: 'Nothing the God of bio-mechanics wouldn't let you in heaven for'. The point, of course, is that there is *nothing* that this God of bio-mechanics wouldn't let you into heaven for.

All of Tyrell's creations are in different ways more impressive than their human creator. Where Dick had imagined his androids as inferior to humans, Scott's replicants are more nearly superhuman. The film's prologue informs us that: 'The NEXUS 6 *Replicants* were superior in strength and agility, and at least equal in intelligence, to the genetic engineers who created them'. And the greatest of these genetic engineers is Tyrell, who explains to Deckard that 'more human than human is our motto'. In the confrontation with Batty, Tyrell is even more explicit:

> You were made as well as we could make you. The light that burns twice as bright, burns half as long. And you have burned so very, very brightly, Roy.

Deckard, too, is the best at his bloody trade: as Bryant tells him, 'I need you, Deck.... I need the old blade runner, I need your magic'. And, if Rachael 'is an experiment, nothing more', in Tyrell's words, then this experiment is nonetheless that to produce the most convincing Nexus 6 yet. Where Tyrell is the God of Scott's 'hell-on-Earth', then, as Desser rightly observes, Deckard, Rachael and Batty are, respectively, its Adam, Eve and Satan (Desser 1991: 54–5, 58). But since this Los Angeles is precisely a hell rather than a heaven, their problem is not how to remain in Paradise but how to escape it. And yet each falls, Deckard and Batty through the sin of murder, Rachael through the dawning realisation that she is replicant rather than human. Thereafter, however, each finds a way toward both personal redemption and escape.

For Batty, redemption and escape come simultaneously in the moment when he saves Deckard's life and surrenders his own. Roy Batty is surely more obviously the hero of *Blade Runner* than Satan was ever that of *Paradise Lost*. Though the film's narrative movement is initially carried by Deckard, the focus shifts progressively towards Batty: he organises and directs the escaped replicants; he forces the issue of their mortality in the confrontation with Tyrell; he propels the narrative towards its climax in the film's most powerful scene, that of his own death. Unlike Satan, Batty defeats both his creator, Tyrell, and his rival creation, Deckard: it is as if Satan had not only seduced Eve and thence Adam, but also successfully stormed Heaven. And then, in the gesture that most clearly reverses Dick's intended humanism, Batty shows mercy to Deckard, to the blade runner who has shown none either to Pris or to any of the other replicants. In terms of the film's own internal morality, this gesture somehow cancels out all Batty's previous killing. His last speech reasserts the extraordinariness of his own superhuman individuality and yet also announces a final acceptance of mortality:

> I've seen things you people wouldn't believe. Attack ships on fire off the shoulders of Orion. I watched C beams glitter in the dark near the Tanhauser Gate. All those moments will be lost in time, like tears in rain. Time to die.

Which leaves Deckard and Rachael, Scott's Adam and Eve, the monster and the bride he has not yet been cheated of. For both, redemption comes through love: she has saved him from Leon; he will save her from the blade runners. But escape is another matter, depending very much on which of the film's two endings we use. In both, the original release and Scott's director's cut, the rival blade runner, Gaff, tells Deckard: 'It's too bad she won't live. But then again, who does?' In both, the line is later repeated. In both, Deckard asks for and receives from Rachael the promise of love and trust. In both, they discover Gaff's origami unicorn and thus realise he has previously found Rachael but nonetheless not killed her. The director's cut ends with a lift door closing on Deckard and Rachael, that is, on the ambiguous possibility of their escape from Los Angeles. The original theatre release version is much more explicit, however, leading to a subsequent sequence of their flight over what is clearly a deliberately Edenic countryside, with a voice-over explaining, not only that Gaff has let Rachael go, but also that she has no 'termination date'. There have been numerous objections to this ending, not least from Scott, the most obvious being the improbability of such an Eden existing within striking distance of so peculiarly hellish a Los Angeles.

Interestingly, Heldreth has argued that, although the first release ending 'may seem intellectually contrived and out of tone with the rest of the film,...it's the emotional ending we want' (1991: 51). In the most literal of senses, he is absolutely right: the studio chose this ending precisely because it was preferred by their pre-release sample audiences. But Heldreth prefers it for quite explicitly humanist reasons: 'At the end of the film', he writes, 'Deckard [is] no longer trying to remain a human being while he kills the very emotional responses that define his humanity.... Deckard, i.e., man, is presented as a human being who makes his escape into the new Eden with a new Eve' (ibid.: 51). Deckard and Rachael are indeed a new Adam and a new Eve, escaping into a new Eden. But Rachael is certainly not a woman and, if Scott is to be believed, nor is Deckard a man: these are replicants, the first of Frankenstein's race of devils. And if this is indeed the ending 'we' want, this can be so only for reasons precisely the obverse of Heldreth's – in short, because 'we', meaning the postmodern audiences of the late-capitalist world of the late twentieth century, were no longer at all persuaded of our own evolutionary superiority as a species. As Boozer says of *Blade Runner*, 'This near-future tech *noir* edition of...the postmodern city...is...in an advanced state of decay. Rather than reharmonizing itself with nature through knowledge, the world of Tyrell is further removed than ever' (1991: 219). And this is exactly how 'we' have increasingly come to see 'our' cities, as the mounting wreckage of a civilisation nearly beyond repair. In 1982 the *Blade Runner* solution still seemed quite staggering in its audacity: to give up on humanity in a wager on the prospects for a posthuman future, a post-lapsarian cyborg redemption, Eden for the replicants. The 1992 version spells out this replicant solution more explicitly, in almost every respect except the choice of ending. The director's cut concludes with a knowing gesture toward film noir, the characteristically postmodern move of intertextuality for its own sake, which distracts from the originality of the film's actual narrative resolution in the cyborg option.

For all its remarkable technical finesse, *Blade Runner*'s more general cultural significance is as a harbinger of this cyborg option. If postmodern cultural theory had begun to moot the possibility of a posthuman condition as early as the late 1970s, this had remained an essentially academic conceit. But *Blade Runner* marked a shift in popular and literary sensibilities that would register most powerfully, not so much in film as in the cyberpunk novel. Scott's Los Angeles is the prototype for 'the Sprawl' in Gibson's *Neuromancer* trilogy (1984, 1986, 1988), a debt widely acknowledged in much secondary criticism (cf. Benford 1992: 224; Clute and Nicholls 1993: 288). McHale even described *Blade Runner* as 'the most influential example of cyberpunk poetics in any medium' (1992: 229). Cyberpunk inherited at least three of its more distinctive sub-generic motifs from *Blade Runner*: a 'retro-fitted' vision of the future as always-already 'trashed'; a populist acceptance of the givenness of commodity aesthetics; and a persistent curiosity about the possibilities and potentialities for posthuman existence. If postmodernism is the cultural dominant of multinational late capitalism, then the Gibson trilogy was its 'exceptional literary realization', Jameson observed, 'as much an expression of transnational corporate realities as...of global paranoia' (Jameson 1991: 38). This sense of cyberpunk in particular, and contemporary SF more generally, as somehow peculiarly 'postmodern' has been much echoed elsewhere (Sobchack 1987: 246–50, 299–300; Broderick 1995: 103–9).

Jameson's is a determinedly 'dialectical' reading, in which cyberpunk is at once both 'reality' and 'paranoia', and much the same might be said of the cyborg moment within cultural theory. Haraway, for example, argued that a cyborg world would represent either 'the final imposition of a grid of control on the planet' or, alternatively, a world where 'people are not afraid of their joint kinship with animals and machines' (Haraway 1991: 154). Part of the power of *Blade Runner* and of the *Neuromancer* trilogy is in their capacity to represent this near-future from both perspectives. At one level this was absolutely necessary: the political struggle for a future can only ever be fought on the future's terrain. As Haraway observed: 'The cyborg would not recognise the Garden of Eden; it is not made of mud and cannot dream of returning to dust' (ibid.: 151). Yet, these alternatives are not simply logical possibilities; they are also socio-historical potentials, their effectivity conditioned by the balance of historical probabilities and social forces. It is at this level that the dystopian reading seems more persuasive than the utopian, since cyberspace is surely more likely to be dominated by Rupert Murdoch and Bill Gates than by cyberpunk hackers. In *Towards 2000* Williams had coined the term 'Plan X' to describe the New Right's 'new politics of strategic advantage', in contrast to older forms of political conservatism. Their 'real politics and planning', he concluded, will be centred 'on an acceptance of the indefinite continuation of extreme crisis and extreme danger' (Williams 1983: 244). This was an uncharacteristically alarmist remark and is, no doubt, easily dismissed as an old man reaching for the panic button. But Williams was neither much given to panic nor very old.

The years since his untimely death have witnessed a continuing and cumulative diminution of the sense of alternative possibilities within our culture. In part, this has been an effect of the collapse in 1989 of the Soviet Union, which, for all its brutalities, had appeared to many as empirical evidence for the feasibility of working alternatives to American corporate capitalism. Not that the United States, as a state, somehow 'won' the Cold War. Quite the contrary, the United States, as a state, has exhibited something close to paralysis under successive administrations, incapable of bringing to heel Al Qaeda, the great oil corporations or even the National Rifle Association. The 'victors' have not been these United States, then, but rather the great transnational corporations, Gibson's *zaibatsu*, the referential counterparts to the Tyrell Corporation or 'the Company' in Scott's *Alien*. The degeneration of the erstwhile utopianism represented in the figure of Haraway's cyborg, both into militarism and into commodification, thus ominously prefigured a posthumanism very different from hers. This has been apparent, moreover, from the founding moment of cyberpunk: for all their post-punk anarchism, Gibson's narratives were structurally organised around the inevitability of (a peculiarly fast-moving) process, rather than the instant of meaningful choice. As Landon observed, 'The real message of cyberpunk was inevitability – not what the future might hold, but...what the future could not fail to be' (Landon 1988: 245, cited in Csicsery-Ronay 1992: 38). And, as Ross notes, this future is 'recognizably extrapolated from...present trends that reflect the current corporate monopoly on power and wealth' (Ross 1991: 152).

The X-Files and *Buffy the Vampire Slayer*

Thus far, we have traced the development of the Frankenstein myth in twentieth-century theatre and cinema, that is, in two very public arts. But, as we noted in Chapter 3, these media were progressively superseded by the cultural forms and technologies of mobile privatisation, the most important of which were televisual. Television was perhaps the most truly global mode of cultural consumption in human history, but its production processes were more effectively dominated by American (or, in the specific case of News Corporation, Australo-American) media corporations than film, theatre or the novel. I want to conclude this chapter, then, with an analysis of how the Frankenstein story was retold in two of the most successful American television series of the last decade of the twentieth century and the first of the twenty-first: *The X-Files*, which ran from 1993 until 2002; and *Buffy the Vampire Slayer*, which ran from 1997 until 2003. We move very shortly to an analysis of particular episodes from each: 'The Postmodern Prometheus', which first went to air in November 1997, as part of the fifth season of *The X-Files*; and the 'Adam' sequence from *Buffy*'s fourth season, a set of four linked episodes, comprising 'The I in Team', 'Goodbye Iowa', 'The Yoko Factor' and 'Primeval', first broadcast during 2000, on 8 and 15 February and 9 and 16 May, respectively. But, first, let us say something about the more general characteristics of the two series.

The X-Files was produced by Chris Carter for Murdoch's American Fox Network; *Buffy* by Joss Whedon's own production company, Mutant Enemy, and broadcast on the Warner and Paramount networks, though its wider distribution was also handled by Fox. By televisual standards, both were subject to and acknowledge unusually strong claims to authorship. The credits for *The X-Files* described it as 'created' by Carter, he was its executive producer, he wrote the scripts for the first two episodes (and for nine out of twenty-four in the first season, two as co-author) and he directed many key episodes. Whedon was listed as 'creator' and 'executive producer' for *Buffy* and, during the first five seasons, directed sixteen episodes and wrote twenty-two. Both series were immensely successful. In February 1995, during its second season, the *X-Files* episode entitled 'Fresh Bones' reached some 10.8 million American homes (Lowry 1995: 247). This success was repeated elsewhere, in Britain for example, both on the BBC and News Corporation's Sky TV, and in Australia on Channel 10 and Murdoch's Foxtel. *Buffy* had a similar impact, again not only in the US, but also in Britain, again on the BBC, and in Australia, on Channel 7 and again on Foxtel. Both generated a considerable secondary spin-off industry of 'collectible' toys, comics and books (often published by News's HarperCollins), for *The X-Files* a film, and for *Buffy* the *Angel* television series.

The 'X-Files' provided Carter's programme with its title and central organising motif: each individual episode was supposed to be a file from the American Federal Bureau of Investigation's inquiries into the paranormal. For most of the series, the investigators were Agent Fox Mulder, played by David Duchovny, and Agent Dana Scully, played by Gillian Anderson. In the penultimate series Duchovny was for the main part replaced by Robert Patrick, in the role of Agent John Doggett. The episode that concerns us is taken from the main body, however, featuring Duchovny and Anderson. As the title makes clear, it is a self-consciously postmodern retelling of SF's founding text, *Frankenstein, or The Modern Prometheus*. Carter had never been entirely happy with the notion that *The X-Files* was SF: in a 1995 on-line interview, he insisted he 'never was a science fiction fan' and had 'never seen an episode of "Star Trek"' (Badley 1996: 150n.). But *Star Trek* provides only a very limited model of the science fictive and, for the main part, *The X-Files* met even Suvin's fairly restrictive criteria. Its long-run story arc was provided by a threatened alien invasion and collaboration by sections of the American elite, both entirely compatible with 'cognitive logic'. And, even where the paranormal became less obviously rational in content, Scully would seek to explain it through the cognitive logic of medical science. We should qualify these observations, by adding that this was distinctly 'postmodern' SF, not only in the obvious sense that Jameson and Baudrillard see SF and television as characteristically postmodern cultural phenomena, but also because the programme displayed postmodern characteristics of its own, which we will explore below.

Buffy the Vampire Slayer was not SF as Suvin had understood it, but rather Gothic fantasy, descended from Shelley's Geneva by way of a rather different genealogy. The Southern Californian town of Sunnydale, where the series is set, is a 'Hellmouth', the entrance to a world of ancient books and archaic weapons, bibles and wooden stakes, vampires, demons and magic. This Hellmouth is a Suvinian novum, but of the distinctly non-cognitive variety. The central protagonist, Buffy Summers, is a Vampire Slayer by nature and destiny, but a thoroughly contemporary Californian young woman by upbringing and preference. The conflict between nature and nurture had generated much of the narrative drive and comic effect in the 1992 film that inspired the television series. Directed by Fran Rubel Kuzui for Twentieth Century Fox, with Whedon as its scriptwriter, it was set in 'Southern California: the Lite Ages', as opposed to the Dark Ages, and was overwhelmingly comic in register. Kirsty Swanson played Buffy, Donald Sutherland her guide, Merrick, and Rutger Hauer the chief vampire, Lothos. In the television series this conflict between nature and nurture is significantly occluded through the naturalisation of the fantastic as an everyday feature of Southern Californian life. Television's Buffy, played by Sarah Michelle Gellar, graduated year by year, season by season, through Sunnydale High School and the University of California, Sunnydale, as one fresh-faced middle-class youngster amongst others, situated within and contextualised by an ensemble of friends (the 'Scooby Gang') and lovers. The friends included Nicholas Brendon as Xander, Alyson Hannigan as Willow and Charisma Carpenter as Cordelia; the lovers, David Boreanaz as Angel, the vampire with a soul, Marc Blucas as Riley, of whom more later, and James Marsters as Spike, the vampire eventually deprived of his capacity to kill humans. The programme's central adult authority figure, a direct counterpart to the film's Merrick, was provided by Buffy's 'watcher', Giles, played by Anthony Stewart Head, here nicely naturalised as the high school librarian.

This naturalisation of the supernatural suggests how closely SF and fantasy had come to overlap in 'New Age' late twentieth- and early twenty-first-century America. It is significant here that the US-based 'World Science Fiction Society', which for decades had made its annual Hugo Awards on near-Suvinian criteria, would award the 2001 prize for the best book to Rowling's *Harry Potter and the Goblet of Fire* (2000), for the best dramatic presentation to Ang Lee's *Wo hu cang long*, in English *Crouching Tiger, Hidden Dragon* (2000). The latter award went to Peter Jackson the following year for *The Fellowship of the Ring*, the first in his *Lord of the Rings* trilogy. It was divided into two separate classes in 2003, a long-form version, which went to Jackson once again, this time for *The Two Towers*, and a short-form version, which went to *Buffy*, for the 2002 episode 'Conversations with Dead People', written by Jane Espenson and Drew Goddard, directed by Nick Marck. This developing uncertainty over the distinction between SF and fantasy penetrated even into academic science fiction studies. As Parrinder pointedly observed: 'Suvin's poetics has...outlived its moment..."Cognitive estrangement" may be taken to be a fact about the 1970s, just as T. S. Eliot's "dissociation of sensibility" was a fact about the 1920s' (Parrinder 2000: 10). The empirical force of this convergence between SF and fantasy need not necessarily provide its own justification: prescriptively, there may still be much to be said for Suvin. But descriptively, convergence had simply become a 'fact' of contemporary cultural life. The *Buffy* episodes that concern us here are unusually close, nonetheless, to SF. In these and the immediately contiguous episodes, the programme's monsters and vampires were both rationalised and naturalised as 'HSTs', or Hostile Sub Terrestrials, pursued and hunted down by the ultra-scientific 'Initiative', which planned to use their body parts to create a cyborg, the demonoid 'Adam'. Here, as in 'The Postmodern Prometheus', the linking theme is a postmodern retelling of the *Frankenstein* story.

Buffy's main interests were in vampires, however. Vampire legends have a very long history, but entered into English prose fiction only comparatively recently, on the night that Frankenstein was conceived: Polidori's *The Vampyre* was published, under the name 'Lord B', only a year after *Frankenstein.* Its hero, Aubrey, travelled to Greece rather than Transylvania, its vampire was a lord rather than a count, Lord Ruthven, but the prototype for Bram Stoker's *Dracula*, the most famous of all vampire novels, had been established nonetheless. Stoker was Anglo-Irish, born, brought up and educated in Dublin, but as part of the Anglican Protestant ascendancy rather than the Catholic majority. First published in 1897 by Archbald Constable and Company, his *Dracula* introduced readers to the vampire Count and his dark Transylvanian home, but also to the isolated port of Whitby, where Dracula first steps ashore in England. Here readers first encountered the now familiar characters: Jonathan Harker, the hero, Van Helsing, the vampire hunter, Lucy Westenra and Mina Harker, both of whom Dracula desires, though only Lucy dies, whilst Mina eventually survives. In a scene that would recur throughout the history of cinema, Jonathan famously killed the Count at Castle Dracula just as the sun was setting.

There is a strange parallelism to the subsequent histories of the Frankenstein and Dracula myths. Like *Metropolis*, the first silent film version of the Dracula story was a product of German Expressionist cinema, Murnau's 1921 *Nosferatu*, released in English under the title *Dracula*. The first talkie version, also entitled *Dracula* and starring Bela Lugosi as the Count, was directed by Tod Browning in the same year and for the same studio as Whale's *Frankenstein*. It too triggered a series of sequels: *Dracula's Daughter* (1936), *Son of Dracula* (1943), *House of Dracula* (1945) and *The Return of Dracula* (1958). The Count was variously played by Lon Chaney Jr and John Carradine as well as Lugosi. Hammer's 1958 *The Horror of Dracula* was actually directed by Terence Fisher and featured Christopher Lee as the Count and Peter Cushing as Van Helsing. The Hammer sequels included *The Brides of Dracula* (1960), *Dracula – Prince of Darkness* (1965) and *Taste the Blood of Dracula* (1970). Lee played the Count, not only for Hammer, but also in other film versions, such as Pedro Portabella's 1970 *Vampir*, made for the Spanish Films 59. There is thus good reason to take seriously Moretti's argument that these are somehow archetypally modern myths: 'The fear of bourgeois civilization is summed up in...Frankenstein and Dracula...the two horrible faces of a single society...the disfigured wretch and the ruthless proprietor (Moretti 1988: 83). Like Baldick (1987: 148), I am by no means convinced that the Count is quite so modern a figure as Moretti suggests: there are clear continuities between Dracula, Ruthven and the historical figure of the feudal lord. But, equally, the vampire continues to strike terror into modern and postmodern audiences. I am inclined to read these two extremes rather differently, then, as fear of science and fear of anti-science. In short, this is a fictional – literary and cinematic – dialectic of Enlightenment and anti-Enlightenment.

Returning to the television programmes, but remaining for the moment with Adorno and Horkheimer, we should note that, although the special effects are technically proficient, the ideas were clearly more important, not in the sense that they were necessarily 'serious', but rather that they make the shows 'work'. The sheer range of ideas was crucial to the distinctive appeal of *The X-Files* and *Buffy*: in both, the viewer could never be quite certain what would happen next. By the standards of American television, this is a strong claim to make. The tension between idea and effect, which Adorno and Horkheimer identified in their critique of Hollywood cinema, seems to be resolved differently in television, primarily because of the low-budget nature of the medium. At one level, financial constraints clearly militate against both idea and effect, which is why so much television is interesting as neither. But ideas can come more cheaply than their specularisation, which leads to the possibility that television might sometimes reverse the cinematic prioritisation of effect over idea. This may well be the case here. At the very least, we need to note that these were unusually adventurous and interesting programmes.

Their novelty functioned at the level of form, moreover, as well as content. In *Television: Technology and Cultural Form*, Williams identified three main forms in television drama: the series, the serial and the single television play, the latter often part of an anthology (Williams 1974: 57–61). The first is a set of discrete stories built around a shared repertoire of characters and locations; the second, a set of linked episodes in a continuing narrative, which necessarily entails some continuity in both character and location; the third, either a separate production in its own right or a collection of entirely distinct stories, connected by the frame device of the anthology. All three have been used in SF, though the third seems to have become less common over time, probably because its use of different combinations of production and performance personnel for each episode makes it relatively high-cost. Formally, *The X-Files* and *Buffy* were neither pure series, serial nor anthology, but, rather, examples of what Reeves, Rodgers and Epstein described as 'episodic/serial straddle', that is, 'a sort of mini-serial within the series' (Reeves *et al.* 1996: 33–4). There were discrete episodes, but also multi-part episodes (such as 'Duane Barry' and 'Ascension' in *The X-Files* or the Adam sequence in *Buffy*). More importantly, a range of developing story-lines continued from episode to episode: in *The X-Files*, Mulder and his sister's abduction, Scully and her father, the Cancer Man (William B. Davis) and the conspiracy in high places; in *Buffy*, the mother/daughter relationship between Joyce Summers (Kristine Sutherland) and Buffy, the romances with Angel, Riley and Spike, Willow's lesbian relationship with Tara (Amber Benson), the Scooby Gang's steady progress through high school and university. Such long-term story arcs allowed for a cumulative character development unavailable to the conventional series as a form.

The X-Files and *Buffy* were examples of late-capitalist relations of cultural production in two interesting aspects: both were the product, simultaneously, of transnational capitalism and niche marketing. The transnational character of *The X-Files* is perhaps most readily apparent: Fox Broadcasting, which produced, broadcast, syndicated and marketed the programme, was a subsidiary of News Corporation, the Australian-based media conglomerate; its key 'stars' were American; but all except the last series were made in Canada, with mainly Canadian labour, including the actors playing the minor roles; and its audience was near-global. *Buffy* was less obviously transnational in production, but nonetheless had a distinctly transatlantic accent: Buffy, Willow and Xander – and Sunnydale – were firmly Californian; but Giles, Spike and Buffy's second Watcher, Wesley (Alexis Denisof), were played as English rather than American. Like *The X-Files*, *Buffy* also acquired a global market. That *The X-Files* belonged to Fox was more than merely coincidental: it also explains something of its success. Reeves, Rodgers and Epstein distinguish between what they term 'TVI', which lasted from the 1950s to the 1970s, and 'TVII', which dated from the 1980s and 1990s (ibid.: 24–5, 29). In the former, American television was dominated by three major 'free-to-air' networks, ABC, NBC and CBS, each producing programmes for very large 'mass' audiences. To survive in this market, a programme had to command something like one-third of the American television audience. Children's television aside, SF and fantasy could rarely manage this: even *Star Trek* lasted for only two seasons. TVII was characterised by the development of alternative outlets, such as satellite TV, cable TV and home video recording. During this period, the audience share commanded by the big three networks fell from 90 to 60 per cent (ibid.: 30), creating the space, not only for SF, but also for News Corporation to create its fourth network. Murdoch's company used *The X-Files* as a flagship for the Fox Network and as a key resource for its other satellite and cable interests, such as Sky in Britain and Foxtel in Australia. Similarly, *Buffy* was broadcast on the minor Warner network, which was itself part of a larger international media conglomerate, Time-Warner.

Both series were spectacular cult – that is, niche market – successes. Both were aimed at a target demographic of late teenagers and young adults, rather than 'mature' adults or children: in the United States, the peak audience for *Buffy* was in the 18–34 range, the average age 29 (Ono 2000: 165). Both seemed to be pitched at a disproportionately female audience. Both also acquired a 'fan' following of the kind we discussed in Chapter 4. By comparison with other sub-genres, SF does seem to inspire unusually strong loyalties amongst relatively clearly defined and demarcated audiences and hence tends to acquire this kind of 'cult' status. This is true even of the written medium, which has its

'SF Community' or 'Fandom' and their World Conventions (cf. Sanders 1994), but is much more the case for television. The first convention of 'X-Philes' was held in San Diego in June 1995, some 2,500 people attending, with twenty conventions in total scheduled for the same year across the USA. Both series generated a proliferation of collectibles and other spin-offs, and an extraordinarily well-developed on-line fandom, devoted to 'The Truth' or the 'Buffyverse'. In 1995 something like 25,000 people per month logged on to *X-Files* sites (Lowry 1995: 239–40).

Both series exhibited at least three characteristically postmodern tropes: 'politically correct' identity politics; intertextual aesthetics; and the posthuman as thematic. As to the first, Scully and Buffy were instances of the late twentieth-century fashion in American television for 'powerful women', which extended to include Xena the Warrior Princess and Captain Janeway from *Star Trek: Voyager*. In *The X-Files*, Scully was the more rational, scientific and sceptical, Mulder the more prone to 'believe', in part because he believed his sister to have been abducted. This is 'gender bending' of a kind, except insofar as the narrative tended to support his credulity as much as her scepticism. But the play with gender was real, nonetheless, and it was thus unsurprising that the show should have had a very large female audience. Shots of Mulder sometimes invited a female gaze as surely as anything in *Blade Runner* had invited the male. Moreover, as Wilcox and Williams approvingly observe, for the lead characters themselves: 'Their looks acknowledge each other as subjects rather than fetishizing or denying the other person' (1996: 120). *Buffy* was similarly non-homophobic and unsexist: witness the sympathetic treatment of the Willow/Tara relationship; or Buffy's capacity to take the initiative, not only in encounters with vampires and demons, but also in her relations with Riley and Angel. So it was Buffy, rather than Riley, who initiated their mutual seduction in 'The I in Team'. Shots of Riley during their subsequent lovemaking not only invite a female gaze, but also actually acquired one from within the televisual frame, when the camera panned away from a screen-within-the-screen, to reveal Professor Maggie Walsh as the female voyeur. No doubt sections of the male audience could gaze along with her, albeit at Buffy rather than Riley. But the more general success of these powerful women had arisen precisely from their capacity to function simultaneously as male sex objects and positive female role models.

If intertextuality is indeed the central postmodern aesthetic effect, then it is as evident in these shows as anywhere. In *The X-Files*, Mulder and Scully clearly refer to Woodward and Bernstein in *All the President's Men*, just as their initial insider contact with a penchant for meetings in car parks refers to the original 'Deep Throat'. But Mulder also borrows from Dale Cooper, the FBI agent in *Twin Peaks*, and Scully from Agent Starling in *The Silence of the Lambs* (Lowry 1995: 14–150). *Buffy* rifles through the horror and teen movie genres, borrowing everything from werewolves to graduation days, so that in the television series, as in the earlier film, much of the humour derives from running the two genres against each other. In both programmes, intertextual aesthetics are often combined with a posthuman thematic. In *The X-Files* these anxieties typically revolved around themes of alien abduction and/or invasive scientific experimentation on the human body. Buffy is actually a superhuman, but supposedly stands in a long line of Slayers, each human rather than posthuman. Riley and Adam, however, are more properly posthuman and, as we shall see, in these episodes the anxieties over posthumanism centre on the linked themes of monstrous rebellion and irresponsible scientific experimentation.

'The Postmodern Prometheus' and the biomechanical demonoid

The core narrative in 'The Postmodern Prometheus' tells how Mulder and Scully are summoned by Shaineh Berkowicz, a plump, mid-Western fan of *The Jerry Springer Show*, played by Pattie Tierce, to investigate claims that she has suffered two completely unwanted pregnancies, one contemporary, the other eighteen years previously. In both, she fears she might have been drugged and impregnated by some kind of monster, apparently to the accompaniment of music by Cher Bono. The FBI agents proceed to consider claims that the town has indeed been the unwitting home to a resident monster, the Great Mutato, played by Chris Owens; and, thence, to investigate the genetic researches of a prominent local scientist, Professor Polidori, played by

John O'Hurley. Represented by herself and by Polidori as a 'scientist', Scully's response is to insist that this is merely a populist hoax:

> Isn't it obvious? I think what we're seeing here is an example of the culture for whom daytime talkshows and tabloid headlines have become a reality against which they measure their lives, a culture so obsessed by the media and a chance for self-dramatisation that they'll do anything in order to gain a spotlight.

Mulder is less sure:

> I'm alarmed that you would reduce these people to a cultural stereotype. Not everybody's dream is to get on *Jerry Springer*.

Even setting aside its title, the programme is characteristically postmodern, both in the thematic concern for the posthuman and in a strong sense of intertextuality as fun. The referent, the real to which the sign refers, was pretty well suppressed in most *X-Files* episodes, but here the focus fell even more than usual on the interplay of signifiers. This is apparent, for example, from the way the episode deliberately signals its own fictionality. It was the only X-File to be filmed in black and white, rather than in colour, a device to alert the audience to its cinematically fictional aspects. It had a well-defined frame narrative, another obviously fictional device, not simply Carter's own, but the frame-within-a-frame provided by *The Great Mutato* comic book, written by Shaineh's son, Izzy, performed by Stewart Gale. It played with the problem of how fiction constructs endings by allowing Mulder to object to a likely unhappy ending, then contriving the happy ending he asked for. More fundamentally, the entire narrative is structured around the opposition between high and popular culture, here represented through different forms of textuality, the one as literature (Shelley's *Frankenstein*) and science (Polidori's research), the other as comic book (*The Great Mutato*), television (*The Jerry Springer Show*) and recorded music (Cher).

Moreover, the programme comprises a tissue of intertextual references to Shelley's novel, to the occasion of its composition and to subsequent film adaptations, especially Whale's. The name of the

Frankenstein figure in Carter's retelling, Polidori, refers, of course, to Byron's physician and secretary. The first meeting between this Polidori, Scully and Mulder is introduced by a headline from the university newspaper: 'PROFESSOR CREATES OWN MONSTERS'. The meeting is shot, not simply in black and white, but to the accompaniment of thunder and lightning flashes, which quote directly from Whale's *Frankenstein*. When the professor brings the interview to a close, he explains that he will be travelling that night to the University of Ingolstadt to give an international address. There is no university at Ingolstadt, nor has there been since 1800, but it was nonetheless there that Shelley's Victor Frankenstein had been educated (M. Shelley 1980: 42, 235n.). Polidori's wife, we later learn, is an Elizabeth, just as Frankenstein's would be. By no means all viewers spot the intertextual references. But for those who don't, Mulder, representing literature as against science, spells them out to Scully:

> When Victor Frankenstein asks himself 'Whence did the principle of life proceed?' and then, as the gratifying summit to his toils, creates a hideous phantasm of a man, he prefigures the postmodern Prometheus, the genetic engineer, whose power to reanimate matter – genes – into life – us – is only as limited as his imagination is.

It remains for Scully to spell out the joke:

> Mulder, I'm alarmed that you would reduce this man to a literary stereotype.

The references to Whale are also important. So, when Mulder discovers the family album of Mutato photographs and exclaims: 'It's Alive!', he quotes from the movie, rather than the novel, where this line never actually appears. The town mob's pursuit of the monster, in an angry torch-burning procession, with Polidori at their head, is yet another quotation from Whale. Modern film and postmodern television programme end differently, however, the first in a serious endorsement of small-town mob violence, the second in a comic resolve to live and let live with the monstrously posthuman. Whale's monster had been killed in a windmill set alight by the vigilantes' torches, burnt to death in scenes that invited audience complicity with sadistic violence. But Carter's escapes the burning barn and is rescued from mob vengeance by his own eloquent plea in self-defence:

> What we did was wrong, but in our trespasses we gave you a loving son. And in your homes I went places I'd never dreamed of. With your books and your records and your home media centers I learned of the world and of a mother's love that I'll never know.

Izzy then speaks for his wronged mother and the entire town, Polidori excepted, when he responds: 'Hey, he's no monster.' He speaks also for ordinariness, Cher and Jerry Springer, as against science and literature. The mother love Mutato invokes here is no mere abstraction, moreover, but rather a specific reference to Bogdanovich's 1985 movie *Mask*, where Cher had played the part of Rusty Denis, the biker mother of a radically deformed teenage boy. Hence the alternative ending nominated by Mulder, in which he and Scully take Mutato to a Cher concert, where the singer, played by Tracey Bell, performs 'Walking In Memphis'. There are at least three good jokes in this closing sequence. First, if this monster was a product of late twentieth-century science, then according to much contemporary popular wisdom Cher too is a substantial tribute to the art of the plastic surgeon. Second, whilst Bell performs Cher performing, the camera cuts to a fictional episode of *The Jerry Springer Show*, where Springer, playing himself, interviews Elizabeth Polidori and Shaineh Berkowicz about their monstrous infants, leading the latter to exclaim: 'What's not to love?' Finally, Mulder and Scully are moved to dance to Cher's music, thus edging towards what could have been their then much-anticipated first screen kiss, only for it to be rendered instantly fictive in the closing frame, as a panel from one of Izzy's comic books.

Whilst Carter directed and wrote 'The Postmodern Prometheus', none of the four episodes in *Buffy*'s Adam sequence were written or directed by Whedon. James A. Contner directed 'The I in Team' and 'Primeval', David Grossman 'The Yoko Factor' and David Solomon 'Goodbye Iowa'; David Fury wrote 'The I in Team' and 'Primeval', Marti Noxon 'Goodbye Iowa' and Douglas Petrie 'The Yoko Factor'.

Where Carter's monster had been a genetically engineered 'mistake', in Polidori's phrase, *Buffy*'s 'Adam', played by George Hertzberg, is a deliberately designed cyborg warrior, a demon–human–machine hybrid. The Frankenstein/God figure here was Buffy's psychology lecturer, Professor Walsh, played by Lindsay Crouse, who is also employed, we later learn, by a top-secret government research facility located beneath the university, the so-called Initiative, where she is working on Project 314, the making of the 'biomechanical demonoid'. That this particular Frankenstein should be female is, of course, an instance of the feminisation of erstwhile masculine authority in postmodern gender bending. Her authority is exercised over male figures, moreover, notably her assistant Dr Angleman, played by Jack Stehlin, and Riley, Buffy's soon-to-be lover, introduced into the show in the first episode of this same season. Riley had first appeared as Walsh's teaching assistant at the university, but we soon learn that he too is employed by the Initiative, as a peculiar kind of commando, subject to full military discipline. Both the commandos and the research are designed to defeat and take advantage of the demon threat to humanity.

The Adam sequence shares with 'The Postmodern Prometheus' both an intertextual aesthetic and a posthuman thematic. References to *Genesis* and *Frankenstein* recur throughout. Whilst the monster's name obviously points to the first, Spike equally obviously gestures towards the second, describing the demonoid as 'big, scary, Frankenstein-looking'. In the 'Goodbye Iowa' episode, the scene where Adam murders the little boy also refers very directly to the killing of the little girl in Whale's *Frankenstein*. The two sequences are almost exactly homologous in narrative structure. In each, a smiling child innocently enters into conversation with the monster; the scene is structured around the physical contrast between their respective heights; the monster then becomes curious to see how the child 'works'; the camera cuts away prior to the killing, in a moment of 'tact' signalling its imminence and its horror; and the cut is to a public arena, the town square in 1931, the television news in 2000, where the death is then announced. The posthuman thematic in the Adam sequence centres on Walsh's various experiments to improve on human life, 'for the greater good', as she says towards the end of 'The

I in Team'. Her motives are thus close to Frankenstein's, not so much evil as hubristic, both by her own account and in Riley's. Despite her choice for his name, Adam is actually a counterpart to the robot in *Metropolis*, the monster in *Frankenstein*, Satan in *Paradise Lost*, that is, the creation who turns on its creator. Planning to rid herself of Buffy and so re-establish Riley's loyalties, Walsh is suddenly and fatally stabbed from behind by the newly conscious Adam. The Biblical and Miltonic figure of Adam is rehearsed more fully, however, in the character of Riley. He too is a significantly augmented, 'posthuman' creation, but one we can identify as still recognisably 'human'; he too disobeys Walsh and the Initiative, but for reasons close to those that prompted Milton's Adam to disobedience, his love for Buffy, the programme's unlikely Eve.

The first encounter between Adam and Riley in 'Goodbye Iowa' is a key exchange for the entire four-episode sequence and can usefully be compared to the confrontation between Frankenstein and his monster on Mont Blanc. Here, the creator is already dead, but, by accessing her software, Adam is able to speak on her behalf. This, in turn, enables him to position Riley, not as Walsh's co-creator, but as his own co-creature. Adam begins by defining himself as a 'kinematically redundant, biomechanical demonoid designed by Maggie Walsh', adding that she 'called me Adam and I called her Mother'. When Buffy observes that he must therefore be made 'from parts of other demons', he agrees, but continues:

> And man. And machine. Which tells me what I am, but not who I am. Mother wrote things down, hard data but also her feelings. That's how I learned that I have a job here and that she loved me.

Riley objects forcefully to this notion that Adam is a mother's son, rather than a scientist's experiment, prompting the demonoid to retort: 'Mother created you too.' The monster then explains just exactly how Walsh had created Riley, most of which is meant to come as a surprise, not only to Buffy, but also to the audience:

> she...shaped your basic operating system. She taught you how to think, how to feel, she fed you chemicals to make you stronger,

> your mind and body. She said that you and I were her favourite children, her art. That makes us brothers, family.

Riley angrily denies the connection, only to be confounded, yet again, by Adam's astute speculation that such discomfiture can have only two possible causes:

> Because your feeding schedule – the chemicals – have been interrupted? Or do you miss her?

The most striking aspect of this exchange, as in its prototype on Mont Blanc, is that the monster has almost all the interesting lines and asks almost all the interesting questions. For Adam is much more concerned than Riley to discover the true nature of their respective identities, to search for the meanings the latter prefers to avoid. Riley's resort to violence, when he brings the dialogue to a close by drawing his gun, underlines his own lack of intellectual curiosity and emotional honesty.

Adam cannot be allowed to excite our sympathies, however, not even to the extent of the monsters in *Frankenstein* or 'The Postmodern Prometheus'. For in *Buffy* the demonic is almost invariably an irreconcilable threat, the solution to which is equally invariably violent extinction. Adam had spoken to Riley of Walsh's 'plan', which gave him his 'job', the details of which remained unclear. But in 'Primeval' we learn that Adam killed Walsh, and later Angleman and others, as part of his own scheme – which had been hers – to use their bodies to create a species of human–demon hybrids, in short, Frankenstein's 'race of devils'. How, then, does the denouement proceed? Unable to defeat Adam from within her own resources, the Vampire Slayer destroys him through magic, a powerful 'enjoining spell', combining her strengths with those of Willow, Xander and Giles, the friends Spike contrived to turn against each other in the immediately preceding episode. This is the problem with fantasy, as against SF: even the most intractable of situations can be readily resolved by means near to, or even identical with, wish fulfilment. Conveniently enough, the Initiative is also destroyed in a mighty battle between soldiers and demons, UC Sunnydale's local version of the *Götterdämmerung*. This resolution is both far too easily bought and fundamentally conservative, closer to Shelley than to Carter. But, as we shall see, its conservatism consists not only in a determination to extinguish the posthuman, but also in the programme's refusal to acknowledge either its own or its audience's deeper fears.

Postmodern Gothic

We noted the presence of 'politically correct' identity politics in *The X-Files* and *Buffy the Vampire Slayer*. Such notions were characteristic features of what Touraine dubbed the 'new social movements' of the late twentieth century (1981: 9–10). Unlike the old social movement, the labour movement, these movements were not in principle anti-capitalist. And it is an important insight in Jameson that postmodernism is not at all post-capitalist, but rather the product of the 'purer capitalism of our own time', which 'eliminates the enclaves of precapitalist organization it...hitherto tolerated and exploited in a tributary way' (Jameson 1991: 36). Understanding postmodernism thus, we can begin to explain the peculiar place occupied within it by the new social movements and their unprecedented attempts to 'decentre' white, straight, male cultural authority. In a culture so commodified, so subject to the logics of the simulacrum, the widening rift between sign and referent produced formidable structural inhibitors to the kind of class consciousness we traced in Milton and Shelley. As Jameson writes: 'For a society that wants to forget about class...reification...is very functional indeed' (ibid.: 315). But this forgetfulness is itself a peculiar kind of class consciousness, he suggests, deriving from the particular new class fraction 'variously...labeled...new petit bourgeoisie,...professional-managerial class, or more succinctly "the yuppies"' (ibid.: 407). I prefer to consider this stratum an intelligentsia, in the sense defined in Chapter 1, but Jameson is right, nonetheless, to point to it as the bearer of postmodern cultural politics. During the late twentieth century, radical politics mutated into identity politics, the preserve of these new movements, whose characteristic narratives typically lacked 'the allegorical capacity to map or model the system' (ibid.: 349).

The movements drew attention to and challenged types of social inequality that, in their most inflexible forms, had become unnecessary and even dysfunctional to the more advanced economies. As late as the early 1960s, class-based relations of exploitation coexisted alongside apparently equally permanent patterns of pre-capitalist social inequality. But since then non-market forms of hierarchy have declined markedly in significance, thus opening up opportunities for what Jameson described as a 'prodigious' expansion of capitalism into 'hitherto uncommodified areas' (ibid.: 35–6). Wittingly or not, the new social movements clearly facilitated this process. They were organised and led, not by a random sample of all women or homosexuals, for example, but precisely by a layer of intellectuals whose unrepresentative class status followed a very clear pattern. This was most easily legitimated, however, both internally and externally, if its significance, that of class, was systematically denied. Ironically, the retreat from class, both in theory and in practical politics, thus expressed the class interests of its advocates, rather than a change in the nature of social reality. As Collini observed:

> In the frequently incanted quartet of race, class, gender and sexual orientation, there is no doubt that class has been the least fashionable in recent years...despite the fact that all the evidence suggests that class remains the single most powerful determinant of life-chances.
>
> (Collini 1994: 3)

Neither Buffy, Mulder nor Scully are exactly new social movement activists, though the latter has been involved in anti-nuclear protests. But both they and their friends clearly provide idealised fictional representations of the late twentieth-century American yuppie. Physically attractive and well dressed, mobile phones invariably at the ready, Scully and Mulder might almost be considered archetypically yuppie heroes. Both are highly educated: he is a former Rhodes Scholar, an Oxford BA in psychology, with academic publications to his credit; she is a medical doctor, with a degree in physics from the University of Maryland and a thesis on Einstein (Lowry 1995: 261, 264). Significantly younger, Buffy and friends are aspirant rather than realised yuppies, physically attractive, but not yet educated, well dressed, but not yet employed. Xander aside, however, they are students at the fictional Sunnydale campus of the real University of California, the more prestigious of the state's public universities. Indeed, Willow has even been offered places at East Coast private universities, but turned these down to attend Sunnydale. Both the Sunnydale setting and the major positive characters, Giles apart, are representative of comfortably middle-class liberal America. Both series also position themselves against what might be the most obvious 'Others' of yuppieness: redneck hillbillies, on the one hand, and Big Government, Big Science and Big Business, on the other. In *The X-Files*, threat tends to come from either or both directions, albeit mainly the latter: one of the key themes is hidden government, extending to the possibility of complicity in alien abduction. *Buffy* is similarly positioned socio-discursively, especially in the Adam sequence, where Big Government and Big Science are cosignified by the Initiative, the lower classes by lowlife 'monsters'.

Noting how difference and identity substitute for each other in the political rhetoric of the new social movements – as simultaneously the 'politics of difference' and 'identity politics' – Jameson concluded that such difference was possible only through the prior consolidation of something like universal identity. Postmodern politics entailed a 'ceaseless alternation' between identity and difference, he concluded, a kind of cultural 'blockage' obstructing any further development through interaction (Jameson 1994: 65–6, 70). Hence the inability to imagine the future, except as 'an eternal present and, much further away, an inevitable catastrophe' (ibid.: 70). Jameson had in mind here the politics of real catastrophe, as in environmental or military disaster, but it is worth noting how both *The X-Files* and *Buffy* construct their fictional worlds thus, alternating between an eternal present which is for ever American and the ultimate catastrophe of alien or demonic invasion. The universalism Jameson detects is, in part, that of the 'empowered' middle-class consumer at play in the marketplace. For, as Žižek insists, the 'dispersed, plural, constructed subject' of postmodernism is the '*form of subjectivity that corresponds to late capitalism*'. Capital itself, he continues, is 'the ultimate power' that undermines the 'traditional fixity of ideological positions (patriarchy, fixed sexual roles, etc.)', in order to eliminate the remaining barriers to the 'unbridled commodification of everyday life' (Žižek 1993: 216).

This peculiar combination of transnational corporate commodification and postmodern cultural politics was powerfully resonant in the last decades of the twentieth century and the first of the twenty-first. In Europe, it led to the 'third way' politics of Blair in Britain, Jospin in France, Schröder in Germany, and to its theorisation by sociologists like Giddens (1998). Arguably, some of this had been anticipated in Australia by the Hawke–Keating governments of the 1980s and early 1990s (Frankel 1997). But its most significant expression was in the US Democratic Party, especially during the Presidency of another Rhodes scholar, Bill Clinton, which ran from 1993 to 2000. It is always risky to postulate close correlations between politics and culture, but I want to argue that this particular political moment was refracted fairly precisely in *The X-Files*, which went to air during the first year of the first Clinton administration, and *Buffy*, which followed in the first year of the second. Chronologically, this is a less than exact fit, but it is sufficiently close to be suggestive. We have observed the post-feminist 'political correctness' of both series. But now we need to note how much this was always a matter of gender and sexuality, rather than class or race-as-class. As Helford observed of the entire cohort of television 'fantasy girls':

> Though we now have female warriors, ship's captains, witches, aliens, and superheroes, they remain overwhelmingly white…, heterosexual, and silent on such issues as class disenfranchisement.
>
> (Helford 2000: 5)

American television's female heroes were never quite so uniformly and explicitly heterosexual as this implies: witness Willow and Tara, or even Xena and Gabrielle. But in general Helford gets it right. Indeed, we might go further: not just white, but blonde or redhead – that is, not dark haired; not just white, but North European in appearance – that is, not Latino; not merely silent on issues of class, but often positively and aggressively middle class. Helford sees this kind of post-feminism as symptomatic of the Clinton years, when the dominant political culture combined a nominally left-wing 'social' liberalism with right-wing economic liberalism. She describes the politics of the period, a little cynically, as 'sameness reconstructed to appear as progressive shift' (ibid.: 6). This is echoed in Kent Ono's argument, elsewhere in the same volume, that, for all its apparent feminism, *Buffy*'s central fear was of difference:

> Normalcy not only regulates Buffy's personal desire to be a normal *human*..., but...also serves as a regulating feature to demarcate appropriate behaviors and privileges affecting all characters.... Because vampires and *other others* are defined as abnormal by the show, it is easy to see them in general through a racial metaphor.
>
> (Ono 2000: 172)

Much the same point might be applied to *The X-Files*, though less obviously so to 'The Postmodern Prometheus' than other episodes. But Helford and Ono both misrecognise the phenomenon, in part, I suspect, due to their complicity with the culture they describe. For there was progress as well as sameness under Clinton; and tolerance, rather than fear, for certain kinds of difference, such as lesbianism and strong women more generally, in *Buffy* and *The X-Files*. Like the postmodern culture which 'hosted' them, to borrow an unusually apposite metaphor, these programmes feared some differences but not others. It was their socio-discursive function, in short, to *police* difference.

If it is easy to read *Buffy* through a racial metaphor, then this is 'race' in a very specific sense. For these vampires, demons and others are coded as neither 'black' nor Native American: relocated to Los Angeles, *Buffy*'s Angel would acquire a black sidekick, Charles Gunn, played by J. August Richards, as keen to hunt demons as anyone in the Buffyverse; confronted by an apparently advanced alien civilisation, Mulder and Scully would repeatedly resort to Navajo traditional wisdom as a key weapon in their armoury. If monsters in *Buffy* and aliens in *The X-Files* are racially coded – and this is a big if – then it is surely as Latino, that is, as descendants of the first Europeans to conquer the region. Both television shows were specifically Californian, not simply in the sense that much American television is financed and marketed in Los Angeles, but at other, more interesting, levels. Their 'authors' were Californians by birth or migration: Carter was born and brought up in Los Angeles; Whedon lived there from shortly after graduating from university. A blond-haired alumnus of California State University with a passion for surfing – he edited *Surfing* magazine for five years – Carter was almost stereotypically Southern Californian Anglo (Lowry 1995: 7–9). This is less true of Whedon, but his *Buffy* was set in a fantastically hyper-Anglophone version of fictionalised Southern California. Even as they aimed at global syndication, both series repressed the most fundamental of facts about their specifically Californian place of origin: that of the structural divide between a largely Anglo middle class and a largely Latino working class. This is a class rather than racial divide, moreover, even though Latinos are racialised in the way Ono describes. For, as Davis observed of late twentieth-century Los Angeles: 'Anglos tend to be concentrated in private sector management and entertainment production, Asians in professions and light manufacturing, African-Americans in the civil service, and Latinos in all other blue-collar occupations' (Davis 1999: 24).

We noted that for Žižek the proper object of ideology critique is, not so much how ideology misrepresents reality, as how the 'spectre' of trauma conceals antagonisms unamenable to symbolisation. He cites Lévi-Strauss's account of the way two main sub-groups in a South American village held radically different perceptions of its physical ground-plan. These differences implied a hidden reference, not to the objective, 'actual' arrangement of the buildings, Žižek continued, but to the 'trauma' around which this 'social reality is structured' (Žižek 1994: 26). We might venture the suggestion that contemporary California is structured analogously: perceived as essentially Anglo by Anglo-Americans and essentially Hispanic by Latino-Americans, with neither able 'to symbolize, to account for, to "internalize", to come to terms with' (ibid.: 26) the 'traumatic kernel' upon which the society is founded. The historical aspect of this trauma is the expropriation of these formerly Spanish, later Mexican, territories by Anglo-Americans during the Californian Revolution of 1846, which briefly established the Republic of California, subsequently incorporated into the United States in 1848. The contemporary aspect is the exploitation of, but also dependence upon, a large and growing Spanish-speaking 'white' working class in California and elsewhere across the American South West. In 1995 Latinos comprised 20.6 per cent of the population of California and 27.6 per cent of Texas; in 1999 the authoritatively predicted figures for 2025 were 43.1 per cent and 37.6 per cent, respectively (Davis 1999: 6). The revolutions that prised Texas and California from Mexico, in 1836 and 1846 were prefigured by large-scale Anglo-American immigration into the region during the period after Mexico become independent from Spain in 1821. Clinton's decision in 1994, during the second season of *The X-Files*, to remilitarise the border – quite specifically, in the first instance, the Californian/Mexican border at San Diego/Tijuana – arose precisely in response to Anglo-American fears about 'uncontrolled immigration' in the reverse direction. Even if the primary demographic driving force is differential fertility rather than migration, there can be no doubting the prospective Latinisation of Los Angeles. As Davis caustically comments: 'The Anglo conquest of California in the late 1840s has proven to be a very transient fact' (ibid.: 26).

None of this registers explicitly in either *The X-Files* or *Buffy*. But the absence of what is actually present should alert us to the traumatic kernel of the ideological fantasy: in 1999 the *Los Angeles Times*, which is published in a city with more than 4.5 million Latino inhabitants, reported that only one in fifty characters on primetime television were Hispanic (ibid.: 7). A trivial but nonetheless striking example of this repression is in the ethnic identity of the university where Buffy meets Walsh and Riley. At the turn of the twenty-first century the real University of California had nine campuses, five located in and named after Hispanically named cities: Los Angeles, San Diego, San Francisco, Santa Barbara and Santa Cruz. Three were located in and named after Anglo-named towns: Berkeley (near San Francisco), Irvine and Riverside. The ninth also had an Anglo name: Davis is a former agricultural college, built on what had once been the Jerome C. Davis farm. Extrapolating probabilistically, one might have expected the tenth fictional campus to bear a Hispanic name. But not only does UC Sunnydale have the most improbably English of names in the whole system, it also seems singularly devoid of Latino faculty, students or even support staff. Repressed at the level of explicit recognition, Hispanic America returns to haunt Anglo-America in its fantasies. If there were aliens bothering the FBI during the late 1990s, they were likely to be Spanish-speaking. If there was a Hellmouth, through which strange monsters poured into Southern California, to inhabit the darker places of its cities and towns, then it was probably somewhere near San Diego. If there were soldiers patrolling the streets of Southern California under the Clinton Presidency, searching for hostiles, they were almost certainly working with the Border Patrol. If there was an Initiative under Clinton, it was the Immigration and Naturalisation Agency. If there were monstrous hybrids, they were probably Chicano-Mexicano-American. And if there was a conspiracy to allow in aliens, whilst pretending to obstruct them, then this, too, would have been directed southward, for the border's function was always to regulate, rather than prohibit, migration. In the second episode of the first season of *The X-Files*, broadcast on 17 September 1993, Deep Throat, played by Jerry Hardin, had warned Mulder that: 'They have been here for a very, very long time'. From well before 1846, certainly, and probably from as early as the sixteenth and seventeenth centuries.

Conclusion: loose canons and fallen angels

In this and the preceding chapter I have attempted to identify a network of intertextual connections between a series of print, film and television texts, each of which has been subject to modes of contextual and textual analysis routinely familiar to comparative cultural studies. How well these particular analyses work is for the reader to judge. But whatever their strengths or weaknesses, it should be apparent that this type of analysis can in fact generate non-trivial hypotheses concerning texts and their institutional and discursive contexts. If this is so, then where exactly does it leave Bloom and the Western Canon? The short answer is in some difficulty, at least in the attempt to define 'literature' as a different order of phenomenon from 'non-literature'. *Frankenstein* clearly straddles the boundaries between elite and popular cultures, literature and fiction, in ways that strongly suggest their impermanence. *Blade Runner* is a film of very real power, which in rather different ways also threatens to straddle these self-same boundaries. Desser has cautiously argued for its inclusion into the canon:

> *Blade Runner* utilizes a popular, contemporary form...to explore and rethink the mythic motifs underlying *Paradise Lost* and *Frankenstein*. All three works began as popular culture; *Paradise Lost* and *Frankenstein* have become transcendent works of art. It is too early to say if *Blade Runner* will enter the realm of high culture (has any film been admitted to the canon?).... But those of us who look to popular art for visions of hope...would do well to look carefully at this film.
>
> (Desser 1991: 64)

But neither *Paradise Lost* nor *Frankenstein* is quite so 'transcendent' as he imagined. As we have seen, both were produced in particular times and places for particular audiences; both found subsequent audiences beyond these immediate contexts, in other particular times and places; and both have often been dismissed, nonetheless, by the institutionalised custodians of the literary-critical canon, especially in England. But whatever the status either of Milton's epic or of Shelley's novel, the answer to the bracketed question is immediately apparent: no, no film has ever been admitted to the canon. And this is so because a canon of sacred texts can never be expanded to include even a single one of even the most interesting or exciting of profane texts. This is the point where Desser should give up on the idea of a canon, the point where it becomes impossible to believe in 'primal aesthetic value', somehow adhering strongly to *Paradise Lost*, but not very much to *Frankenstein* and not at all to *Blade Runner*. For Bennett was right to insist that value is only ever produced, not by the text itself, but by the valuing community that values it. The high canonical status of *Genesis* thus denotes primarily that a great many people believe in Judaism, Christianity or Islam. The relatively low status of *R.U.R.* outside the Czech Republic – though it does warrant a mention in Bloom's longer canon (1994: 558) – suggests above all the problems of writing in a 'minor literature'. And the variable valuations applied over time to *Frankenstein*, and even to *Paradise Lost*, suggest only the variability of community standards. As for *Metropolis*, *Blade Runner* and *The X-Files*, their absence from all known versions of the canon tells us only that most SF fans have better things to worry about.

But *Frankenstein*, *R.U.R.* and *Blade Runner* leave Bennett in some difficulty too, at least insofar as his argument proposed to substitute institutional for textual analysis, or perhaps to subsume the latter under the former. For Bennett, as we have seen, 'literature' is only an institutional arrangement for the processing of texts. In one sense, literature is indeed what the institutions of higher and secondary education, on the one hand, and the book trade, on the other, have chosen to define as such. But it is also a set of particular texts, which still have particular textual properties. Bennett appears not to believe this and therefore seems to have no interest in literary texts, and not much even in popular cultural texts, considered as texts. Having asserted value relativism, he seems to have no further interest in valuing. But there are at least two good reasons for persisting with the study of texts, the one literary-historical, the other contemporary. Literary history is what much of literary studies is actually about, although the habit of criticism tends to obscure this. Once we abandon the effort to work out what is and what isn't 'great', for all times and for all places, then we can get on with the more serious business of using the literary text as a source of often quite privileged insight into a more general history of structures of feeling. This was Williams's point in *The Long Revolution* and it still holds good:

> the arts of a period...are of major importance. For here, if anywhere...[the structure of feeling] is likely to be expressed;...by the fact that here, in the only examples we have of recorded communication that outlives its bearers, the actual living sense, the deep community that makes the communication possible, is naturally drawn upon.
>
> (Williams 1965: 64–5)

As to the contemporary reasons for persisting with texts, these are almost transparently obvious. For even if Bennett prefers to discuss institutions, most of us stubbornly prefer to discuss texts – it is what we do, after all, whenever we debate with others the film we have just seen or the book we have just read. It would be an odd sort of expertise in cultural studies that required its experts to refrain from such debate. Like everyone else, they will apply 'merely relative' values, but there is no reason to suppose this detracts from the importance of the process. We can and we do distinguish between more or less readerly and writerly texts, more or less open and closed texts, more or less ideologically manipulative, more or less patriarchal texts, albeit normally as points on a continuum rather than as binary oppositions. And insofar as these distinctions are acceptable to wider valuing communities, we can and we do engage in meaningful conversation about the value of texts, irrespective of whether or not they are literature. In these terms, Shelley's novel is more writerly and more open, more subversive of the dominant ideologies, including those of patriarchy, than the Fisher, Whale or Branagh films. In my terms, which are not everyone's, but nonetheless not merely mine, that makes it 'better'. And, by a similar token, Čapek's play is better than Lang's film, Carter's television series better than Whedon's.

As we noted in Chapter 1, cultural studies is interested in the interplay between cultural texts, cultural identity and social inequality. From its inception that interest had been intimately bound up with oppositional politics. And much more than is now commonly recognised, all of this has revolved around the central question of class. If Williams taught us much, the lesson we most need to recall today is perhaps that there is no 'getting beyond class politics', that the new issues raised by the new social movements, if followed through, 'lead us into the central systems of the industrial-capitalist mode of production and...into its system of classes' (Williams 1983: 172–3). Which leaves us finally with the tale of yet another Frankenstein monster. Inspired by the initial researches of Professors Williams and Hoggart, the young Stuart Hall laboured long and hard in his Birmingham workshop of filthy creation, stitching together bits of sociology and pieces of literary criticism with the thread of semiology, to produce the monster that is now cultural studies. Much of this is flawed, often hideous and loathsome. But, unlike the Western Canon, it's alive, IT'S ALIVE!

Bibliography and filmography

Texts

Print

Aeschylus (1989) *Eumenides*, ed. and trans. A. J. Podlecki, Warminster: Aris and Phillips.

Anon. (1960) *The Bible*, Authorized Version, Oxford: Oxford University Press.

—— (1988) *Biblia Hebraica Stuttgartensia*, rev. edn, ed. K. Elliger and W. Rudolph, Stuttgart: Deutsche Bibelgesellschaft.

Arnold, M. (1966) *Culture and Anarchy*, ed. J. D. Wilson, Cambridge: Cambridge University Press.

Asimov, I. (1970) *I, Robot*, Greenwich: Fawcett.

Banks, I. (1987) *Consider Phlebas*, London: Macmillan.

—— (2000) *Look to Windward*, London: Orbit.

Blake, W. (1927) *The Marriage of Heaven and Hell*, London: J. M. Dent.

—— (1977) *William Blake: The Complete Poems*, ed. A. Ostriker, Harmondsworth: Penguin.

Branagh, K. (1994) *Mary Shelley's Frankenstein: The Classic Tale of Terror Reborn on Film*, with the screenplay by S. Lady and F. Darabont, London: Pan Books.

Bulgakov, M. (1967) *The Master and Margarita*, trans. M. Glenny, Glasgow: Collins.

Byron, Lord (1991) 'Frame work bill speech', in *The Complete Miscellaneous Prose*, ed. A. Nicholson, Oxford: Oxford University Press.

Čapek, K. (1922) *W.U.R. Werstands Universal Robots*, trans. O. Pick, Prague: Lipsko, Orbis.

—— (1923) *R.U.R. (Rossum's Universal Robots). A Fantastic Melodrama*, trans. P. Selver, New York: Doubleday.

—— (1925a) *Pragmatismus Čili Filosofie Practického Života*, Prague: F. Topic.

—— (1925b) *Letters from England*, trans. P. Selver, London: G. Bles.

—— (1934) *Anglické Listy: pro vetsi nazornost provázené obrázky autorovými*, Prague: Fr. Borovný.

—— (1937) *Bílá Nemoc*, Prague: Fr. Borovný.

—— (1938) *Power and Glory*, trans. P. Selver and R. Neale, London: Allen and Unwin.

—— (1961) *R.U.R. (Rossum's Universal Robots). A Play in Three Acts and an Epilogue*, trans. P. Selver, in The Brothers Čapek, *R.U.R. and The Insect Play*, Oxford: Oxford University Press.

—— (1966) *R.U.R. Rossum's Universal Robots. Kolektivní Drama o Vstupní Komedii a Třech Dějstvích*, Prague: Ceskoslovensky Spisovatel.

—— (1969) *Ctení o T.G. Masrykovi*, Melantrich: V Praze.

—— (1990) *R.U.R. (Rossum's Universal Robots). A Collective Drama in a Comic Prologue and Three Acts*, trans. C. Novack-Jones, in P. Kussi (ed.) *Toward the Radical Center: A Karel Čapek Reader*, Highland Park: Catbird Press.

—— (1999) *R.U.R.*, in *Four Plays*, trans. P. Majer and C. Porter, London: Methuen.

Cervantes Saavedra, M. de (1950) *Don Quixote*, trans. J. M. Cohen, Harmondsworth: Penguin.

Dick, P. K. (1968) *Do Androids Dream of Electric Sheep?*, London: Grafton.

Gibson, W. (1984) *Neuromancer*, London: Victor Gollancz.

—— (1986) *Count Zero*, London: Victor Gollancz.

—— (1988) *Mona Lisa Overdrive*, London: Victor Gollancz.

—— (1994) *Virtual Light*, Harmondsworth: Penguin.

Godwin, W. (1971) *Enquiry Concerning Political Justice*, Oxford: Oxford University Press.

Milton, J. (1651) *Pro Populo Anglicano Defensio, contra Claudii anonymi, alias Salmasii, Defensionem regiam*, London: Typis du Gardianis.

—— (1848a) 'Eikonoklastes', in *Prose Works*, vol. I, London: Bohn.

—— (1848b) 'The tenure of kings and magistrates', in *Prose Works*, vol. II, London: Bohn.

—— (1848c) 'Of Reformation in England', in *Prose Works*, vol. II, London: Bohn.

—— (1848d) 'A treatise on Christian doctrine', in *Prose Works*, vol. IV, London: Bohn.

—— (1848e) 'A defence of the people of England', in *Prose Works*, vol. I, London: Bohn.

—— (1848f) 'Tetrachordon', in *Prose Works*, vol. III, London: Bohn.

—— (1966) *Milton: Poetical Works*, ed. D. Bush, Oxford: Oxford University Press.

Orwell, G. (1951) *Animal Farm: A Fairy Story*, Harmondsworth: Penguin.

—— (1954) *Nineteen Eighty-Four*, Harmondsworth: Penguin.

—— (1966) *Homage to Catalonia, and Looking Back on the Spanish War*, Harmondsworth: Penguin.

—— (1970a) 'James Burnham and the managerial revolution', in *Collected Essays, Journalism and Letters of George Orwell*, vol. 4: *In Front of Your Nose*, ed. S. Orwell and I. Angus, Harmondsworth: Penguin.

—— (1970b) 'Letter to Francis A. Henderson (extract)', in *Collected Essays, Journalism and Letters of George Orwell*, vol. 4: *In Front of Your Nose*, ed. S. Orwell and I. Angus, Harmondsworth: Penguin.

—— (1970c) 'Why I write', in *Collected Essays, Journalism and Letters of George Orwell*, vol. 1: *An Age Like This*, ed. S. Orwell and I. Angus, Harmondsworth: Penguin.

—— (1970d) 'Review of *We* by E. I. Zamyatin', in *Collected Essays, Journalism and Letters of George Orwell*, vol. 4: *In Front of Your Nose*, ed. S. Orwell and I. Angus, Harmondsworth: Penguin.

Rowling, J. K. (2000) *Harry Potter and the Goblet of Fire*, London: Bloomsbury.

Shakespeare, W. (1943) 'Othello, the Moor of Venice', in *The Complete Works of William Shakespeare*, ed. W. J. Craig, Oxford: Oxford University Press.

Shelley, M. (1980) *Frankenstein, or The Modern Prometheus*, ed. M. K. Joseph, Oxford: Oxford University Press.

Shelley, P. B. (1970) 'Preface to Prometheus Unbound', in *Shelley: Poetical Works*, ed. T. Hutchinson, Oxford: Oxford University Press.

—— (1993) 'An address to the people on the death of the Princess Charlotte', in *The Prose Works of Percy Bysshe Shelley*, vol. I, ed. E. B. Murray, Oxford: Oxford University Press.

Wells, H. G. (1996) *The Island of Doctor Moreau: A Critical Text of the 1896 London First Edition*, ed. L. E. Stover, Jefferson: McFarland.

Wollstonecraft, M. (1975) *A Vindication of the Rights of Women*, New York: Norton.

—— (1977) 'A vindication of the rights of men', in J. M. Todd (ed.) *A Wollstonecraft Anthology*, Bloomington: Indiana University Press.

Zamiatin, E. (1970) *We*, trans. B. G. Guerney, London: Jonathan Cape.

Film and television

Branagh, K. (dir.) (1994) *Mary Shelley's Frankenstein*, Tristar: 118 mins.

Carter, C. (dir.) (1997) 'The Postmodern Prometheus', *The X-Files*, Twentieth Century Fox Television: 44 mins.

Contner, J. A. (dir.) (2000) 'The I in Team', *Buffy the Vampire Slayer*, Mutant Enemy Inc./Twentieth Century Fox Television: 44 mins.

—— (dir.) (2000) 'Primeval', *Buffy the Vampire Slayer*, Mutant Enemy Inc./Twentieth Century Fox Television: 44 mins.

Fisher, T. (dir.) (1957) *The Curse of Frankenstein*, Hammer Films: 83 mins.

Grossman, D. (dir.) (2000) 'The Yoko Factor', *Buffy the Vampire Slayer*, Mutant Enemy Inc./Twentieth Century Fox Television: 44 mins.

Jackson, P. (dir.) (2001) *The Lord of the Rings: The Fellowship of the Ring*, New Line Cinema/Time Warner: 178 mins.

—— (dir.) (2002) *The Lord of the Rings: The Two Towers*, New Line Cinema/Time Warner: 173 mins.

Kuzui, F. R. (dir.) (1992) *Buffy the Vampire Slayer*, Twentieth Century Fox: 81 mins.

Lang, F. (dir.) (1926) *Metropolis*, Universum Film Aktiengesellschaft: 180 mins.

—— (dir.) (2002) *Metropolis*, Transit Film/Friedrich Wilhelm Murnau Stiftung: 124 mins.

Lee, A. (dir.) (2000) *Wo hu cang long/Crouching Tiger, Hidden Dragon*, Columbia Pictures: 120 mins.

Marck, N. (dir.) (2002) 'Conversations with Dead People', *Buffy the Vampire Slayer*, Mutant Enemy Inc./Twentieth Century Fox Television: 44 mins.

Sackheim, D. (dir.) (1993) 'Deep Throat', *The X-Files*, Twentieth Century Fox Television: 44 mins.

Scott, R. (dir.) (1982) *Blade Runner*, Blade Runner Partnership/Warner Brothers: 114 mins.

—— (dir.) (1992) *Blade Runner: The Director's Cut*, Blade Runner Partnership/Warner Brothers: 112 mins.

Solomon, D. (dir.) (2000) 'Goodbye Iowa', *Buffy the Vampire Slayer*, Mutant Enemy Inc./Twentieth Century Fox Television: 44 mins.

Whale, J. (dir.) (1931) *Frankenstein*, Universal Studios: 71 mins.

Criticism, history, sociology, theory

Adorno, T. W. (1973) *Philosophy of Modern Music*, trans. A. G. Mitchell and W. V. Bloomster, London: Sheed and Ward.

Adorno, T. W. and Horkheimer, M. (1944) *Dialektik der Aufklärung*, New York: Social Studies Association.

—— (1979) *Dialectic of Enlightenment*, trans. J. Cumming, London: Verso.

Aldiss, B. (1975) *Billion Year Spree: The History of Science Fiction*, London: Corgi.

Alexander, M. (2001) 'Introduction', in *Beowulf: A Verse Translation*, trans. M. Alexander, London: Penguin.

Allen, J. S. (1991) *In the Public Eye: A History of Reading in Modern France, 1880–1940*, Princeton: Princeton University Press.

Althusser, L. (1971) *Lenin and Philosophy and Other Essays*, trans. B. Brewster, London: New Left Books.

Althusser, L. and Balibar, É. (1970) *Reading Capital*, trans. B. Brewster, London: New Left Books.

Altick, R. (1978) 'The sociology of authorship', in P. Davison, R. Meyersohn and E. Shils (eds) *Literary Taste, Culture and Mass Communication*, vol. 10: *Authorship*, Cambridge: Chadwyck-Healey.

—— (1998) *The English Common Reader: A Social History of the Mass Reading Public, 1800–1900*, 2nd edn, Columbus: Ohio State University Press.

Anderson, B. (1991) *Imagined Communities: Reflections on the Origins and Spread of Nationalism*, rev. edn, London: Verso.

Anderson, P. (1974) *Passages from Antiquity to Feudalism*, London: New Left Books.

—— (1992) *English Questions*, London: Verso.

—— (1998) *The Origins of Postmodernity*, London: Verso.

Appadurai, A. (1986) 'Introduction: commodities and the politics of value', in A. Appadurai (ed.) *The Social Life of Things: Commodities in Cultural Perspective*, Cambridge: Cambridge University Press.

Apter, E. (2003) 'Global *translatio*: the 'invention' of comparative literature, Istanbul, 1933', *Critical Inquiry*, 29: 253–81.

Arac, J. (2002) 'Anglo-globalism?', *New Left Review* (II) 16: 35–45.

Auerbach, E. (1953) *Mimesis: The Representation of Reality in Western Literature*, trans. W. R. Trask, Princeton: Princeton University Press.

—— (1965) *Literary Language and its Public in Late Latin Antiquity and in the Middle Ages*, trans. R. Manheim, London: Routledge and Kegan Paul.

Australia Council (1983) 'Appendix I: statistical tables', in *The Artist in Australia Today: Report of the Committee for the Individual Artists Inquiry*, Sydney: Australia Council.

—— (1995) *Books: Who's Reading Them Now? A Study of Book Buying and Borrowing in Australia*, Sydney: Australia Council.

Badley, L. (1996) 'The rebirth of the clinic: the body as alien in *The X-Files*', in D. Lavery, A. Hague and M. Cartwright (eds) *Deny All Knowledge: Reading the X-Files*, London: Faber.

Bakhtin, M. (1981) *The Dialogic Imagination: Four Essays*, trans. C. Emerson and M. Holquist, Austin: University of Texas Press.

Baldick, C. (1983) *The Social Mission of English Criticism 1848–1932*, Oxford: Oxford University Press.

—— (1987) *In Frankenstein's Shadow: Myth, Monstrosity and Nineteenth-Century Writing*, Oxford: Oxford University Press.

Barrett, M. (1988) *Women's Oppression Today: The Marxist/Feminist Encounter*, London: Verso.

—— (1999) *Imagination in Theory: Essays on Writing and Culture*, Cambridge: Polity Press.

Barthes, R. (1957) *Mythologies*, Paris: Seuil.

—— (1970) 'To write: an intransitive verb?', trans. R. Macksey and E. Donato, in R. Macksey and E. Donato (eds) *The Languages of Criticism and the Sciences of Man*, Baltimore: Johns Hopkins University Press.

—— (1972) 'The structuralist activity', in R. T. de George and F. M. de George (eds) *The Structuralists: From Marx to Lévi-Strauss*, New York: Anchor.

—— (1973) *Mythologies*, trans. A. Lavers, St Albans: Paladin.

—— (1974) *S/Z*, trans. R. Miller, New York: Hill and Wang.

—— (1975) *The Pleasure of the Text*, trans. R. Miller, New York: Hill and Wang.

—— (1977) 'The death of the author', in *Image–Music–Text*, trans. S. Heath, New York: Hill and Wang.

Bassnett, S. (1993) *Comparative Literature: A Critical Introduction*, Oxford: Blackwell.

Baudrillard, J. (1975) *The Mirror of Production*, trans. M. Poster, St Louis: Telos Press.

—— (1983) *In the Shadow of the Silent Majorities, or, The End of the Social and Other Essays*, trans. P. Foss, J. Johnston and P. Patton, New York: Semiotexte.

—— (1988) *America*, trans. C. Turner, London: Verso.

—— (1993) *Symbolic Exchange and Death*, trans. I. Hamilton Grant, London: Sage.

—— (1994) *Simulacra and Simulation*, trans, S. F. Glaser, Ann Arbor: University of Michigan Press.

Bauman, Z. (1992) *Intimations of Postmodernity*, London: Routledge.

Beck, U. (1992) *Risk Society: Towards a New Modernity*, trans. M. Ritter, London: Sage.

—— (1994) 'The reinvention of politics: towards a theory of reflexive modernization', trans. M. Ritter, in U. Beck, A. Giddens and S. Lash, *Reflexive Modernization: Politics, Tradition and Aesthetics in the Modern Social Order*, Cambridge: Polity Press.

Belsey, C. (1988) *John Milton: Language, Gender, Power*, Oxford: Blackwell.

Benford, G. (1992) 'Science fiction, rhetoric, and realities: words to the critic', in G. Slusser and T. Shippey (eds) *Fiction 2000: Cyberpunk and the Future of Narrative*, Athens: University of Georgia Press.

Benjamin, W. (1973a) 'Theses on the philosophy of history', in *Illuminations*, trans. H. Zohn, Glasgow: Collins.

—— (1973b) 'The work of art in the age of mechanical reproduction', in *Illuminations*, trans. H. Zohn, Glasgow: Collins.

—— (1977) *The Origin of German Tragic Drama*, trans. J. Osborne, London: New Left Books.

Bennett, T (1979) *Formalism and Marxism*, London: Methuen.

—— (1983) 'Texts, readers, reading formations', *Literature and History* 9(2): 214–27.

—— (1985) 'Really useless "knowledge": a political critique of aesthetics', *Thesis Eleven* 12: 28–52.

—— (1989) 'Holding Spaces', *Southern Review* 22(2): 85–8.

—— (1990) *Outside Literature*, London: Routledge.

—— (1992) 'Useful culture', *Cultural Studies* 6(3): 395–408.

—— (1998) *Culture: A Reformer's Science*, London: Sage.

Bennett, T. and Woollacott, J. (1987) *Bond and Beyond: The Political Career of a Popular Hero*, London: Macmillan.

Bennett, T., Emmison, M. and Frow, J. (1999) *Accounting for Tastes: Australian Everyday Culture*, Melbourne: Cambridge University Press.

Berger, P. L. and Luckman, T. (1971) *The Social Construction of Reality: A Treatise in the Sociology of Knowledge*, Harmondsworth: Penguin.

Bhabha, H. K. (1994) *The Location of Culture*, London: Routledge.

Bloom, H. (1973) *The Anxiety of Influence: A Theory of Poetry*, New York: Oxford University Press.

—— (1976) *Poetry and Repression: Revisionism from Blake to Stevens*, New Haven: Yale University Press.

—— (1979) 'The breaking of form', in H. Bloom, P. de Man, J. Derrida, G. H. Hartmann and J. H. Miller, *Deconstruction and Criticism*, New York: Seabury Press.

—— (1994) *The Western Canon: The Books and School of the Ages*, New York: Harcourt Brace & Co.

—— (1999) *Shakespeare: The Invention of the Human*, London: Fourth Estate.

Boozer, Jr, J. (1991) 'Crashing the gates of insight: *Blade Runner*', in J. B. Kerman (ed.) *Retrofitting 'Blade Runner': Issues in Ridley Scott's 'Blade Runner' and Philip K. Dick's 'Do Androids Dream of Electric Sheep?'*, Bowling Green: Bowling Green State University Popular Press.

Bourdieu, P. (1974) 'The school as a conservative force: scholastic and cultural inequalities', in trans. J. C. Whitehouse, J. Eggleston (ed.) *Contemporary Research in the Sociology of Education*, London: Methuen.

—— (1977) *Outline of a Theory of Practice*, trans. R. Nice, Cambridge: Cambridge University Press.

—— (1984) *Distinction: A Social Critique of the Judgement of Taste*, trans. R. Nice, London: Routledge and Kegan Paul.

—— (1988) *Homo Academicus*, trans. P. Collier, Cambridge: Polity Press.

—— (1989) 'The corporatism of the universal: the role of intellectuals in the modern world', trans. C. Betensky, *Telos* 81: 99–110.

—— (1993) 'The production of belief: contribution to an economy of symbolic goods', trans. R. Nice, in P. Bourdieu, *The Field of Cultural Production: Essays on Art and Literature*, ed. R. Johnson, Cambridge: Polity Press.

—— (1996a) *The State Nobility: Elite Schools in the Field of Power*, trans. L. C. Clough, Cambridge: Polity Press.

—— (1996b) *The Rules of Art: Genesis and Structure of the Literary Field*, trans. S. Emanuel, Cambridge: Polity Press.

—— (1998) *Acts of Resistance: Against the New Myths of Our Time*, trans. R. Nice, Cambridge: Polity Press.

Bourdieu, P. *et al.* (1999) *The Weight of the World: Social Suffering in Contemporary Society*, trans. P. P. Ferguson, S. Emanuel, J. Johnson and S. T. Waryn, ed. A. Accardo, Cambridge: Polity Press.

Bradbury, M. and McFarlane, J. (1976) 'The name and nature of modernism', in M. Bradbury and J. McFarlane (eds) *Modernism 1890–1930*, Harmondsworth: Penguin.

Brailsford, H. N. (1961) *The Levellers and the English Revolution*, London: Cresset Press.

Broderick, D. (1995) *Reading by Starlight: Postmodern Science Fiction*, London: Routledge.

Browitt, J. (1996) 'From "sociology of consciousness" to "sociology of the text": French sociocriticism', *Southern Review* 29(1): 69–86.

Bürger, P. (1984) *Theory of the Avant-Garde*, trans. M. Shaw, Minneapolis: University of Minnesota Press.

Butler, E. M. (1935) *The Tyranny of Greece over Germany*, Cambridge: Cambridge University Press.

Butler, J. (1990) *Gender Trouble: Feminism and the Subversion of Identity*, London: Routledge.

—— (1999) 'Merely cultural', *New Left Review* (I) 227: 33–44.

Callari, A. and Ruccio, D. F. (eds) (1996) *Postmodern Materialism and the Future of Marxist Theory: Essays in the Althusserian Tradition*, Hanover: Wesleyan University Press/University Press of New England.

Callinicos, A. (1989) *Against Postmodernism: A Marxist Critique*, Cambridge: Polity Press.

Chalaby, J. K. (1997) 'No ordinary press owners: press barons as a Weberian ideal type', *Media, Culture and Society* 19(4): 621–41.

Cixous, H. (1981) 'The laugh of the Medusa', trans. K. Cohen and P. Cohen, in E. Marks and I. de Courtivron (eds) *New French Feminisms: An Anthology*, Brighton: Harvester.

Cixous, H. and Clément, C. (1986) *The Newly Born Woman*, trans. B. Wing, Minneapolis: University of Minnesota Press.

Clute, J. and Nicholls, P. (eds) (1993) *The Encyclopedia of Science Fiction*, London: Orbit.

Collini, S. (1994) 'Escape from DWEMsville', *Times Literary Supplement*, 27 May.

Collins, D. (1982) 'The 1920s picture pallace', in S. Dermody, J. Docker and D. Modjeska (eds) *Nellie Melba, Ginger Meggs and Friends: Essays in Australian Cultural History*, Malmsbury: Kibble Books.

Collins, J. (1992) 'Television and postmodernism', in R. C. Allen (ed.) *Channels of Discourse Reassembled: Television and Contemporary Criticism*, Chapel Hill: University of North Carolina Press.

Coser, L. A., Kadushin, C. and Powell, W. W. (1985) *Books: The Culture and Commerce of Publishing*, Chicago: University of Chicago Press.

Couturier, M. (1991) *Textual Communication: A Print-Based Theory of the Novel*, London: Routledge.

Crick, B. (1980) *George Orwell: A Life*, London: Secker and Warburg.

Cros, E. (1988) *Theory and Practice of Sociocriticism*, trans. J. Schwartz, Minneapolis: University of Minnesota Press.

Cross, N. (1985) *The Common Writer: Life in Nineteenth-Century Grub Street*, Cambridge: Cambridge University Press.

Csicsery-Ronay, Jr, I. (1992) 'Futuristic flu, or, the revenge of the future', in G. Slusser and T. Shippey (eds) *Fiction 2000: Cyberpunk and the Future of Narrative*, Athens: University of Georgia Press.

—— (2003) 'Science fiction and empire', *Science Fiction Studies* 30(2): 288–45.

Curran, J. (1997) 'Press history', in J. Curran and J. Seaton, *Power Without Responsibility: The Press and Broadcasting in Britain*, 5th edn, London: Routledge.

Curtain, J. (1993) 'The media industries: book publishing', in S. Cunningham and G. Turner (eds) *The Media in Australia: Industries, Texts, Audiences*, Sydney: Allen and Unwin.

Curtius, E. R. (1953) *European Literature and the Latin Middle Ages*, trans. W. R. Trask, New York: Pantheon.

Davis, M. (1990) *City of Quartz: Excavating the Future in Los Angeles*, London: Verso.

—— (1999) 'Magical urbanism: Latinos reinvent the US big city', *New Left Review* (I) 234: 3–43.

de Certeau, M. (1984) *The Practice of Everyday Life*, trans. S. Rendall, Berkeley: University of California Press.

Derrida, J. (1970) 'Structure, sign and play in the discourse of the human sciences', trans. R. Macksey, in R. Macksey and E. Donato (eds) *The Languages of Criticism and the Sciences of Man*, Baltimore: Johns Hopkins University Press.

—— (1978) *Writing and Difference*, trans. A. Bass, Chicago: University of Chicago Press.

—— (1987) *The Truth in Painting*, trans. G. Bennington and I. McLeod, Chicago: University of Chicago Press.

—— (1994) *Spectres of Marx: The State of the Debt, the Work of Mourning, and the New International*, trans. P. Kamuf, London: Routledge.

Desser, D. (1991) 'The new Eve: the influence of *Paradise Lost* and *Frankenstein* on *Blade Runner*', in J. B. Kerman (ed.) *Retrofitting 'Blade Runner': Issues in Ridley Scott's 'Blade Runner' and Philip K. Dick's 'Do Androids Dream of Electric Sheep?'*, Bowling Green: Bowling Green State University Popular Press.

Dollimore, J. (1991) *Sexual Dissidence: Augustine to Wilde, Freud to Foucault*, Oxford: Oxford University Press.

Dollimore, J. and Sinfield, A. (eds) (1994) *Political Shakespeare: Essays in Cultural Materialism*, Manchester: Manchester University Press.

During, S. (1999) 'Introduction', in S. During (ed.) *The Cultural Studies Reader*, 2nd edn, London: Routledge.

—— (2002) *Modern Enchantments: The Cultural Power of Secular Magic*, Cambridge, Mass.: Harvard University Press.

Durkheim, E. (1964) *The Rules of Sociological Method*, trans. S. A. Solovay and J. H. Mueller, New York: Free Press.

Dworkin, A. (1981) *Pornography: Men Possessing Women*, London: Women's Press.

Eagleton, T. (1976) *Criticism and Ideology*, London: New Left Books.

—— (1989) 'Introduction', in T. Eagleton (ed.) *Raymond Williams: Critical Perspectives*, Cambridge: Polity Press.

—— (1990) *The Ideology of the Aesthetic*, Oxford: Blackwell.

—— (1995) *Heathcliff and the Great Hunger*, London: Verso.

—— (1996a) *Literary Theory: An Introduction*, 2nd edn, Oxford: Blackwell.

—— (1996b) *The Function of Criticism: From 'The Spectator' to Post-Structuralism*, London: Verso.

—— (2000) *The Idea of Culture*, Oxford: Blackwell.

—— (2003) *Sweet Violence: The Idea of the Tragic*, Oxford: Blackwell.

Easthope, A. (1988) *British Post-Structuralism since 1968*, London: Routledge.

—— (1991) *Literary into Cultural Studies*, London: Routledge.

Eco, U. (1981) *The Role of the Reader: Explorations in the Semiotics of Texts*, London: Hutchinson.

—— (1986) *Travels in Hyperreality*, trans. W. Weaver, San Diego: Harcourt Brace Jovanovich.

Ehrenreich, B. and Ehrenreich, J. (1979) 'The professional managerial class', in P. Walker (ed.) *Between Labour and Capital*, Hassocks: Harvester Press.

Eliot, T. S. (1962) *Notes Towards the Definition of Culture*, London: Faber.

—— (1968) *Milton: Two Studies*, London: Faber.

Elliott, A. (2003) 'Slavoj Žižek', in A. Elliott and L. Ray (eds) *Key Contemporary Social Theorists*, Oxford: Blackwell.

Engels, F. (1970) 'Special introduction to the English edition of 1892 to "Socialism: utopian and scientific"', in K. Marx and F. Engels, *Selected Works*, Moscow: Progress Publishers.

Escarpit, R. (1966) *The Book Revolution*, London: George Harrap.

—— (1971) *The Sociology of Literature*, trans. E. Pick, London: Cass.

Euromonitor (1989) *The Book Report 1989*, London: Euromonitor.

Evans-Pritchard, E. E. (1940) *The Nuer: A Description of the Modes of Livelihood and Political Institutions of the Nilotic People*, Oxford: Oxford University Press.

—— (1951) *Kinship and Marriage among the Nuer*, Oxford: Oxford University Press.

—— (1956) *Nuer Religion*, Oxford: Oxford University Press.

Feather, J. (1993) 'Book publishing in Britain: an overview', *Media, Culture and Society* 15(2): 167–81.

Febvre, L. and Martin, H.-J. (1976) *The Coming of the Book: The Impact of Printing 1450–1800*, trans. D. Gerard, ed. G. Nowell-Smith and D. Wootton, London: New Left Books.

Fehér, F. (1986) ' Is the novel problematic?', in A. Heller and F. Fehér (eds) *Reconstructing Aesthetics: Writings of the Budapest School*, Oxford: Blackwell.

Felperin, H. (1985) *Beyond Deconstruction: The Uses and Abuses of Literary Theory*, Oxford: Oxford University Press.

Findlater, R. (1978) 'What are writers worth?', in P. Davison, R. Meyersohn and E. Shils (eds) *Literary Taste, Culture and Mass Communication*, vol. 10: *Authorship*, Cambridge: Chadwyck-Healey.

Forry, S. E. (1990) *Hideous Progenies: Dramatizations of Frankenstein from Mary Shelley to the Present*, Philadelphia: University of Pennsylvania Press.

Foucault, M. (1965) *Madness and Civilisation: A History of Insanity in the Age of Reason*, trans. R. Howard, New York: Vintage Books.

—— (1970) *The Order of Things: An Archaeology of the Human Sciences*, London: Tavistock.

—— (1973) *The Birth of the Clinic*, trans. A. M. Sheridan, London: Tavistock.

—— (1977) 'What is an author?', in *Language, Counter-Memory, Practice*, trans. D. F. Bouchard and S. Simon, ed. D. F. Bouchard, Ithaca: Cornell University Press.

—— (1978) *The History of Sexuality*, vol. 1: *An Introduction*, trans. R. Hurley, New York: Random House.

—— (1980) 'Truth and power', trans. C. Gordon, in *Power/Knowledge: Selected Interviews and Other Writings, 1972–1977*, ed. C. Gordon, Brighton: Harvester Press.

—— (1991) *The Foucault Effect: Studies in Governmentality, with Two Lectures by and an Interview with Michel Foucault*, ed. G. Burchell, C. Gordon and P. Miller, Chicago: University of Chicago Press.

Frankel, B. (1997) 'Beyond labourism and socialism: how the Australian Labor Party developed the model of "New Labour"', *New Left Review* (I) 221: 3–33.

Freadman, A. (1988) 'Untitled: (on genre)', *Cultural Studies* 2(1): 67–99.

French, J. M. (1938) 'The Powell–Milton bond', *Harvard Studies and Notes* 20: 61–73.

Frow, J. (1986) *Marxism and Literary History*, Oxford: Blackwell.

—— (1995) *Cultural Studies and Cultural Value*, Oxford: Oxford University Press.

Fukuyama, F. (2002) *Our Posthuman Future: Consequences of the Biotechnology Revolution*, New York: Farrar, Straus & Giroux.

Gadamer, H.-G. (1990) *Truth and Method*, trans. J. Weinsheimer and D. G. Marshall, New York: Crossroad.

Gallagher, C. and Greenblatt, S. (2000) *Practicing New Historicism*, Chicago: University of Chicago Press.

Garnham, N. (1983) 'Towards a theory of cultural materialism', *Journal of Communication* 33(3): 314–29.

—— (1988) 'Raymond Williams, 1921–1988: a cultural analyst, a distinctive tradition', *Journal of Communication* 38(4): 123–31.

George, A. (1999) 'Introduction', in *The Epic of Gilgamesh: The Babylonian Epic Poem and Other Texts in Akkadian and Sumerian*, trans. A George, London: Penguin.

Giddens, A. (1991) *Modernity and Self-Identity: Self and Society in the Late Modern Age*, Stanford: Stanford University Press.

—— (1994a) 'Living in a post-traditional society', in U. Beck, A. Giddens and S. Lash, *Reflexive Modernization: Politics, Tradition and Aesthetics in the Modern Social Order*, Cambridge: Polity Press.

—— (1994b) *Beyond Left and Right: The Future of Radical Politics*, Cambridge: Polity Press.

—— (1998) *The Third Way: The Renewal of Social Democracy*, Cambridge: Polity Press.

Gilbert, S. M. and Gubar, S. (1984) *The Madwoman in the Attic: The Woman Writer and the Nineteenth-Century Literary Imagination*, New Haven: Yale University Press.

Goethe, J. W. (1950) 'Bezüge nach außen', *Gedenkausgabe der Werke, Briefe und Gespräche*, vol. 14, Zurich: Artemis-Verlag.

—— (1973) 'Some passages pertaining to the concept of world literature', in H.-J. Schulz and P. H. Rhein (eds) *Comparative Literature: The Early Years*, Chapel Hill: University of North Carolina Press.

Goldmann, L. (1964) *The Hidden God: A Study of Tragic Vision in the 'Pensées' of Pascal and the Tragedies of Racine*, trans. P. Thody, London: Routledge and Kegan Paul.

—— (1970a) *The Human Sciences and Philosophy*, trans. H. V. White and R. Anchor, London: Jonathan Cape.

—— (1970b) 'Structure: human reality and methodological concept', trans. R. Macksey and E. Donato, in R. Macksey and E. Donato (eds) *The Languages of Criticism and the Sciences of Man*, Baltimore: Johns Hopkins University Press.

—— (1971) *Immanuel Kant*, trans. R. Black, London: New Left Books.

—— (1975) *Towards a Sociology of the Novel*, trans. A. Sheridan, London: Tavistock.

Goodwin, K. (1986) *A History of Australian Literature*, London: Macmillan.

Graff, H. J. (1987) *The Legacies of Literacy: Continuities and Contradictions in Western Culture and Society*, Bloomington: Indiana University Press.

Gramsci, A. (1971) *Selections from Prison Notebooks*, trans. Q. Hoare and G. Nowell Smith, London: Lawrence and Wishart.

Green, M. (1959) 'British decency', *Kenyon Review* 21(4): 509–32.

Greenblatt, S. (1990) *Learning to Curse: Essays in Early Modern Culture*, London: Routledge.

—— (1994) 'Invisible bullets: Renaissance authority and its subversion, Henry IV and Henry V', in J. Dollimore and A. Sinfield (eds) *Political Shakespeare: Essays in Cultural Materialism*, Manchester: Manchester University Press.

Griest, G. (1970) *Mudie's Circulating Library and the Victorian Novel*, Indiana: Indiana University Press.

Grosz. E. (1989) *Sexual Subversions: Three French Feminists*, Sydney: Allen and Unwin.

—— (1990) *Jacques Lacan: A Feminist Introduction*, London: Routledge.

—— (1994) 'Experimental desire: rethinking queer subjectivtiy', in J. Copjec (ed.) *Supposing the Subject*, London: Verso.

Guldberg, H. H. (1990) *Books – Who Reads Them? A Study of Borrowing and Buying in Australia*, Sydney: Australia Council.

Gunew, S. (1994) *Framing Marginality: Multicultural Literary Studies*, Melbourne: Melbourne University Press.

Habermas, J. (1971) *Knowledge and Human Interest*, trans. J. J. Shapiro. Boston: Beacon Press.

—— (1975) *Legitimation Crisis*, trans. T. McCarthy, Boston: Beacon Press.

—— (1985) 'Modernity – an incomplete project', trans. S. Ben-Habib, in H. Foster (ed.) *Postmodern Culture*, London: Pluto Press.

—— (1989) *The Structural Transformation of the Public Sphere: An Inquiry into a Category of Bourgeois Society*, trans. T. Burger, Cambridge: Polity Press.

—— (1994) *The Past as Future*, ed. and trans. M. Pensky, Cambridge: Polity Press.

—— (1998a) *A Berlin Republic: Writings on Germany*, trans. S. Rendall, Cambridge: Polity Press.

—— (1998b) 'There are alternatives', *New Left Review* (I) 231: 3–12.

Hall, S. (1993) 'Culture, community, nation', *Cultural Studies* 7(3): 349–63.

—— (1996) 'New Ethnicities', in D. Morley and K.-H. Chen (eds) *Stuart Hall: Critical Dialogues in Cultural Studies*, London: Routledge.

Hall, S. and Jefferson, T. (eds) (1976) *Resistance Through Rituals: Youth Subcultures in Post-War Britain*, London: Hutchinson.

Hall, S., Critcher, C., Jefferson, T., Clarke, J. and Roberts, B. (1978) *Policing the Crisis: Mugging, the State, and Law and Order*, London: Macmillan.

Halperin, D. (1995) *Saint Foucault: Towards a Gay Hagiography*, Oxford: Oxford University Press.

Haraway, D. J. (1991) *Simians, Cyborgs, and Women: The Reinvention of Nature*, New York: Routledge.

Harding, D. W. (1957) 'The character of literature from Blake to Byron', in B. Ford (ed.) *The Pelican Guide to English Literature*, vol. 5: *From Blake to Byron*, Harmondsworth: Penguin.

Hardt, H. (1988) 'The accommodation of power and the quest for enlightenment: West Germany's press after 1945', *Media, Culture and Society* 10(2): 135–62.

Hardt, M. and Negri, A. (2000) *Empire*, Cambridge, Mass.: Harvard University Press.

Hassan, I. (1977) 'Prometheus as performer: toward a posthumanist culture? A university masque in five scenes', in M. Benamou and C. Caramello (eds) *Performance in Postmodern Culture*, Madison: Coda.

Hawthorn, J. (1992) *A Concise Glossary of Contemporary Literary Theory*, London: Edward Arnold.

Hayles, N. K. (1999) *How We Became Posthuman: Virtual Bodies in Cybernetics, Literature and Informatics*, Chicago: University of Chicago Press.

Hebdige, D. (1979) *Subculture: The Meaning of Style*, London: Methuen.

Hegel, G. W. F. (1975) *Philosophy of Fine Art*, vol. 4, trans. F. P. B. Osmaston, New York: Hacker Art.

Heldreth, L. G. (1991) 'The cutting edges of *Blade Runner*', in J. B. Kerman (ed.) *Retrofitting 'Blade Runner': Issues in Ridley Scott's 'Blade Runner' and Philip K. Dick's 'Do Androids Dream of Electric Sheep?'*, Bowling Green: Bowling Green State University Popular Press.

Helford, E. R. (2000) 'Introduction', in E. R. Helford (ed.) *Fantasy Girls: Gender in the New Universe of Science Fiction and Fantasy Television*, Lanham: Rowman and Littlefield.

Hill, C. (1977) *Milton and the English Revolution*, London: Faber.

—— (1985a) 'Censorship and English literature', in *The Collected Essays of Christopher Hill*, vol. 1: *Writing and Revolution in 17th Century England*, Brighton: Harvester.

—— (1985b) *The Experience of Defeat: Milton and Some Contemporaries*, Harmondsworth: Penguin.

Hitchens, C. (2002) *Orwell's Victory*, London: Allen Lane.

Hoggart, R. (1957) *The Uses of Literacy*, London: Chatto and Windus.

—— (1958) *The Uses of Literacy*, Harmondsworth: Penguin.

Hollinger, V. (1999) 'Contemporary trends in science fiction criticism, 1980–1999', *Science Fiction Studies* 26: 232–62.

Horkheimer, M. (1972) *Critical Theory: Selected Essays*, trans. M. J. O. O'Connell, New York: Seabury Press.

Hunter, I., Saunders, D. and Williamson, D. (1993) *On Pornography: Literature, Sexuality and Obscenity Law*, London: Macmillan.

Huyssen, A. (1988) *After the Great Divide: Modernism, Mass Culture and Postmodernism*, London: Macmillan.

Irigaray, L. (1985) *This Sex Which Is Not One*, trans. C. Porter with C. Burke, Ithaca: Cornell University Press.

Jacka, E. (1997) 'The media industries: film', in S. Cunningham and G. Turner (eds) *The Media in Australia: Industries, Texts, Audiences*, 2nd edn, Sydney: Allen and Unwin.

Jakobson, R. (1960) 'Closing statement: linguistics and poetics', in T. A. Sebeok (ed.) *Style in Language*, Cambridge, Mass.: MIT Press.

James, E. (1994) *Science Fiction in the Twentieth Century*, Oxford: Oxford University Press.

Jameson, F. (1981) *The Political Unconscious: Narrative as a Socially Symbolic Act*, London: Methuen.

—— (1982) 'Progress v. utopia; or, can we imagine the future?', *Science Fiction Studies* 9(2): 147–58.

—— (1984) 'Postmodernism, or the cultural logic of late capitalism', *New Left Review* (I) 146: 53–92.

—— (1985) 'Postmodernism and consumer society', in H. Foster (ed.) *Postmodern Culture*, London: Pluto Press.

—— (1990) *Late Marxism: Adorno, or, the Persistence of the Dialectic*, London: Verso.

—— (1991) *Postmodernism, or The Cultural Logic of Late Capitalism*, London: Verso.

—— (1992) *The Geopolitical Aesthetic: Cinema and Space in the World System*, Bloomington: Indiana University Press.

—— (1994) *The Seeds of Time*, New York: Columbia University Press.

—— (1998) *The Cultural Turn: Selected Writings on the Postmodern, 1983–1998*, London: Verso.

Jauss, H. R. (1982) *Toward an Aesthetic of Reception*, trans. T. Bahti, Brighton: Harvester.

Jenkins, H. (1992a) '"Strangers no more, we sing": filking and the social construction of the science fiction fan community', in L. Lewis (ed.) *The Adoring Audience: Fan Culture and Popular Media*, London: Routledge.

—— (1992b) *Textual Poachers: Television Fans and Participant Culture*, New York: Routledge.

Johnson, B. (1982) 'My monster/my self', *Diacritics* 12: 2–10.

Jones, P. (1999) '"The problem is always one of method...": cultural materialism, political economy and cultural studies', *Key Words* 2: 28–46.

Kadrey, R. and McCaffery, L. (1991) 'Cyberpunk 101: a schematic guide to storming the reality studio', in L. McCaffery (ed.) *Storming the Reality Studio: A Casebook of Cyberpunk and Postmodern Science Fiction*, Durham: Duke University Press.

Kautsky, K. (1983) 'Terrorism and communism', in *Karl Kautsky: Selected Political Writings*, ed. and trans. P. Goode, London: Macmillan.

Kettle, A. (1967) *An Introduction to the English Novel*, vol. 1: *To George Eliot*, London: Hutchinson.

Kinyon, K. (1999) 'The phenomenology of robots: confrontations with death in Karel Capek's *R.U.R.* ', *Science Fiction Studies*, 26, 3: 379–400.

Klaić, D. (1991) *The Plot of the Future: Utopia and Dystopia in Modern Drama*, Ann Arbor: University of Michigan Press.

Kolb, W. M. (1991) 'Script to screen: *Blade Runner* in perspective', in J. B. Kerman (ed.) *Retrofitting 'Blade Runner': Issues in Ridley Scott's 'Blade Runner' and Philip K. Dick's 'Do Androids Dream of Electric Sheep?'*, Bowling Green: Bowling Green State University Popular Press.

Konrád, G. and Szelényi, I. (1979) *The Intellectuals on the Road to Class Power*, trans. A. Arato and R. E. Allen, Brighton: Harvester.

Kristal, E. (2002) '"Considering coldly"...a response to Franco Moretti', *New Left Review* (II) 15: 61–74.

Kristeva, J. (1984) *Revolution in Poetic Language*, trans. M. Waller, New York: Columbia University Press.

Lacan, J. (1977a) *The Four Fundamental Concepts of Psycho-Analysis*, trans. A. Sheridan, London: Hogarth Press.

—— (1977b) *Écrits: A Selection*, trans. A. Sheridan, London: Tavistock.

Lacy, D. (1970) 'The economics of publishing, or Adam Smith and literature', in M. C. Albrecht, J. H. Barnett and M. Griff (eds) *A Sociology of Art and Literature*, London: Duckworth.

Landon, B. (1988) 'Bet on it: cyber/video/punk/performance', *Mississippi Review* 47/48(16): 245–51.

—— (1991) ' "There's some of me in you": *Blade Runner* and the adaptation of science fiction literature into film', in J. B. Kerman (ed.) *Retrofitting 'Blade Runner': Issues in Ridley Scott's 'Blade Runner' and Philip K. Dick's 'Do Androids Dream of Electric Sheep?'*, Bowling Green: Bowling Green State University Popular Press.

Lane, A. (1978) 'Books for the millions', in P. Davison, R. Meyersohn and E. Shils (eds) *Literary Taste, Culture and Mass Communication*, vol. 12: *Bookselling, Reviewing and Reading*, Cambridge: Chadwyck-Healey.

Lane, M. (1970) 'Books and their publishers', in J. Tunstall (ed.) *Media Sociology: A Reader*, London: Constable.

Lash, S. (1990) *Sociology of Postmodernism*, London: Routledge.

—— (1999) *Another Modernity, a Different Rationality*, Oxford: Blackwell.

Laurenson, D. T. and Swingewood, A. (1972) *The Sociology of Literature*, London: MacGibbon and Kee.

Le Doeuff, M. (1989) *The Philosophical Imaginary*, trans. C. Gordon, London : Athlone Press.

—— (1991) *Hipparchia's Choice: An Essay Concerning Women, Philosophy, etc.*, trans. T. Selous, Oxford: Blackwell.

Leavis, F. R. (1948) *Education and the University: A Sketch for an 'English School'*, London: Chatto and Windus.

—— (1962a) *The Common Pursuit*, Harmondsworth: Penguin.

—— (1962b) *The Great Tradition*, Harmondsworth: Penguin.

—— (1972a) *Revaluation*, Harmondsworth: Penguin.

—— (1972b) *Nor Shall My Sword: Discourses on Pluralism, Compassion and Social Hope*, London: Chatto and Windus.

Leavis, Q. D. (1979) *Fiction and the Reading Public*, Harmondsworth: Penguin.

Lévi-Strauss, C. (1963) *Structural Anthropology*, vol. 1, trans. C. Jacobson and B. G. Schoepf, New York: Basic Books.

—— (1966) *The Savage Mind*, Chicago: University of Chicago Press.

—— (1976) *Structural Anthropology*, vol. 2, trans. M. Layton, New York: Basic Books.

Lovell, T. (1987) *Consuming Fiction*, London: Verso.

Lowry, B. (1995) *The Truth Is Out There: The Official Guide to 'The X-Files'*, London: Harper Collins.

Lucas, S. (2003) *Orwell: Life and Times*, London: Haus.

Lukács, G. (1962) *The Historical Novel*, trans. H. and S. Mitchell, London: Merlin Press.

—— (1971) *The Theory of the Novel: A Historico-Philosophical Essay on the Forms of Great Epic Literature*, trans. A. Bostock, London: Merlin Press.

Lyotard, J.-F. (1984) *The Postmodern Condition: A Report on Knowledge*, trans. G. Bennington and B. Massumi, Minneapolis: University of Minnesota Press.

McGuigan, J. (1996) *Culture and the Public Sphere*, London: Routledge.

McHale, B. (1992) *Constructing Postmodernism*, London: Methuen.

Macherey, P. (1978) *A Theory of Literary Production*, trans. G. Wall, London: Routledge and Kegan Paul.

Maclean, M. (1994a) 'Monstre et signature: Mary Shelley et le pouvoir procréateur', trans. D. Davatchi and P. Anderson, *Romantisme: revue du dix-neuvième siècle* 85: 27–36.

—— (1994b) *The Name of the Mother: Writing Illegitimacy*, London: Routledge.

McLennan, G. (1995) 'After postmodernism – back to sociological theory?', *Sociology* 29(1): 117–32.

Mann, P. H. (1971) *Books: Buyers and Borrowers*, London: Andre Deutsch.

—— (1982) *From Author to Reader: A Social Study of Books*, London: Routledge and Kegan Paul.

Marx, K. (1973) 'The eighteenth Brumaire of Louis Bonaparte', trans. B. Fowkes, in *Surveys from Exile*, Harmondsworth: Penguin.

—— (1974) *Capital*, vol. III, London: Lawrence and Wishart.

—— (1975) 'Appendix B. Preface (to a contribution to the critique of political economy)', in *Early Writings*, Harmondsworth: Penguin.

Marx, K. and Engels, F. (1959) 'Manifest der kommunistischen Partei', *Werke*, vol. 4. Berlin: Dietz Verlag.

—— (1967) *The Communist Manifesto*, trans. S. Moore, Harmondsworth: Penguin.

—— (1970) *The German Ideology*, part 1, trans. W. Lough, C. Dutt and C. P. Magill, ed. C. J. Arthur, London: Lawrence and Wishart.

Mauss, M. (1989) *The Gift: The Form and Reason for Exchange in Archaic Societies*, trans. W. D. Halls, London: Routledge.

Millett, K. (1977) *Sexual Politics*, London: Virago.

Milner, A. (2002) *Re-Imagining Cultural Studies: The Promise of Cultural Materialism*, London: Sage.

Milner, A. and Browitt, J. (2002) *Contemporary Cultural Theory: An Introduction*, 3rd edn, London: Routledge.

Moers, E. (1978) *Literary Women*, London: Women's Press.

Moi, T. (1985) *Sexual/Textual Politics*, London: Methuen.

Moore, M. (2002) *Stupid White Men…and Other Sorry Excuses for the State of the Nation!*, London: Penguin.

Moretti, F. (1987) *The Way of the World: The Bildungsroman in European Culture*, trans. A. J. Sbragia, London: Verso.

—— (1988) *Signs Taken for Wonders: Essays in the Sociology of Literary Forms*, 2nd edn, trans. S. Fischer, D. Forgacs and D. Miller, London: Verso.

—— (1996) *Modern Epic: The World System from Goethe to García Márquez*, trans. Q. Hoare, London: Verso.

—— (1998) *Atlas of the European Novel 1800–1900*, London: Verso.

—— (2000) 'Conjectures on world literature', *New Left Review* (II) 1: 54–68.

—— (2003) 'More conjectures', *New Left Review* (II) 20: 73–81.

Muecke, S., Davis, J. and Shoemaker, A. (1988) 'Aboriginal literature', in L. Hergenhan (ed.) *The Penguin New Literary History of Australia*, Melbourne: Penguin.

Mulvey, L. (1989) *Visual and Other Pleasures*, London: Macmillan.

O'Flinn, P. (1986) 'Production and reproduction: the case of *Frankenstein*', in P. Humm, P. Stigant and P. Widdowson (eds) *Popular Fictions: Essays in Literature and History*, London: Methuen.

Ong, W. J. (1988) *Orality and Literacy: The Technologizing of the Word*, London: Routledge.

Ono, K. A. (2000) 'To be a vampire on *Buffy the Vampire Slayer*: race and ('other') socially marginalizing positions on horror TV', in E. R. Helford (ed.) *Fantasy Girls: Gender in the New Universe of Science Fiction and Fantasy Television*, Lanham: Rowman and Littlefield.

Orsini, F. (2002) 'Maps of Indian writing: India in the mirror of world fiction', *New Left Review* (II) 13: 75–88.

Page, B. (2003) *The Murdoch Archipelago*, London: Simon and Schuster.

Palmer, D. J. (1965) *The Rise of English Studies*, Oxford: Oxford University Press.

Parkin, F. (1979) *Marxism and Class Theory: A Bourgeois Critique*, London: Tavistock.

Parla, J. (2004) 'The object of comparison', *Comparative Literature Studies* 41(1): 116–25.

Parrinder, P. (2000) 'Introduction: learning from other worlds', in P. Parrinder (ed.) *Learning from Other Worlds: Estrangement, Cognition and the Politics of Science Fiction and Utopia*, Liverpool: Liverpool University Press.

Parsons, T. (1949) *The Structure of Social Action*, New York: Free Press.

Patterson, A. (1984) *Censorship and Interpretation: The Conditions of Writing and Reading in Early Modern England*, Madison: University of Wisconsin Press.

Pavlyshyn, M. (1994) 'On the possibility of opposition under glasnost', in C. Worth, P. Nestor and M. Pavlyshyn (eds) *Literature and Opposition*, Melbourne: Centre for Comparative Literature and Cultural Studies, Monash University.

Penley, C. (1997) *NASA/TREK: Popular Science and Sex in America*, London: Verso.

Perry, B. E. (1967) *The Ancient Romances: A Literary-Historical Account of their Origins*, Berkeley: California University Press.

Peter, J. (1960) *A Critique of Paradise Lost*, London: Longman.

Philmus, R. M. (2001) 'Matters of translation: Karel Čapek and Paul Selver', *Science Fiction Studies* 28(1): 7–32.

Poggioli, R. (1968) *The Theory of the Avant-Garde*, trans. G. Fitzgerald, Cambridge, Mass.: Harvard University Press.

Poovey, M. (1984) *The Proper Lady and the Woman Writer: Ideology as Style in the Works of Mary Wollstonecraft, Mary Shelley, and Jane Austen*, Chicago: Chicago University Press.

Posnett, H. M. (1973) 'The science of comparative literature' (first published in 1901) in H.-J. Schulz and P. H. Rhein (eds) *Comparative Literature: The Early Years, An Anthology of Essays*, Chapel Hill: University of North Carolina Press.

Prendergast, C. (2001) 'Negotiating world literature', *New Left Review* (II) 8: 100–21.

Raleigh, Sir W. (1900) *Milton*, London: Edward Arnold.

Reeves, J. L., Rodgers, M. C. and Epstein, M. (1996) 'Rewriting popularity: the cult files', in D. Lavery, A. Hague and M. Cartwright (eds) *Deny All Knowledge: Reading the X-Files*, London: Faber.

Remak, H. (1961) 'Comparative literature, its definition and function', in N. Stallknecht and H. Frenz (eds) *Comparative Literature: Method and Perspective*, Carbondale: Southern Illinois University Press.

Rice, E. (1978) 'The industrialization of the writer', in P. Davison, R. Meyersohn and E. Shils (eds) *Literary Taste, Culture and Mass Communication*, vol. 10: *Authorship*, Cambridge: Chadwyck-Healey.

Richards, I. A. (1929) *Practical Criticism: A Study of Literary Judgement*, London: Routledge and Kegan Paul.

Rickman, G. (1991) 'Philip K. Dick on *Blade Runner*: "They did sight simulation on my brain"' in J. B. Kerman (ed.) *Retrofitting 'Blade Runner': Issues in Ridley Scott's 'Blade Runner' and Philip K. Dick's 'Do Androids Dream of Electric Sheep?'*, Bowling Green: Bowling Green State University Popular Press.

Ross, A. (1991) *Strange Weather: Culture, Science and Technology in the Age of Limits*, London: Verso.

Ryan, K. (1996) 'Introduction', in K. Ryan (ed.) *New Historicism and Cultural Materialism: A Reader*, London: Arnold.

Said, E. W. (1993) *Culture and Imperialism*, London: Chatto and Windus.

—— (1994) *Representations of the Intellectual: The 1993 Reith Lectures*, London: Vintage.

—— (1995) *Orientalism*, Harmondsworth: Penguin.

Sanders, J. (ed.) (1994) *Science Fiction Fandom*, Westport: Greenwood.

Sartre, J.-P. (1976) *Critique of Dialectical Reason*, trans. A. Sheridan-Smith, London: New Left Books.

Saurat, D. (1924) *Milton: Man and Thinker*, London: Cape.

Saussure, F. de (1974) *Course in General Linguistics*, trans. W. Baskin, Glasgow: Collins.

Schleiermacher, F. D. E. (1985) 'General hermeneutics', in K. Mueller-Vollmer (ed.) *The Hermeneutics Reader: Texts of the German Tradition from the Enlightenment to the Present*, trans. J. Duke and J. Forstman, New York: Continuum.

Schultz, J. (1997) 'The media industries: the press', in S. Cunningham and G. Turner (eds) *The Media in Australia: Industries, Texts, Audiences*, 2nd edn, Sydney: Allen and Unwin.

Schutz, A. (1972) *The Phenomenology of the Social World*, trans. G. Walsh and F. Lehnert, London: Heinemann.

Schwarz, R. (1992) 'Misplaced ideas', in J. Gledson (ed.) *Misplaced Ideas: Essays on Brazilian Culture*, London: Verso.

Segal, L. (1999) *Why Feminism?*, New York: Columbia University Press.

Seymour, M. (2001) *Mary Shelley*, London: Picador.

Shiner, L. (1992) 'Inside the movement: past, present, and future', in G. Slusser and T. Shippey (eds) *Fiction 2000: Cyberpunk and the Future of Narrative*, Athens: University of Georgia Press.

Shklovsky, V. (1965) 'Art as technique', trans. L. Lemon and M. Reis, in L. Lemon and M. Reis (eds) *Russian Formalist Criticism: Four Essays*, Lincoln: University of Nebraska Press.

Showalter, E. (1978) *A Literature of Their Own: British Women Novelists from Brontë to Lessing*, London: Virago.

—— (1989) 'A criticism of our own: autonomy and assimilation in Afro-American and feminist literary theory', in R. Cohen (ed.) *The Future of Literary Theory*, London: Routledge.

Sinfield, A. (1992) *Faultlines: Cultural Materialism and the Politics of Dissident Reading*, Oxford: Oxford University Press.

—— (1994) *Cultural Politics, Queer Reading*, London: Routledge.

—— (1997) *Literature, Politics and Culture in Postwar Britain*, 2nd edn, London: Athlone Press.

—— (1998) *Gay and After*. London: Serpent's Tail.

Slusser, G. (1992) 'The Frankenstein barrier', in G. Slusser and T. Shippey (eds) *Fiction 2000: Cyberpunk and the Future of Narrative*, Athens: University of Georgia Press.

Sobchack, V. (1987) *Screening Space: The American Science Fiction Film*, New York: Ungar.

Spearman, D. (1966) *The Novel and Society*, London: Routledge and Kegan Paul.

Spender, D. (1986) *Mothers of the Novel: 100 Good Women Writers before Jane Austen*, London: Pandora.

Spivak, G. C. (1987) *In Other Worlds: Essays in Cultural Politics*, London: Methuen.

—— (1993) 'Reading *The Satanic Verses*', in M. Biriotti and N. Miller (eds) *What is an Author?*, Manchester: Manchester University Press.

—— (1999) *A Critique of Postcolonial Reason: Toward A History of the Vanishing Present*, Cambridge, Mass.: Harvard University Press.

—— (2003) *Death of a Discipline*, New York: Columbia University Press.

Stephen, Sir L. and Lee, Sir S. (eds) (1921) *Dictionary of National Biography*, vol. XVIII, Oxford: Oxford University Press.

Sterling, B. (1990) 'Cyberpunk in the nineties', *Interzone: Science Fiction and Fantasy* 38: 39–41.

Sutherland, J. A. (1976) *Victorian Novelists and Publishers*, London: Athlone Press.

—— (1982) *Offensive Literature: Decensorship in Britain 1960–1982*, London: Junction Books.

Suvin, D. (1979) *Metamorphoses of Science Fiction: On the Poetics and History of a Literary Genre*, New Haven: Yale University Press.

—— (2000) 'Novum is as novum does', in K. Sayer and J. Moore (eds) *Science Fiction, Critical Frontiers*, Basingstoke: Macmillan.

Sykes, J. B. (ed.) (1976) *The Concise Oxford English Dictionary*, Oxford: Oxford University Press.

Thomas, D. (1969) *A Long Time Burning: The History of Literary Censorship in England*, London: Routledge and Kegan Paul.

Thomas, M. (1976) 'Manuscripts', in L. Febvre and H.-J. Martin, *The Coming of the Book*, trans. D. Gerard, ed. G. Nowell-Smith and D. Wootton, London: New Left Books.

Thompson, E. P. (1963) *The Making of the English Working Class*, London: Victor Gollancz.

Thomson, G. (1978) *The Prehistoric Aegean*, London: Lawrence and Wishart.

Touraine, A. (1981) *The Voice and the Eye: An Analysis of Social Movements*, trans. A. Duff, Cambridge: Cambridge University Press.

Tulloch, J. and Jenkins, H. (1995) *Science Fiction Audiences: Watching 'Dr Who' and 'Star Trek'*, London: Routledge.

Turner, B. (ed.) (2002) *The Writer's Handbook 2003*, London: Macmillan.

UNESCO (1984) *UNESCO Statistical Yearbook 1984*, Paris: UNESCO.

—— (1989) *UNESCO Statistical Yearbook 1989*, Paris: UNESCO.

—— (1990) *UNESCO Statistical Yearbook 1990*, Paris: UNESCO.

—— (1993) *UNESCO Statistical Yearbook 1993*, Paris: UNESCO.

—— (1999) *UNESCO Statistical Yearbook 1999*, Paris: UNESCO.

Van Hise, L. (1982) 'Interview: Philip K. Dick on *Blade Runner*', *Starlog* 55: 19–22.

Watt, I. (1963) *The Rise of the Novel: Studies in Defoe, Richardson and Fielding*, Harmondsworth: Penguin.

Weber, M. (1930) *The Protestant Ethic and the Spirit of Capitalism*, trans. T. Parsons, London: Unwin.

—— (1948) 'Class, status, party', trans. H. H. Gerth and C. W. Mills, in H. H. Gerth and C. Wright Mills (eds) *From Max Weber: Essays in Sociology*, London: Routledge and Kegan Paul.

—— (1949) *The Methodology of the Social Sciences*, trans. E. A. Shils and H. A. Finch, New York: Free Press.

—— (1952) *Ancient Judaism*, trans. H. H. Gerth and D. Martindale, New York: Free Press.

—— (1964) *The Theory of Social and Economic Organization*, trans. A. M. Henderson and T. Parsons, New York: Free Press.

Wellek, R. and Warren A. (1976) *Theory of Literature*, Harmondsworth: Penguin.

West, C. (1999) 'The new cultural politics of difference', in C. West (ed.) *The Cornel West Reader*, New York: Basic Books.

Wilcox, R. and Williams, J. P. (1996) ' "What do you think?": *The X-Files*, liminality and gender pleasure', in D. Lavery, A. Hague and M. Cartwright (eds) *Deny All Knowledge: Reading the X-Files*, London: Faber.

Williams, R. (1958) *Culture and Society 1780–1950*, London: Chatto and Windus.
—— (1963) *Culture and Society 1780–1950*, Harmondsworth: Penguin.
—— (1965) *The Long Revolution*, Harmondsworth: Penguin.
—— (1973a) *Drama from Ibsen to Brecht*, Harmondsworth: Penguin.
—— (1973b) *The Country and the City*, New York: Oxford University Press.
—— (1974) *Television: Technology and Cultural Form*, Glasgow: Collins.
—— (1976a) *Keywords: A Vocabulary of Culture and Society*, Glasgow: Collins.
—— (1976b) *Communications*, Harmondsworth: Penguin.
—— (1977) *Marxism and Literature*, Oxford: Oxford University Press.
—— (1979a) *Modern Tragedy*, 2nd edn, London: Verso.
—— (1979b) *Politics and Letters: Interviews with New Left Review*, London: New Left Books.
—— (1980) *Problems in Materialism and Culture: Selected Essays*, London: New Left Books.
—— (1981) *Culture*, Glasgow: Collins.
—— (1983) *Towards 2000*, London: Chatto and Windus.
—— (1984) 'Seeing a man running', in D. Thompson (ed.) *The Leavises: Recollections and Impressions*, Cambridge: Cambridge University Press.
—— (1989a) 'A defence of realism', in N. Belton, F. Mulhern and J. Taylor (eds) *What I Came to Say*, London: Hutchinson Radius.
—— (1989b) *The Politics of Modernism: Against the New Conformists*, ed. T. Pinkney, London: Verso.
Williams, R. and Said, E. W. (1989) 'Appendix: media, margins and modernity', in R. Williams *The Politics of Modernism: Against the New Conformists*, ed. T. Pinkney, London: Verso.
Willis, P. with Jones, S., Canaan, J. and Hurd, G. (1990) *Common Culture: Symbolic Work at Play in the Everyday Culture of the Young*, Milton Keynes: Open University Press.
Wilson, S. (1995) *Cultural Materialism: Theory and Practice*, Oxford: Blackwell.
Wolff, J. (1990) *Feminine Sentences: Essays on Women and Culture*, Cambridge: Polity Press.
—— (1993) *The Social Production of Art*, 2nd edn, London: Macmillan.
Wright, E. O. (1978) *Class, Crisis, and the State*, London: New Left Books.
Zima, P. V. (2000) *Manuel de sociocritique*, Paris and Montréal: l'Harmattan.
Žižek, S. (1989) *The Sublime Object of Ideology*, London: Verso.
—— (1991) *Looking Awry: An Introduction to Jacques Lacan through Popular Culture*, Cambrige, Mass.: MIT Press.
—— (1992) *Everything You Always Wanted to Know about Lacan: (But were Afraid to Ask Hitchcock)*, London: Verso.

—— (1993) *Tarrying with the Negative*, Durham: Duke University Press.

—— (1994) 'Introduction: the spectre of ideology', in S. Žižek (ed.) *Mapping Ideology*, London: Verso.

—— (1997) 'Multiculturalism, or, the cultural logic of multinational capitalism', *New Left Review* (I) 225: 28–51.

—— (2001) 'Postface', in G. Lukács, *A Defence of 'History and Class Consciousness': Tailism and the Dialectic*, trans. E. Leslie, London: Verso.

Index

INDEX